THE POLITICAL ARRAYS OF
AMERICAN INDIAN LITERARY HISTORY

The Political Arrays of American Indian Literary History

JAMES H. COX

University of Minnesota Press
Minneapolis
London

The University of Minnesota Press gratefully acknowledges the financial assistance provided for the publication of this book by the President's Office of the University of Texas at Austin.

An earlier version of chapter 1 was published as "'Yours for the Indian Cause': Gertrude Bonnin's Activist Editing at *The American Indian Magazine*, 1915–1919," in *Blue Pencils and Hidden Hands: Women Editing Periodicals, 1830–1910*, ed. Sharon M. Harris, 173–201 (Boston: Northeastern University Press, 2004); reprinted by permission of University Press of New England. An earlier version of chapter 2 was published as "'Learn to Talk Yaqui': Mexico and the Cherokee Literary Politics of Will Rogers and John Milton Oskison," *Western American Literature* 48, no. 4 (Winter 2014): 400–421; reprinted by permission of University of Nebraska Press. An earlier version of chapter 3 was published as "The Cross and the Harvest Dance: Lynn Riggs' and James Hughes' *A Day in Santa Fe*," *Quarterly Review of Film and Video* 32, no. 4 (2015): 384–98; reprinted by permission of Taylor and Francis. An earlier version of chapter 5 was published as "Native American Detective Fiction and Settler Colonialism," in *A History of American Crime Fiction*, ed. Chris Raczkowski, 250–62 (New York: Cambridge University Press); reprinted by permission of Cambridge University Press.

Copyright 2019 by the Regents of the University of Minnesota

All rights reserved. No part of this publication may be reproduced, stored in a retrieval system, or transmitted, in any form or by any means, electronic, mechanical, photocopying, recording, or otherwise, without the prior written permission of the publisher.

Published by the University of Minnesota Press
111 Third Avenue South, Suite 290
Minneapolis, MN 55401–2520
http://www.upress.umn.edu

Printed in the United States of America on acid-free paper

The University of Minnesota is an equal-opportunity educator and employer.

Library of Congress Cataloging-in-Publication Data
Names: Cox, James H. (James Howard), author.
Title: The political arrays of American Indian literary history / James H. Cox.
Description: Minneapolis : University of Minnesota Press, [2019] | Includes bibliographical references and index. |
Identifiers: LCCN 2018055519 (print) | ISBN 978-1-5179-0601-6 (hc) | ISBN 978-1-5179-0602-3 (pb)
Subjects: LCSH: American literature—History and criticism. | American literature—Indian authors—History and criticism. | Politics and literature—United States—History and criticism.
Classification: LCC PS153.I52 C68 2019 (print) | DDC 810.9/897—dc23
LC record available at https://lccn.loc.gov/2018055519

CONTENTS

INTRODUCTION Political Arrays — 1

CHAPTER 1 Indigenous Editing — 25
Gertrude Bonnin, Lee Harkins, and American Indian Periodicals

CHAPTER 2 Transnational Representations — 73
Mexico and the Cherokee Literary Politics of John Milton Oskison and Will Rogers

CHAPTER 3 A Good Day to Film — 113
Lynn Riggs, Sherman Alexie, and Independent Indigenous Cinema

CHAPTER 4 Academic Networks — 143
John Joseph Mathews and the Politics of Indigenous Correspondence

CHAPTER 5 Crimes against Indigeneity — 177
The Politics of Native American Detective Fiction

CONCLUSION Speculative Arrays — 207

Notes — 213
Bibliography — 235
Index — 255

INTRODUCTION
Political Arrays

The Political Arrays of American Indian Literary History proposes and demonstrates a method of reading the works produced by American Indian writers in an always vexingly politicized literary context. While all writers must anticipate the prospect of unsatisfactory or even infuriating interpretations of their work, Native authors face a bafflingly capricious literary critical landscape defined by what Muscogee Creek and Cherokee literary scholar Craig Womack calls "the interdependency of politics and literature" (17). Were Fredric Jameson to enter the "Homeric battlefield" of interpretation in Native American and Indigenous literary studies, he might find at least some pleasure in encountering a prioritization of "the political interpretation of literary texts" (13, 17). Yet Native texts, whether novels or newspaper columns, short stories or screenplays, resist efforts to read them as advocating singular political positions. Moments of startling militancy might erupt in a work conventionally understood as assimilationist, while a Red Power novel might contain retrograde views, for example, of women, gay men, or Mexican Americans. With equal attention given to both recovered and canonical texts, *The Political Arrays of American Indian Literary History* takes as its central focus what Native texts say and do politically and proposes that literary scholars approach single texts, collections of texts by the same author and by multiple Native authors, and conversations among Native and non-Native writers about their works as political arrays: confounding but also generative collisions of conservative, moderate, and progressive ideas that together constitute the rich political landscape of American Indian literary history.[1]

I define literature capaciously in this book. In the Introduction to *Literary Theory* (1996), Terry Eagleton entertains the possibility that literature means "any kind of writing which for some reason or another somebody values highly" (9). *The Political Arrays of American Indian*

Literary History adopts a position shared by many scholars who value all writing by American Indians for a wide range of formal and political reasons, whether the writing appears in private letters, periodicals, or petitions or between the covers of a novel or collection of poems. Cherokee literary studies scholar and creative writer Daniel Heath Justice speaks eloquently to the commitment within Indigenous literary studies to value and listen carefully to Indigenous voices wherever and however they appear. In response to Anishinabe poet Marie Annharte Baker's observation regarding the silencing of her mother's generation of First Nations women, Justice asserts:

> Our literatures are just one more vital way that we have countered those forces of erasure and given shape to our own ways of being in the world. Our mindful stories, in all their forms and functions—and whether vocalized, embodied, or inscribed—honour the sacrifices of those who came before us and who made it possible for us to continue the struggle today as specific peoples in relation with the world. They help us bridge the gap of human imagination between one another, between other human communities, and between us and other-than-human beings. Fundamentally, they affirm Indigenous presence—and our *present*. (*Why Indigenous Literatures Matter*, xix)

Justice situates Indigenous literatures, "in all their forms and functions," as central both to the survival of Indigenous communities and to resistance to anti-Indigenous forces. By defining all the forms of writing under my consideration as literature and as significant contributions to American Indian literary history, I claim for them a specific value—cultural, historical, and political—deriving in part from the extraordinary effort required even to find a voice and make it heard in powerfully anti-Indigenous cultural, historical, and political contexts, especially prior to the civil rights era.

By politics, I mean the struggle for and conflict over power, which political scientist Robert Dahl defines generally as a relation among people in which some have the resources to force others to act or live in ways they otherwise would not, specifically in colonial and settler-colonial contexts.[2] Eagleton concludes his meditation on the definition of literature by positioning the act of making value judgments as part of this struggle and conflict, since these value judgments, he argues, "refer in the end not simply to private taste, but to the assumptions by which certain social groups exercise and maintain power over others" (16). Justice addresses this struggle and conflict, too, in the passage quoted above and consistently and in specific detail throughout the book from which it comes, *Why Indigenous Literatures Matter* (2017). Indeed, he conceives of the book as "avowedly political," and after drawing on Menominee poet Chrystos's rejection of "poetry without politics," he observes, "To argue for and produce Indigenous writing *as such* is necessarily to engage in political struggle and to challenge centuries of representational oppression" (xvii–xviii). This struggle and conflict sit in the foreground of almost all scholarship in Native American and Indigenous literary studies. We ask, frequently first and foremost, how do writers participate in this struggle and conflict? It is an enduring and perplexing question, one uniting scholars in the field in a common purpose but also dividing us when we disagree not about the cultural or historical significance of a work of literature but about the political positions we judge an author, or our fellow critics, to have taken.

The Political Arrays of American Indian Literary History introduces political arrays as a concept that helps answer this central question in the field by illuminating the nuances, ambiguities, and ambivalences of the politics of Native American and Indigenous writing. Textual evidence of these arrays exists in public, readily accessible places, such as in poems and novels or book reviews and journal articles, as well as in the not quite as convenient manuscripts housed in libraries. They appear as intratextual, intertextual, intratribal, intertribal, transracial, trans-Indigenous, and transnational, for example, with the forms and genres used by American Indian authors shaping them in unpredictable ways. As readers, we cannot predict the politics of a personal letter or detective novel. No form or genre emerges as more conservative or progressive than another. Also, while some political arrays emerge in conversations among American Indian authors, scholars can stage these conversations by identifying and tracing political arrays, some discrete and others expansive and sprawling, across space and time. These diachronic political arrays generated by literary critics have their own politics, or, at least, the critics constructing them will have their own political goals driving their work. How we treat these political arrays as distinct from each other, or how we treat their relative significance or validity, depends, too, on our own political allegiances.

Consider the array generated by Louise Erdrich's novels in the mid-1980s, when Erdrich, who as a citizen of the Turtle Mountain Band of Chippewa has carefully navigated the politicized world of American Indian literature throughout her career, became one of the highest-profile Native writers. This particular array originates in the richly textured political worlds of the novels, and it includes personal letters, in which Erdrich takes an explicitly pro-Indigenous position in the struggle for and conflict over power in a settler–colonial context, and a book review by revered Laguna Pueblo writer Leslie Marmon Silko. On August 15, 1984, Erdrich wrote to Peter Matthiessen, who during a prolific career wrote at times on American Indian and environmental causes and won the National Book Award three times, to thank him for his kind words about her novel *Love Medicine* (1984). She took the opportunity to comment on Matthiessen's work: "I was at Leonard Peltier's trial in Fargo, and found the verdict shameful and incredible. Your book *In the Spirit of Crazy Horse* prompted the same reaction in many, many people. Thank you for that, too" (Erdrich to Matthiessen, August 15, 1984). Peltier's defense team and prominent supporters, including Matthiessen, believed that the federal government had framed the activist, but the jury found Peltier guilty of killing FBI agents Jack Coler and Ronald Williams. Matthiessen's book had sparked Erdrich's memory of and outrage over the 1977 trial.

The following year, Erdrich responded to Mathiessen's invitation to join an event in support of Peltier. She tells him, with a hint of anxious regret:

> I would like to be of use where Leonard Peltier is concerned, and although I can't come to Washington this June there may be some other way I can help. I'd like to help. I've contacted the Minneapolis support group for a list of people to whom I might write in support of Leonard's case. I don't know Leonard personally, but was at his trial in Fargo and was convinced that his trial was mishandled and manipulated by the government. (Erdrich to Matthiessen, May 18, 1985)

In response to a query from Matthiessen, she states that she did not model *Love Medicine*'s Gerry Nanapush on Peltier but adds that "after the trial I put some specific events that resembled what happened in South Dakota because the injustice rankled" (Erdrich to Matthiessen,

May 18, 1985). Erdrich refers here to the appearance of Nanapush, like Peltier a member of the American Indian Movement (AIM), at Pine Ridge. Nanapush kills a state trooper and, as Peltier did in July 1979, escapes from prison.[3] Erdrich ends the letter with another apology for declining the invitation to the Peltier event and a comment on her work with her husband Michael Dorris on fetal alcohol syndrome, "which has become near epidemic on some reservations" (Erdrich to Matthiessen, May 18, 1985). The shift in focus from her inability to attend the Peltier event to her dedication to ameliorating the damage caused by alcohol consumption in Native communities indicates possible concern that Matthiessen might judge her as insufficiently committed to the Peltier cause. She wants to help with Peltier but cannot, and she implies that Matthiessen need not question her political or activist credentials. She has another, possibly more significant, social problem to face.

The publication of Erdrich's second novel, *The Beet Queen* (1986), which focuses primarily on a non-Native family, elicited more correspondence, but without any discussion of explicitly political issues, between the two authors. In a letter handwritten in hybrid print and cursive, Erdrich tells Matthiessen, "You are tremendously kind to have written in response to *The Beet Queen*. It means a very great deal to me, and I thank you" (Erdrich to Matthiessen, January 21, 1987). Fetal alcohol syndrome must have been on Erdrich's mind daily two years after her initial exchange of letters with Matthiessen. Upon her marriage to Dorris in 1981, she had become mother to his three adopted Native children with FAS, and Dorris was still deep in the project that eventually reached publication in 1989 as *The Broken Cord* and won a National Book Critics Circle Award.

The sentiments expressed in this private component of the array contrast sharply with the public statements by Silko, who had a less sanguine view than Matthiessen of *The Beet Queen*. In her October 7, 1986, review of the novel, Silko compliments its aesthetics but condemns its deplorable politics: "Self-referential writing has an ethereal clarity and shimmering beauty because no history or politics intrudes to muddy the well of pure necessity contained within language itself" (179). Silko implies in this passage a tension, perhaps irresolvable, between the clarity, beauty, and purity of Erdrich's artistic expression and history and politics, represented figuratively as mud, in a U.S. colonial and settler-colonial context. She specifies Erdrich's failures later in the review:

In Erdrich's hands, the rural North Dakota of Indian-hating, queer-baiting white farmers, of the Depression, becomes magically transformed.... What Erdrich, who is half-Indian and grew up in North Dakota, attempts to pass off as North Dakota may be the only North Dakota she knows. But hers is an oddly rarified place in which the individual's own psyche, not racism or poverty, accounts for all conflict and tension. In this pristine world all misery, suffering, and loss are self-generated, just as conservative Republicans have been telling us for years. (180–81)

Silko's reading of *The Beet Queen* as a conservative literary document, as a perpetuation of the racial politics of Ronald Reagan's administration, sits in stark juxtaposition to Erdrich's political self-representation in her correspondence with Matthiessen at the same time in the mid-1980s.

The review of *The Beet Queen* in the *Washington Post* by author, critic, and literary magazine editor Wendy Lesser contributes another node, and another political perspective, to the array:

Whereas Love Medicine derived a great deal of its originality (and also, one fears, a portion of its critical success) from the fact that it chronicled the previously unexamined lives of American Indians, The Beet Queen uses the Chippewa stories only as it uses everything else—as supporting material in the creation of fascinating personalities. Admittedly, the eponymous agricultural monarch—a girl named Dot Adare—is one-quarter Chippewa; yet the most interesting part of her family is not the Kashpaws, but the crazy white Adares. ("Louise Erdrich's Plains Song")

In the parenthetical comment about the critical response to *Love Medicine*, Lesser laments that some readers valued a novel for its dedication to illuminating "the previously unexamined lives of American Indians." To many readers, such an observation sounds uninformed, since it suggests a lack of familiarity with writers such as Silko, N. Scott Momaday (Kiowa), and James Welch (Blackfeet and Gros Ventre), among many others. At the same time, Lesser's words resonate as politically reactionary, since she rejects precisely the reason why so many readers value the work of Native American and Indigenous writers: they challenge what Justice calls "those forces of erasure" and break a coerced historical silence.

Silko found herself at the center of another, similar political array several years after her review of *The Beet Queen* when fellow Laguna Pueblo writer Paula Gunn Allen objected to Silko's use in *Ceremony* of Laguna Pueblo oral traditions. Allen claims, "To use the oral tradition directly is to run afoul of native ethics, which is itself a considerable part of the tradition. Using the tradition while contravening it is to do violence to it. The ethical issue is both political and metaphysical, and to violate the traditional ethos is to run risks that no university professor signed up for in any case" (379). The scholarly examination of the oral traditions in *Ceremony* exacerbates Allen's dismay: "I believe I could no more do (or sanction) the kind of ceremonial investigation of *Ceremony* done by some researchers than I could slit my mother's throat. Even seeing some of it published makes my skin crawl" (383). Allen offers the following ominous assertion in response to Silko's ethical and political transgressions: "Telling the old stories, revealing the old ways can only lead to disaster" (384). This warning appears to draw upon one of the most compelling and frequently cited moments in Silko's novel, the gathering of witches during which a powerful conjuror calls white people into existence. When the other witches express their fear of these violent thieves and killers, their powerful confederate tells them, "*It's already turned loose. / It's already coming. / It can't be called back*" (138). While in the earlier array Silko characterizes Erdrich's novel as a 1980s conservative Republican document, in this new array Allen positions Silko as a dangerous and potentially very destructive witch aligned with colonial and settler-colonial forces, including academic ones.[4]

This array shares a node—Peter Matthiessen—with the first example. Allen's article on *Ceremony* appeared in 1990 as Silko worked to complete *Almanac of the Dead,* a novel widely perceived as the most explicitly anticolonial and politically insurgent work of fiction by a Native American writer. Acoma Pueblo author Simon Ortiz read *Almanac of the Dead* the following fall, and in a letter to Matthiessen three months prior to its publication, he observes, "I am now reading the galley copy of Leslie Silko's *Almanac of the Dead*. It is quite a novel, a dark wonder, insightful with a terrible and powerful rage, dealing with 'white' people and America as honestly as possible. Upon its release this fall, it will raise a storm I expect. I've only read the first 150 pages of a 1500 page book, but I expect the rest is just as wonderful" (Ortiz to Matthiessen, August 24, 1991). This private praise from a legendary figure, honored as a poet but also as the author of the "foundational" essay "Towards a National Indian Literature: Cultural Authenticity in Nationalism," coheres with the dust jacket blurb by Larry McMurtry on the novel's first edition: "A brilliant, haunting, and tragic novel of ruin and resistance in the Americas. In a long dialectic, tinted with genius and compelled by a just anger, Leslie Silko dramatizes the often desperate struggle of native peoples in the Americas to keep, at all costs, the core of their culture: their way of seeing, their way of believing, their way of being."[5] Silko dedicated the book to McMurtry, whose "pathological" Blue Duck from *Lonesome Dove* (1985) appalled scholars of Native literatures such as Louis Owens.[6]

These letters, novels, reviews, articles, and paratexts form an array of political positions on and investments in American Indian literary expression, and they illustrate the political minefield into which all Native authors step when they begin to write. The tribal national, colonial, and settler–colonial contexts in which they write produce urgency and anxiety in many readers, who often respond to an alleged textual lack as powerfully as they do to the words on the page. Silko comments, for example, on what she perceives as a glaring absence in *The Beet Queen*: "After all, the Wounded Knee Massacre is only 42 years and 400 miles south of Sita and the others in Erdrich's novel" (Review of *The Beet Queen*, 182). Even a 763-page novel with strong activist bona fides such as *Almanac of the Dead* faces similar criticism from Crow Creek Dakota scholar Elizabeth Cook-Lynn, a luminary in Native literary studies. While she praises Silko's *Almanac* for "engag[ing] in and insist[ing] upon the nationalist's approach to historical events and in the process seems to put any so-called pandering ordinarily required of the storyteller in its place," Cook-Lynn also asserts that the novel "fails in this nationalistic approach, since it does not take into account the specific kind of tribal/nation status of the original occupants of this continent" (*Why I Can't*, 93). Silko demands explicit resistance from Erdrich; Cook-Lynn demands a better kind of resistance from Silko. The political stakes of Indigenous writing, of giving voice to Indigenous peoples and their histories, make John Updike's first rule for reviewing books—"Try to understand what the author wished to do, and do not blame him for not achieving what he did not attempt" (xviii)—sound naive.[7]

We might consider such responses not as condemnations, however, but as articulations of the desire for differently political Indigenous literatures. Silko's and Cook-Lynn's political desires align them with many scholars of American Indian literatures, including this one, who also read for resistance and search for and find explicitly anticolonial and decolonial narratives, often in surprising places: in a petition posted by Abenakis outside an English fort in 1747; in the late 1830s or early 1840s in Rome, Italy, in a conversion narrative by Pablo Tac, a young Native man from California; in a letter between the quarreling lovers Gertrude Simmons and Carlos Montezuma in June 1901.[8] Such narratives appear more readily identifiable during and following the civil rights era and the emergence of the Native American Renaissance, when the historical fact of direct action by Native activists, and the widespread coverage of it in the dominant media, coincides generally with an ostensibly greater number of Native writers getting their work into print and earning accolades. Yet as Silko and Cook-Lynn suggest, and Erdrich's correspondence with Matthiessen demonstrates, resistance even during the Renaissance takes many forms.

The more dramatic acts of resistance take center stage in American Indian literary studies. An event such as the occupation of Alcatraz from November 20, 1969, to June 11, 1971, serves as a political touchstone that for some scholars shapes this new cultural and literary era. Sean Teuton's *Red Land, Red Power: Grounding Knowledge in the American Indian Novel* (2008) and Dean Rader's *Engaged Resistance: American Indian Art, Literature, and Film from Alcatraz to the NMAI* (2011), to take two inspirational studies as examples, foreground the significance of the occupation of Alcatraz in late 1969 as a key moment in Native American political and cultural expression. Following epigraphs from Clyde Warrior, a Ponca activist and one of the founders of the National Indian Youth Council in 1961, and Momaday, Teuton opens the introduction to his book at the beginning of a compelling moment of direct action: "On 9 November 1969, a young American Indian student dove from a borrowed sailboat into the frigid waters of San Francisco Bay and swam 250 yards against swift currents to reclaim Alcatraz Island as Indian land" (1). This moment works as the narrative catalyst for Teuton's literary critical assertions: "During the era of Red Power, Native writers imagined a new narrative for Indian country, and they did so neither by longing for an impossibly timeless past nor by disconnecting Indians' stories from the political realities of their lives. Instead, writers of the era struggled to better interpret a colonized world and then offered this new knowledge to empower the people" (2). Teuton traces the roots of Red Power activism to Pontiac and Tecumseh, Ottawa and Shawnee leaders, respectively, who led intertribal military alliances against colonials and settler colonials. "Red Power activists," Teuton argues, "developed a new, more sophisticated form of resistance to American imperialism. Boldly intellectual, they were better trained than their forebears to translate their culture-specific tribal values to European Americans" (5). In the chapters that follow, Teuton identifies Momaday's *House Made of Dawn*, Welch's *Winter in the Blood,* and Silko's *Ceremony* as Red Power novels. While he makes a persuasive argument, we could productively think of these novels also, or instead, as explorations and revelations of the roots of Red Power. All three authors set their novels before the Red Power era, and the novels do not, therefore, engage Red Power politics directly. As Teuton notes, too, *House Made of Dawn* appeared in print a year before the events at Alcatraz; some of it appeared as much as three years earlier, in Momaday's "Three Sketches from *House Made of Dawn*" in the Autumn 1966 issue of the *Southern Review,* where the contributor's note describes the novel as "recently completed" (933). The January 1967 issue of the progressive periodical the *Reporter* and the Summer 1967 issue of *New Mexico Quarterly* also published excerpts. It was complete prior to the founding of the American Indian Movement in Minneapolis in 1968, as well as before Richard Oakes made his now-famous dive.[9]

The effort "to better interpret a colonized world" also involved healthy disagreement among Native writers, intellectuals, and activists. Revered scholars such as Alfonso Ortiz, an anthropologist from San Juan Pueblo, and Beatrice Medicine, an anthropologist from Standing Rock, along with Vine Deloria Jr., D'Arcy McNickle, Momaday, Simon Ortiz, and many others, attended the First Convocation of American Indian Scholars at Princeton University in March 1970, four months into the occupation of Alcatraz.[10] The meeting produced a political array of entirely Native voices articulating an expansive constellation of views. In the discussion following his talk on American Indian philosophy, Alfonso Ortiz, convocation chairman, comments, "I've seen many nonIndian audiences addressed, particularly in California, by a really fiery Red Power type and, you know, I think nonIndian Americans have become so mesmerized in being insulted that many of them actually enjoy it. This is frightening, you know. They would rather be insulted than informed or intellectually stimulated" (Costo et al., *Indian Voices*, 21). "I think," Ortiz concludes his thoughts on Red Power discourse, "that it really doesn't touch them [nonIndians] inside" (22). Momaday, in the discussion after he delivered "The Man Made of Words," also mentions Alcatraz:

> I had very little hope for it at first. I was very skeptical about it, because I thought it was going to be terminated very quickly, and that the Indian would be left holding the bag, and simply the scapegoat in that whole venture. It turned into something rather more serious than that, and there is no way at this point to realize just what it's going to be. But *symbolically,* it's very important at this moment, and the kind of sympathy for the Indian that has been generated in the Bay Area is really quite remarkable and quite impressive. (Costo et al., *Indian Voices*, 71)

In his presentation on Native American Studies programs, W. Roger Buffalohead, previously of UCLA's American Indian Culture Program but at the time a new faculty member in the University of Minnesota's Indian Studies Department, remarks on the destructive factionalism that had developed in the UCLA program over whether to focus on the "remedial or revolutionary material" (Costo et al., *Indian Voices*, 165). His contribution to the conversation following his talk includes this observation: "If you are going to teach students to be involved and to be activists, as was done at California, can you then draw a line and say to them: You've got to come back from Alcatraz and learn your lessons? Those of us who had approved this involvement at Alcatraz were caught in a fix. What could we say?" (172). During the same discussion, Medicine laments that her students at San Francisco State "who went to Alcatraz didn't keep up their studies" and comments that the "revolutionaries . . . really aren't doing much in terms of intellectual growth or in social movement either" (179). Rupert Costo, president of the Steering Committee, concludes the summation of his panel, titled "Forms and Uses of Tribal Government," by objecting, "Some of the young Indian people are relentlessly alienating the older folks, who would normally be their staunchest supporters and allies. This is a needless posture to take. Not everybody can picket. Some of us are fighting just as hard, on other fronts, in other ways, in directions equally important" (Costo et al., *Indian Voices,* 297). Medicine later delivered two talks at the convocation, including one entitled "Red Power: Real or Potential?" in which she asserts, "[Red Power's] positive aspects have never been universal in the Indian world. Many Indian people consider it a misnomer; some consider it as action; picketing; destroying property; capturing islands. Some consider it stupid" (Costo et al., *Indian Voices,* 303). She adds that some students of Red Power "have not made the transition from confrontation politics to the exacting studies, which possibly are a better step to effective power" (303), before stating her preference for the cultivation of Native "intellectual power," which "would stem from wisdom and an awareness of the structure of power in the dominant society" (305). As the chair of a panel titled "The Urban Scene and the American Indian," Deloria refers to the "alleged Red Power movement, which is just in Stan Steiner's head, and only occasionally outside of that area" (Costo et al., *Indian Voices,* 333–34). Ortiz's, Momaday's, Buffalohead's, Costo's, Medicine's, and Deloria's distinct views on Alcatraz and Red Power, as well as the many positions expressed by the participants in the spirited conversations following Medicine's presentation on Red Power and Deloria's, titled "The Urban Scene," demonstrate that the intellectual and political contexts of this era resist generalization.

Rader draws the same direct correlation between grassroots activism and a new era of Native literary and other artistic expression. "Engaged Resistance: Alcatraz," chapter 1 of *Engaged Resistance,* begins with an epigraph from a poem by an anonymous "poet-occupier" at Alcatraz and a photo of a tepee on the grounds of the prison. Rader defines engaged resistance as "a fundamentally indigenous form of aesthetic discourse that engages both Native and American cultural contexts as a mode of resistance against the ubiquitous colonial tendencies of assimilation and erasure" (1). After a paragraph in which he comments on Simon Ortiz's aforementioned essay, Rader continues, "The book demonstrates that Native-produced texts like poetry, fiction, movies, paintings, and sculpture are fundamental products and processes of American Indian sovereignty" and "explores how Native cultural expression comprises a strategy of aesthetic activism fashioned by Natives for both Native and Anglo publics" (1). Alcatraz, Rader contends, makes this kind of aesthetic and literary activism possible: "I argue that Alcatraz marks a movement away from cultural segregation in favor of cultural engagement, enabling Natives to reclaim identity on their own terms. By 'cultural segregation,' I mean not only reservations but also various other ways of marginalizing Indians and even rendering them invisible or dead. The occupation of Alcatraz enables not only reclamation of identity but also public, visible, rhetorically sophisticated performances of this reclamation for both Native and non-Native audiences" (3). Rader takes readers through the resistance at work in paintings, novels, films, poems, and public art before finishing with the National Museum of the American Indian. As with the three novels at the center of Teuton's study, the first three novels under Rader's consideration—Charles Red Corn's *A Pipe for February* (2002), Debra Magpie Earling's *Perma Red* (2002), and Louise Erdrich's *The Plague of Doves* (2008)—have pre-civil-rights-era settings. These Native authors also imagine acts of resistance—singing an Ojibwe song, learning from an Osage elder, committing an act of vigilantism, or surviving—before the Red Power era and illuminate the world that shaped these acts and circumscribed other forms of resistance.[11]

The literary critical and political act of marking a specific historical moment after which Native people imagined new narratives, interpreted the experience of colonialism more productively, moved from cultural segregation to cultural engagement, reclaimed their identities, and publicly performed those identities risks implicating previous generations—and perhaps primarily the most immediately prior one—in the failure to imagine, interpret, reclaim, and perform in particular ways. These literary critical and political acts also reinforce the perception of the Native American Renaissance as a rupture. *The Political Arrays of American Indian Literary History* does not question the literary, artistic, and political significance of either the Renaissance or the post-Renaissance era from the mid-1990s to the present.[12] However, it seeks to challenge our understanding of the Renaissance as a literary and political break with the past.

This book looks to the Native writers and intellectuals of the early and middle decades of the twentieth century for the literary historical and political contexts that informed the development of different forms of resistance by activists and writers of the next generation. It foregrounds continuities among the writers of the first two decades of the Renaissance and the writers of the generations to either side of the 1970s and 1980s. For example, Silko's condemnation of *The Beet Queen* and Allen's excoriation of *Ceremony* place both Erdrich and Silko in the company of many pre-Renaissance Native writers who face the displeasure and dissatisfaction of late-twentieth- and early-twenty-first-century scholars over their lamentable politics, especially their failures to affirm an Indigenous identity culturally and politically distinct—or distinct enough—from non-Natives. While Choctaw author Todd Downing does not center Indigenous identity and politics in his crime novels published in the 1930s, to the chagrin of critics such as Wolfgang Hochbruck, his novels are no less an expression of a Choctaw author interpreting the experience of colonialism or moving from cultural segregation to cultural engagement than Momaday's *House Made of Dawn* or Silko's *Ceremony*, or, to keep the comparison within the crime-fiction genre, Choctaw author D. L. Birchfield's *Black Silk Handkerchief* (2006) or Cherokee author Sara Sue Hoklotubbe's series of Sadie Walela mysteries (2003–14). We might also look to Cherokee writer John Milton Oskison's cleverly subversive *Tecumseh and His Times: The Story of a Great Indian* (1938) as a work of nonfiction that anticipates Deloria's Red Power–era manifesto *Custer Died for Your Sins* (1969) in its expression of an enduring hope for an Indigenous future that runs from Tecumseh and Hiawatha to "the obscure Osage communicant in his peyote lodge today" and its celebration of the "long tradition of protest against subjection" of the Shawnees (*Tecumseh*, viii, 4). Oskison mentions at the end of the biography a prophecy of Tecumseh's return, and he expresses a desire for a leader like him, one of the "champions of the ideal of Indian sovereignty" and "a crusader for Indian rights" (4, 80), capable of building the peyote "movement into one of active protest against a rubber-stamp Christian civilization" (236–37). Such an emphatic statement leads readers to wonder what Oskison would have thought of some of the chapters in Deloria's *Custer* or *Red Earth, White Lies* (1997).

Downing's crime novels and Oskison's *Tecumseh*, among many other works in the twenty years before and after World War II, resist generalizations of these eras as literarily and politically impotent, tentative, or assimilationist. Just as the most revered writers of the Renaissance, such as Silko and Erdrich, produce literary moments that read as unsatisfying or dangerously conservative to other writers and prominent scholars, pre-Renaissance writers produce literary moments that under the same political criteria read as satisfying: "Now Mexico is an Indian country," Downing declares in 1940 in *The Mexican Earth*, "where the white man is rapidly being bred out" (320). Ewing Hartshorne, a young Choctaw writer whose "Indian Lore Quiz" appeared in a few issues of the monthly magazine the *American Indian,* included the following question in one of the quizzes: "When were battles and raids between the whites and Indians called massacres?" (August 1927, 4). His answer is a clever revelation of non-Native control of dominant historical narratives and a reminder of successful Indigenous resistance: "When the Indians won" (6). Just as the literary works of the first two decades of the Renaissance do not consistently, explicitly, or rigorously express orthodox Red Power politics—again, *House Made of Dawn, Ceremony,* and *Winter in the Blood,* to take three celebrated novels as examples, are set before Alcatraz and the rise of AIM—their predecessors did not consistently, explicitly, or rigorously promote assimilation as the only course forward for Indigenous people. Even in hindsight in her memoir, *Crazy Brave* (2012), acclaimed first-generation Renaissance writer Joy Harjo (Mvskoke) does not tell of a young adult life shaped by Red Power politics. Though Red Power emerged in her formative late-teen years, she mentions Alcatraz only once. Instead, Harjo emphasizes what she calls at one point "the drudgery of survival"—young motherhood, poverty, domestic abuse, alcoholism—and her search to fulfill "the need for artistic expression" (135). In her own memoir, *The Turquoise Ledge* (2010), Silko acknowledges that "anyone who dared to reveal ceremonial secrets"—the transgression that Allen accused Silko of committing in *Ceremony*—"risked severe reprisals from the supernatural world" (51). However, she did not conceive of *The Turquoise Ledge* as a political work: "I had decided before I started the memoir that I wanted as much as possible to avoid unpleasantness and strife and politics" (170). This decision explains the absence of any references to American Indian activism, even in the late 1960s and early 1970s, when Silko attended the University of New Mexico and taught at Navajo Community College. All these authors, pre- and post-Renaissance, worked or continue to work in vexing and at times exciting political contexts. They generally respond to these contexts not with blunt political statements but with nuanced discussions of how Indigenous peoples might best navigate them. *The Political Arrays of American Indian Literary History* turns its attention to these textual and extratextual arrays to foreground the broad diversity of political voices in the most recent hundred years of American Indian literary history.

The Politics of American Indian Literature

Scholars in American Indian literary studies agree that literature by American Indians within colonial and settler–colonial contexts always has an urgent political component. However, many unacknowledged assumptions about American Indian politics guide how scholars in the field evaluate literary texts. These assumptions originate in the central role played by the civil rights activism of the late 1960s and early 1970s, the early Native American Renaissance period, in defining what constitutes desirable or ideal political positions for American Indian authors to adopt and scholars in the field to endorse. One of the more common assumptions, for example, is that a literary work is not political, or not political enough, if it fails to convey explicitly prosovereignty and anticolonial messages. In American Indian literary studies, "political" almost always means "progressive," and much of our understanding of a text's value derives from the critical pressure that we exert to make it politically appealing. Contemporary Native American literary criticism does not, as Jameson would have it, so much "rewrite selected texts" (17), though that happens, as preselect texts for attention based on rather narrow political positions that often do not map well onto even the most radically insurgent piece of writing.

The ahistorical treatment of politics, or the imposition of one era's political contexts onto another era, often produces compelling—and even important—scholarship. However, it does not necessarily produce clarity about either the literary or political significance of works by American Indian writers. In addition, it obscures formal, cultural, and political continuities in American Indian literary history between pre- and post-civil-rights-era writers.[13] In its approach to writing by American Indian authors, *The Political Arrays of American Indian Literary History* resists this flattening of the politics of American Indian literary expression and, in so doing, joins a conversation among scholars such as Lisa Brooks, Kirby Brown, Joanna Hearne, Shari Huhndorf, Maureen Konkle, Joshua Nelson, Robert Dale Parker, Beth Piatote, Phillip Round, Cheryl Suzack, Kiara Vigil, Amy Ware, and Jace Weaver, many of whom appear in the following pages. As Huhndorf and Suzack explain in their introduction to *Indigenous Women and Feminism* (2010), Indigenous feminists have played an especially crucial role not only in diversifying Indigenous political activity, with sustained efforts to resist male dominance in American Indian activist organizations and tribal national governance and to draw attention to the "systematic disempowerment of Indigenous women" under colonialism and settler colonialism, but also in challenging reductive narratives of Indigenous politics (5). In fact, Huhndorf observes in "Indigenous Feminism, Performance, and the Politics of Memory in the Plays of Monique Mojica," her contribution to *Indigenous Women and Feminism,* "Native cultural authenticity and political resistance have been gendered male" (183). *The Political Arrays of American Indian Literary History* takes into account the contemporary historical and political contexts to which American Indian authors respond, the political positions that they take in their writing, and the political perspectives that implicitly or explicitly shape the scholarship on their work. The book also insists on the historicizing of the political contexts in which authors write and will foreground the literary strategies authors use to represent and explore the political lives of American Indians.

The Political Arrays of American Indian Literary History examines the full range of political expression by American Indian writers beyond the literature of the late 1960s and early 1970s that, by serving as the field's primary political touchstone, has obscured the rich political diversity of the last hundred years of American Indian literary history. It challenges both the powerful assumptions about American Indian politics that structure scholarly discourse in the field and the literary criticism those assumptions produce. Despite what much of the criticism suggests, even the most revered American Indian writers of the civil rights era rarely incorporated Red Power politics into their work. Indeed, in their early Renaissance novels, Silko's and Momaday's main political concern is the interference by settler–colonial forces (church, federal government, military) in Pueblo life in New Mexico during the interwar and early Cold War periods rather than pan-Indian organizing against police brutality, treaty violations, or the incompetence of the Bureau of Indian Affairs and federally controlled tribal governments. American Indian literary history also includes, for instance, Gertrude Bonnin's grassroots activism and antipeyotism, Will Rogers's interwar noninterventionism, John Milton Oskison's conservative Cherokee exceptionalism, Todd Downing's Indigenous transnationalism, and Sherman Alexie's and Thomas King's simultaneously hopeful and skeptical liberalism.[14]

This Introduction and a Conclusion on the political alliances between Gerald Vizenor (White Earth Anishinabe) and Alexie (Spokane and Coeur d'Alene) frame chapters devoted to novels, short stories, films, letters, crime fiction, and columns and editorials published in the middle decades of the twentieth century. The book has particular sympathy for writers and texts neglected by mainstream American Indian literary criticism and therefore follows the lead of scholars, such as Brooks, Konkle, Parker, Piatote, Round, and Matt Cohen, who study Native voices in overlooked sites of writing and prepare some of the ground for identifying provocative political alliances, and sometimes less satisfying political tensions, among Native writers. Some of the literary and cultural productions under consideration in *The Political Arrays of American Indian Literary History* will enter the contemporary scholarly conversation for the first time in this book. Each chapter will also develop diachronic arrays by emphasizing links between pre-Renaissance and post-Renaissance writers and filmmakers.

While scholars of American Indian literary studies have opened the field to a wide variety of texts, from notes written on birch bark to winter counts and earthworks, nonfiction published in periodicals remains unexamined as significant Native writing. Periodicals produced and edited by American Indians contain a profusion of political arrays, with the implicit or explicit political views in editorials, columns, and advertisements, for example, often in tension with each other. "Indigenous Editing," the first chapter, considers the *American Indian Magazine* (1913–20), the publication of an intertribal organization called the Society of American Indians, and the *American Indian*, a magazine published in Tulsa from 1926 to 1931 almost entirely by an American Indian editorial board and staff. The former periodical was conceived specifically to influence federal Indian policy on the national stage and had as editors both Arthur C. Parker (Seneca) and Gertrude Bonnin (Dakota); the latter was a general-interest publication attuned to the political, cultural, and economic concerns of a regional audience in northeastern Oklahoma. The *American Indian*, edited by Lee F. Harkins (Choctaw), contains the work of nearly unknown or entirely forgotten Native writers such as Joe Bruner (Creek), James Culberson (Choctaw), Ewing Hartshorne (Choctaw), Annetta Lohmann (Osage), Emily P. Robitaille (Chippewa), and Muriel Wright (Choctaw).[15] These periodicals set the stage for journals such as the *Indian Historian / Wassaja* (1967–80) and literary magazines such as *Sun Tracks,* which ran as a periodical from 1971 until 1979 before becoming a book series.

Chapter 2 considers transnational Cherokee political arrays in the work published in national periodicals by childhood friends Will Rogers and John Milton Oskison, with what Cherokee Nation scholar Kirby Brown calls the "trans/national stateswomanship" of their contemporary, Ruth Muskrat Bronson, as well as Brown's scholarship on it, providing additional nodes in the array. While their childhood in the Cherokee Nation influenced their political views, they developed political identities later in life primarily in response to World War I and its aftermath. Rogers came to oppose both military and cultural intervention by the United States, and Oskison increasingly embraced ethnic nationalism. When he writes about Mexico, for example, Rogers expresses nostalgia for a simpler, premodern life while also constantly needling the U.S. federal government for its coercive and in some cases violent interventions in Mexican national life. While Rogers used his commentary on Mexico to promote noninterventionism, Oskison produces a familiar depiction of a turbulent, uncivilized Mexico and ignorant, incompetent Mexicans of various ethnic groups and social classes. Oskison's political history, which suggests a concern for the social welfare of minority ethnic communities, does not prepare readers for such lamentable depictions. The politics of his posthumously published autobiography, "A Tale of the Old I.T.," help contextualize his views of Mexico and Mexicans. His portrait of the Cherokee Nation in the autobiography distinguishes Cherokees from other Indigenous Americans and asserts rural forms of labor, elite eastern education, law and order, and literacy as the key features of national Cherokee life. Socially, culturally, and politically, Oskison aligns an exceptional Cherokee Nation with the United States rather than with other tribal nations. Their divergent representations of Mexico anticipate a post-Renaissance political array with the same transnational focus in Silko's and Momaday's first novels as well as in Alexie's incisive, and often playful, references to indigeneity in Mexico.

Chapter 3 considers the surprising anticolonial politics of the shooting script of the Lynn Riggs and James Hughes film *A Day in Santa Fe* (1931) and of the film itself, and it identifies and develops a transhistorical array linking *A Day in Santa Fe* to films by late-twentieth- and early-twenty-first-century independent Indigenous filmmakers. The European and immigrant European American interest in Indigenous

American artifacts within a historical context of colonial Spanish and Catholic dominance defines much of Part I of the script and film. Part II of the script and film, however, decenters the colonial authority and primitivist orientation of Santa Fe in Part I by asserting a specifically Pueblo way of being in and knowing the land. The chapter argues that the film is a work of both Indigenous primitivism and the Cherokee avant-garde that challenges stereotypical caricatures in other silent films from the era, such as *Redskin* (1929) and *The Silent Enemy* (1930). Late-twentieth-century and early-twenty-first-century films such as Arlene Bowman's *Navajo Talking Picture* (1986) and Dustinn Craig's experimental *4wheelwarpony* (2008) consider remarkably similar concerns about privacy, cultural continuity, and the history of colonial violence in the Indigenous Southwest.

Though biographers of Native writers such as Bonnin, McNickle, and Riggs draw heavily on their correspondence, there are few studies of the art and politics of personal letters by American Indian writers, with only Silko's correspondence with poet James Wright earning mention by scholars.[16] Wright initiated the correspondence with a remarkable letter dated August 28, 1978, in which he struggles to convey how much he admires *Ceremony*: "I think I am trying to say that my very life means more to me than it would have meant if you hadn't written *Ceremony*" (in Anne Wright, *The Delicacy and Strength of Lace*, 3). In his next letter, Wright asks Silko to consider applying for a Guggenheim Fellowship and offers to write a letter of recommendation for her (*Delicacy*, 5). This invitation into a network of writers recalls Simon Ortiz's request for a recommendation for the same award from Matthiessen: "Peter, this year I am applying for a Guggenheim, and I am submitting your name as a reference to make a comment about me and my work" (Ortiz to Matthiessen, August 24, 1991). Neither Silko nor Ortiz have won a Guggenheim, though Silko won a MacArthur Genius grant in its first year along with writers such as Cormac McCarthy, Derek Walcott, and Robert Penn Warren. This Renaissance-era correspondence between Native and non-Native writers replicates exchanges in the previous generation, such as the one between Charles Alexander Eastman and the Pulitzer Prize–winning writer Hamlin Garland, who, for example, wrote to Eastman with praise for *Indian Boyhood* (1902).[17]

The letters from Wright to Silko and Ortiz to Matthiessen evince the private, delicate diplomacy in which Indigenous writers engage as they navigate the settler–colonial politics of what literary studies scholar James F. English calls "the economy of prestige (the economy of symbolic cultural production)" and the institutions controlling it (75). In their letters to scholars and fellow writers, including mutual non-Native friend and University of Oklahoma English professor Walter S. Campbell / Stanley Vestal, John Joseph Mathews and Riggs speak frankly and eloquently about their lives and art while also working within but in opposition to the dramatically asymmetrical relations of privilege and power between self-supporting Native writers and non-Native writers employed at flagship universities. Though their letters, the subject of Chapter 4, do not produce public political arrays, they speak directly to the history and politics of literary studies in the academy. Their letters also add many more pages of writing to mid-twentieth-century American Indian literary history, and they reveal, along with the surprisingly diverse bibliographies of southwestern literature produced by their correspondents and other scholars, their contributions to the emergence of a modestly progressive for the time, but to this point unrecognized, mid-twentieth-century academic network inclusive of American Indian writers.

The letters between Mathews and non-Native Texas folklorist J. Frank Dobie provide a particularly intimate look into this network. Mathews's social conservatism might have delayed his appreciation by scholars of American Indian literatures, but Dobie, along with other academics, advocated for him in the 1940s and 1950s. Mathews's commitment to documenting Osage life eventually, following Robert Warrior's *Tribal Secrets* (1995), made him a central writer and intellectual in American Indian literary studies at the end of the twentieth century. Riggs had equally rich if not as well documented friendships with Campbell and Pulitzer Prize–winning playwright Paul Green. He even sent his short drama manifesto about socially conscious theater as a seventeen-page letter to the latter. The Vine Theatre, Riggs argued, would resist "the triumphant, arrogant state" that "by pogrom, by discriminatory laws—and the other tools of inhumanity and cruelty" crushes all opposition to it (Riggs to Green, March 5, 1939). Riggs's friendship with Green and Mathews's with Dobie extended into the 1950s. Late in that decade, Yvor Winters, who crossed paths with Riggs in the 1920s in Santa Fe and who expressed in his poetry admiration for if also an imperfect understanding of Indigenous cultures, became Momaday's mentor at

Stanford.[18] Momaday identifies this moment as his "first big break."[19] During the last few decades before the end of legal segregation and in an anti-Indigenous settler–colonial world, Mathews and Riggs established in their private correspondence with non-Native writers a set of political arrays that anticipates and helps to contextualize later moments in American Indian literary history such as Momaday's "first big break" and Ortiz's appeal to Matthiessen.

Chapter 5, "Crimes against Indigeneity," examines the diachronic political arrays circulating within and among detective novels by Native authors, with a primary focus on Todd Downing, Sara Sue Hoklotubbe (Cherokee), and Carole laFavor (Ojibwa).[20] In the golden age of detective fiction almost sixty years before the passage of the Native American Graves Protection and Repatriation Act or U.S. Public Law 101-601, Downing wrote several novels in which criminals steal Indigenous Mexican artifacts and human remains to sell on the black market to museums in the United States. By using crime fiction to illuminate the transgressions committed against Indigenous peoples and, in some cases, to expose a legal system indifferent or antagonistic to them, Downing anticipates the work of post-civil-rights-era crime novels by American Indian authors, especially Hoklotubbe and laFavor but also Alexie, Thomas King, Louis Owens, Marcie Rendon (White Earth Anishinabe), and Ron Querry (Choctaw). The focus of these authors on crimes against Indigenous peoples and communities establishes a robustly progressive political array linking the pre- and post-Renaissance eras.

The conclusion, "Speculative Arrays," turns to an example that highlights the always self-conscious, selective critical work informing the identification and development of any political array in American Indian literary history. In the collection of essays *Mixedblood Messages* (1998), Louis Owens observes, "Gerald Vizenor and Sherman Alexie are at opposite ends of the spectrum of contemporary Indian writing" (81). He objects in particular to Alexie "posing militantly while giving the white audience what it already knows and desires" (81). In subsequent interviews, Alexie confirms that he also sees a distinction between his work and Vizenor's, commenting, for example, "If Indian literature can't be read by the average 12-year-old kid living on the reservation, what the hell good is it? You couldn't take any of [Vizenor's] books and take them to a rez and teach them, without extreme protestation" (Purdy and

Alexie, "Crossroads" 7). While significant formal and cultural distinctions exist between Vizenor's and Alexie's writing, they at times fall in the same place politically on Owens's contemporary Indian spectrum. If we shift our focus from the spectrum model of politics and approach Vizenor's and Alexie's writing as full of arrays that both diverge and meet, however, we would produce an interpretation that more precisely conveys how their work takes, rejects, and explores a range of political positions for our consideration. Vizenor's writing on Thomas James White Hawk in 1968 and Alexie's 1996 novel *Indian Killer,* for example, approach the same political issues, especially assimilation, within the context of homicides committed—or alleged to have been committed—by Native people, and Vizenor's reporting in the early 1970s on the American Indian Movement includes representations of activists and concerns about their tactics that align closely with Alexie's representation of Native activists in *Flight* (2007).[21] This discussion provides the final example of the way literary scholars elide the political diversity within single literary texts and among a single author's various publications and obscure the political continuities among the works of Native writers, even ones as ostensibly distinct as Vizenor and Alexie.

To draw a coherent picture of a Native writer's politics—of any writer's politics—requires isolating and emphasizing parts of texts and ignoring others and selectively organizing historical and cultural contexts to produce a convincing and compelling background. How might our view of the political array generated by Erdrich in the mid-1980s change if we take into consideration "A Time for Human Rights on Native Ground," an editorial in the *New York Times* published on December 29, 2000, on the anniversary of the massacre at Wounded Knee, in which she announces her "political leanings were all surface, consisting mainly of fashion statements" at the time of the Peltier trial ("A Time"). She also reveals that, following the trial, she was "ambivalent about Mr. Peltier and the attendant posturing of other leaders of the American Indian Movement" ("A Time"). While "not persuaded of his innocence," Erdrich explains, "I was positive that on the basis of what I'd heard in court that there was reasonable doubt as to his guilt and that he should not have been convicted" ("A Time"). The publication of *The Round House* (2012), a National Book Award winner directly engaged with conversations about the Violence against Women Act (VAWA), as well as her *New York Times* opinion piece "Rape on the Reservation" on

February 26, 2013, makes situating Erdrich as a politically conservative writer quite the challenge. David Treuer's still recent critique of Erdrich's "syntactical concessions" in her use of Anishinabemowin in *The Antelope Wife* (1998) and other novels, however, serves as a reminder that very few if any Native writers will pass every litmus test of their insurgent credentials (Treuer, *Native American Fiction*, 60). As this book argues, critics in Native literary studies might productively bring these challenging political moments into conversation in an effort to demonstrate the full richness of the politics in American Indian literary history and Indigenous communities and to derive from that conversation ideas about how best to confront enduring, deeply entrenched settler–colonial states.

CHAPTER 1

Indigenous Editing

Gertrude Bonnin, Lee Harkins, and American Indian Periodicals

As multimedia forms with distinct voices appearing alongside each other in every issue, periodicals often contain wonderfully rich political arrays. When under the control of Native publishers, editors, and writers, they provide an especially diverse range of political views within and among American Indian communities.[1] This study begins with a reading of the political arrays in two American Indian periodicals, one national and the other local. They circulated during an era with a political landscape that Native literary studies scholars tend to overgeneralize as produced primarily by a small group of boarding school graduates committed to assimilation. Many Native writers and intellectuals of this period considered assimilation as one strategy to manage and survive the struggle for and conflict over power in a settler–colonial context. However, debate always existed over what assimilation meant for Indigenous communities, present and future, and writers and intellectuals might give way in one arena (e.g., educational or economic) while holding firm in another (e.g., political, legal, or religious). They also changed their minds throughout their careers and adopted more or less progressive positions as they assessed new challenges. In addition, at times they expressed—or, in the case of Indigenous editors of periodicals—helped circulate, anti-settler-colonial political views. The polyvocality of these periodicals makes them ideal texts to demonstrate the concept of political arrays as a hermeneutic that illuminates the careful maneuvering of American Indian writers through always deeply vexed political contexts.

American Indians already had a long history of printing newspapers and periodicals, as Daniel F. Littlefield Jr. and James W. Parins have documented, by the time the Society of American Indians (SAI) published the first issue of its quarterly journal on April 15, 1913. These periodicals contain a rich and undertapped reserve of Native writing and political perspectives. A few, such as the *Cherokee Phoenix*, make irregular appearances in scholarship, and literary scholars have examined the work of a handful of writers, such as John Milton Oskison (Cherokee), Alexander Posey (Creek), and Will Rogers (Cherokee), who published in newspapers and magazines.[2] Robert Dale Parker's *Changing Is Not Vanishing: A Collection of American Indian Poetry to 1930* (2011), which contains the work of eighty-two Native poets and information on approximately sixty more, demonstrates the extent of unexamined Native writing in periodicals. Parker observes, "Most of the poems in this collection come from newspapers and magazines, not from books of poetry," and he comments on a "vast quantity of forgotten early American Indian fiction" uncovered in his research (7). In addition to poetry and fiction, periodicals contain editorials and other opinion pieces, biographies, legends, letters, short histories, personal testimonies, and examples of humor by Native writers. Indigenous editors, such as Carlos Montezuma (*Wassaja*, 1916–22), Marie Mason Potts (*Smoke Signal*, 1948–78), Howard Uyagaq Rock (*The Tundra Times*, 1962–97), Jeannette Henry (*The Indian Historian / Wassaja*, 1967–80), and Tim Giago (*Lakota Times / Indian Country Today*, 1981–92; 1992–98), also controlled the content of and therefore shaped the political debates in their periodicals.[3]

Gertrude Bonnin and Lee F. Harkins, as the editors of the *American Indian Magazine* (1915–19; formerly the *Quarterly Journal of the Society of American Indians*), and the *American Indian* (1926–31), respectively, published a wide range of Native voices and political perspectives. Bonnin approached editorial work as an extension of her community and political activism, in which she had been involved, most extensively with the Northern Utes on the Uintah and Ouray Reservation in Utah, for many years before joining the Society of American Indians. She differed from her friend and predecessor, Arthur C. Parker (Seneca), in exercising a less imperious editorial practice that allowed for a greater diversity of Indigenous political views.[4] At the age of twenty-eight, Harkins became the founding coeditor of the *American Indian* after studying journalism at the University of Oklahoma and working on several newspapers.[5] With the help of exclusively or almost exclusively Native editorial boards, Bonnin and Harkins used their magazines to make claims about Indigenous pasts, presents, and futures in tribal-nation-specific, pantribal, intertribal, trans-Indigenous, transnational, and settler–colonial contexts. They constructed a narrative of Indigenous America culturally, historically, and politically distinct in content, if not always in form, from dominant beliefs about what Indigenous Americans had been (childlike, primitive, savage), currently were (still benighted, incompetent government wards unworthy of citizenship) and would become (indistinguishable from European Americans). At the same time, these dominant views appeared in both magazines, especially in Harkins's, making generalizations about their political commitments difficult.

Bonnin and Harkins worked as editors in the later years of an era, 1877–1934, in which federal policies of assimilation targeted Native land as well as Native social, political, and cultural structures and practices and, therefore, radically compromised many sites of potential protest.[6] At the same time, to advocate for assimilation into the settler–colonial state meant taking a progressive position against segregation and certain forms of institutional racism, if not necessarily against the deep-rooted ideology of European and Anglo American superiority that informed the progressive as much as the reactionary position in the debates over Indigenous futures. While their periodicals promote this progressive agenda—national belonging for American Indians in the United States within a cultural context overwhelmingly defined by capitalism, Christianity, and representative democracy—and express varying degrees of condescension toward or rejection of Indigenous cultural beliefs and practices, this agenda is neither consistent nor monolithic. These periodicals also contain assertions of the rights of self-determination and self-representation as well as, for example, celebrations of resistance fighters and condemnations of non-Native depredations. Political emphases shift within and between issues, in some cases on the same page and in a rather jarring fashion. The periodicals contain, in other words, arrays of Indigenous political views circulating through the urgent conversations orchestrated by the editors and authors about indigeneity in the 1910s and 1920s in the United States.

Gertrude Bonnin's Activist Editing at the *American Indian Magazine*, 1915–19

Bonnin's literary reputation rests primarily on her work in the years 1900–1902, when Bonnin, in her midtwenties and under the self-given Lakota name Zitkala-Ša (Red Bird), published articles in *Harper's Magazine, Atlantic Monthly,* and *Everybody's Magazine* and a collection of *ohunkakan* titled *Old Indian Legends* (1901).[7] The articles were collected and published twenty years later as *American Indian Stories* (1921). Literary scholars have assessed Bonnin's work by focusing their attention on this three-year period of literary production that preceded her conversion to Catholicism, her role as an activist and public intellectual in the SAI, and her campaign against peyote with other prominent Native intellectuals, including Arthur C. Parker and Charles Alexander Eastman (Mdewakanton Dakota), and General Richard Henry Pratt, the non-Native founder of Carlisle Indian Industrial School. The "old legends" and "stories" tell only a small part of Bonnin's history. From 1915 to 1919, Bonnin was also a contributing editor and, for four issues, the editor general of the SAI's magazine. A consideration of her service as an editor provides the opportunity to review her fiction and autobiographical essays within a broader political and intellectual context, and the expanded focus on her entire career as author and activist illustrates that her relationship to both Native and non-Native cultural and intellectual traditions was a constant negotiation characterized by many shifts between acceptance of, resistance to, and compromise with those traditions. In many camps and, simultaneously, in a camp all her own, Bonnin participated in an array of divergent political scenes and networks. She moved between coalitions and alliances, western and eastern states, and tribal nations and pan-Indian communities, in a career as activist and writer that continued until her death. Any attempt to characterize Bonnin as consistently defying or accommodating a single political position obscures the diverse strategic views she adopted throughout her career in her search for a viable future for American Indians in the United States. While her own writing and activism constitute a remarkably nuanced political array—like, as Kirby Brown demonstrates, Ruth Muskrat Bronson's—the first part of this chapter focuses on the arrays she generates through her work as an editor of the *American Indian Magazine*.

Bonnin worked as an editor near the end of the first of four major periods, as categorized by Robert Warrior, for public Native intellectuals in the twentieth century. During the first of these four periods, which for the purposes of Warrior's study runs from 1890 to 1916, prominent Native intellectuals such as Eastman and Montezuma (Apache) helped form the SAI. The members of the SAI, Warrior explains, were part of a generation "faced with the prospect of total dispossession if Natives continued to resist the U.S. government" (7), and their efforts to organize represented "the first coming together of Native intellectuals in a specific political project" (10). In her study of Bonnin and three other major Indigenous intellectuals of this period, Kiara Vigil describes this "coming together" as occurring variously within social, intellectual, political, and cultural networks. While scholars have understood the SAI's project primarily as integrationist and assimilationist, as Vigil observes and challenges, the history of the organization's magazine, called first the *Quarterly Journal of the Society of American Indians* and then the *American Indian Magazine,* reveals a lively public discussion among American Indians about what integration and assimilation meant.[8] In particular, the accommodationist tone of the early issues shifted substantially when, in 1918, the year Carlisle closed as an Indian boarding school and the Native American Church incorporated in Oklahoma, Bonnin became the editor for four of the final five issues. Bonnin addressed a set of concerns shared by most Native intellectuals at the time: education, religious worship, literary self-representation, political self-determination, treaty rights, sovereignty, the legal status of Native Americans, the social and cultural status of Native women, and the social and cultural disruption of Native lives. She understood this disruption as the direct result of the Indian boarding school system, the government-ward status of most American Indians, the dictatorship of a corrupt Office of Indian Affairs (OIA), the reservation system, and peyote use.

Bonnin's life, spent almost entirely in the era in which the federal government aggressively enforced assimilation as its official policy, spanned a series of often abrupt changes in Indian Country that helped define the historical context in which she addressed these issues. She was born in 1876, the year that Lakota and Cheyenne warriors under the command of the Hunkpapa Lakota leader Sitting Bull defeated General George Armstrong Custer at the Battle of the Greasy Grass.[9] The military victory over invading U.S. troops did not lead to future successes for Indigenous communities on the plains or for the many bands of the Dakotas, including Bonnin's own people on the Yankton Reservation.[10] The assassination the following summer of the Oglala Lakota leader Crazy Horse and, in 1890, the assassination of Sitting Bull and the massacre of Big Foot's band of Minneconjou Lakotas at Wounded Knee discouraged continued military resistance on the plains.

Bonnin experienced firsthand the federal government's assimilation policy as a student at missionary and boarding schools—a bilingual Presbyterian school at Yankton; the Quaker-run White's Manual Labor Institute in Wabash, Indiana; Santee Normal Training School, founded by the Reverend Alfred Riggs in Santee, Nebraska—and as a teacher at Carlisle.[11] She witnessed the height of Dakota participation in the Ghost Dance; the suppression of traditional Native religious practices, such as the Sun Dance on the Uintah and Ouray Reservation, where she spent fourteen years; and the creation of the Native American Church.[12] She also defended in print her "pagan" beliefs, then converted to Catholicism.[13] In the legislative arena, Congress passed both the Manypenny Agreement, which in 1877 claimed the Black Hills for the United States and reinforced Dakota dependence on the federal government, and the General Allotment Act, which instituted a policy that continued until 1934 of allotting tribal lands to families and individuals. Native Americans continued to face various challenges to efforts at self-representation during this era. The Wild West shows, in which Sitting Bull participated, gained international popularity, while non-Native scholars and "friends of the Indian" reform organizations dominated by non-Natives continued to have a significant influence on the ways in which the general public viewed Indigenous people. The reform organizations also influenced federal policy. Immediately prior to the granting of citizenship to all Native Americans in 1924, Bonnin investigated the Osage Reign of Terror, during which non-Natives murdered Osages for their oil headrights, and she saw the publication in 1928 of the Meriam Report, which contributed substantially to a reform of Indian policy that became the Indian New Deal.[14] Before Bonnin died in 1938, the administration of John Collier began at the OIA, and, in 1934, Congress passed the Indian Reorganization Act or Wheeler–Howard Act, which, Standing Rock Dakota author Vine Deloria Jr. writes, "gave the reservations their first taste of self-government in nearly half a century" (*Custer,* 55).[15] This brief history should suggest neither unremitting disaster nor a life that ended at a point of clear reversal of the U.S. government's policies of assimilation, treaty abrogation, land seizure, and cultural warfare. As a Native intellectual and community activist throughout her life, Bonnin actively engaged in this tumultuous history that shaped her writing and editorial work.

Negotiating with the Civilizing Machine, 1900–1915

Two critical readings of Zitkala-Ša's work during the three years she published in mainstream magazines tend to dominate the scholarship on her. Scholars have an interest in her subversion of sentimental literary modes and in the ways in which her *Atlantic Monthly* essays overtly defy the federal government's assimilation program in the Indian boarding schools. These articles assess Zitkala-Ša in reference to Anglo women authors, with the exception of P. Jane Hafen (Taos Pueblo), who in "Zitkala Ša: Sentimentality and Sovereignty" situates Zitkala-Ša's work within the context of her commitment to tribal sovereignty, and Dorothea Susag, whose article "Zitkala-Sa (Gertrude Simmons Bonnin)" traces Zitkala-Ša's Native language and culture in the autobiographical essays.[16] More recently, Bonnin's biographer, Tadeusz Lewandowski, calls these essays "'a political autobiography' of sorts" (37). Generally, scholars view Zitkala-Ša's *Old Indian Legends* as an affirmation of Dakota culture and a subversive critique of colonialism. Jeanne Smith reads *Old Indian Legends* from a more specifically Native critical position by explaining the ways in which "Zitkala-Ša explores both the enabling and the destructive potential of the trickster for the future of her culture" (47). These articles contribute to our understanding of Zitkala-Ša within a contemporary critical context in which finding politically insurgent material in the work of marginalized authors is a common project. Zitkala-Ša's rejection of assimilation, of the violence of the "civilizing machine," helps establish her reputation as, at least during this time of her life, an anti-assimilationist (Bonnin, *American Indian Stories*, 66). In the final line of her series of three essays about her experience as a student and teacher, she writes, "Few there are who have paused to question whether real life or long-lasting death lies beneath this semblance of civilization" (99). Following her two years as a teacher at Carlisle, Bonnin intended to collect stories at Yankton in an effort of cultural affirmation that would have directly challenged her boarding school experiences.

Bonnin's literary career does not end with the publication of the legends and stories, her marriage at Yankton in 1902 to Captain Raymond T. Bonnin (Yankton Dakota), and her subsequent move to Utah. In addition to publishing poems in the SAI's periodical, Bonnin collaborated in 1913 with William F. Hanson, a music professor at Brigham Young

University, on *The Sun Dance Opera*.[17] The opera negotiates Native and non-Native cultural traditions in order to validate Native lives and beliefs within the context of a medium of creative expression privileged by the majority culture and, as Katherine Evans demonstrates, within the context of a particular kind of Native stage performance in the final two decades of the nineteenth century and first two decades of the twentieth.[18] Hafen observes, "*The Sun Dance Opera* reveals the sometimes turbulent cultural waters that Bonnin navigated in her life. Often she seemed caught between validating her indigenous beliefs and seeking public approval" (*Dreams*, xx). The performance of a religious ritual in a Western medium and for a mostly non-Native audience would have made the opera controversial even in the second decade of the twentieth century; this kind of public display of Indigenous religious practice frequently falls under scrutiny in early-twenty-first-century Native intellectual contexts. In *Manifest Manners* (1999), Gerald Vizenor comments on what he calls "the consumer sun dances" that for some members of the American Indian Movement became a performance of resistance rather than a serious spiritual ceremony (154). The consumer sun dances are also popular with "wannabes," non-Native cultural tourists who make playing Indian a weekend hobby.[19] Religious ceremony in a nonreligious context—on a theater stage, in front of television cameras, or for the benefit of tourists—no longer qualifies as a religious ceremony, Vizenor argues.

Though Bonnin and Hanson left places in the opera for the performance of Native songs and dances, the possibility of the exploitation of Native peoples and cultures might have troubled her future colleagues in the SAI, particularly Chauncey Yellow Robe (Sicangu Lakota), who contributed an article censuring Wild West shows to the magazine.[20] *The Sun Dance Opera* relies on a sentimental plot with a male villain, Sweet Singer, and two women under duress, the abandoned Shoshone Maid and Winona; Winona loves Ohiya but must contend with Sweet Singer's unwanted courtship. Contemporary Native scholars such as Craig Womack and Elizabeth Cook-Lynn suggest that aesthetic success or failure might be less important for assessing the value of the opera to Native communities than the fact that Bonnin fashions a response to colonial incursions into Indian Country—in this case, the suppression of the Sun Dance in Utah. Indeed, Lewandowski argues for the opera's subversive "political dimensions" (88). This theatrical performance of the Sun Dance also functions as a refusal either to capitulate to the majority culture's aesthetic expectations or to surrender a tribal worldview.[21]

Vizenor's observations on Luther Standing Bear (Oglala Lakota), the author, actor, teacher, and activist whose shifting challenges to and accommodations of the majority culture parallel Bonnin's, apply equally well to Bonnin's pre-SAI work.[22] In *Manifest Manners,* Vizenor identifies Standing Bear as his first example of a post-Indian warrior and asserts, "The postindian warriors encounter their enemies with the same courage in literature as their ancestors once evinced on horses, and they create their stories with a new sense of survivance. The warriors bear the simulations of their time and counter the manifest manners of domination" (4). Zitkala-Ša performs similar acts of courage in her early writing, as she works in her stories toward survival and resistance—or, to use Vizenor's term, survivance—and she counters the domination of her culture and people by making strategic forays into the enemy's territory: sentimental literature, opera.[23] The opera is the only creative work Bonnin made public during her fourteen years in Utah, where her work in the community of Uintah-Ouray eventually led to her membership in the SAI and a national presence in American Indian politics.

Liberating the "Little Peoples," 1915-19

The SAI originated at a meeting organized by Fayette A. McKenzie, a professor of economics and sociology, in April 1911 at Ohio State University.[24] McKenzie invited to campus a group of "progressives," American Indians who desired a reform organization run by American Indians and who, Hazel Hertzberg explains, "believed in education, hard work, and in adapting their attitudes, values, and habits of life to those of the larger American society" (31).[25] The organization began publishing the *Quarterly Journal of the Society of American Indians* in 1913, with Arthur C. Parker as the editor. In his discussion of the early years of the journal, Gregory Smithers identifies "education and citizenship," specifically birthright citizenship, as the primary political concerns of Parker and the contributing authors (265). He also highlights Parker's determination to keep the journal independent from the federal government, advertisers, and non-Native reform organizations while refining "the journal's message of uplift, self-help, and race-pride"

(276). Smithers asserts that to Parker and many other Native Americans at the time, "'assimilation' in the context of education and political activism meant giving Native Americans the cultural, linguistic, and civic foundations upon which to rise from 'tribalism' and unite to awaken the Indian 'soul.' To Indigenous readers of the journal, the invocation of the 'soul' bespoke a commitment to 'traditional' beliefs and cultural practices" (277). By situating "assimilation" within the context of Native political and cultural discourses in the second decade of the twentieth century, Smithers establishes a historically specific working definition of one of the key terms governing the discussion of any political array in Native American literary history.

Parker, a great-nephew of General Ely S. Parker, the author of the surrender ending the Civil War and the first American Indian to serve as commissioner of the OIA, edited the magazine during its first five and a half years of publication.[26] In his editorials, Parker insists that the responsibility for solving the "Indian problem" rests with Indigenous people, who need to "awaken" and "improve" themselves. As Smithers explains, the magazine took the editorial position that Native traditionalists "should be divested of their local political power and cultural influence" in order to make this awakening and improving possible (Smithers, 265). This observation about the journal's politics exists in uncomfortable tension with Smithers's working definition of assimilation, and it suggests that readers of the journal under Parker would have heard mixed messages about their beliefs and ceremonies. Parker's other interests included equal access to all levels of education and U.S. citizenship for all Native people. He also advocated for the creation of a court of claims specifically for American Indians, a codification of the laws and policies that applied to American Indians, and the gradual termination of the OIA. Most urgently, he believed in the value of the SAI as a pan-Indian community and as a group of American Indians determining their own future, and he protected the SAI by demanding loyalty to the organization and struggling vigorously to obviate any factionalism.

Bonnin became an editor during Parker's tenure, and her editorial work establishes a political array with his vision for the magazine and his ideas about the future of American Indians. She did not as readily forgive attacks on Native Americans. She also more stridently condemned injustice and corruption and more directly pursued the resolution of local, tribal nation grievances rather than focusing on the organization's national platform. The magazine's content, whether or not authored by Bonnin, became less conciliatory but more romanticized. As editor, Bonnin also foregrounded her interests in literature and community activism. In terms of policy, she used her position as editor to publicize her antipeyote stance, which developed in response to some appalling events at Uintah and Ouray.[27] Finally, in the issues she edited, Bonnin gave a more prominent position to the Native and non-Native women who played a role in local, national, and global affairs. An overall assessment of her editorial work suggests that she understood editing as a continuation of her role as an activist invested in the future of Native communities. However, as in her literary production, her editorial work neither consistently resisted nor consistently accommodated non-Native attempts to compromise, assault, or annihilate those same Native communities.

Parker's voice dominates the magazine beginning with the first issue in January–April 1913. Though the initially all-male editorial board included influential thinkers and writers such as Montezuma and Oskison, Parker appears to have solely authored the frequently long editorials (twenty or more pages) that begin each issue. Parker establishes the political position of the magazine by focusing his editorials on the "uplift" of the race and its necessary assimilation into the society and culture of the United States. He claims in the "Editorial Comment" in the first issue that the aim of the all-Native organization is "to place the race in the position of a constructing, producing factor in civilization" (7). Along with many of the writers published in the magazine, Parker saw education as the key to uplifting the race. By education, he did not mean the limited curriculum at Indian boarding schools but the formalized Western education to which many non-Natives had greater access. The vocational education of the boarding schools, in the SAI's opinion, inadequately prepared American Indians to compete in a world largely controlled by non-Natives. Parker wanted access to more Western education.

Parker develops a defensive, apologetic, and paternalistic argument for assimilation. In the April–June 1913 issue, he opines, "The fundamental principle of Americanism since its earliest beginning has been to produce a uniform civilization. The base of that civilization, better termed *ethnic culture,* was and is English" ("The Editor's Viewpoint," 104). He continues by discussing a hypothetical immigrant from

Finland: "Later, as he became acculturated, he might return to a consideration of the ways of his fathers and seek to commemorate them, but purely as a matter of racial pride or patriotic interest, and not as something to be revived and made again an active culture to be lived and followed" (104). Parker assures his audience that American Indians have little interest in remaining Indians. Following complete assimilation, he suggests, they will identify as Indigenous biologically or historically but not culturally or politically. In this second editorial, in a section subtitled "The Social Tyranny of Tribal Life," Parker even distances himself rhetorically from "the Indian people":

> It is not difficult to see why the student carefully educated, trained and taught in all the ways of civilized life does not prosper as he should normally in normal communities when he returns to the reservation. He alone can not always compel all the rest of the community to see that he is right and that they are wrong.... This brings to the proposition, then, that to bring about the civilization we desire to the Indian people, where they are, we must make the social life of the reservation the same as that found in communities we are pleased to call civilized. (108)

Parker views Anglo culture as normative, and he sees no future for American Indians in the distinct cultural and political worlds on reservations. The SAI advocated for the settlement of land claims, but not in order to strengthen reservation communities. Instead, the SAI wanted the Department of the Interior to allow "competent" American Indians to control individual allotments.[28]

Throughout his tenure as editor, Parker qualifies his theories of assimilation and race relations by drawing contrasts between American Indians and African Americans or recent groups of immigrants, for example, but he steadfastly maintains his focus on the issues important to him and the SAI. Direct criticism of Anglo settlers, Indian agents, and other government officials occurs more frequently with each issue, both in his own editorials and in the articles. Parker delivers his strongest reproach to Europe while discussing World War I. In the January–March 1917 editorial, he wonders if "the civilization of which the European has boasted is after all a defective thing" (8). But several issues later, he returns to commenting upon the ignorance and superstition of "savage tribes" and insisting that complete loyalty to the United States is the only hope for American Indians ("Editorials," 7). Fearful of creating factions within and political difficulties outside the organization, Parker attempted to avoid controversy by adhering tenaciously to the organization's political platform.[29]

As soon as she became a contributing editor in the October–December 1915 issue, the last under the title *Quarterly Journal of the Society of American Indians,* Bonnin made her first appearance in its pages as a community organizer and activist. Her presence as a contributing editor did not lead to changes in the magazine's format and content, with the exception of the promotion of her community-center project and the publication of her poems. When he first mentions Bonnin, Parker uses her as an example of those Native people who have benefited from education in non-Native schools. The next two references to her reveal Bonnin's interest in publicizing her community work at Uintah–Ouray. In a section devoted to the SAI's Fifth Annual Conference, held in Lawrence, Kansas, the editors note that the community center exemplifies what American Indians can do to help themselves. Regardless of Bonnin's own ideas about the role of the center, the editors interpret her work according to the SAI's platform of American Indian self-help.

Bonnin describes the community center from her own perspective in the same issue in "A Christmas Letter from Zit-kal-a-sa: Describes Her Community Improvement Work among the Utes." She expresses a primary concern for the welfare of the community's women elders, for whom the community center sewing class made some garments, though Bonnin also requested that the women pay for the materials used. The sewing class also began serving lunch to Utes who came to the agency for the Monday disbursal of government checks. Prior to the intervention of the sewing class, the underpaid Native government employees at the agency faced an overwhelming number of requests for hospitality. The remainder of the letter describes what soon became her well-known opposition to peyote, which she had already started to oppose publicly. In her discussion of peyote, Bonnin most closely approximates Parker's patronizing tone toward American Indians on reservations: she describes the Utes as "easy victims because of their ignorance, superstitions and degradation" ("A Christmas Letter," 324). She has, she notes, asked a state senator, a Mr. Colton, to join the SAI as an associate member and to help with legislation to prohibit the importing of peyote into Utah.

Bonnin viewed her antipeyote position as intimately connected to her community-center work. Her article "Chipeta, Widow of Chief Ouray, with a Word about a Deal in Blankets" appears in the July–September 1917 issue, following Ouray's obituary. The inclusion of the obituary establishes the context for the antipeyote statement. First, Bonnin assures her readers that both Ouray and Chipeta befriended and even defended white settlers. Then she describes her visit to Chipeta to warn her of the destructive effects of peyote. Bonnin believes that neither Chipeta nor her brother, McCook, will stop using peyote because the government has not told them that, like liquor, peyote is unhealthy. After she criticizes the government's attempt to honor Ouray's widow with a gift of two trading-store shawls that they require the Ute tribe, and therefore Chipeta, to purchase, Bonnin constructs Chipeta as an infantile and abused loyalist to the government and an uninformed abuser of peyote. As in her previous statements against peyote use, Bonnin uses the conventional social reform discourses of Native inferiority and helplessness. Her use of this discourse advances her political interest in prohibiting the use of peyote but undermines other attempts to demonstrate the strength of Native women. She concludes her article by explaining that water rights, title to Ute land, or a letter from the government against peyote use would have been better gifts than two shawls. This conclusion contains what we might call a microarray: a demand for sovereignty (water rights, land claims) but also a request for colonial imposition (prohibition of Native religious practices). Bonnin sees an American Indian future with self-determination in terms of ownership and control of the land but without peyote use, which she believed threatened the ability to own and control the land wisely.

Bonnin's literary contributions to the magazine during her tenure on the editorial board promote the SAI's stated goals, though occasionally they hint at challenging Parker's more conciliatory position. "The Red Man's America" offers revised lyrics to "My Country 'Tis of Thee" that change the song into a request for citizenship and voting rights and an overt demand for the passage of bills that would abolish a corrupt Indian Office and criminalize peyote use. "A Sioux Woman's Love for Her Grandmother" appears in what came to be known as the "Sioux

Number" in October–December 1917. In the poem, set just prior to the Battle of the Greasy Grass, Bonnin focuses on the relationships between women as constitutive of Native community: a grandmother, defying Custer's troops, remains behind to wait for her lost granddaughter as her community retreats. "The Indian's Awakening" is Bonnin's most politically nuanced literary contribution. The title draws on one of the most familiar words in the discourse of racial progress. If an awakening has occurred in the poem, however, the poetic persona has emerged from sleep into a nightmare. The opening lines recall her first days at boarding school, when school employees cut her long hair into an Anglo style and took her traditional clothing. But those who attempted this violent imposition of Anglo identity "Left heart all unchanged; / the work incomplete" (line 3). These lines convey a less sanguine view of assimilation than Parker's.

The following lines, the second and third stanzas from "The Indian's Awakening," offer a more forceful challenge to Parker's editorials and other articles in the magazine such as the award-winning essays written by boarding school students about the value of their educations. They repudiate both Bonnin's own boarding school experience and the title of the poem:

> My light has grown dim, and black the abyss
> That yawns at my feet. No bordering shore;
> No bottom e'er found by hopes sunk before.
> Despair I of good from deeds gone amiss.
> My people, may God have pity on you!
> The learning I hoped in you to imbue
> Turns bitterly vain to meet both our needs.
> No Sun for the flowers,—vain planting seeds.
>
> I've lost my long hair; my eagle plumes too.
> From you my own people, I've gone astray.
> A wanderer now, with no where to stay.
> The Will-o-the-wisp learning, it brought me rue.
> It brings no admittance. Where I have knocked
> Some evil imps, hearts, have bolted and locked.
> Alone with the night and fearful Abyss
> I stand isolated, life gone amiss. (Lines 9–24)

The promised enlightenment or awakening remains unrealized; the learning she has received helps neither herself nor her people. If they read it carefully, the poem must have made Parker, Eastman, Montezuma, Pratt, and the other regular contributors wonder about Bonnin's political commitment to the SAI's platform. However, Bonnin also uses the conventional note of excessively articulated anguish at cultural loss prevalent in non-Native literary endeavors about American Indians. This tone might have made the poem more acceptable.

The rest of the poem refigures the meaning of a racial "awakening" as used by Parker and many of the other contributors to the magazine. In the poem, the persona has a spiritual awakening that requires a journey to visit her ancestors. A divine voice assures the persona that life has meaning and refreshes her before she climbs on a saddled horse and rides through the cosmos, the realm of what she calls the Great Spirit. In this cosmos, she encounters

> A village of Indians, camped as of old.
> Earth-legends by their fires, some did review,
> While flowers and trees more radiant grew. (Lines 66–68)

At this camp, an elder tells her that the people she sees are now souls, distant from their life on earth in traditional Dakota lands but still connected to the living by memory. The persona then makes a joyous return to earth. Figuratively, the persona has "gone back to the blanket," the derogatory expression used by adherents of the boarding school system to describe a student who returns to the reservation and rejects non-Native education.[30] The poem hints provocatively, too, at the promise of the Ghost Dance in the persona's discovery of a spirit world in which her ancestors live in the old ways without Europeans.

Bonnin's letter describing her community activism and the poems illustrate two of the many ways that she managed and responded to political issues in Native communities.[31] The Christmas letter shows her working with a vibrant community to address problems created by an intrusive government bureaucracy. In addition to organizing Indian Office employees, missionaries, and Utes in order to alleviate a strain on the community's resources, she expresses anxiety about the threat of peyote to the community's health. The poem contains, in contrast, an image of a village of elders living a happy, idealistic existence, and it does not represent Native belief systems as superstitions or American Indians unfamiliar with Anglo educational expectations as ignorant or degraded. The letter and poem suggest two paths towards "uplift," with one drawing inspiration from older generations and the other from dedicated activists. They form an array of political perspectives and demonstrate Bonnin's willingness to use a range of tactics and discourses to defend Native people.

Bonnin's role as contributing editor and eventual election as the SAI's secretary and treasurer provide her with the opportunity to interject herself more forcefully into debates within the SAI and diversify the political arrays generated by the organization. In the September 1916 issue of the magazine, the editors publish a transcription of a debate at the Sixth Annual Conference, in Cedar Rapids, Iowa, on the loyalty of the Indian employees of the OIA to "the race" and the government. Against the attacks of those who want to abolish the OIA immediately, Bonnin defends those working for the government so that they can stay on the reservation and help their people. Her contribution to the debate, informed by her own work at Uintah–Ouray, challenges those who have not remained "in the wilderness" to help their people with daily needs. She asserts, "In justice to those Indians who wish to be citizens of our beloved America, to be true to the Government of America, to be civilized men and women, to be loyal to their own who are not so far along as they are, these Indian employees are glad to work under the Indian Bureau" ("Open Debate on the Loyalty of Indian Employees," 255). Bonnin places enormous political value on committing to work inside Indigenous communities, which explains in part why she shifted her focus away from her literary efforts for so many years.

The context in which Bonnin became the editor of the magazine demonstrates this commitment to tribal national or local and regional activism and her willingness to risk factionalism to address specifically tribal national rather than more generally pan-Indian concerns. Hertzberg explains that Parker's frustration with increasing factionalism led him to consider taking the magazine from the SAI or making the SAI subsidiary to the magazine (168, 172). As political disagreements and personal animosity exacerbated the conflicts at the Sixth Annual Conference over the abolition of the OIA and the prohibition of peyote use, Parker grew increasingly anxious about the organization. With Parker engrossed in the factionalism, Bonnin began to assert her position on the editorial board in late 1917 with the publication of the "Sioux Number." Hertzberg explains that the issue was

> in all likelihood... evidence of Gertrude Bonnin's Sioux patriotism. For as Parker took less interest and devoted less time to the affairs of the Society, Mrs. Bonnin gave more.... She was by no means willing to sit by and watch the Society expire or allow it to become merely an adjunct of the *American Indian Magazine*. While she agreed with Parker on many issues, being especially vehement against peyote, she was increasingly inclined to take a stronger line against the Indian Bureau than he did. (173)

Following the publication of the "Sioux Number," Bonnin aligned with Eastman to organize a conference in 1918 in Pierre, South Dakota, in the middle of Dakota country. Parker did not attend the conference, where he was ousted as president. The ensuing issues of the magazine include an unprecedented emphasis on a single American Indian group, the Dakotas: Bonnin included pictures of Eastman and Captain Bonnin; added Margaret Frazier, Ben Brave, and Elaine Goodale Eastman, an author and Charles Eastman's Anglo wife, to the editorial staff; and foregrounded past (Sitting Bull's assassination) and present (the Black Hills land claim; the death of the Eastmans' daughter) events in the region.[32] Tribal national ties remained strong for these members of the SAI, even if Bonnin or Eastman, for example, did not chose to return permanently to their communities.

The voice of the magazine, if not necessarily its politics, changed abruptly when Bonnin claimed the editorship of the Autumn 1918 issue, following the conference in Pierre. Hertzberg explains that at the Pierre conference, "Parker was asked to remain as editor of the *Magazine* should he desire to do so; otherwise, Mrs. Bonnin was to become editor, as she informed him shortly after the conference.... While he hesitated, Mrs. Bonnin acted, notifying him that since she had received no reply from him, she was assuming the editorship herself" (176). Bonnin provides a different version of events in her first editorial, which begins by explaining that military duty prevented Parker from attending the conference. Her description of the conference also puts a benign public facade on the factionalism that led to Parker's ousting. Bonnin claims, "The spirit of a great united American brotherhood fighting in a common cause,—the defense of world democracy, pervaded the whole affair" ("Editorial Comment," 113). Like Parker, Bonnin read the war in Europe as directly relevant to American Indians, though she articulated this view in more strident language:

> Surely, the flaming shafts of light typifying political and legal equality and justice,—government by the people, now penetrating the dark cloud of Europe are a continuous revelation. The light grows more effulgent, emanating as it does from the greatest of democracies,—America. The sunburst of democratic ideals cannot bring new hope and courage to the small peoples of the earth without reaching the remotest corners within America's own bounds. (113–14)

This insistent demand for liberation, conveyed in the characteristic paternalism of reform discourse, illustrates the clearest distinction between Parker's and Bonnin's approaches to Native politics.

Bonnin locates her interest in tribal or local activism in a global context. In contrast to Parker, she focuses much less on cultivating the organization itself and more on using the organization and the magazine to make as direct interventions as possible in the daily lives of American Indians. In her editorial for the Winter 1919 issue, Bonnin reiterates her position on the recently ended war in Europe. The exultant tone contrasts sharply with Parker's in his long pieces on the need to embrace the organization's "ideals." Bonnin exclaims, "Under the sun a new epoch is being staged! Little peoples are to be granted the right of self-determination! Small nations and remnants of nations are to sit beside their great allies at the Peace Table; and their just claims are to be duly incorporated in the terms of a righteous peace" ("Editorial Comment," 161). Bonnin's optimism about the Paris Peace Conference implies an equal hope that American Indians will have their "just claims" addressed in the United States. She continues, "The universal cry for freedom from injustice is the voice of a multitude united by afflictions. To appease this human cry the application of democratic principles must be flexible enough to be universal. Belgium is leading a historic procession of little peoples seeking freedom!" (161–62). The subtext, as articulated for years by the SAI and Bonnin and by Eastman in an article that follows her editorial, is that the OIA produces afflictions by defying the democratic principles to which Bonnin refers. Bonnin hints at possible coalitions, too, as she mentions members of labor organizations, women, and African Americans (including W. E. B. Du Bois, an associate member of the SAI) as petitioners for justice. She ends her editorial with a request for citizenship for American Indians and a query as to who will represent her people in Paris. With a more tribal-nation oriented editorial board providing a message in a broader global context, Bonnin locates herself in a political and intellectual place distinct from Parker's.

Bonnin also expresses without apology more interest in the "old ways" than did Parker, who, in an effort to keep his intellectual focus on the future "awakening" of his race, rarely mentioned older generations.[33] She follows her first editorial with "Indian Gifts to Civilized Man," an article previously published in the July 1918 issue of the *Indian Sentinel*. The article foregrounds American Indian religious beliefs: the powerful Navajo deity Changing Woman, Bonnin explains, provided humans with both corn and potatoes, which, in turn, helped alleviate the hunger around the world that was one consequence of the war. After shifting to global events, Bonnin defends American Indians as patriotic and loyal, even though they did not have citizenship, and offers gratitude that the military did not segregate American Indian soldiers. She believes "a close companionship promises mutual benefits," as American Indians, in her estimation, had an inherited sense of direction which made them good guides ("Indian Gifts," 116). Bonnin suggests the possibility of a mutual and equal, perhaps idealized, cultural exchange within the context of a pro-integration position that is not necessarily antitribal. In addition, in this issue she published a letter she wrote to the third assistant secretary of war requesting that he not close Carlisle as a boarding school. The letter indicates the emergence of a strategic alliance with her former nemesis, Pratt, with whom she shared an opposition to peyote.

Bonnin's greater willingness to honor Indigenous beliefs complements her self-representation as a well-read and politically and intellectually engaged Native woman involved in world events and pushing for reform. Following her "Editorial Comment" and a short article by Eastman in the Winter 1919 issue, she published "America, Home of the Red Man," a personal narrative about her travel to the Pierre conference that she wrote for the *Home Mission Monthly*. In the narrative, a "paleface" traveler accosts Bonnin in order to ask about the service pin she wears. Bonnin explains that the pin belongs to her husband, "a member of the great Sioux Nation, who is a volunteer in Uncle Sam's Army" (165). The man replies, "Oh! Yes! You are an Indian! Well, I knew when I first saw you that you must be a foreigner" (165). Rather than responding to the man, Bonnin has a vision of thousands of American Indian soldiers in France. She watches the soldiers and thinks, "The Red Man of America loves democracy and hates mutilated treaties" (165). The vision continues with the image of a Ute grandmother donating five hundred dollars to the Red Cross, an American Indian soldier who refuses to quit after he receives multiple wounds, and "little French orphans, babes with soft buckskin moccasins on their tiny feet. Moccasins that Indian women of America had made for them, with so much loving sympathy for an anguished humanity" (166). A call for the emancipation of American Indians from the OIA and the paternalism of the U.S. government provides the vision's denouement. Following the vision, Bonnin interrogates the traveler about what he has read recently, but, obviously intimidated, he withdraws, and she suggests that the world will pass by the traveler and leave him behind. The white man, like so many literary Natives, fades off the page in the face of the politically and intellectually astute Native woman.

As the image of the fading paleface traveler suggests, Bonnin's editorial position allowed her to provide a greater presence for a favored constituency, both Native and non-Native women. She substantially alters the content of the magazine by the cumulative influence of her editorial decisions: pictures of and eulogies for Angel DeCora Dietz (Winnebago), the artist who illustrated *Old Indian Legends*; newspaper clippings about women's temperance and suffrage movements; excerpts from a speech in which she insists that more women, the teachers of Native children, should be involved in the SAI; use of the term "sisters" to describe her companions in reform. In her third contribution to the Winter 1919 issue, "The Coronation of Chief Powhatan Retold," Bonnin privileges the role of women in global affairs and shows the subversive rhetorical moves she used so frequently in the autobiographical essays and *ohunkakans*. Bonnin takes as her topic a European visit by President and Mrs. Woodrow Wilson. She explains that the first lady, Edith Bolling Galt Wilson, is a direct descendant of Pocahontas and that therefore the hosting of the Wilsons by the royal families of Europe reenacts the reception given to Pocahontas and John Rolfe three centuries previously.[34] Bonnin, however, had less interest in international diplomacy than in reiterating the message of her previous editorial. She places the Wilsons' visit in historical context: "Springing from the tribal democracies of the new world, Pocahontas was the first emissary of democratic ideas to caste-ridden Europe. She must have suffered untold anguish when King James was offended with her sweetheart husband, Rolfe, for his presumption in marrying the daughter of a king—a crowned head too!" (179). In this historically subversive narrative, Bonnin suggests that Europeans destroyed democracy in the Americas, just as they had done in Europe during World War I. We should reject European claims about bringing civilization to the Americas, Bonnin implies. Rather, a Native woman, Pocahontas, brought civilization to Europe, and Mrs. Wilson, her descendant and the wife of the man trying to establish the League of Nations, occupies the same role contemporarily. The second part of the article reinforces the point: the crown and royal costume sent by King James I through John Smith to Powhatan, a "liberty loving soul," left this Indigenous leader unimpressed (180). Bonnin says the English "resorted to trickery" to get Powhatan to accept the gifts and dress as a European monarch (180). In Bonnin's narrative, liberty resides in the "primeval forest," not the European metropolis, and coercing Powhatan to mimic the metropolis in the forest signals the beginning of the European attempt to remake the Americas in its image. Pocahontas and Mrs. Wilson, with help from their male relatives, offer the greatest resistance to European barbarism. The Pocahontas article explores all the issues of interest to Bonnin and the SAI, from education to treaty rights to citizenship. The citizenship issue, for example, when read through the lens of this article, becomes a request for *re*entrance into a democratic world destroyed by Europeans.

Bonnin makes a direct plea to tribal national political leaders in her final contribution to the Winter 1919 issue, "Letter to the Chiefs and Headmen of the Tribes." The brief letter focuses on learning English and protecting Indigenous land as urgent political issues. The title has an asterisk that alerts readers to a message from Bonnin at the bottom of the page: "Dear Reader into whose hands this letter has fallen, will you do a kind act by reading and explaining it to an Indian who cannot read or speak English?" (196). The message appears to solicit sympathy for the "poor Indians" of conventional reform discourse, the same stereotype that Parker mocked by referring to his representative American Indian by the first name "Lo," as in "Lo, the Poor Indian."[35] Yet the body of the letter contains a call by a bilingual Native activist for strategic language acquisition. Learning English will facilitate political organizing across tribal national borders and, Bonnin implies, will help American Indians retain ownership of their land "for the sake of our children's children" (197). She signs the letter "Yours for the Indian Cause" (197). Her "Indian cause"—Indigenous leaders from all tribal nations using English to organize and to defend Indigenous land—anticipates a future that comes to pass.

Bonnin's last issue as editor, Summer 1919, features an emphasis on religion not evident in the previous issues, though she still addresses many of the topics that held her interest in the previous editions: her tribal nation, the loyalty of American Indian soldiers, the benefits of integration, and blatant racial discrimination, in this case against Eastman, whom the OIA prevented from entering the Menominee Reservation and speaking about citizenship. In "An Indian Praying on the Hilltop," Bonnin thanks the Great Spirit for providing her with individual consciousness and protecting her. The next two paragraphs state that this same power awakens her from nightmares of friendless poverty in a dangerous land. A reader could interpret this dangerous land as an America invaded by colonial European powers, as the factionalized SAI, or as reservations, which Bonnin saw as unpleasant environments. The prayer ends with Bonnin rejoicing: "I see the dawn of justice to the Indian, even upon earth: and now, Great Spirit, my heart is full of joy!" (92). While optimism often follows statements of potential despair in her work in the magazine, Bonnin leaves many questions unanswered. Readers might take the prayer as a statement in support of traditional American Indian religious practices, though only the reference to a Great Spirit instead of God distinguishes it as a possibly more Native than Christian ritual expression. The prayer might also sound to some readers like a performance of humility for her acquaintances in Christian reform organizations. It is not even clear whether Bonnin intended "An Indian Praying" as autobiographical or fictional. The message's ambiguity, however, makes it only one of Bonnin's many routine articulations of an often elusive but always compelling intellectual and political view of American Indian life in the early twentieth century.

The report on the conference at the end of the Fall 1919 issue includes an address by Bonnin in which God, rather than the Great Spirit, plays a significant role within the context of Bonnin's belated plea for unity within the organization, which she claims had doubled in membership in the last year. In apparent contradiction of her personal optimism about the organization, her career in it culminated at the conference. In the officer elections, Thomas Sloan (Omaha), a well-known peyotist, defeated Eastman and Captain Bonnin by a vote of 25 to 8 to 5. The following transcription of events shows Bonnin declining her nomination by Sloan to remain as secretary and treasurer. Her protest of ill health also serves as her resignation as editor of the magazine:

> I feel that I must at this time make a public statement about my own health which, under ordinary circumstances, I would not mention. I have been glad to serve in some capacity these past four years and I think you all know it but I have continued the work against my physician's instructions. I have been very ill and he says that if I expect to recover or keep well I must rest. I shall not be able to serve you in any way I fear. I am honored to have my name mentioned again but my name will have to be withdrawn because of my health. (180)

Following her statement, Captain Bonnin declines a nomination, too, and Eastman and Montezuma both decline, "absolutely," to serve as editors of the magazine (181). The hasty withdrawal of this group, led by Bonnin, appears to result from Sloan's election as president. As quickly as Bonnin claimed the editorship from Parker, she lost it and her power within the organization to Sloan.

Lobbying and Organizing for the Indian Cause, 1920–38

Sloan's differences with the outgoing officers and editors manifest in a vastly different political orientation for the magazine. In the last issue, non-Native writers predominate. Parker's and Bonnin's efforts to cultivate Native voices make an abrupt retreat as non-Native authors—such as Mary Roberts Rinehart, a non-Native initiated into the Blackfeet tribal nation and given the name Pitamakan, or Running Eagle; Walter Hough, the curator of ethnology at the United States National Museum; Clark Wissler, the curator-in-chief in the Division of Anthropology and the curator in North American ethnology at the American Museum of Natural History; and Lew Sarett, a "noted author of Indian verse"—

present to readers conventional vanishing-race discourses and exoticized Indians. Sloan even sold space in the magazine for advertisements, including one for Stetson, the company famous for its iconic hats associated with life in the western United States.

Though her involvement with the SAI ended, Bonnin's career helping what she called the "little peoples" continued unabated. In 1921 and 1922, Bonnin lobbied for Indian causes, often under the auspices of the General Federation of Women's Clubs (GFWC), which added a national committee on Indian welfare. As William Willard explains in his discussion of Bonnin's political activism, the chair of the GFWC's Indian welfare committee hired John Collier, the future commissioner of the OIA, to research the social conditions under which many American Indians lived. While Collier went to New Mexico to fight the Bursum Bill, Bonnin traveled to Oklahoma in November and December 1923 to investigate the abuse of probate laws by legal authorities, especially county judges, and professional guardians to dispossess Indigenous people in eastern Oklahoma. Her research led to the publication by the Indian Rights Association of *Oklahoma's Poor Rich Indians* (1924), coauthored with Charles H. Fabens and Matthew K. Sniffen.[36] Both Willard and Vigil show that Bonnin's political activity increased dramatically following her exit from the SAI. Willard explains that Bonnin used her connections with Republicans, including wealthy philanthropists such as the Du Ponts and Rockefellers, in the "efforts of the Yankton Sioux tribal government to secure claims reparations from the federal government for land lost and infringed upon in Minnesota, Iowa, and South Dakota" (12). With her husband, she campaigned in the West for congressional candidates, and in 1928 their efforts led to the addition of a plank in the Republican platform. Willard explains, "The plank called for two things: (1) a presidentially appointed commission to investigate and report to Congress on the administration of Indian affairs; (2) guarantees of treaty and property rights to the Indians of the United States, any law or administrative practice which was prejudicial to these rights should be repealed" (12). She eventually served in Collier's American Indian Defense Association and then formed her own organization, the National Council of American Indians, in 1926. In 1932, she gave testimony before the Senate Indian Committee, with a particular focus on the abuse by reservation superintendents of their complete control over the leasing of American Indian land to non-Indians. In the same year, she abandoned Herbert Hoover and joined Will Rogers in supporting Franklin D. Roosevelt, who made Collier the commissioner of Indian affairs.

Bonnin's work as editor illustrates her diverse interests and wide-ranging knowledge of tribal national, local, and global concerns related to the struggle for liberation. She devoted much of her work to alleviating immediate suffering without explicitly committing to any particular political position, though she took a strong political stance against peyote. As Susan Bernardin observes, "As forecast by her autobiographical stories, Zitkala-Ša constructed and ultimately claimed a self that thwarted reductive interpretations of her life and writing as simply either assimilationist or subversive" (230). Her editorial work also defies the efforts of contemporary scholars seeking to characterize her politics as one-dimensional. Lewandowski, for example, describes Bonnin as "one of a new generation of Sioux resistance fighters" and "a forerunner of Red Power" (16). After World War I, he argues, she developed "a proto-Red Power platform of resistance to white rule" (16, 150). Yet it is the array of political positions that Bonnin embraced, abandoned, and in some cases reaffirmed as the political circumstances around her constantly changed that most accurately conveys her full life not as a symbol for a single political perspective but as a dedicated political worker and activist.

Indigenous Modernity at Lee F. Harkins's *American Indian*, 1926–31

Lee F. Harkins's editorial work also generates a robust constellation of political arrays in another understudied source of Indigenous writing. Four years before the birth of fellow Choctaw and future crime novelist Todd Downing in 1898 in Atoka, Oklahoma, Harkins was born nearby at Boggy Depot in the Choctaw Nation, Indian Territory. Choctaw historian Muriel Wright traces Harkins's life after Oklahoma Territory and Indian Territory became the state of Oklahoma in 1907 through high school in Tishomingo, Oklahoma, service in World War I, and two years at the University of Oklahoma, where he prepared for a career as a journalist. Throughout his adult life, Wright explains, "Lee Harkins was a writer, editor and publisher at different times though he continued as a printer by trade, a member of the Newspaper Printing Corporation, in the composing room of *The Tulsa Tribune* for many years" (285). Wright contributed articles to the magazine, which she calls "his great venture," before adding, "He was always proud of the files of his *American Indian* though it took him several years to make up the deficit of the expense for its publication" (285). The *American Indian* had a progressive agenda, as Harkins and many of his authors repeatedly assert, but it contains a diverse collection of political perspectives and an exciting number of nearly or entirely forgotten Native writers trying to maintain and assert modern indigeneity through stories, histories, and biographies, among other genres, in a world both between the Indian Citizenship Act of 1924 and the Indian Reorganization Act of 1934 and between World War I, in which thousands of American Indians served with distinction, and the Great Depression. Will Rogers held the attention of the entire nation in print, on the radio, and on the silver screen, and Chickasaw director Edwin Carewe was making his "best-known and most lucrative films," including *Resurrection* (1927), *Revenge* (1928), *Ramona* (1928), and *Evangeline* (1929), from screenplays by his brother, Finis Fox, and with star Mexican actress Dolores del Río.[37] Charles D. Curtis of the Kaw Nation served as vice president of the United States from 1929 to 1933, and Jim Thorpe, already recognized as one of the world's greatest athletes, continued to establish his Hall of Fame credentials in professional football and to barnstorm with the World Famous Indians basketball team.[38] Near the tail end of an era Phil Deloria calls "the founding years and the boom years of the sound of Indian," operas regularly featured Native themes, and performers such as Tsianina Redfeather / Florence Tsianina Evans (Creek), Princess Watawaso / Lucy Nicolar (Penobscot), and Princess Atalie / Iva Josephine Rider (Cherokee) were popular (*Indians in Unexpected Places*, 218–19). Harkins produced his magazine in this context, in which a handful of Native people had a national voice and visibility but most others, like the Utes at Uintah–Ouray served by Bonnin or those Indigenous people facing the competency commissions created under the Burke Act of 1906, continued in poverty and poor health and remained under the control of capricious and predatory federal and state governments.[39]

Harkins ran the *American Indian* as a sixteen-page monthly with a distinctly local Tulsa and regional Oklahoma flavor, though he also published some stories of national, continental, and occasionally international interest. Baby pictures along with wedding and death announcements for Tulsa-area residents sit alongside stories about Native activities in New York, Chicago, and Hollywood; federal legislation; archaeological digs on the West Coast; and, for example, travel to the Middle East. He created regular features and then abandoned them, often very quickly, for others: a Hall of Fame of Native leaders mentioned in the first issue but not brought to fruition; the Indian Lore Exam for You, which ran for three issues from July 1927 to September 1927; the Poetry Page, which debuted in September 1928; themed issues or "numbers" (on Cheyenne, Haskell-Tulsa Football, Kiowa–Apache–Comanche, Okmulgee) from October 1928 to January 1929; and the First American's Page for young readers, which first appeared in April 1930. Harkins also devoted many pages to long pieces of generally uninspired fiction and nonfiction, including thirteen installments on Washington Irving's 1832 tour of Oklahoma and nine installments of a pre-Columbian story of adventure and warfare by John Brown Jewett.[40] Throughout its five years in print, the *American Indian* maintained a consistent focus on a narrow selection of topics: business and economics, education (Pratt casts a long shadow across the magazine's pages, as do boarding schools, such as Carlisle and Chemawa, and colleges, especially Bacone and Haskell); history of warfare and removal; land claims; missionary work, past and present; and racial identities and representations. The writing on each topic had political implications—and in several cases, such as land claims, political urgency—for Native people in the struggle for and conflict over power in tribal national and settler–colonial contexts.

Harkins filled the magazine with a diversity of Native voices, but most of them came from the Native nations of Oklahoma. His voice—firm in promoting "progress" for Native people—emerges most clearly in the editorials. On occasion, he used the editorial page to publish the work of other writers in letters or reprinted articles. In the magazine's main body, he included many Native writers, some now forgotten even if respected in their own time. These writers include Joe Bruner (Creek), James Culberson (Choctaw), R. T. Hanks (Cherokee), Ewing Hartshorne (Choctaw), Robinson Johnson / Whirling Thunder (Winnebago), Annetta Lohmann (Osage), Emily P. Robitaille (Chippewa), Anne Turman VanNoy (Chickasaw), William T. Ward (Chickasaw), Harriette Johnson Westbrook (Mohawk), and Muriel Wright (Choctaw), among others, as well as the following poets identified and analyzed by Robert Dale Parker in *Changing Is Not Vanishing*: Stella LeFlore Carter (Chickasaw), De Witt Clinton Duncan (Cherokee), Winnie Lewis Gravitt (Choctaw),

Gust-ah-yah-she (Menominee), James Harris Guy (Chickasaw), Mary Hartshorne (Choctaw), William J. Kershaw (Menominee), Ben D. Locke (Choctaw), Alice C. Oshkosh (Menominee), Iva Josephine Rider as Sunshine Rider (Cherokee), Elise Seaton (Cherokee), and Julia Carter Welch (Chickasaw).[41] From January 1930 to June 1930, Harkins put together the most politically and culturally compelling series of issues. While the magazine folded as the result of a defamation lawsuit, Harkins always struggled to keep the magazine in production, and it eventually folded as the result of a defamation lawsuit.[42] More issues such as this group of six—thoughtfully organized, forcefully resistant to attacks on Native dignity, and consistently concerned with sharing a range of Native voices—might not have saved the magazine, but they would have secured Harkins a legacy more on par with other prominent Indigenous cultural producers of the era.

"To All Indians in North America" or "The Palefaces Came Like Blackbirds"

The *American Indian* debuted in October 1926, with a masthead and cover photo of Osage leader and former principal chief Bacon Rind illustrating a balance between Indigenous pasts, presents, and futures that Harkins attempted to achieve in the pages of his magazine. The title, with *The* in script and *American Indian* in block letters flowing like a small wave, runs above three tepees on the left and the skyline of Tulsa on the right with two American bison in a small circle in the middle and two U.S. flags hanging from a tomahawk and a pipe and flying at forty-five-degree angles over the camp and the city, respectively. Journalism scholar John M. Coward, who reads the *American Indian* as promoting "a progressive, thoroughly assimilated Indian identity for Native Americans during the early twentieth century," observes, "Since Harkins worked downtown, it seems clear that he saw the city as the place for the Indian present—and future" (4, 8). If in fact Harkins envisioned "the Indian present—and future" as urban, as Coward argues, he shared this view with many other Indigenous people, including, to use one famous example, the Mohawk ironworkers moving in large numbers to New York City in the 1920s.[43] Harkins also did not necessarily see cities as inherently non-Native. As historians such as Rosalyn Lapier and David Beck, Nicolas Rosenthal, and Coll Thrush and literary critics such as Laura Furlan have documented, many Indigenous people in the

United States rejected the incommensurability of indigeneity and urban life.[44] In one editorial, Harkins traces "the lineal line of the Indian" to the "Mayan and Aztec stages of civilization" ("Culture of the Indian," 4). Without taking into account his sketchy outline of Indigenous migration in North America, Harkins might have understood a movement by American Indians into Tulsa as a return to urban life.

The photo of Bacon Rind in a formal, stiff-backed studio pose and ceremonial dress also conveys a multilayered political message. Bacon Rind, according to Jon May, "was politically progressive and favored the allotment of the Osage Reservation and the development of its oil and natural gas resources. He remained a traditionalist in customs, however, and always wore native dress and an otter-skin hat." May adds, "Bacon Rind was a gifted speaker of the Osage language" ("Bacon Rind"). In the epic history of his people, *The Osages: Children of the Middle Waters* (1961), John Joseph Mathews refers to Bacon Rind as one of the last widely respected Osage leaders:

> He was much over six feet tall and very handsome, embodying all the physical attributes that calendar artists had conceived. Like most of the fullbloods, he wore his traditional buckskin leggings and moccasins and his otter bandeau with an eagle feather stuck between it and his Peyote long hair. He wore beautiful blankets and colored silk shirts. He wore the *wah-sha-she-skah,* the disk gorget carved from the fresh-water mussel, representing Grandfather the Sun, and he wore a large crucifix hung about his neck. He walked each day in the eyes of Grandfather, but also in the eyes of the impressionable journalists and magazine writers. (779–80)[45]

Bacon Rind, May and Mathews suggest, had adapted to modern life; he could, simultaneously, boldly proclaim his Osage identity and religious practice while also successfully maneuvering within an emergent culture of modern American celebrity.

Harkins had optimistic, ambitious plans for the magazine. The dedication at the top of the table of contents of the first issue promises a continental and then hemispheric scope: "To all Indians in North America in whose veins flow the blood of the 'Oldest Aristocracy' of the western hemisphere and more especially to those stoic and faithful leaders who have passed beyond the 'pale frontiers of life', The American Indian is dedicated" ("Dedication," 1). His reference to the "Oldest Aristocracy" hints at one of the magazine's main strategies for establishing Indigenous equality with Europeans and European-descended settlers: claiming civilization as Indigenous. In his thoughts on the older generation of Osage men that serve as an introduction to comments on Bacon Rind in *Wah'kon-tah: The Osage and the White Man's Road* (1932), Mathews calls them all "old aristocrats" (322). By self-fashioning identities as princesses, an act informed by but distinct from colonials and settler colonials exoticizing Native women, female Native celebrities and performers also took part in this cultural and political strategy.[46]

Harkins might not have acknowledged that such claims, such appropriations of discourses of civilization and aristocracy, carried a political message about Indigenous belonging in the Americas, since they were self-evident to him. Indeed, he viewed the magazine's enterprise as non-political. "Our Code of Ethics," which he published in the first issue, asserts, "The magazine is non-political, non-sectarian and non-partisan. We endorse any move that will be beneficial to the advancement of the Oklahoma Indian. This magazine desires to become the 'voice' of all Indians in expressing their ideas for the intellectual advancement of Oklahoma society" (4). Yet the content of the magazine belies the claim that the magazine does not take political positions. Like the SAI's journal, the *American Indian* adopted a politically progressive editorial position. In fact, Harkins immediately caught the attention of Arthur Parker, who sent a letter to the magazine that Harkins published in the second issue. Articles by Parker also appear occasionally in the pages of Harkins's magazine throughout its run. After praising the magazine in his letter, Parker opines, "Our Indian brethren need a deepened consciousness of their rich heritage and of their responsibilities. It is what our people do constructively that is going to win for them a present day place in the sun. I am glad that your periodical is emphasizing what the modern Indian is doing, rather than what he did years ago" (Letter to the editor, 8). Harkins and Parker are literally and figuratively on the same historical and political page: the "rich heritage," an aristocratic one to writers like Harkins and Mathews, forms the basis for Indigenous modernity.

However, Harkins's commitment to publishing the points of view of many different Native writers and documenting the various activities of American Indians across the country made sustaining a dogmatic progressive position impossible. Next to Parker's letter, the photograph of Little Sugar Brown, a four-year-old Otoe and champion powwow dancer in full regalia, generates political tension on the first editorial page. The photographer showed Brown in action during a performance at an event at Haskell Institute identified by Gloria A. Young and Erik D. Gooding as one possible beginning of "the era of the modern powwow on the Southern Plains" (Young and Gooding, 1013).[47] The photo conveys, in Parker's words, "what the modern Indian is doing," in this case finding a way to continue "what he did years ago," that is, maintain traditions, some of which had been banned by Commissioner of Indian Affairs Hiram Price at the urging of Secretary of the Interior Henry Teller in 1883. Punishment for violating the ban included either the loss of rations or imprisonment.[48] The Office of Indian Affairs had recently—in 1921 and 1923—published circulars that encouraged agents to enforce these regulations on traditional dances.[49] Thus Little Sugar Brown, as well as the other dancers at the event and their supporters, helped perform a future into which early Red Power activists like fancy dancer Clyde Warrior (Ponca) could ceremoniously and joyfully step.

Even the celebratory affirmation of the central role of Indigenous people in the journal's production makes an important political statement about Indigenous self-determination. An unsigned article entitled "Introducing 'Ye Editor'" appears on the editorial page of the first issue. The author, perhaps Harkins writing about himself, identifies the editor as "one-half Choctaw-Chickasaw Indian" and "an employee of The Tribune mechanical department" ("Introducing 'Ye Editor,'" 4). After asserting that the magazine "will endeavor to express ideas of the Indians, their views and opinions," the author shares endorsements from well-known supporters, both Native (Cherokee congressman W. W. Hastings and Kaw senator and future vice president Charles D. Curtis) and non-Native (Choctaw Nation–born Colonel Patrick Hurley and the Pawhuska, Oklahoma, attorney T. J. Leahy). The author then turns to Harkins's biography, noting accomplished male ancestors on both sides of his family (his maternal grandfather Captain Benjamin Smallwood and his paternal grandfather Colonel G. W. Harkins) and his professional experience at Tishomingo, Norman, and Tulsa. The biography ends with the quaint remark that Harkins lives with his mother in Tulsa, after which the author lists the members of the nearly all-Native editorial board and, for the Native editors, their tribal nation citizenship.

Articles by Native writers such as Joe Bruner, Annetta Lohmann, and Emily Robitaille form an especially diverse array of political perspectives; Bruner was a particularly entertaining and provocative storyteller of narratives of glorious Creek exceptionalism. Bruner, identified in the caption beneath his photograph as a "prominent member of the Creek Tribe, who lives at Sapulpa," made his first appearance in the sixth issue, in March 1927, with an article reprinted from the *Tulsa Tribune*, "Interesting Legend Tells Indian Came from So. America" (10). A transcription of a talk Bruner delivered at a Kiwanis Club lunch, "Interesting Legend" begins with an origin story of "the Indian" in a place Bruner calls "the Happy Land." "This land of happiness," Bruner explains, "is the heaven of the Redmen.... There, millions of Redmen are. Men and women, and they are all as happy as the Creator can make them." These ancestors, who lived in an idyllic Indigenous past, came to this world through a tunnel in a mountain. Once their people began to die, they tried, unsuccessfully, to rediscover the tunnel. Only the dead, Bruner observes, "join their people in this beautiful and happy land that they once left." He anticipates some resistance to the story but asserts, "The Redman has a right to his own belief as other people. He does not believe that he is a descendent of the baboon or a monkey; he says as far back as it has been handed down to him from mouth to ear he has always from the beginning been an Indian man and woman" (10).[50] While Bruner tells a romanticized and generalized rather than Creek-specific emergence story, he uses it to claim an Indigenous religious point of view in contrast to both Christianity and evolution.[51] With the 1924 Scopes trial still a recent memory, Bruner's audience would have seen his article as participating in this debate about human origins.

Bruner shifts from a cosmological to a historical perspective in the next section, in which he situates Creek emergence in South America. Creeks lived there "for hundreds of years," he observes, before game became scarce. In response, the Creeks, or "Spo-Ko-Gee nation," divided into four tribes and two towns and eventually moved north through Panama, Mexico, Texas, and the North before returning to a warmer climate and settling in the Southeast (10). Their illustrious history included conquering and adopting many other tribes, without ever sustaining a military loss; losing and then finding their seed corn; and fighting with "a species of Indian ... much lighter in color than they had ever seen before" (11). These "white redmen" or "race of white Indians," in Bruner's words, built the mounds in what is now the U.S. Midwest. The Spo-Ko-Gees, Bruner says, routed the mound builders by driving them to the southern tip of Florida. Surrounded, they constructed boats to flee the Creeks by sea, though the Spo-Ko-Gees "expected that the first storm would sink every Mound Builder" (11). The story of a "red race" so soundly defeating and even destroying a "white race" by driving it into the sea probably pleased some readers and deeply troubled others. Harkins, who endorsed and perhaps even articulated "a happier relationship between the Indian and his white brother" as a goal of the magazine ("Introducing 'Ye Editor,'" 4), must have assumed that many readers would not recognize the potentially subversive claim to Indigenous American superiority.

Harkins published seven more of Bruner's articles, in which he continues to celebrate Creek history and culture, in the next eight issues. In articles with titles such as "The Indian Women Served as the Official 'Scalp Takers'" (May 1927), "A Creek's Uncles Always Selected His Companions in Life" (July 1927), "E-Nah Is Said to Be the Discoverer of the Tobacco Weed" (September 1927), and "The Indian Hunter Prized Very Highly His Flint and Steel" (October 1927), Bruner presents Creeks as strong, militant, and socially well-organized as well as healthier and more virtuous than non-Natives. "The Indian Women," for example, begins with the Spo-Ko-Gees sending "the last of the Mound Builders" a farewell volley of arrows (8). Bruner curiously claims that some of the Mound Builders, and "little squads" of Spo-Ko-Gee, Cherokee, Choctaw, and Chickasaw allies, survived a sea voyage to the Philippines and returned to the Americas at the Chicago World's Fair in 1893.[52] He shifts from this history of Indigenous global migration to ethnographic descriptions of Creeks dressing deer skins, making *sofkee* and soups, and using charms before ending the article with a discussion of apparently fearsome Creek women killing and scalping prisoners in preparation for the Scalp Dance.[53] His comments on *sofkee*—"As long as an Indian can drink sofkee there is hope for him to live"—in a section entitled "The Red Man's Eats" indicates a strong, enduring connection to Indigenous foodways, and the assertions about Creek women, made in an almost deadpan prose, reinforce the representation of Bruner's people as powerful and willing to defend themselves aggressively.[54]

As he continues to shift between Creek culture and history, Bruner maintains a matter-of-fact, difficult to generalize political voice. In

"Legends and Traditions of Muskogee Indians Revealed" (June 1927), he covers in detail the Green Corn Dance, which he calls, with cavalier disregard for the facts, "the only religious ceremony of the Redman" (6). After a careful description of the ceremony on a "great worship day," he comments on the Redman's "superstitions" (6). He distinguishes, therefore, between organized, institutional religious practice and folk beliefs involving hunting, for example, within Native communities. In "A Creek's Uncles," he draws a distinction between prophets (those who diagnose) and medicine men (those who provide a remedy) and segues into "some never failing remedies among the Red Men's Medicine Men" for gunshot wounds, appendicitis, snake and spider bites, and the like (8). The discussion of remedies leads to thoughts on the wellness of contemporary Indigenous people in "Many Clans Were Formed in Ranks of Native American" (August 1927). Bruner observes, "Since the Red Man built him a house to live in and began to eat hog and beef and to take strong drink he is no good any more. God made him to live in the open air and eat and live on wild meat. But the change to civilization has ruined his health" (10). His thoughts recall Bonnin's in her "Letter to the Chiefs and Headmen of the Tribes":

> Many times as I walk on the paved streets of the city, I long for the open Indian country in which I played as a child. I wondered how our White brothers can be content, being born and bred In-doors. I understand that it is their fast increasing population that necessitates building houses, larger and higher, to accommodate them. The White man is a wonderful builder of stone houses, which to me are better to look upon from the outside than to live in, as they shut out the sky and sunshine. (197)

While Bonnin suffered from chronic ill health, she celebrates outdoor life not as a healthy alternative to indoor life but as a component of her case for maintaining Indigenous land ownership. Bruner, however, argues that adapting to colonial or settler–colonial lifeways has had a severe impact on Native physical and even moral health: "The Redman on his native heath was truly an honest man. God never made a man of any color that was more honest than the Redman, nor did he make a more virtuous woman than the Indian woman" ("Many Clans Were Formed," 10). Bruner concludes by characterizing assimilation as a fall: "The modern civilization of the white man as the Redman embraced it has been a downfall to the red man and woman" (10). While he appears to have developed some non-Native prejudices against certain Creek cultural practices, Bruner does not embrace or advocate for assimilation.

Indeed, his contributions to the magazine read like cautionary tales that often celebrate Native political and military leaders such as Wild Cat (Coacoochee). A Seminole resistance fighter in Florida during the 1830s, Wild Cat, according to Bruner, swam back to the continent with his followers after their exile to Cuba ("Removal of Five Tribes to Oklahoma Is Historical Event," November 1927).[55] After removal, "It was said that Wild Cat was not satisfied with the country that now is Oklahoma and penetrated the wilderness to Old Mexico and that it was here he lived his remaining days—still unconquered by the white man" (6). Bruner calls postremoval life in Oklahoma initially happy for the Indigenous peoples of the Southeast, if not for their slaves, but the Civil War caused a rift between pro-Union and pro-Confederate Creek factions. He celebrates Hopothe Yohala (Opothleyahola) for insisting that the Creeks remain neutral "because the north and south were raging a war merely because of the negro and that the Indian always got the worst of it when it came to making treaties with the white man" (6). After declaring his neutrality, Hopothe Yohala led a group of his people westward, along with Cherokees, Chickasaws, Choctaws, and Osages. During their flight, Confederate General James McQueen McIntosh attacked and overwhelmed him.[56] The Creeks, Bruner asserts, lived with the animosity between the two factions, which included the occasional spilling of blood, for many years. Coacoochee and Hopothe Yohala represent models of strong Indigenous leaders who face similar fates despite making different political and military decisions to benefit their people.

After praising Indigenous resistance fighters and condemning "civilization" as unhealthy for Indigenous people, the final paragraphs of Bruner's series sound politically timid. Now the Indian "is progressive" and "for the upbuilding of the community in which he resides," he argues before adding as a final note that "during the late World war the Indian went across the seas, sacrificing his life in order to make this a better world to live in—which reveals his warpath days are over and that he has become a worthy citizen striving to do nobler things in life" ("Removal of Five Tribes," 6). The language appears ambiguous or generic enough, though, to leave readers wondering precisely what Bruner means by "upbuilding" and "nobler things," especially since in his articles he positions "nobility" in an Indigenous past.

Whereas Bruner situates Native people, and especially Creeks, of the 1920s in a sometimes comfortably mundane and sometimes glorious and even epic past, Emily Peake Robitaille (White Earth Ojibwe), a contributor as well as an editorial board member, and Annetta Lohmann (Osage), a contributor of eight articles, give readers the views of a younger, more eagerly progressive generation. Robitaille, a student at Carlisle earlier in the same decade that Bonnin arrived as a teacher and, later, a teacher at Carlisle herself, wrote three articles in support of Pratt and his educational system.[57] In her first, "Chippewas Benefitted by the 'White Man's Education,'" Robitaille makes an elusive argument about the way residents of White Earth faced and overcame settler–colonial forces such as rapacious timber interests, which play such an important role in Louise Erdrich's novels *Tracks* (1988) and *Four Souls* (2001) and White Earth Ojibwe author and political activist Winona LaDuke's novel *Last Standing Woman* (1997), and the federal bureaucracy. While Robitaille does not make clear how boarding school education aided them, she claims that following their dispossession by the timber corporations, White Earth residents left the reservation and established themselves "coast to coast and from Canada to Mexico" (6). "The talk about 'starving Chippewas' is propaganda," she argues. Instead, she writes, "It is safe to say that none of them will be found living in the slums of any community," and "from out the chaos self reliance has come to them" (6). She concludes the article by arguing that all Indigenous people in North America will have the same experience as these Chippewas. In preparation, they should have the same kind of education as non-Native people, preferably, she proposes, at a new institution called either Carlisle University or Pratt University. Bonnin must have wondered about the efficacy of her own coherently and passionately argued positions in the face of such poorly constructed assertions about the recent history and contemporary social and political status of American Indians. At the same time, Bonnin had reconciled and joined forces with Pratt before his death in 1924 over their shared antipeyote stance, and she objected to the closing of Carlisle in 1918.[58] She might have had mixed feelings, therefore, about Robitaille's proposal to honor the founder of Carlisle with a university named after him.

Robitaille also successfully advocated and raised funds for a memorial, "erected in loving memory by his students and other Indians," to Pratt at Arlington National Cemetery ("Memorial Erected," 6). In subsequent issues, the *American Indian* listed in very small print the names of some of the six hundred contributors. Those contributors include Charles Alexander Eastman, Thomas Sloan, Fred Lookout, Arthur C. Parker, Chief Standing Bear, Bacon Rind, Joe Bruner, Sylvester Long Lance, and many other locally and nationally known Indigenous people.[59] Robitaille even posted an advertisement for "Carlisle Sweaters" in the July 1927 issue, on sale, evidently, to raise money for the university. The ad reads: "Be a booster for Carlisle University and order a Carlisle Sweater" ("Carlisle Sweaters," 16). She returns as a contributor in August 1927, with the first installment of a biography of Pratt titled "General Pratt's Friendship for the Indian Led to Establishment of Carlisle College" (11). The biography, a short puff piece, takes readers from his birth to the founding of Carlisle. In ensuing installments, equally full of praise and admiration, she describes Pratt's "disheartening" struggles, "untiring efforts," and "grim determination" on behalf of the school and its students ("General Pratt Encountered Many Struggles," 13). Comments in this article, such as "So great was Pratt's influence with his students that he induced them to subscribe to funds from their savings account to help with improvements to the school," suggest an unwillingness to address the dramatic power imbalance between Pratt and the students (13). Based on what Bonnin wrote about her educational experiences, she might have seen Pratt taking money from students as outright theft.

Annetta Lohmann adds a richly textured node to the political array generated by Bruner and Robitaille. Identified as a "promising journalist" and "a member of the Osage tribe" living at Pawhuska in an editor's note before her first article, "Holy Jerusalem Is the 'Shrine City' of the Entire World," Lohmann contributed a series of eight articles on her trip to the Middle East in 1924 as part of a group, including other family members, going to attend the dedication of a basilica at Mount Tabor. This "American Indian Abroad Narrative," to use Dean Rader's term for several of the chapters in LeAnne Howe's *Choctalking on Other Realities* (2013), appears almost seventy years before Howe's title story about her own visit to Jerusalem. Rader's sense in the foreword that Howe's travel essays "birth a new genre" suggests how much Renaissance and post-

Renaissance writing shapes American Indian literary history (iv). Even Will Rogers, to whom Rader compares Howe as a humorist, published "American Indian Abroad Narratives" in the 1920s, such as *Letters of a Self-Made Diplomat to His President* (1926) and *There's Not a Bathing Suit in Russia* (1927).[60] While Howe explains in the second paragraph of "Choctalking," the title story, that she visited "Israel/Palestine as an academic tourist on a university-sponsored tour" (*Choctalking on Other Realities*, 79), Lohmann does not tell readers the reason for her visit until near the end of her narrative in the seventh article, and she emphasizes the significance of her Osage identity, and her Osage ceremonial dress, only in the final two. Her decision to structure the articles in this way prompts readers to consider the earlier articles within the context of the revelation in the later ones of her pride in her Osage family.

While Bruner celebrates Creek culture and history, and, in one article, explicitly rejects Judeo-Christian and scientific explanations of Indigenous origins, Lohmann roots her identity in Judeo-Christian culture and history. A Christian pilgrim and representative of the Osage Nation, Lohmann writes throughout the articles in the voice of Christian and American superiority. Though she notes in her first article in July 1927 that "the Holy Land is under the rule of Great Britain," she does not connect British imperialism in the Middle East, or the British occupation of Jerusalem, to the history of European colonialism in the Americas ("Holy Jerusalem," 2).[61] Upon arriving in Palestine, Lohmann engaged in an orientalist discourse evident throughout the series. Even the "large, round, orange moon" sits in the sky as an exotic marker of "the Orient" (2). As an awe-inspired Christian pilgrim walking in Christ's footsteps, she visits a long series of sites, beginning with the Basilica of Mount Saint Sepulchre, Mount Calvary, and Golgotha, before exiting through the Damascus Gate to the Mount of Olives. She continues the series in the next issue, which features a photograph of her on the cover. As she documents her pilgrimage step-by-step in the voice of a devout Christian speaking to other devout Christians, only her identification as Osage in the editor's note before the first article and on the cover of the August 1927 issue beneath her photograph draws attention to the significance of her tribal nation citizenship.

The title of the second article appears motivated to generate Christian outrage and anti-Muslim sentiment: "Mohammedans Forbid Christian Worship in Their Mosque." Such outrage at the suppression of religious practices circulated at the same time in Indian Country, where Indigenous people in 1924 had faced another attempt by the federal government to prohibit their ceremonies. Yet, again, Lohmann's alliances appear strictly Christian. Her group attends the Church of the Pater Noster, the Chapel of the Ascension, the site of Mary's birth, and the Garden of Gethsemane, and she comments on the healing waters of the Pool of Bethesda and the site of the execution of the Apostle James on "the spot where the first apostolic blood was shed in the cause of Catholicity" ("Mohammedans," 2). James's death precedes several paragraphs in which Lohmann stokes Christian grievance: at the Chapel of the Angels, Christ "was struck in the face by the mailed fist of a cowardly soldier" and "made the sport of soldiers"; at the House of Caiaphas, "we gazed upon the prison of Christ, the dark, cold bastile where He was chained by His neck to a prison wall" (2). While she acknowledges the sincerity of Jewish people praying at the Wailing Wall, she observes that "they are blindly asking for the Christ who has already come down from heaven—and returned" (2). Immediately thereafter, the group goes to the scene of the Last Supper, now a mosque where "no Christian dare bow his head or bend his knee in prayer, for the Mohammedans will not tolerate these outward signs of Christianity" (2). Within a few lines, in the same column of print, Lohmann expresses her own religious intolerance and then condemns religious intolerance, while also missing an opportunity to reject the religious intolerance of the Office of Indian Affairs.

The six additional installments continue in the same vein with expressions of myopic American exceptionalism and occasionally evocative observations of life in Palestine. In the September 1927 issue, Lohmann describes a context of intense paranoia between adherents of the different faiths who struggle for control of the region. She adopts the voice of the superior American: "The Jerusalem of today seems to be the meeting place of all the religionists of the world. Men and women walk about mumbling something that may be charitably construed as prayer. In America such behavior would cause anyone to be termed insane. In Jerusalem, it is perfectly logical" ("Many Denominations," 2). Camel trains, people in colorful dress, and "ragged men, smelly camels, or stupid-looking donkeys" complete the picture of an exotic, primitive world inside Jerusalem, while, Lohmann says, the modern exists only outside the walls (2). In these passages, Lohmann represents her religion's sacred homeland in the same way many writers depict Indigenous American religious beliefs and practices.

Indeed, Lohmann suggests that the sacred Christian homeland has not changed since the era of the religion's emergence in the region. In the October 1927 issue, which features on the cover Ruth Shields Downing, Choctaw author Todd Downing's sister, Lohmann visits Bethlehem, "the center of the earth," and the Grotto of the Nativity ("Christ," 2). She slows the narrative and patiently describes the mise-en-scène in a way that evokes place more powerfully than the catalogs of historic sites in the previous columns. These more careful observations, however, do not change her view that she has walked into a Christian past as well as a Christian space. In November 1927, she reiterates her claim that Bethlehem appears unchanged from two thousand years ago. At the Virgin's Well, she "watched the native women carrying water from the well in earthen pots balanced gracefully upon their heads" ("Many Places," 2), and she compliments a group of women cleaning their clothes by soaking them in a bag and beating them with clubs. She follows this praise with another condescending gesture of American superiority: "It was the only evidence of cleanliness that I saw in the Holy Land" (2). The "mudhut settlement" of El Mejdel, purportedly the site of Mary Magdalene's birth, she concludes, was "squalid and uninviting" (2), and the "waste land" around the Dead Sea leaves her unimpressed (2). In "Nazareth—Scene of Christ's Childhood—Has Cabaret" in the December 1927 issue, we learn of a "dance hall" that, Lohmann insinuates, serves the local Muslim population (2).[62] Lohmann resists romanticizing; her Palestine appears paradoxically rich in Christian history but fallen, even postapocalyptic, and in need of salvation.

Her group of pilgrims brings the means of this salvation with them. They will, she explains in "Nazareth," dedicate a "new basilica built on Mount Thabor" (2). She avers, "As the church was built with American money, an American archbishop was asked to dedicate it" (2). With this high-ranking representative of the Catholic Church, the archbishop of Santa Fe, New Mexico, they present to the region "a living memento to American faith" and "an American gift to Almighty God" (2). As if to provide a final reminder of the necessity of American salvific charity, Lohmann observes that Muslims control the Grotto of Elias (the prophet Elijah) and have turned it into a "pagan mosque" (2). Lohmann appears for the most part uninterested in the region's long history of occupations, religious wars, and political intrigue. Her Christian grievances sound petty—unclean locals, a dance hall, a pagan mosque—and they undermine any sense of awe that she generates with exclamations about how these sites move her.

Yet in her final two contributions to the *American Indian*, Lohmann conveys as much pride in her Osage heritage as in her U.S. citizenship. After her emotive farewell to the Holy Land in "Nazareth," Lohmann returned to the magazine two months later in February 1928 with "Aboriginals at Dedicatory Services on Mount Thabor," a story accompanied by a picture of her, her mother and father, and several other travelers holding an American flag. "Aboriginals" begins with a description of a visit to the region thirty years ago by a group of American Catholics. In response to "the forlorn conditions in Palestine" and the "poverty and dire need which they had witnessed in the Holy Land" (2), the pilgrims decided to raise funds to build a basilica on Mount Tabor. Lohmann and her family members made the trip in 1924 in order to attend the dedication of the basilica. Lohmann asserts:

> And at this solemn dedication, at this holy place on sacred ground, the real Americans were represented, for among the pilgrims were five Americans in whose veins flowed the blood of the Osage Indian. These five Indians, who were none other than my relatives and I, had brought with them from America an American flag made of silk and gaily decorated with fringe; ... My brother, dressed in the uniform of an American army officer, and I, dressed in the tribal costume of the Osage Indian, presented the American flag to the basilica.... We represented the true Americans—the soldiers who risked, and so often gave their lives for their country; and the Indians, to whom America originally belonged before the invasion of the white men. ("Aboriginals," 2)

For the first time in these articles, Lohmann foregrounds her indigeneity and the settler–colonial context in which she travels. By excluding non-Indigenous people from her definition of "real" Americans, and by describing European colonialism as an "invasion," she also hints at her sympathy for more pro-Indigenous, anticolonial politics than the earlier articles suggest.

During the most memorable moment of the journey, meeting the head of the Catholic Church, she also presented herself as an Osage. "Memory of Blessing Received from Eminent Pope Pius XI," published in March 1928, contains another picture of the pilgrims, this time at the Vatican, where they attended a mass led by the pope on Sunday afternoon, May 25, 1924. Lohmann observes, "My aunt, Mrs. W. B. McGill of San Antonio, Texas, and I, however, were allowed to wear the costume of the Osage Indian" and adds, "Pope Pius was deeply impressed by the Indian costumes which my aunt, Mrs. McGill, and I wore." She concludes, "He said we were the first American Indians he had ever seen and that, according to his knowledge, we were the first Indians ever to visit the Vatican in our native costume. He told the Archbishop that he would like to do something for us, who were representatives of America's oldest known inhabitants. Accordingly, he gave us both the honorary title of 'princess'" (2). While an important though underdeveloped component of her politics as an American Indian writer, Lohmann's self-presentation as Osage appears both tentative and belated. Nor did she express pride in her Osage citizenship, as a writer such as John Joseph Mathews did, despite his own sense that the world of the older generations of Osages would soon pass.

Harkins's magazine continued to feature diverse political arrays until the end of its run, though for a series of issues beginning in January 1930 he and several of his writers developed a more focused and sustained protest against various affronts to the dignity of Indigenous peoples. In the editorial for this issue, for example, Harkins comments, "It gets rather disgusting to a reader when an author refers to the Indian as a 'savage or barbarian' as if he never had a real cultural background. The Indian did not just 'happen' but must have gone through as many stages in man development as his white brother" ("Culture of the Indian," 4). He also persists in favorably comparing the development of Indigenous peoples to Anglo-Saxons. While he states that at some point "the Indian's civilization was retarded in some manner," he "can point with pride to his cultural background, ever remembering that he represented the oldest aristocracy in this so called new world. The name 'barbarian' is a misnomer applied to him by any Anglo-Saxon writer, whose folk at one time were clothing themselves in skins and sleeping in drifted leaves of the forest" (4). This editorial marks a surprisingly abrupt shift in tone. Perhaps the stock market crash a few months earlier made Harkins and his fellow American Indian businessmen in the Apela Club anxious about the ability of Hoover and Curtis to help the economy recover, or perhaps the rising tide of criticism of federal paternalism and assimilation policies, as expressed most publicly and extensively in 1928 in the Meriam Report, on which the magazine occasionally reported, led Harkins to wonder about the kind of progressive politics for which he advocated for American Indians.

Yet the shift in political perspective was almost comically brief. The headline "Viscount Chateaubriand's Adventures with Muscogulges," an article by historian Carolyn Thomas Foreman, greeted readers turning the page. The first line reads, "The French took a deep interest in their vast provinces beyond the Atlantic, and many adventurers braved the perils of storm, hunger, disease and savages to explore the empire along the Gulf of Mexico" (6). Several pages later—in an article reprinted from the *Dartmouth Alumni Magazine* that references Pauline Johnson's poem "The Corn Husker," Samson Occom's "A Sermon Preached at the Execution of Moses Paul, an Indian," and speeches by Hiawatha, Captain Pipe / Hopocan, Red Jacket, and Black Hawk—Jason Almus Russell celebrated American Indian oratory by first referencing the "noble savage" before comparing Occom favorably to the "*unlearned* savage" ("Soul of the Indian," 10). Next to Russell's piece on oratory, a short article about Mount Shasta includes references to "superstitious Indians," "a primitive tribal legend," and an example of Hollywood Indian-speak: "Heap big mountain not blow up now" ("Snow Averts Eruption of Mt. Shasta," 11). The issue, however, also includes articles by Mohawk writer Harriette Johnson Westbrook / O-Jan-Jan-Win and Winnebago writer Robinson Johnson / Whirling Thunder, a prominent figure in American Indian cultural and political circles in Chicago. Johnson adopts a much more respectful tone in his article on Indian sign language. "When well done," Johnson says, "the gestures are graceful and beautiful and expressive," and he adds, "It possesses a beauty and an imagery that can be found in but few other languages, and is the foremost gesture language the world has ever produced" ("Some 200 Signs," 14). Articles lauding the Toltecs and ancient Peruvians, with the former drawing distinctions between civilized and "savage" Indigenous groups, also appear to contribute to the issue's more forceful defense of Indigenous American history and culture. The latter article even includes a rejection of "those Bible fairy tales" used by Christian authors to claim Indigenous descent from Adam and Eve (Layson, 15). This issue of the magazine contains a particularly tangled array of political perspectives in Native America at the beginning of the 1930s in the early months of the Great Depression and before both the Dust Bowl and the Indian Reorganization Act.

Harkins continues his more vigorous defense of American Indians in the February 1930 issue, which features Choctaw leader Pushmataha on the cover. Pushmataha, like Tecumseh, with whom he refused to join in the fight against the United States in the War of 1812, stands for many Native writers of this era as one of the most important Indigenous leaders. Tom Meagher, the non-Native author of the article on the Toltecs in the previous issue, returns with this issue's first story about the origins of the Chah-tah, both Pushmataha's and Harkins's people, and the Chica-sah, Cow-ih-tah, and Cus-ih-tah. This issue thus begins with emergence, though in the map accompanying his article, Meagher puts the emergence place on the Red River rather than at Nanih Waiya. In his editorial, titled "Sentimental Civilization," Harkins distinguishes between progressive whites and sentimental, "communistic" Natives. He praises Indigenous Americans for building public works—temples, "huge swinging bridges," water routes—and discovering cocaine, rubber, coal, and oil. They also, Harkins claims, "developed the 'community chest' idea first in this country and looked after the poor." There were, indeed, "no orphans among his people" (4). Such a characterization, celebratory and with some of Harkins's familiar disregard for historical accuracy, resonates in the early Depression years as an opaque but nevertheless prophetic political platform. Native communities, Harkins suggests, provide working models for addressing social and economic problems. John Collier, at this moment a prominent reformer and activist, would have agreed.

The editorial page also features an article by Indian Territory–born syndicated journalist Mrs. Walter Ferguson objecting to the whitewashing of American history. In "Patriots Blind to Past of United States—History Reveals Much That Is Wrong," reprinted from the January 20, 1930, *Congressional Record,* she asserts, "We should not forget our plunder of the red man. Even our histories have covered up that deplorable tale to make it decent reading for children" (4). After comparing the dominant historical narratives of "The Battle of the Washita," a massacre perpetuated by Custer, and "The Custer Massacre," a battle precipitated by Custer's aggressive tactics, Ferguson opines:

> If you want to keep your sons filled with a false idea of patriotism—
> that silly belief that one's country can do no wrong—instead of teaching them to look facts in the face in order to learn finer judgment and justice, never allow them to read of the shameful capture of Osceola, the famous Seminole. Lured from his stronghold in the Florida Everglades by an American flag of truce, he was heinously murdered. Don't give into their hands that rare book of Helen Hunt Jackson called "A Century of Dishonor," wherein is told the bald, bad tale of all our broken treaties with the red man. (4)

Ferguson's strident condemnation of military and discursive attacks on Native people complements the political message conveyed by the cover portrait of Pushmataha. Harkins also prints and expresses the Apela Club's disapproval of House Resolution 7963, a bill to establish a U.S. Court of Indian Claims, which did not move beyond the committee.[63] A reprinted article by DeWitt Clinton Duncan, in which he argues for a skill-based rather than knowledge-based education, provides another Native voice, this one of an aging Indigenous progressive, to the array.

The March 1930 issue represents the zenith of the magazine's potential as a diverse, robust voice for Native political conversation. Harkins's editorial, "The Indians' Vote," focuses on Native people as a powerful voting bloc. The Poetry Page features a poem by Chickasaw author Julia Carter Welch, and an article by Chickasaw writer Will Ward tells the story of young Chickasaw men sent from the Harley Institute to study at Vanderbilt University in the 1890s. Mohawk writer Harriette Johnson Westbrook has another story in the issue, "Interesting Sioux Legend of the White Buffalo Calf Pipe," and a brief article on Indian art actually mentions Native artists, the Kiowa Five at the University of Oklahoma. Arthur C. Parker and Chauncey Yellow Robe also make appearances in the issue. In an article on Freemasonry reprinted from the *Six Nations,* a magazine published on the Seneca Nation's Cattaraugus Reservation, Parker celebrates various Native leaders, including Clinton Rickard, a "truly heroic figure" who vehemently protested for free passage by members of the Six Nations across the U.S.–Canadian border. However, Parker also expresses antiblack racism in his objection to certain "fake Indians" ("Indians and Freemasonry," 12). Yellow Robe, having recently completed his last picture, *The Silent Enemy* (1930) with Mary Alice Nelson Archambaud / Molly Spotted Elk (Penobscot) and Chief Buffalo

Child Long Lance, appears as the storyteller behind a "Sioux Legend of Creation" (16).[64] The issue is the most richly textured culturally and politically of the magazine's entire run.

While the next few issues make some compelling political gestures (Sequoyah appears on the cover of the April 1930 issue, along with a passage in Cherokee type), Harkins does not sustain the momentum. An editorial in May 1930—in which he laments that "the Indian is losing his identity so quickly," advocates for "the Indian to come into his own from a publicity standpoint," and objects to novels about only either Herculean or Satanic Native people—might have generated more interest in the first rather than one of the last of the magazine's issues ("Two Pulitzer Prizes," 4). Other than two stories on a battle between the Fort Belknap Reservation's tribal council and local public schools that refused to enroll their children; a letter to the editor from Reverend Dr. Barnabas objecting to the racism of the Improved Order of Red Men; and a story, "An Indian Code," by Chickasaw writer Stella LeFlore Carter, the final issues offer more of the same. Coincidentally, along with Arthur Parker and Will Rogers, Barnabas names Mrs. Gertrude Bonnin as an "outstanding citizen" worthy of admittance to the organization (Barnabas, Letter to the editor, 4). One can imagine Bonnin scoffing at the compliment.

As a product of the civil rights era, the collected issues of the *American Indian* entered an afterlife in a political era ostensibly quite distinct from the one in which it emerged. As museum director Ke Mo Ha (Patrick Patterson) writes in the preface to the collected edition of the magazine that he fondly recalls reading as a young man, "This was a magazine for Indians, and mostly by Indians" (Ke Mo Ha, Preface).[65] John M. Carroll, the researcher who brought the magazine back into print in 1970, found them in the summer of 1969 at Jim Edwards's Abalache Book Store in Oklahoma City. Carroll also learned the main reason for the demise of the journal: "an objection lodged by an individual over alleged character defamation, an objection which eventually grew into a lawsuit, and subsequently caused the magazine's cessation as an organ for the American Indian" (Carroll, Introduction). Carroll observes, in response to both Patterson's preface and the dedication by Louis R. Bruce, the Mohawk and Dakota commissioner of the Bureau of Indian Affairs, "They both recognize the fact that the story of the Indian then, as today, is a story of youth and vibrancy," and he calls Harkins "an early pioneer in human rights" (Carroll, Introduction). Bruce served as commissioner from 1969 to 1972 during the occupation of Alcatraz and the Trail of Broken Treaties and the subsequent occupation of the Bureau of Indian Affairs building, after which President Richard Nixon fired him.

The back cover of the final issue (February–March 1931) has a full-page advertisement for the Wirt Franklin Petroleum Corporation of Ardmore, Oklahoma, in the heart of Harkins's mother's Chickasaw Nation. A statue of a Native man, dressed in a loin cloth and with one arm raised in greeting, stands on what appears to be a rock with the words "A FRIEND" inscribed on it. The rock sits on a pedestal with two plaques announcing the company's gasoline product. Wirt Franklin had come to Indian Territory as a member of the Dawes Commission and stayed to practice law and work in the oil business. While Harkins attempted to ingratiate himself and his magazine with the businesses of eastern Oklahoma, this concluding page of his publishing project conveys, in the single palatable image in red ink of a friendly, welcoming Native, the many political negotiations and compromises he felt he had to make. While the political impact of the magazine appears negligible, and its legacy questionable, the magazine remains a remarkable and remarkably vexed record of middle-class, upwardly mobile American Indians marking their history and charting, with considerable optimism, an Indigenous future.

A picture of the diverse Indigenous political terrain of the 1910s and 1920s emerges when we place the work of editors such as Parker, Bonnin, and Harkins and writers such as Lohmann and Mathews, Lohmann and Robitaille, or Lohmann and Harkins, for example, in conversation with each other. These conversations form arrays of Native voices all working on a daily basis through the issues facing them and their communities as the settler–colonial state relentlessly asserts its dominance. While surface and symptomatic readings of many Native writers will reveal moments that appear either anticolonial or proassimilation, for example, approaching their work as part of political arrays focuses our interpretations on how their views continuously developed and changed in specific, vibrant political contexts. By deferring general political judgments about eras and authors, readers will see more political nuance and texture in Indigenous literary history.

CHAPTER 2

Transnational Representations
Mexico and the Cherokee Literary Politics of John Milton Oskison and Will Rogers

While Lee Harkins and Gertrude Bonnin devoted their efforts to developing and shaping Indigenous media outlets publishing diverse Native voices, two Cherokee writers, John Milton Oskison and Will Rogers, made their mark in the non-Native print media of the early decades of the twentieth century. As Lionel Larré explains, "Oskison had a long career in New York journalism. He worked first as a reporter for the *New York Evening Post* from 1903 to 1906. He then worked as a financial editor for *Collier's Magazine* from 1909 to 1914" (2).[1] During his time at *Collier's*, Oskison became a founding member of the Society of American Indians. He served on the editorial board of the organization's journal beginning with the first issue, January–April 1913, under Arthur C. Parker, and published three articles in it.[2] Oskison was still on the editorial board when Bonnin joined it for the October–December 1915 issue, and he served with her for one issue after she took the journal's reins for the Autumn 1918 issue. He left the board only when Bonnin completely overhauled it for the next issue. Rogers, Oskison's friend since their school days in the Cherokee Nation, reached an enormous audience—"over sixty million," according to political biographer Richard D. White Jr.—in the 1920s and 1930s with his syndicated newspaper columns and articles. White describes Rogers as "the most incisive political commentator of his era who, beneath his humor, provided his countrymen a critically honest appraisal of American politics and world affairs" and calls him "a true political insider with the power to shape public opinion and ultimately influence public policy" (xx). Oskison's and Rogers's interests rarely converge on the same political issues, at least in print. Yet their commentary on and representation of Mexico, during an era in which many other American Indian, European American, and European writers traveled there, form transnational, and in some cases trans-Indigenous, political arrays that demonstrate the diversity of political thought within a single tribal nation in the early twentieth century.[3]

Mexico figures prominently in Cherokee historical and political imaginaries as a legendary homeland, site of migration, and potential sanctuary from U.S. settler–colonial violence. Cherokee historian Emmet Starr included a well-known story of their migration from Mexico in his 1921 *History of the Cherokee Indians and Their Legends and Folk Lore*.[4] In his own history of the Cherokee Nation published in 2005, Cherokee writer Robert Conley summarizes a related story first published in 1973 by Nighthawk Keetowah Cherokee Levi Gritts. Gritts situates the Cherokee homeland on an island off the coast of South America and relates a northern migration through Central America and Mexico into the U.S. Southeast.[5] From the 1820s to the 1910s, through the removal and allotment eras, Cherokee leaders such as Richard Fields, John Ross, John Brown, Bird Harris, and Redbird Smith considered Cherokee migration to Mexico to escape the United States and the myriad forms of state and state-sanctioned violence that secured and extended its domination.[6] Sequoyah, the famous inventor of the Cherokee syllabary, even took a journey to Mexico at the end of his life in search of lost relatives.[7]

As a site of historical and political inquiry for Cherokee writers, Mexico also presents an opportunity to intervene in the conversations, overwhelmingly shaped by racist and xenophobic U.S. perceptions of its southern neighbor, about its Indigenous and mestizo populations. The view of Mexico as a "backward" or "primitive" nation enables its economic exploitation and aggressive, hostile treatment by the United States. As citizens of a tribal nation with a long history of conflict with the same powerful settler–colonial nation, Oskison and Rogers occupied a position potentially sympathetic to Mexico and, more specifically, to Indigenous Mexicans. Oskison (born 1874) and Rogers (born 1879), as well as Ruth Muskrat Bronson (born 1897) and Lynn Riggs (born 1899), whose writings provide opportunities to expand the Cherokee political arrays under consideration in this chapter, were born into the Cherokee Nation in Indian Territory prior to Oklahoma statehood in 1907.[8] They witnessed the devastation of allotment and the dissolution of their tribal nation's government. Riggs usually represents the Cherokee Nation and Indian Territory in his plays as grim and violent places, but Oskison in his novels and Rogers in his books, daily telegrams, and weekly articles convey pride in and nostalgia for the Cherokee Nation as it existed in Indian Territory. These contrasting views remain in their writing on Mexico. Riggs imagined Indigenous Mexicans as the main actors in an anticolonial revolution, and neither their experiences in nor nostalgia for the prestatehood Cherokee Nation made Oskison or Rogers political allies of other internally colonized Indigenous people. Their political allegiances rarely aligned with those of Indigenous Mexicans, a people sometimes viewed by Native Americans—for example, by early-twentieth-century Choctaw writer Todd Downing—as historical and cultural kin.[9] Bronson did not write about Mexico, but her comparison of American Indians to Koreans during the Japanese occupation from 1910 to 1945 parallels Riggs's views of Indigenous Mexicans as potential political allies. It also constitutes one of the most explicit links between Cherokees and other colonized peoples within the transnational Cherokee political imaginary of the middle decades of the twentieth century.[10]

Rogers usually spent his time in Mexico either with the nation's economic and political elite, with whom he played polo, or with affluent foreigners, such as William Randolph Hearst, who owned a ranch in the Mexican state of Chihuahua.[11] When Rogers made an official trip to Mexico with aviator Charles Lindbergh in 1927 at the request of Dwight Morrow, the new U.S. ambassador to Mexico, he gave a speech to Morrow and Mexican president Plutarco Elías Calles at a dinner at the American embassy. The speech, with jokes about diplomacy evidently written specifically for this occasion, includes a startling piece of advice for Calles and other Mexican elites: "Make your rich, every time they send a Child to Paris to learn 'em to talk French—make them send one to Sonora to learn to talk Yaqui. They are the ones you have to live and get along with, not the French" (Rogers, *The Autobiography of Will Rogers,* 172–73). Rogers makes this suggestion at the end of a year in which the Mexican military had finished a campaign, complete with aerial bombing, against the Yaquis in Sonora, and he does so in a familiar tone developed by U.S. writers over the previous five decades: "Wealthy elites of Mexico were treated with kid gloves, although more often than not in rather unflattering terms" (G. González, 9). At the same time, it is a bold reference to, if not a clear indictment of, Mexican federal Indian policy, though such references are anomalous in Rogers's commentary on Mexico. Indeed, as Nicole Guidotti-Hernández explains, "Yaqui struggles for autonomy, pre and post revolution (1901–1910 and 1920–1935) were, and continue to be, written out of the history of the Mexican nation" (69–70). Scholars have also largely ignored violence committed by "U.S., Mexican American, and Mexican state actors against Yaqui peoples" (70). Without focusing on Yaquis or other Indigenous Mexicans, Rogers expresses nostalgia for an ostensibly simpler, premodern life in Mexico while also constantly needling the U.S. federal government for its coercive and in some cases violent interventions in Mexican national life. Oskison, who attended Willie Halsell College in Vinita, Oklahoma, with his more famous compatriot, did not share Rogers's views of Mexico.[12] Instead, he produced, especially in the "fictionalized biography" *A Texas Titan: The Story of Sam Houston* (1929), a familiar depiction of a turbulent, uncivilized Mexico and ignorant, incompetent Mexicans of various ethnic groups and social classes.[13]

In contrast to his fellow Cherokee authors from Indian Territory, dramatist Lynn Riggs produced Cherokee representations of Mexico and Indigenous Mexicans that cohere with a Cherokee-specific understanding of that southern region as a possible sanctuary or site of Indigenous revitalization. Riggs found Mexico full of exciting potential for the social transformation of Indigenous worlds during the 1930s. He wrote two plays, *A World Elsewhere* (circa 1934–37) and *The Year of Pilár* (circa 1935–38), in which Indigenous Mexican revolution and land reclamation figure prominently. *World* is a satire of U.S. tourists and a U.S.-educated Mexican general and hacendado. The tourists romanticize Indigenous Mexican people and material culture, while the general leads a failed counterrevolution against the government of President Lázaro Cárdenas and its agrarian reform program, which involved the redistribution of land from the haciendas to Indigenous communities.[14] As the counterrevolution begins in Mexico City, the soldiers fighting for the Mexican economic and political elites use machine guns against a crowd of people. In *Pilár*, which culminates in Mayans reclaiming their land and, in some cases, killing hacendados, the son of a hacendado condemns the slavery, torture, and sexual assault that characterize life on the henequen plantations of Yucatán.

While Riggs's dramas of revolutionary Indigenous Mexico, which I examine fully in *The Red Land to the South: American Indian Writers and Indigenous Mexico* (2012), are politically compelling, especially to a post-civil-rights and post–American Indian literary Renaissance audience, they tell only a small, selective part of the literary, political, and intellectual history of mid-twentieth-century Cherokee and American Indian writing.[15] By imagining Indigenous revolutions, Riggs disrupts the conventional assessment of American Indian literature of the early twentieth century as assimilationist or politically impotent.[16] This discussion of Oskison and Rogers, however, illuminates the Mexico of this era's Cherokee literature as not exclusively revolutionary but, rather, multidimensional politically, in both progressive and reactionary ways. The Cherokee view to the south generates a diverse array of political positions on indigeneity, settler colonialism, and racial representations and an especially well-developed component of a transnational and global Cherokee literary politics in the first half of the twentieth century.

"Lazy" Mexicans and Doomed Texas Cherokees in the Borderlands

Oskison's reputation has suffered from the prevailing critical view that he was an uncompromising assimilationist, though Cherokee scholar Kirby Brown persuasively argues for a more nuanced understanding of Oskison's politics. Brown demonstrates that the setting of Oskison's 1926 novel *Black Jack Davy* is "a fully functioning, multicultural, politically autonomous, and sovereign Cherokee state firmly rooted in its own constitutional and legal traditions" (80). Within this Cherokee Nation context, Brown asserts, Ned Warrior's determined defense of his community against land grabbers from the United States "stands as a profoundly symbolic assertion—and, within the narrative arc of the text, restoration—of the collective sovereignty of the Cherokee Nation" (97).[17] Oskison does not as insistently express his support for Cherokee political sovereignty in the novels *Wild Harvest* (1925) and *Brothers Three* (1935), and all three novels express a cautious optimism about the transformation of the Cherokee Nation and Indian Territory by statehood. During the wedding ceremony between two non-Native immigrants to the Cherokee Nation that ends *Wild Harvest,* Henry Bear translates the words of his father, the "Indian preacher" Tall Bear: "He says times has changed since he was a young man like him an' his old woman was a girl like her an' they got married out in the woods, but he ain't sorry old ways are goin', because we got to have new ways an' good men an' women from the outside to help build up this Eenyan country" (297–98).[18] Brown also acknowledges that Oskison does not accommodate Cherokees with

African ancestry in his visions of Cherokee national continuity. Indeed, in the article "In Governing the Indian, Use the Indian!," published in *Case and Comment* in 1917, Oskison celebrates Cherokee attorney and congressman William Wirt Hastings's determined effort in court to challenge claims against the Cherokee Nation made by Cherokee freedmen. Oskison does not make clear the specific freedmen claims against which Hastings fought. Presumably, though, his description of the freedmen's "vague claims and theories" refers to their attempts to secure Cherokee Nation citizenship and receive allotments (441). In addition, Oskison's vexed representations of dark-skinned Cherokees in his novels, particularly women such as Rose Lamedeer in *Black Jack Davy* and Es-Teece in *Brothers Three* but also the heavy-drinking "half-breed" Joe Tiger in *Wild Harvest*, suggest that Oskison's racialism was more powerful than his progressive politics.[19]

Beth Piatote (Nez Perce) and Larré join Brown in this reassessment of Oskison. Piatote demonstrates that Oskison's "The Problem of Old Harjo," a story about Creek polygamy published in 1907 in the *Southern Workman*, "exposes the power of coverture law in American marriage to objectify women as property and asserts Creek family formation, and the laws that produce it, as valid" (*Domestic Subjects*, 42). In addition, she argues, "the story implicates the machine of assimilation policy that would equally 'pulverize' indigenous lands and families" (44). By rejecting conventional narratives about Indian Territory, Oskison "not only gives shape to the Indian Territory as a distinct geopolitical and cultural space but also offers an alternative vision of what it is and what it could be" (45). Larré takes a broader view of Oskison's writing, in which he sees more political nuance than the term "assimilation" conventionally conveys. Oskison, Larré asserts, believed that "the only struggle worth fighting was the struggle against the ultimate dehumanization that the paternalistic reservation system tended to accomplish" (15), and his "counter-representations of Indian modernity were the acts of resistance that Oskison, Eastman, and other Indian intellectuals of the time accomplished in their writings" (16). Without entirely repudiating "assimilationist" as an accurate description of Oskison's politics, Larré works admirably, though with limited success, to recover some anticolonial political program in Oskison's work. The terms that he substitutes for "assimilation," either his own ("integration," "adjustment," "inserting") or Oskison's ("absorption," "amalgamation," "merging") differ so insubstantially from "assimilation" as to reinforce the conventional scholarly assessment of Oskison. Tribal-nation sovereignty and citizenship also do not appear as either realities or options in Larré's account of Oskison's politics; early-twentieth-century Indigenous people, Larré appears to suggest, would either adopt an ethic of "personal responsibility" and choose to integrate, adjust, or amalgamate, or do so under coercion. In Larré's narrative, the responsibility for their state—poverty, ill health, homelessness—falls disproportionately on Indigenous people.

Brown's and Piatote's claims, both more nuanced and more narrowly focused than Larré's, illuminate an array of political perspectives in Oskison's writing. These efforts to recover political scenes in this Cherokee author's oeuvre that more readily conform to early-twenty-first-century progressive contexts require careful, determined interpretation. While Oskison depicts the title character in "The Problem of Old Harjo" as dignified, though also childlike in his wide-eyed embrace of Christianity, most of his fiction conveys frequently patronizing and demeaning views of Indigenous people. In "A Schoolmaster's Dissipation," a schoolteacher in the Indian Territory struggles to communicate through "crazy signs" with older American Indians while teaching the "grimy" Indigenous children living in the lamentable "sanitary conditions of the Indian home" (159–60). The teacher's loneliness drives him to become a morphine addict, but after a young female doctor arrives in the "half-savage land" and saves him, he learns, following the example of old man Panting Bear, to appreciate the "simple beauty of his life and surroundings" (161, 163). Hanner the Runt, the protagonist of "Only the Master Shall Praise" and, the narrator explains, "a half-breed Cherokee cowboy," had "the stoicism of the Indian" (165). Naive and simple-minded, Hanner confesses to robbing a stagecoach to save his friend. Upon learning that the law hanged Hanner for the crime, his friend calls him "a poor little fool" (176). In "When the Grass Grew Long," Oskison represents a Cherokee family as "unconcerned and delighted" by the spectacle of a massive prairie fire and prepared to fight it with a wet grain sack, wet cloth, and two buckets of water (179). They refuse to attempt to escape, despite the cries of Billy Wilson, the cowboy in love with the daughter: "Don't be such awful fools! Are you crazy?" (180). After the daughter saves Billy's life but dies in the fire, Billy exclaims, again, "Fools!" Even a short story such as the 1913 *Collier's* publication "Walla Tenaka—Creek," which describes a Creek system of justice and therefore affirms one mode of tribal-nation sovereignty, also perpetuates stereotypes of drunk and stoic American Indians and allows readers to anticipate the execution, pitiable as it is, of a Creek man. "The Man Who Interfered," in which a white man convinces a Native woman to return to her white husband, "a cow-country bum and wife beater," could be read as a condemnation of white male dominance over Native women (312). However, this 1915 *Southern Workman* piece suggests that, in pursuit of "the general good which comes from preserving the social order," Lizzie Squirrel should return to her abusive husband rather than seek sanctuary with the family and community that she left to attend white schools (307). "Preserving the social order" by keeping a marriage intact in "The Man Who Interfered" does not have the same salutary consequences or political implications for Indigenous people that it does in "The Problem of Old Harjo."

"The Singing Bird," published in 1925 in *Sunset Magazine* and Oskison's first story to see print after the passage of the 1924 Indian Citizenship Act and the demise of the SAI, aligns politically with "The Problem of Old Harjo" as delineated by Piatote. Though the title, a reference to an unfaithful wife, suggests infidelity as the plot's central conflict, a disagreement about the future of the Cherokee Nation drives the suspense instead. As the "Cherokee tribal council was meeting in the boxlike brick capital," outside in the square Kee-too-wah leader Jim Blind-Wolfe makes a speech in protest of the Cherokee Nation leasing land to white men: "I tell you, Kee-too-wah fellows don't like this lease business. You lease your land to the white man, and pretty soon you don't have any land; white man crowd you out! This here country is Eenyan (Indian) Country, set aside for Eenyans. We want to keep it alwaysfor Eenyans. Such is belief of Kee-too-wahs, and I am Kee-too-wah!" (333). When Lovely Daniel, "a wild half-breed neighbor" of Blind-Wolfe, objects to the speech and calls the Kee-too-wahs "fools," Blind-Wolfe knocks him unconscious (332, 333). With vengeance in mind, Daniel courts Blind-Wolfe's wife, Jennie Blind-Wolfe, whom he comes to trust enough to tell her that he plans to kill Blind-Wolfe. Initially, Jennie appears to encourage Daniel, only to lead him into a trap and expose him to her husband. With an opportunity to kill his political and romantic rival, Blind-Wolfe offers Daniel a choice: exile or suicide. Daniel chooses the latter. While Oskison celebrates the Kee-too-wahs for "carrying out the ancient command to maintain among the Cherokees the full-blood inheritance of race purity and race ideals" as well as for working to protect the Cherokees from outlaws both within and without the Nation, he does so at the expense of Cherokees with lower blood quantum, specifically "half-breeds" like Daniel. At the same time, the story accurately depicts the vexing blood politics at work in the Cherokee Nation before concluding with domestic harmony in the Blind-Wolfe home, which stands as the site of a fatal political conflict over the appropriate Cherokee national response to encroaching settler colonials.

The essays pose an equally difficult challenge to readers in search of explicit anticolonial politics or even generally more anti-assimilation, pro-Native self-determination positions in Oskison's writing. His 1902 short essay "Cherokee Migration" puts a sanguine spin, even in the title, on the coerced, traumatic removal of the Cherokees from the Southeast and celebrates the Cherokee Nation's "progress toward the higher civilization" and "high state of cultivation" on the eve of Oklahoma statehood in the first decade of the twentieth century (352). In "The President and the Indian," published in the same year, Oskison praises both the progressive U.S. president, Theodore Roosevelt, for his informed perspective on Indian affairs and the settler–colonial government for working in Indian Territory "to make the transition from tribal superstition and prejudice to national citizenship as smooth as possible" (353). He aligns his authorial voice with the settler–colonial position throughout the article in references, for example, to "the crudity and inefficiency of Indian courts" and to "the more hotheaded among the native leaders [who] talked somewhat vaingloriously of armed opposition" (355). He expresses some concern for "the peculiar needs of those who still live in the old full-blood style" but embraces "leaders in the movement toward amalgamation," many of whom, Oskison asserts without a trace of regret, had been "trained to see the point of view of the whites in their colleges and universities" (356, 357). The article culminates with an ominous comment about the settler–colonial government no longer "permitting" boarding school graduates to "go back to the blanket" (357). These essays collectively affirm, with apparent satisfaction, the military, legal, political, and cultural dominance of the United States.

Oskison makes even more explicitly alarming statements in subsequent essays. In "The Outlook for the Indian," from a 1903 issue of the *Southern Workman*, he observes, "The next inevitable step is the complete absorption of the Indian into the white race, which will result in the ultimate amalgamation of the two" (359). In this process of "complete absorption," they will need help: "We cannot close our eyes to the fact that they are still children, with all of the child's ignorance of modern life, with the child's helplessness in practical affairs" (359). He concludes, "The Indian problem, so far as the tribes of the Territory are concerned, is being solved by extinguishing the Indian as a distinctive individual and merging him with his white neighbors and competitors" (361). In "The Closing Chapter: Passing of the Old Indian," published in *Munseys* in 1914, Oskison observes, "The real Indians are disappearing" (429). Later in the article, he asserts, "In another ten years 90 percent of all our Indians will have become taxpayers; *politically,* the absorption into American life will then be nearly complete. Another generation ought to see the end of the reservation system. So, the American Indian is entering upon the final stage of his history; and what a lurid, picturesque history it has been!" (429, 431; emphasis added). Even if Oskison defines "absorption" and "amalgamation" as distinct from "assimilation," his pronouncements sound ominous and, if fulfilled, would mean the disappearance of Indigenous people.

When Oskison recognizes the social issues Indigenous people face, he recommends further assimilation into settler–colonial political, legal, and cultural systems rather than the strengthening of Indigenous ones. In "Friends of the Indian," a 1905 article in the *Nation,* he asserts that Indigenous people require "real standing in the courts" and enfranchisement to protect them (363). They need better "press agents" as well, though, perplexingly, in "The Need of Publicity in Indian Affairs," Oskison suggests that the settler–colonial descendants of European immigrants, not American Indians, face the most unfairly one-sided representations (369). He objects to Helen Hunt Jackson's condemnation of settler–colonial depredations in *A Century of Dishonor* (1881) and *Ramona* (1884) and argues that newspaper editors need the facts to demonstrate that "the white people are not all villains in their treatment of Indians" (370). He then comments that these editors are "in sympathy with the whites, you know, because the average editor is a white man and believes thoroughly in his race. The facts are there; there is no trouble about that. The Indian question is nearer settlement than ever before, the development is satisfactory, and the head of the department is satisfactory, as everyone is saying" (370). Rather than read Jackson, claims Oskison, they should consult reports distributed by the Lake Mohonk Conference, one of the "friends of the Indian" organizations that urged passage of the Dawes Act in 1887, legislation coauthored by one of the conference's attendees, Senator Henry L. Dawes. Oskison's blithe assessment of the state of Indigenous America at the turn of the century continues in "Remaining Causes of Indian Discontent," published in 1907 in the *North American Review*. He begins this article by using White River Utes who staged an "angry protest" against allotment as examples of "a vanishing type of discontented Indian" (372). Oskison dismisses a significant anti-settler-colonial act by the relatives of the Utes to whom Bonnin had committed years of her life as a community activist. Oskison and Bonnin met years later as members of the SAI, but at this point in their careers, their political commitments, at least as expressed in their writings, diverge dramatically. Oskison continues in the article to argue, "Only one big distinctively Indian problem—the distribution of Indian Trust and Treaty Funds—remains to be settled by Congress" (372). It is an astonishingly inaccurate comment by a generally well-informed writer. The rest of the article undermines this initial observation, too, as Oskison mentions irrigation, sanitation, education, usury, fraud, the trade in and consumption of alcohol, and poor record-keeping as significant issues in Indigenous communities. Oskison also touches on these urgent social issues and the attendant precarity of Indigenous communities in "Making an Individual of the Indian," another article published in 1907.

In several articles, Oskison urges the federal government and tribal nations to allow young Native people to become leaders, a position that suggests a commitment to tribal national self-determination. However, Oskison advocates for young Native leaders, in articles such as "A Bigger Load for Educated Indians" from 1915 and "In Governing the Indian, Use the Indian!" from 1917, in order to further what he sees as the salutary goal of eroding the power of an older, more conservative generation. He observes in "The New Indian Leadership," one of his three articles published in the SAI's journal, that the traditional council has become a meeting in Native communities and that, in these meetings, outsiders would witness "the old Indians giving up their ceremonial pipes and their right to speak the first word, and the younger people, equipped with the white man's language and instructed in his ways, reaching forward timidly and awkwardly for the leadership" (448). These young men, Oskison reflects with apparent approval, repeat the words of the reservation superintendent and express "the white man's impatience of the 'conservatism' of the old men" (450). Oskison appears to define "strong Indian leaders of the new generation" as the most assimilated young American Indians who willingly adopt and advocate for the federal government's position on important social and political issues (456). Throughout his stories and essays, Oskison remains consistent: for Indigenous people, the preferred path forward involves continuing to break with the Indigenous political, legal, and cultural forms under attack by the federal government's official assimilation program.

Oskison's racialism and whitewashing of Indigenous American futures, as well as the racial, cultural, and class politics of his incomplete and posthumously published autobiography, "A Tale of the Old I.T.," and three novels, help explain his retrograde representations of Mexico, Mexicans, and the United States–Mexico borderlands. Though the title emphasizes "the Old I.T." as the narrative's most significant geographic and geopolitical space, the autobiography begins with his father's birth "on a tenant farm somewhere in England" rather than with his mother's birth in Indian Territory ("A Tale of the Old I.T.," 65).[20] Indeed, his immigrant English father overwhelmingly shaped Oskison's worldview, in part because his mother died when he was only four years old. When he tells readers about Cherokees, he distinguishes them from other Indigenous Americans and asserts rural forms of labor, elite Eastern education, law and order, and literacy as the key features of national Cherokee life:

> The Indians he [Oskison's father] came to know in Indian Territory were not all like the nomadic hunters he had seen on the plains. They were farmers, stockmen, merchants; they ran gristmills and sawmills and saltworks. They had good neighborhood schools and, at Tahlequah, two high schools—the Male and Female Seminaries—staffed by competent teachers from New England. They had a complete system of government under a constitution modeled on that of the United States, district courts and a supreme court, and law enforcement officers. Their chief was a well-educated man, a graduate of Princeton. Among the tribal judges, senators, and councilmen were other graduates of eastern colleges, Dartmouth and Princeton. They published *The Cherokee Advocate*, a weekly newspaper printed

half in English and half in the Cherokee characters devised more than forty years before by Sequoyah. (67)

Socially, culturally, and politically, Oskison aligns the Cherokee Nation with the United States rather than other tribal nations. He reorients the Cherokee Nation's cultural and historical roots from the Southeast to the Northeast, and more specifically to New England, from where the competent, non-Cherokee teachers of Cherokee children come and readers will find the prestigious institutions that educated their judicial, legislative, and executive leaders.

The cultural points of reference remain almost entirely English or English settler–colonial throughout the autobiography. "At home," Oskison comments, "I read Dickens, Scott, and Reade" (75). Of the inexpensive editions that he bought with his friend Clara, he remembers three in particular for their literary quality: "Stevenson's *Treasure Island* and Kipling's *Plain Tales from the Hills* and *Soldiers Three*" (82). After watching a stage adaptation of *East Lynne* (1861), a best-selling sensation novel by English writer Ellen Wood, he relates the experience to reading the "mushy romances" of American writer E. D. E. N. Southworth, only to compare both *East Lynne* and Southworth's works unfavorably to those of Stevenson and Kipling. From his time at Stanford, he recalls discovering "Chaucer and the Anglo-Saxon bards" (93). After Stanford, Oskison attended Harvard in the intellectual center of the New England world that so auspiciously shapes the Cherokee Nation. Though "he wrote short stories in every spare hour" (106), the "Indian Territory tales" to which he dedicated so much of his literary effort throughout his life, the experience at Harvard only reinforced his cultural, intellectual, and political biases.

As a political progressive, Oskison often found himself in the company of social reformers, including those working for the social welfare of minority ethnic communities. He even met the leader of the progressives, President Theodore Roosevelt, who remembered Oskison's brother from his service in the Rough Riders.[21] Oskison lived, for example, for one year at the University Settlement, an organization on New York City's Lower East Side that served Jewish immigrants. He observes:

> The thousands upon thousands of Jewish families that for twenty years had been pouring in from Poland, Russia, Austria, and

Hungary, unrestricted by immigration quotas, made it outwardly a bedlam. Our settlement workers, however, found the universal hunger for betterment that had caused their uprooting from Europe led them, here, to urge their children to seize avidly every opportunity to get ahead in this strange new world where no bars to their advancement existed. ("A Tale of the Old I.T.," 117)

The first statement, with its anxiety about the lack of immigration quotas and the chaos it causes on the Lower East Side, has a hint of xenophobia in it, but the second expresses sympathy imbued with progressive idealism. While the immigrants inspired or "stimulate[d]" Oskison and his fellow workers to help them, Oskison also pauses to comment that they "were poorly dressed; they washed all over infrequently; they talked clamorously, pushed and milled all over the place once they got over their first shyness" (118). He sympathized with immigrants, but he neither particularly liked them nor understood the severe constraints of their poverty. He imagined himself and his settlement coworkers as model citizens worthy of emulation: "They were quick to note that we resident workers bathed daily, dressed neatly, spoke grammatically, did not shout to make ourselves heard, seemed to know how to behave correctly at parties, and were equipped to tell them a good deal about America's history and way of living" (118). He expected them, without prompting or coercion, to see the superiority of his way of life and assimilate to it.

Oskison's description of Mexican people, the single time they appear in the autobiography, is similar to his portrayal of the Jewish immigrants of the Lower East Side. In the summer between Stanford and Harvard, Oskison made a trip to Gallina in northern New Mexico to visit a family friend intent on having the Oskisons join him. Oskison hired José Nutrias to take him on the final stage of his journey and spent the night at Nutrias's home. The experience left Oskison unimpressed: "For a brief time I tried to sleep on a rolled-out mattress on the dirt floor, sandwiched between him and another of his numerous family, with the door and the room's one small window closed. When the smell of unwashed Mexicans became overpowering, however, I sneaked out to make a nest in the hay he had heaped in the wagon he was to drive next day" (101). Though Oskison had lived on farms throughout his childhood, he objected the next day to the "rank smell of raw goat flesh" that lingered after his host prepared him a meal. During the tour of the area, he observes, "The whole setting—sun-baked huts, shy dark-skinned children, the inevitable strings of red peppers against whitewashed walls, ubiquitous goats, twisted cedars and scrub pines of the scantily grassed mesa—seemed like something out of the Old Testament, the end of nowhere, an ideal refuge for a refugee from civilization" (101). Oskison felt utterly out of place in this world, approximately eight hundred miles west from Tahlequah, Oklahoma, and judged it as alien, as a "nowhere," a dead end. Instead, he identified aggressively with the more geographically distant, and more ethnically Anglo, cities of Palo Alto, California, and Cambridge, Massachusetts.

Oskison draws upon the Cherokee Nation–specific view of Mexico as historically and politically significant in several of his turn-of-the-century short stories, the posthumously published novel *The Singing Bird* (circa 1935–45), and his biography of Sam Houston. Oskison entertains but dismisses Mexico as a Cherokee sanctuary in the short story "Tookh Steh's Mistake" and *The Singing Bird*. He published "Tookh Steh's Mistake," which Larré calls "probably the most political" of his stories (41), in the *Indian Chieftain* in 1897. Daniel F. Littlefield Jr. and James W. Parins explain, "'Tookh Steh's Mistake' ... is the story of a full blood who cannot adapt to social changes that will come with the imminent dissolution of the tribal government; he decides, like many of his historical counterparts did, to emigrate to Mexico but, ill-equipped to make such a trip, starves to death en route" (32). A Cherokee Nation resident, Tookh Steh lives to see an increase in "intruding whites" and the dawn of the allotment era, during which the United States finally expressed its wish "to stamp out tribal government in the Cherokee Nation" ("Tookh Steh's Mistake," 153). The narrator's sympathy initially appears to reside with the agents of the federal government and against the politicians, some presumably Cherokee, who "left the impression that the United States meant to rob the poor Indian outright" (154). Tookh Steh attends a meeting with the members of the commission during which a "full-blood spokesman" passionately objects to allotment, after which a commissioner "told the full-bloods that they had no choice in the matter" (155, 156). Oskison carefully conveys the positions and convictions of both sides of the allotment debate. Tookh Steh, represented by Oskison as a man in whom politicians had no interest, decides that "he would not live in a country where his old freedom would be restricted.... He would go to Mexico. He had heard that there one could find boundless freedom, amid mountains more rugged than any he had ever seen" (156). His journey ends tragically: a letter arrives in the Cherokee Nation explaining that "an old Indian who called himself a seeker after freedom, and who babbled foolishly about Mexico and deer and turkeys, had died in a small Texas town" (156). Tookh Steh "had a principle to back him" and held strong "convictions," but the story ends with the narrator condemning him as "foolish" (157). While Tookh Steh makes multiple mistakes in the story, Oskison draws attention to the most significant one: his character's belief that Mexico, rather than the United States, offered him freedom. Oskison draws on the prevailing late-nineteenth- and early-twentieth-century belief in Mexico's inferiority to the United States to reinforce the foolishness of Tookh Steh's siding with the passionate full-blood over the reasonable commissioner and leaving the Cherokee Nation on a quest to Mexico.[22]

In *The Singing Bird* (2007), a novel hailed by Cherokee literary critic Daniel Heath Justice as "the most fully realized of any of his fictions, and the most devoted to representing the Cherokee context of Indian Territory" (*Our Fire*, 115), Oskison draws on Sequoyah's search in Mexico both for another band of Cherokees and ancient Cherokee sacred objects stolen by the Delawares. Timothy B. Powell and Melinda Smith Mullikin, the editors of the recovered novel, observe, "Three of the noted early historians of Cherokee culture—James Adair, Cephas Washburn, and James Mooney—all confirm the existence" of these objects (xxxvii).[23] They see Oskison's incorporation of this history into his novel as his effort "to dispel the myth that Native Americans lacked 'civilization'" and "to dismantle the problematic idea that Indian culture before white contact was 'prehistoric' and thus not part of American literary history" (xxxii). Indeed, they argue that "Oskison's sophisticated experiment of infusing the novel form with a Native American vision of history can be seen as one of the earliest examples of a narrative technique that would reach fruition in some of the Native American Literary Renaissance's finest works" (xlii). On the journey, Sequoyah works on a written history of the Cherokees. He arrives in Mexico and finds the "self-exiled Cherokees" (Oskison, *The Singing Bird,* 140), though he does not return with either the Cherokee religious items or the history of his tribal nation. His attempt to recover the old traditions apparently fails, and the narrator assumes he is dead. Oskison leaves readers with an image of Sequoyah heading into the mountain territory of the Yaquis, famous for their resistance to the Spanish invasion and, well into the twentieth century, to Mexico's federal government. Mexico remains in the novel an unimagined, mysterious landscape.

A more violent, desolate, and anti-intellectual Mexico emerges in the 1901 short story "The Biologist's Quest" and *A Texas Titan*. "The Biologist's Quest" tells the story of Jake Lake, a collector for the Smithsonian and the British Museum, who has been assigned to determine if a species of short-tailed rat still exists in Lower California.[24] The task is dangerous: his predecessor "was killed by a superstitious Mexican" (182). Jake hires Kitti Quist, a Yuma, and "Joe" Maria, a Mexican guide, to take him into Mexico by boat. Quist informs Lake that he had been a powerful medicine man, but "the Yumas grew poorer, less energetic, and careless of the fame of their great man" (183). Early in the trip, Lake impresses Quist with his ability to capture lizards and rats. Quist attempts to assert his authority by capturing a rattlesnake bare-handed and then taming and killing it. The hypermasculine posturing establishes a social equivalence between Lake and Quist. Quist's successful performance, however, cannot compensate for the loss of his social and spiritual status within the Yuma community. Within the context of the loss of his authority on a tribal national scale, Quist's determination to impress Lake, or his attempt to assert masculine authority on such a small personal scale, conveys desperation. If Quist is one of the best of the Yumas, a formerly respected tribal-nation leader, then his people have a grim future.

Oskison represents Mexico's geography in the story as dangerously inscrutable. Once Lake disembarks, he has trouble reading the coastal landscape. When foul weather forces the boat out to sea, stranding Lake on the shore, he nearly panics. He survives for two days and nights but refuses to drink the remaining fresh water in his canteen. When Quist and Maria eventually make land, Quist suggests that they follow Lake's tracks: "But Joe Maria was lazy," Oskison writes, "and suggested that they set off a great blast of gunpowder" (190). Oskison then repeats this characterization of Maria. As Lake emerges from the salt grass, he sees "a nut-faced old Indian staring at him, and a lazy Mexican waving his sombrero frantically" (190). This representation aligns with the dominant convention of the era. U.S. writers frequently imagined "lazy and feckless Mexicans," asserts Cecil Robinson, and, "along with expressions of racial aversion, nineteenth-century American writers on Mexico covered pages expounding on Mexican lying, stealing, violence, cowardliness, dirtiness, sensuality, and superstition" (3, 4). The representation contrasts sharply, however, with the sympathetic portrayal of the Mexican working class a generation later in Riggs's plays. Lake finally gives his equipment to his two guides and says he will not return to Mexico, and Oskison announces at the end that the short-tailed rat "never existed except in the imagination" (57). This turn-of-the-century depiction of Mexico as a primitive, hostile terrain coheres with the dominant U.S. view of Mexico, thoroughly documented by Gilbert G. González, as helpless without U.S. ingenuity and capital. The politics of such representations, González asserts, were imperial: U.S. writers mobilized these representations to justify a "peaceful conquest" or "peaceful invasion" of Mexico by U.S. entrepreneurs and corporations (23, 63). By generating such representations and justifying, implicitly or explicitly, the United States's imperial designs on Mexico, Oskison maintains his consistent political alliance with the settler–colonial state.

The Mexican American world of northern New Mexico in "Koenig's Discovery," published in 1910 in *Collier's* and set in the mid-nineteenth century, appears equally hostile (268). Heinrich Koenig and Fritz Schaefer vie for the attentions of the "black-eyed, flashing" Rachel Garcia, with Koenig winning her hand but Schaefer her heart as well as her father's trust. As Koenig seeks revenge, he ponders "the quality of this border life into which he had so eagerly and zestfully plunged" (268). Koenig thinks, "It was not all romance; it was not even half romantic. There was an unexpected grimness about it. Instead of the blithe, careless, adventurous people that he had pictured while still following the sun over the mountains, he found them close-mouthed and unsmiling—at least those with whom he had been thrown. In them he found a wolfish quality" (268). Deciding that he must live by this borderland's "devil's creed," Koenig ambushes Schaefer, murders him, and leaves him on display for Rachel in a silent landscape that he views as a "graveyard . . . big enough to hold the dead of a continent" (269). The body reminds Koenig that "in the primitive man's country, to have means to hold" (270), and the narrator observes that travelers passing by the corpse will assume Indigenous people had punished a tribal member. Oskison's U.S. Southwest borderlands region derives its unforgiving and sinister character from Mexican and Indigenous inhabitants. Discursively and representationally, it closely resembles the Mexico of the early-twentieth-century U.S. borderlands imaginary.

By writing a Texas cultural hero into Cherokee history in *A Texas Titan: The Story of Sam Houston,* Oskison generated an opportunity to challenge, on both historical and political grounds, settler- and Texas-centric narratives about Indigenous inferiority and heroic U.S. expansion into Mexico and the U.S. West. However, this fictional biography of Houston, "a Cherokee . . . by choice, marriage, and adoption, if not by blood," works primarily as propaganda celebrating a superior U.S. empire that overwhelms uncivilized Comanches and Mexicans (180).[25] As Brown persuasively argues, while Oskison subverts Western generic conventions by claiming law, order, and civilization for the Cherokees, he reserves that civilization for his own Indigenous American people. Though he published the biography of Houston in 1929, Oskison continued to perpetuate the conventional late-nineteenth- and early-twentieth-century representation of Mexico and Mexicans identifiable in "The Biologist's Quest." He divided the book into three sections: Tennessee, Arkansas, and Texas. The Texas section tells the story of Houston's role in the war with Mexico, the creation of the Republic of Texas, the annexation of Texas by the United States, and the Civil War. Prior to his departure to Texas, Houston tells his mentor, Andrew Jackson, "Sir, . . . the natural southwestern boundary of our country is the Rio Grande! North of the river, Mexico has only a handful of population, and so few soldiers that they cannot even control the Comanche horse thieves. There lies for our taking an empire" (141). Mexican tyranny and incompetence also justify military action. Oskison explains, "[Houston] warmed to the true pioneers, men who needed elbow room, who loved the vast unbroken stretches of prairie and dreamed of them sometimes under the plough, whose eyes lifted to the horizon with the look of conquerors. . . . Here then was the human material out of which to make a revolution; here the hardened, reckless men to oppose to the death the aggressions of the Mexican government" (164). Mexico is a land of revolution for Oskison, though that revolution is Anglo and imperial rather than Indigenous and anticolonial. In support of this revolution, Oskison's Sam Houston uses the same implicit and explicit rationales for violating Mexican sovereignty and dispossessing Mexicans that representatives of Georgia and the United States used against the Cherokee Nation. Surprisingly, the biography does not feature a critique of Andrew Jackson, one of the most unpopular U.S. politicians in the Cherokee Nation and the president who signed into law the Indian Removal Act of 1830.

A Texas Titan becomes in its final third a patriotic, xenophobic narrative of U.S. superiority, with the Indigenous people of northern colonial Mexico as the familiar villains of narratives of U.S. expansion and conquest: "The Comanches kept the people in constant fear, and along the Gulf coast was another tribe of huge squalid Indians, the 'Cronks,' who smeared their bodies with alligator grease as armour against mosquitos, and raided or begged as opportunity offered" (161–62). Oskison then conflates Indigenous people with Mexicans: "Everywhere, the Mexican soldiers garrisoning the string of ramshackle posts from Anahuac, on the Gulf east of Galveston, to San Antonio, on the western plain, were growing even more menacing than the Indians" (162). A local squatter, who acknowledges that his community lives illegally on the land, also reports that Mexicans dressed like Indians attacked them. Unnamed Texans refer to the Mexican soldiers that they have defeated as "fice" (small dogs) and "lice," and the Mexicans act indolently after defeat and express their awe of the Texans. The Mexican general Santa Anna, Oskison asserts, develops "a genuine affection for, and admiration of, his conqueror" (213). Even the military leader of the conquered Mexicans, like so many American Indian leaders in U.S. storytelling traditions, recognizes the superiority of the invaders, the Anglo Texans.

Only the Texas Cherokees disrupt, albeit briefly, the consistency of the book's celebration of U.S. settler–colonial expansion. After Houston moves to Nacogdoches and advertises his services as an attorney, he tours the colonies in Texas and meets with Comanches before coming into contact with "a Texas band of Cherokees under an old half-breed named Boles" (156). Oskison provides a brief history of Boles's band: "They had been established for some years on land granted by Mexico; and Boles wore not only the title of colonel but fragments of a once splendid Mexican uniform to support his claim to the rank" (156). The description of Boles reinforces the previous suggestion that Mexicans are an Indigenous or mestizo and therefore inferior race: Boles dresses in the tattered clothes of a Mexican soldier, just as earlier in the narrative Mexicans dressed like American Indians to attack Anglo settlements.[26] Houston hopes to have the allegiance or at least the neutrality of the Cherokees when war with Mexico comes. Boles complains to Houston,

"The Mexican government's agents were venal and negligent; they either could not or would not keep off the Cherokee grant American settlers who boldly claimed the Indians' cultivated fields under other grants" (156). Houston advises Boles to prepare a petition to the Mexican government requesting the removal of the white squatters; it is a "hopeless mission," Houston believes (157). Oskison's Sam Houston has limited sympathy for the Cherokees and a casual disregard for their fate. Indeed, he fights with the American settlers against whom Boles lodges his grievances.

Following the defeat of Santa Anna, Oskison depicts Houston making another effort to aid the Texas Cherokees despite his belief in their imminent doom. As president of Texas, Houston sets his agenda:

> Texas must have a sufficient army, he insisted, to guard the Rio Grande border and control the freebooter factions that threatened her peace from within. Finally, he made his plea for fair treatment of the Indians—the most hopeless plea a man could make in Texas.... Only in his Indian programme did he meet defeat. He wanted not only to protect those fragments of friendly tribes, like Boles's band of Cherokees, already in Texas, but he hoped to bring others under the protection of the Republic. But the Texans were fixed in their enmity to all Indians; to the rallying cry of 'Texas for the Texans,' they proposed to repudiate the treaty made with Boles, run the Cherokees out, and get rid of the Comanches by killing them. Sam was able to prevent aggressive action during the rest of his term. (249)

Oskison again tempers the apparent sympathy for the Cherokees by commenting on their grim future: "He must be honest with the Indians, try to prepare them for the tragic time that must come after he stepped down from the presidency" (250). He has a moment of regret that he cannot remain in power and help them, but he retreats from that position. Only a free, democratic Texas matters, even if its future leaders include Indian haters, like the Georgia-born Mirabeau Buonaparte Lamar, who intended to remove or exterminate all Indigenous peoples. Lamar and other early Texas leaders represent more successful versions of the fictional Jerry Boyd, his son Cale, and the bandit Jack Kitchin, the criminals in *Black Jack Davy* who try to murder Ned Warrior and take his land.

In *Black Jack Davy,* Oskison celebrates Cherokee law and condemns U.S. immigrants who break it. His outrage over the violation of a nation's sovereignty and territorial integrity does not translate, however, to the Mexico–Texas and Mexico–United States conflicts in which Sam Houston played such an important role. Instead of continuing to express his support for the citizens of less powerful nations who face aggressive, expansion-minded U.S. settlers, Oskison celebrates the Texan and U.S. assaults on Mexico. In the Houston biography, he depicts this settler–colonial nation in the same way that U.S. politicians and other commentators for so long represented American Indian nations: as primitive and incapable of governing itself. Indeed, *Black Jack Davy,* as Kirby Brown explains, contains a nuanced rejection of this view of American Indian nationhood. Oskison also does not claim the Texas Cherokees as part of a sovereign Cherokee Nation. The attack on them is lamentable but less important than the rise of the Republic of Texas and its eventual annexation by the United States. Oskison's writing, across years and genres, includes a remarkably divergent array of political positions. In the case of *A Texas Titan: The Story of Sam Houston,* Oskison aligns himself with the supporters of Manifest Destiny.

In notable contrast to Oskison, the quarter-century-younger Riggs positions himself politically as an artist in alliance with Indigenous people in the United States–Mexico borderlands and Mexico and in opposition to settler colonials in both nations. As I discuss in chapter 3, Riggs's *Russet Mantle* forcefully mocks the Anglo elites of Santa Fe, New Mexico, and their explicitly settler–colonial view of the region and its Indigenous peoples. In *A World Elsewhere* and *The Year of Pilár,* Riggs represents Indigenous Mexicans as active, astute, anticolonial political agents. With different emphases—in the former on a family from the United States on tour in Mexico D.F. during a reactionary counterrevolution by Mexican elites; in the latter on an elite Mexican family returning to their hacienda immediately prior to an Indigenous revolution—these plays show Riggs's characteristic sympathy for the working classes, specifically Indigenous in *A World Elsewhere* and *The Year of Pilár,* as well as his consistent resistance to assumptions of settler–colonial political, cultural, and racial superiority. Riggs's youth relative to Oskison does not determine but only partially explains the differences in their borderlands and transnational politics, for Riggs shared with Will Rogers, twenty years his senior, a political affinity for working-class Native and non-Native people, if not, however, the inclination for revolution.

"Meddling in Mexico," a U.S. Sport

As Richard D. White Jr. argues in *Will Rogers: A Political Life* (2011), Rogers held significant influence in U.S. politics, especially from the beginning of the 1920s until his death in 1935. He had friendships "with every president from Theodore Roosevelt, whose family delighted at his rope tricks on the White House lawn, to Franklin Roosevelt, whom he openly supported" (xxii), and he visited with them frequently. Following his travels around the world and meetings with world leaders, White explains, Rogers often upon his return immediately traveled to Washington, D.C., to debrief with presidents, cabinet officials, senators, and congressmen. He also attended and reported to the country on many of the national political conventions, beginning with the 1920 Republican Convention in Chicago. At the 1932 Democratic National Convention in Chicago, he even received twenty-two votes from the Oklahoma delegation during the second round of voting.

Rogers leaned progressive, as defined in that era, but he held political views along the entire political spectrum. He opposed U.S. intervention in Latin America, including the military occupations of the Dominican Republic from 1916 to 1924 and Nicaragua from 1912 to 1933 (White, 15, 101), and he vigorously attacked prohibition, but he did not support women's suffrage (23). As a tireless humanitarian, Rogers also raised funds, for example, for victims of the 1927 Mississippi River flood, after which he successfully advocated for the passage of the Flood Control Act (122–23), and he organized an extensive relief effort for families hit by the drought in the early months of 1931. He favored a strong military and criticized what he considered a soft criminal justice system but advocated for gun control. He supported unions, according to White, but usually not strikes (261). At the same time, White observes, Rogers admired Benito Mussolini and complimented Spanish dictator Miguel Primo de Rivera (94–96, 97), yet "other than Franklin Roosevelt himself, Rogers possibly did more than any other American to convince the public to accept the overall New Deal" (xxvii). His response to the Great Depression reveals Rogers as "essentially a Jeffersonian who mistrusted big government, blamed the dire economy on a bloated federal bureaucracy, an impotent Congress, greedy industrialists and bankers, and Wall Street financiers" (173). Rogers was a walking array of political positions; indeed, as White demonstrates, he appears to have angered the Far Left and the Far Right equally. Rogers's political positions on issues especially urgent to Indigenous and ethnic minority communities are more difficult to trace, with the exception of oil exploration and extraction, which he tended to consider from various tribal-nation perspectives. In 1929, he successfully advocated for the construction by the federal government of a hospital in Claremore, Oklahoma, for Native people. White also notes, "Will Rogers at times revealed a deep-seated anger about the inhumane treatment of Indians" (140). When he spoke to thousands of Eastern Cherokees in 1928, he broke from his script to attack Andrew Jackson, whom Oskison spared from criticism in *A Texas Titan*. According to one report, Rogers railed for several minutes against Jackson and removal (White, 141–42). He conceived of his constituency as the poor, regardless of tribal-nation citizenship or ethnicity, but he publicly betrayed a prejudice against African Americans. White reflects, too, that while Rogers denounced the Ku Klux Klan, "he never spoke out against lynchings" (264). Though Mexico became one of his favorite foreign countries to visit and support in his writing, he mentions Mexican Americans much less frequently.

Rogers's views of Mexico also have roots in his childhood in the Cherokee Nation in Indian Territory. He frequently identified himself as Cherokee, including in his first weekly article, and he made almost entirely celebratory and often nostalgic references to his homeland in the Cherokee Nation, Indian Territory, and to towns such as Oologah and Claremore.[27] A weekly article from February 18, 1923, begins with a comment about U.S. troops finally returning from Germany before Rogers shifts to a discussion of one of his favorite topics: U.S. politics. He compares Congress to a Hollywood movie studio, "the Capital Comedy Company," and the legislative process to the production of comedies and, occasionally, tragedies (*Weekly Articles*, vol. 1, 25). His subsequent observations on water management eventually turn to Oklahoma: "Now I am off my Senators from Oklahoma, especially Robert Owen who is part Cherokee like myself (and as proud of it as I am). Now I got names right there on my farm where I was born that are funny, too, and Owen don't do a thing to get me a Harbor on the VERDIGRIS river at OOLAGAH in what used to be the District of COOWEESCOOWEE, (before we spoiled the best Territory in the World to make a State)" (*Weekly Articles,* vol. 1, 27). Rogers repeats his observation about the regrettable legacy of Oklahoma statehood in an article from January 27, 1924: "There is a good deal in the papers about giving my native state of Oklahoma back to the Indians. Now I am a Cherokee Indian and very proud of it, but I doubt if you can get them to accept it—not in its present state. When the white folks come in and took Oklahoma from us, they spoiled a mighty happy hunting ground" (*Weekly Articles,* vol. 1, 185). A discussion of the increasing popularity of football in a weekly article from September 29, 1929, entitled "Story of a Misspent Boyhood" leads to a reflection on one of his childhood educational experiences. Rogers recalls the all-Indian school that he attended: "It was all Indian kids went there and I being part Cherokee (had enough white in me to make my honesty questionable)" (*Weekly Articles,* vol. 4, 67). The school, called Drumgoole, was in a one-room log cabin in Indian Territory. Rogers laments the school's demise, which he argues was a consequence of its excessive focus on academics and its failure to field a good football team. However, he takes the opportunity to remind readers in an aside that "the Cherokee Nation, (we then had our own Government, and the name Oklahoma was as foreign to us as a Tooth Paste)" (*Weekly Articles,* vol. 4, 68). Several other references in the weekly articles to his Cherokee identity and the Cherokee Nation also include the addendum that he takes pride in both, and his discussion of political scandals in Oklahoma reinforces his view that the state was not an improvement on the Territory.[28]

The United States, like the state of Oklahoma, does not fare well in comparison to Indian Territory. On September 20, 1925, Rogers expresses concern with the proliferation of firearms, particularly automatic pistols:

> I was born and raised in the Indian Territory, at Claremore to be exact. (A town that has cured more people than Florida has swindled.) Well, that country, along about the time I was a yearling was supposed to have some pretty tough men. Of course, as I grew up and began to be able to uphold law and righteousness, why these men gradually began to thin out and drift on down to Politics, a big part of them becoming Governors. Well, even in those days out there it was against the law to carry guns and every once in awhile the Sheriff

would search a fellow to see if he was overdressed, and they fined 'em heavy. Mind you, that was men carrying guns that knew what they were; knew the danger of them, and knew how to use them. (*Weekly Articles*, vol. 2, 81)

While Indian Territory had reasonable gun laws, and the people who had weapons knew how to use them, New York, Rogers says, has drug addicts and unhappy wives who do not know how to shoot and fire their weapons indiscriminately. This commentary reverses the familiar Wild West–civilized East binary that structures much of the dominant historical and literary discourse about the settler-colonization of the West. Rogers longed for Indian Territory, a place governed better than Oklahoma and less dangerous than the United States. This view of Indian Territory and the Cherokee Nation aligns with Oskison's in *Black Jack Davy*; both authors assert the political superiority of the Cherokee Nation to the Oklahoma and U.S. governments and celebrate the social order that Cherokee governance produced.

Rogers adopts a more explicitly nostalgic tone in a weekly article about a visit to Texas entitled "Will Rides Back to the Good Old Times." The itinerary included Galveston, Houston, and Austin—where he met with Governor James E. Ferguson and saw the bed of adopted Cherokee Sam Houston—as well as stops in Temple, Breckenridge, and Amarillo. The ranching culture and economy of Texas elicits the following expression of longing: "I have always regretted that I didn't live about 30 or 40 years earlier, and in the same old Country, the Indian Territory. I would have liked to got here ahead of the 'Nestors,' the Bob wire fence, and so called civilization" (*Weekly Articles*, vol. 2, 160–61). Racism in the Cherokee Nation and the United States also informs this nostalgia. Rogers reminisces in an article from September 25, 1932: "I used to love to sing coon songs and was the first fellow in Cooweescoowee district, Cherokee Nation, Indian territory, that ever did the cake walk" (*Weekly Articles*, vol. 5, 188). Rogers joined many others singing these songs during what historian James Dormon calls the "national fascination" with them, or the "craze," between 1890 and 1910 (450, 453). These songs, Dormon explains, "were calculated to be hilariously funny" but "were based in caricature" of African American life (453). It was "*happy* music," he adds, "despite the grossly offensive lyrics as judged by modern sensibilities" (453). The vaudeville world that welcomed Rogers in

1904 also embraced these songs. Rogers even faced a protest by the National Association for the Advancement of Colored People (NAACP) after he used a racial slur on the air on January 21, 1934. Rather than apologizing, Rogers used "darky" instead during the following week's program.[29] As both Amy Ware, in "Will Rogers's Radio," and Mvskoke Creek scholar Tol Foster, in "Of One Blood," argue, this racism is, to quote Foster, "homegrown" in the Cherokee Nation (286). Rogers's use of racial slurs and the ensuing conflict with the NAACP recalls Oskison's depictions of darker-skinned Cherokees and Mexicans as well as his apparent aversion to incorporating Cherokees with African ancestry into his imagined Cherokee Nation.

Like Riggs's dramatic representations of Mexico, which share readily identifiable characteristics with the representations of Indian Territory in many of his plays, Rogers's Mexico reads as a political cognate of the Indian Territory of his childhood but without explicitly identified Indians. Amy Ware explains this apparent unwillingness to identify with Indigenous Mexicans. Although in his writing Rogers frequently expresses pride in his Cherokee roots, she observes, he viewed Cherokees as distinctly superior to and, in Rogers's words, more "educated and civilized" than other, less assimilated Indigenous American people (quoted in Ware, "Unexpected Cowboy, Unexpected Indian," 18). Yet Rogers, like Riggs, sees in Mexico another territory under siege by an aggressive United States. Daniel Heath Justice observes of Rogers, "His critique of U.S. imperialist policies toward Puerto Rico, Hawai'i, Cuba, and the Philippines—policies which mirrored and perfected the brutal erasure of Indian sovereignty in the former Indian Territory—are particularly pointed and often utilize language familiar in Indian Country as the language of embattled tribal sovereignty" (*Our Fire Survives the Storm*, 124). Foster concurs: "Tribal figures like the Cherokee writer Will Rogers are historically situated actors who utilize the counternarratives of their communities as a theoretical base from which to conduct anticolonialist and cosmopolitan critique" (267). The language that Rogers uses to discuss Mexico to his U.S. reading public also evokes Indian Territory history.

Rogers set the tone for his observations about Mexico in his sixth weekly article, published on January 21, 1923. On the occasion of President Warren G. Harding's order that U.S. servicemen in Germany return home, Rogers took the opportunity to discuss U.S. interference abroad. From a comment about unofficial representatives sent to influence the governments of foreign nations, he shifts his focus to larger-scale acts of aggression: "Nations never seem to get much nourishment out of these Unofficial invasions. If memory don't fail me I think we made a pilgrimage into Mexico unofficially. All we got was Sand in our eyes" (*Weekly Articles,* vol. 1, 15). Rogers recollects in this passage the 1916–17 invasion of Mexico by General John J. Pershing in pursuit of Pancho Villa. On Villa's death later that same year, Rogers mocks the fascination with Villa and the multiple, inaccurate reports of his death in U.S. newspapers. He then celebrates the revolutionary: "He was personally responsible for our only losing war. Of course, after losing it, we changed the name of it from a war to a punitive expedition" (*Weekly Articles,* vol. 1, 103). Rogers appears to take particular joy in relating Pershing's inability to catch Villa and recalling the humiliation earned by the United States during this violation of Mexican sovereignty; he repeats the story in condensed form in his weekly article from February 17, 1924, and mentions it briefly again on January 25, 1925.[30]

Rogers's observations on U.S. oil companies operating in Mexico and the Mexican plan to expropriate its oil reserves gave readers an opportunity to see Indigenous contexts more clearly informing his politics. When President Harding observed that the United States was cultivating good relations with Mexico, the only nation in the Western hemisphere with which the United States was not friendly, Rogers wryly noted, "Mexico must have struck more oil" (*Weekly Articles,* vol. 1, 63). The oil industry had considerable power in Oklahoma, particularly in the Osage Nation to the west of the Cherokee Nation. The Marland Oil Company and E. W. Marland, the subject of a biography by Osage writer John Joseph Mathews, owned one of the major oil fields, the Burbank, in the Osage Nation. Rogers made frequent comments about Osage wealth derived from oil leases.[31] On May 25, 1924, Rogers also reports, "I hear the Navajos have struck oil on their reservation. That will give the white man a chance to show his so-called 100 percent Americanism, by flocking in and taking it away from the Indians" (*Weekly Articles,* vol. 1, 238). His support of the expropriation of Mexico's oil reserves resonates within this context: "They give America 50 years to get the oil out from under the land, and then they want to divide the land up with the Natives. Now that don't seem so unreasonable to give you fifty years. We say it's against our laws. Our Laws! What's our laws got to do with Mexico?"

(*Weekly Articles,* vol. 3, 8). Rogers's nostalgia for Indian Territory informs both the personal and historical context of his outrage.

The political conflicts between the Cherokee Nation and the United States that characterized Rogers's childhood and adolescent years in Indian Territory also have cognates in Mexico. He frequently references past and present political turmoil in Mexico and ties it to U.S. interference, through arms sales, for example, or through the simple diplomatic process of the official U.S. recognition of a new Mexican government.[32] Rogers relentlessly protests this constant interference in articles such as the June 28, 1925, piece "Meddling in Mexico, a Summer Sport." Rogers tells the story of Secretary of State Frank Kellogg, the federal prosecutor representing the United States in the 1911 antitrust case of *Standard Oil Company of New Jersey v. the United States* and a future winner of the Nobel Peace Prize in 1929, who anxiously wants to establish diplomatic relations with some other nation. He asks a member of his staff, "What about Mexico? I have always heard that when the U.S. couldn't find anybody else to pick on that they picked out Mexico." His staff member replies, "I know, Mr. Secretary, but Mexico hasn't done anything; in fact they have been behaving themselves almost beyond recognition. They are so peaceful you would hardly think they were a Republic" (*Weekly Articles,* vol. 2, 47). But Secretary Kellogg remains determined:

> Well, you send them the following: "America is getting very tired of your Nation down there not paying us what you owe us for land we claim was taken by the Revolutionists from some of our respectful Citizens. It's funny to me you can't control these Revolutions. Now, we want Americans protected. Remember, MEXICO IS ON TRIAL BEFORE THE EYES OF THE WORLD." Remember this is a friendly Note. (47)

The rest of the article lacks Rogers's characteristic humor. He chastises the United States and its citizens for interfering in Mexico—"Why don't you let every Nation do and act as they please? What business is it of ours how Mexico acts or lives?"—and for using and abusing its southern neighbor for financial gain (48). This section of the article culminates with this assertion: "The difference in our exchange of people with Mexico is: they send workmen here to work, while we send Americans there to *work* Mexico" (48–49). After he presciently predicts that Germany will soon start another war, Rogers extrapolates the lesson about interfering in the life of other sovereign nations: "There is only one way in the World to prevent war, and that is, FOR EVERY NATION TO TEND TO ITS OWN BUSINESS" (49). Rogers does not deviate from this specific indictment of U.S. intervention in Mexico and what he sees as the related interference in Nicaraguan affairs. His objections to aggressive U.S. foreign policy run consistently through the weekly articles.

Though the articles about Mexico and his commentary on the Cherokee Nation in Indian Territory create a dialogue about invaded territories, Rogers rarely recognized the Indigenous population of Mexico specifically. When the United States planned to lift an embargo and sell weapons to Mexico, Rogers fretted about another revolution fought by "ignorant Peons" (*Weekly Articles,* vol. 3, 6). For U.S. authors, Gilbert G. González explains, "peons" meant "the poorest of the Mexican population" and "an obstacle to modernization." "Peon" also became "synonymous for Indian" (80). González observes, "So distinctive were their alleged characteristics that peons were essentially perceived as a racial category unto themselves" (80). Rogers makes his observation about a large mass of impoverished Indigenous Mexicans without the ostensible concern for the Yaquis in his speech at the American embassy. The socioeconomic and racial category "peon" even denies Indigenous Mexicans their specific communal identifications and political affiliations.

A January 1, 1928, article titled "Mexico and Oklahoma in the Limelight" leaves implicit the connection between Indian Territory and Mexico as sovereign geographies in which the United States interferes. In this article, Rogers's report on Lindbergh's visit to Mexico becomes a defense of Mexican politicians against accusations of dishonesty, after which Rogers comments on "Cuckooland," one of his names for Washington, D.C., and a political scandal in Oklahoma (*Weekly Articles,* vol. 3, 114–16). Yet in this article he mentions the Cristero War, the conflict in Mexico between the government and the Catholic Church that Choctaw author Todd Downing incorporates into his 1935 novel *Vultures in the Sky,* and he returns to it earnestly two weeks later in an article he wrote as a letter to Governor Al Smith of New York:

> Mexicans are fine people. They don't do everything our way or like we do. But why should they? Maybe their way is best, who knows? And if I ever was serious in my life I am serious in all I am saying to you.

I honestly believe you are the best equipped and the most logical person in the world today to settle this great question.... And as for us and our relations with Mexico, it would mean everything. And most of all it would be giving those poor peons down there something, that through no fault of theirs they are now denied. You know most of the population down there are poor, and they work hard, and they don't get a whole lot, and their church services and their fiesta days is about all they get out of it. That and to be let alone is all they ask. (*Weekly Articles*, vol. 3, 122)

His defense of the impoverished and disenfranchised would have sounded familiar to his regular readers, though here it also includes a defense of a large exploited working class comprised of "peons" or Indigenous Mexicans.

Despite the absence of an explicit connection between the two geographies, this defense of and affection for Mexico has the distinct character of his commentary on Indian Territory. He completes an article from March 17, 1929, on various small rebellions and the executions in which they culminate with the following observation: "It makes you sick to hear of these things happening down there. For they are no difference from us. They love peace just as much, they love Life, and they want to be let alone.... I hope they get straightened out, for they are an awful nice people. Hospitality is their middle name. If I wasent acting a Fool here in New York and have to stay I would be in Mexico in 24 hours. I would try to kid em out of fighting. So Viva Mexico" (*Weekly Articles*, vol. 4, 3). The article that follows, "A History of Mexico," satirizes the violence that characterized the recent history of Mexican politics. The satire remains focused on Mexican leaders; the Mexican population—especially the vaqueros and the ropers—earn Rogers's praise and admiration (*Weekly Articles*, vol. 4, 3-5). His depiction in "Over Your Shoulder" of an elderly Mexican man who sleeps well at night, untroubled by "over production, unemployment, second mortgages, poor movies, and a thousand and one things that bite us and keep us awake at nights," captures the equivalence between Rogers's representation of Indian Territory and Mexico as desirable landscapes (*Weekly Articles*, vol. 5, 199). "Riding back to the good old times" and going down to Mexico produce the same emotional and political responses in Rogers and involve a temporal as well as a spatial movement. The movement back in time to an Indian Territory ruined by statehood and across a settler–colonial border to a Mexico constantly in conflict with the United States illuminates possible political alliances between Cherokees and Mexicans, but only once, and briefly, between Cherokees and Yaquis or any other specific Indigenous Mexican group.

Though working in a much different literary form from Rogers's, Lynn Riggs distinguished himself from his fellow Cherokee Nation citizen by developing these potential trans-Indigenous alliances between Cherokees and Indigenous Mexicans and, in *The Year of Pilár*, specifically Màyans in Yucatán. Indeed, setting plays in Mexico appears to have empowered Riggs to imagine Indigenous people taking political control of their future. In his plays set in Indian Territory and the post-statehood Cherokee Nation, especially *The Cherokee Night*, young Cherokees struggle to find their way. In *The Year of Pilár*, however, Beto, a young Mayan man, seizes an opportunity to help his people. At the end of the play, he agrees to work with the federal government to redistribute land long held by settler colonials to Mayans. Other local Mayans take a different step: they execute the landowners as punishment for their brutal dominance of the region.

Soon after completing the two Mexico plays, Riggs wrote a theater manifesto and included it in a personal letter to his friend, Paul Green, the winner of the 1927 Pulitzer Prize for Drama. In it, he outlines the new Vine Theatre's bold political message:

> In the world today, forces in opposition to the triumphant, arrogant state are demolished by pogrom, by discriminatory laws—and the other tools of inhumanity and cruelty. We do not believe that those forces really achieve their ends. We believe that the way to destroy is not to destroy. The way to change the world is to offer such a living and singing force that all people in whom the germ of truth resides, however deeply, will be drawn and changed by an instinctive need to ally themselves with life instead of death. (Riggs, "The Vine Theatre," 276–77)

While Riggs throughout his career usually aligned himself with economically underprivileged and disenfranchised communities, his experiences traveling in and writing about Mexico brought clarity to these politics. This inspiration occurred, however, on the eve of World War II.

After the war, in which he served in an Army Signal Corps company and worked for the Office of War Information, Riggs appears to have abandoned his plans for the Vine Theatre.

Oskison, Rogers, and Riggs produce an array of three distinct political positions on Mexico while developing a long Cherokee Nation–Mexico connection for a new generation of Cherokees and making that history available to a broader U.S. reading public. The comparative representations of Indian Territory and Mexico invite reconsiderations of past U.S. settler–colonial aggression in the Cherokee Nation in Indian Territory, and scholars could use these reconsiderations as a lens through which to view United States–Mexico diplomatic relations strained by the neocolonial U.S. presence in a settler–colonial Mexico. However, only Riggs used these representations of Mexico to redirect our attention explicitly to American Indian life. Riggs's view of Mexico as promising a better future for Indigenous people contrasts with an Indian Territory devoid of clearly defined Cherokee communities and full of traumatized individual Cherokee characters; Oskison's more conventional depiction of a violent, uncivilized Mexico contrasts with his representation of a strong, effective Cherokee government under duress from U.S. immigrants but still correlating more directly to the revolutionary Texas government and invasive United States than to Mexico; Rogers's affection for what he represented as a simpler life in Mexico correlates directly to his nostalgia for Indian Territory. Together, these authors used Cherokee and Indian Territory history as the foundation of their views of other Indigenous people and of international politics. In these layers of representations, we find overlapping and conflicting histories of race, resistance, diplomacy, and dominance that mutually reveal the strategies that American Indian writers employ to find in occupied Indian Territory landscapes the tools necessary to come to terms with a troubled history, regroup, and build for variously imagined futures. While Oskison did not seriously challenge the trajectory of Indian Territory history, Rogers began the process of intervening in it. Riggs even contemplated what political action might disrupt it to the benefit of Indigenous people and communities.

During the first half of the twentieth century, American Indians from other tribal nations, such as Todd Downing, the Choctaw author of detective novels and a history of Mexico, and D'Arcy McNickle, the

Confederated Salish and Kootenai novelist and anthropologist, wrote books that feature Indigenous Mexicans. John Joseph Mathews spent a year on a Guggenheim Fellowship in Mexico and wrote about the country and Indigenous Mexican people in at least three short stories and in his diary and letters. While this consideration of Rogers and Oskison in comparison to Riggs provides a Cherokee-specific view of international relations with Mexico, the work of these other writers offers a broader, multitribal national picture. Downing's 1940 history of Mexico, *The Mexican Earth*, which includes praise of the unconquerable Yaquis, contains a particularly compelling political statement on the revolutionary potential of Indigenous Mexico. Though Downing spoke Choctaw, English, Spanish, Italian, and French fluently, and though he spends the final chapter of the book talking in Spanish to Luis, a Zapotec from Oaxaca, he did not choose to learn to speak Yaqui. Rogers's admonition to the Mexican elites in attendance at the embassy dinner remained unanswered, literally or politically, even by the American Indian writers whose families and tribal nations shared a traumatic history similar to that of the Yaquis.

Mexico, Renaissance and Post-Renaissance

The tribal national, colonial, and settler–colonial politics circulating through and among the works about Mexico by Oskison, Rogers, and Riggs appear in similar forms in the Renaissance and post-Renaissance eras. At the quincentennial, Gerald Vizenor's *The Heirs of Columbus* (1991) and Leslie Marmon Silko's *Almanac of the Dead* (1991) historically and politically linked Indigenous peoples in the United States and Mexico. Both authors imagine a revolution—peaceful in Vizenor's novel and violent in Silko's—with Mayan roots in Mexico.[33] Curiously, though, more American Indian writers saw political and cultural potential in Mexico in the interwar and immediate post–World War II era than at the end of the twentieth century and beginning of the twenty-first. Of writers from the latter era, Silko, a longtime resident of Tucson, Arizona, most consistently turns her gaze to Mexico. While *Almanac of the Dead* identifies Mexico as the center of a revolution by a coalition of the dispossessed, her earlier novel, *Ceremony*, and her memoir *The Turquoise Ledge* (2010) contain different and more politically conservative representations of Mexico, Mexicans, and Mexican Americans. Like other American Indian writers, Silko produces work that resists political generalizations.

Mexico figures in *Ceremony* both as a source of sacred or supernatural power and as a discourse of adaptive and resilient hybridity associated with the green eyes of several main characters and the semidomesticated Mexican cattle from Sonora that Josiah purchases from Ulibarri. In the process of narrating a story about sexually and supernaturally powerful women, Silko draws on familiar conventional representations of exotic, sensuous Mexican women. The sacred power comes from a character introduced as Josiah's "Mexican girl friend" (32), the Night Swan, and from the medicine man Betonie's grandmother, a "remarkable Mexican" (119). Night Swan easily attracts men, like Josiah, whose heart she leaves "beating like a boy's" (83), and she has the power to punish them as well. When her lover—a man who "could not get enough of her" and whose "eyes would be fevered even after he was limp and incapable of taking any more from her"—condemns Night Swan and returns to his wife, she dances him to death (84–85). Eventually the novel's protagonist, Tayo, also falls for her. When delivering a note to her from Josiah, "he could smell her before he could even see her; the perfume smelled like the ivory locust blossoms that hung down from the trees in the spring" (97). Silko continues with the orientalized representation of Night Swan: after Tayo enters her home, he sees her in a "kimono . . . wrapped around her closely, outlining her hips and belly" (98). Following rapturous sex, she notices his eyes—"Mexican eyes," Tayo says (99)—and becomes the first character to introduce "it" to Tayo, the battle with the destroyers that becomes clear later in the novel (100). When Tayo visits Betonie, the medicine man recognizes Night Swan. After Tayo introduces her to the conversation, Betonie "jumped up. . . . He was excited, and from time to time he would say something to himself in Navajo" (125). He eventually tells Tayo the story of his grandmother, a young Mexican girl discovered by Navajo hunters on "a seductive night" and identified as "the Mexican captive" (146, 148). As she does with Night Swan, Silko presents Betonie's grandmother as supernaturally and, even though "she was only twelve or thirteen," sexually powerful (147). She learns healing arts from a Navajo medicine man, Old Descheeny, and her daughter with him gives birth to Betonie, though Betonie says, "When I was weaned, my grandmother came and took me" (152). Two Mexican women, Night Swan and Betonie's grandmother, thus play a central role in the circulation of sacred, healing power in the novel. After Tayo comes of age in her arms, Night Swan introduces him to the destroyers' scheme. Once Tayo returns from the war, Betonie uses what he learns from his grandmother to set Tayo on a more secure path toward physical and spiritual wellness. Both women, however, are social outcasts, and no other Mexican women appear to put pressure on this representation of mysterious, seductive Latinas as the dominant one in the novel.

Romanticized, exotic, and erotic Mexican women hold at least sacred if not real social power, but Mexican men in the novel appear both unattractive and threatening. Tayo's Auntie Thelma expresses explicitly anti-Mexican sentiment, as when she worries about Josiah's relationship with Night Swan: "It will start all over again. All that gossip about Josiah and about Little Sister. Girls around here have babies by white men all the time now, and nobody says anything. Men run around with Mexicans and even worse, and nothing is ever said" (33). The narrator's voice tends to reinforce Auntie Thelma's view. Mannie, a bartender at an establishment frequented by the veterans, "was a fat Mexican from Cubero who was losing his hair" (42). "The old Mexican man," who serves Tayo menudo and makes a "serious business" of killing flies, appears benign (100, 101), but Silko represents "the Mexicans from the section gang" drinking at a bar as ominous and predatory. As Tayo walks into the bar with Leroy, Harley, and Helen Jean, a young Ute woman, "The Mexicans could see she was drunk, and they were already getting ideas about her" (160). These racially informed anxieties prove prescient, as the Mexican men assault Leroy and Harley and leave the bar with Helen Jean. The novel hints at the possibility of a political coalition between Indigenous and Mexican people, as when Tayo observes that landowners built fences for "a thousand dollars a mile to keep Indians and Mexicans out," recognizes his own internalized racism against other Indigenous people and Mexicans, and overhears a ranch hand equate "greasers and Indians" (188, 191, 202), but it remains unrealized.

While she imagines a large, transethnic and transnational, anticolonial coalition of the dispossessed with its center in Mexico in *Almanac of the Dead*, Silko returns in her memoir, *The Turquoise Ledge*, to more politically conservative representations of Mexico. The work of writer José Díaz Bolio and her interest in Aztecan cosmology and the Nahuatl language shape her imagined Mexico. Despite the criticism directed at

Díaz Bolio by "Maya experts, including Maya people themselves," Silko embraces his work, which argues for the centrality of the rattlesnake to ancient Mayan thought (Silko, *The Turquoise Ledge*, 107). Though she travels to Mexico "to participate in a celebration of the indigenous tribes of Chihuahua and Sonora and other parts of Mexico and the United States," her interest falls primarily on the gods of the Aztecs: Huitzilopochtli and Huracan, for example, but especially Tlaloc. As she paints a series of what she calls "Star Beings," she notes that these figures "expected me to write poetry in Nahuatl although I have no knowledge at all of the language" (138). She eventually suggests that the U.S. Southwest forms part of Mesoamerica: "Such a large pre-Columbian city near Santa Fe helps solidify the Nahua claim to the four corners states of Arizona, New Mexico, Utah and Colorado" (191). She continues to draw connections between "traditional Pueblo and Nahua people" while searching "two Nahuatl dictionaries for coded messages that may inspire me to write. It is possible to do a great deal with a language we don't speak or understand, as long as we freely employ our imagination and have access to good dictionaries" (241). This blithe attitude toward the politics of Indigenous languages in the settler–colonial context of the Americas and her suggestion, later repeated twice, that by writing in Nahuatl she stumbled upon a "rain cloud spell" (242), expose Silko to objections from language revitalization activists as well as writers and scholars concerned about the overwhelming focus on the Indigenous past, not only in her references to Mexico but in her emphasis on those she calls "the ancient ones" or the "ancestors" in the Southwest, rather than on the present and future. In her memoir, Silko adopts a political position that recalls postrevolutionary Mexican *indigenismo*, which embraced Mexico's Indigenous past and material culture but not its living Indigenous people.

The broad range of political positions, from arguably conservative to militantly progressive, in three of Silko's works from the early to the late part of her career does not undermine her significance to either American Indian literary history or the political work American Indian literature accomplishes. Indeed, these shifts link her to earlier Native authors who, one hundred years, more or less, before the publication of *The Turquoise Ledge,* tried to navigate the vexed racial, Indigenous, and gender politics that shaped life in Indian Country by writing about the settler–colonial nation with which the United States shares its southern border. In *Ceremony,* Silko sounds like Oskison, while in *Almanac,* she sounds much like Riggs in his two Mexico plays. In *The Turquoise Ledge,* she sounds more like Todd Downing in *The Mexican Earth,* except that Downing documents contemporary Indigenous Mexican life and looks to a more robust Indigenous Mexican future. Silko's view of Indigenous Mexico in her memoir indicates an interest not in contemporary Indigenous Mexican people but in their distant ancestors. By recognizing the array of political positions in Silko's oeuvre and the work of American Indian writers interested in Mexico, scholars more accurately account for the politics of Native texts and their political potential in the world. If politics remain central to the scholarly assessment of and engagement with Native texts, as the literary critical history suggests that they will, then efforts to draw these distinctions will also remain imperative to scholarly inquiry.

As the shift from this small group of early- and mid-twentieth-century Cherokee writers to Silko demonstrates, political arrays share nodes across eras. Scholarly attention to these nodes reveals often overlooked continuities between pre- and post-civil-rights Native literature. Other possibilities also beckon to contemporary literary critics. Men, and especially Cherokee men, monopolize the formation of the political arrays emerging through their interest in Mexico, for example, but they do not entirely control either the Cherokee or Native transnational political imaginary of their era. Osage writer Annetta Lohmann, published by Lee Harkins in the *American Indian,* and Ruth Muskrat Bronson, whose literary and political work Kirby Brown so thoroughly recovers and analyzes in *Stoking the Fire* (2018), offer the perspectives of two Native women on the place of Indigenous people on a world stage. Bronson's prolific career includes particularly compelling moments, as when she returned from Asia in 1922 and shared these thoughts with an interviewer: "For the Koreans like the Indians see what were formerly their lands ruled by aliens. . . . This reminded her . . . of the time when she sat at the feet of her grandmother and listened to stories in broken English or Cherokee of how the Indians once owned and ranged all this broad country, and how it was taken from them" (quoted in Harvey, 45–46). Approximately a decade earlier than Riggs and Downing, Bronson began to draw transnational and transhistorical political links between the Indigenous people of Indian Territory and another colonized population. Literary scholars could productively treat her reflections on Korea as the origin of a political array that includes Choctaw author LeAnne Howe's essay "I Fuck Up in Japan," in which she relates a not quite as politically inspiring trans-Pacific experience. Such an array would have its own distinct nuances and, like the array that formed around Erdrich's work in the 1980s, would encourage further inquiry into the forms of arrays generated by Native women.

CHAPTER 3

A Good Day to Film

Lynn Riggs, Sherman Alexie, and Independent Indigenous Cinema

Upon its release in 1998, Cheyenne and Arapaho director Chris Eyre's *Smoke Signals* became the *House Made of Dawn* of American Indian cinema, a touchstone film that promised to change dramatically the cinematic landscape for Native filmmakers. The film, written by Sherman Alexie and based primarily on the short story "This Is What It Means to Say Phoenix, Arizona" in *The Lone Ranger and Tonto Fistfight in Heaven* (1993), follows Thomas Builds-the-Fire (Tla A'min Nation actor Evan Adams) and Victor Joseph (Saulteaux actor Adam Beach) on a road trip from the Coeur d'Alene Reservation to Phoenix, Arizona, to retrieve the ashes of Victor's father. *Smoke Signals* figures prominently in Cree director Neil Diamond's *Reel Injun* (2009), a documentary on the history of Hollywood's representations of Native Americans. In the documentary's final section, "The Renaissance," Ojibway film critic Jesse Wente refers to *Smoke Signals* as "another film that came right at the end of the nineties that started the golden age of aboriginal cinema." Dean Rader calls *Smoke Signals* "the most iconic and most revolutionary mainstream American Indian text" (*Engaged Resistance*, 160), and in *Smoke Signals: Native Cinema Rising* (2012), Joanna Hearne begins, "*Smoke Signals* is the most widely recognized and frequently taught film in the field of Native American cinema" (xv). She adds, "The film can be seen as a landmark 'first' in American film history—although it is important to remember the long history of Native filmmaking that came before *Smoke Signals*—and it can also be seen as a self-positioned first introduction to Native perspectives and Native filmmaking for many of its viewers" (xv). Of his work with Eyre at the beginning of the twenty-three-day production, Alexie says, "I think we were immediately aware that we were doing something revolutionary, that it was a revolutionary moment" (Hearne, *Smoke Signals*, 189). As Hearne thoroughly documents, *Smoke Signals* was critically and commercially successful and therefore augured an exciting future for Native film.

Many commentators on the film observe that *Smoke Signals* draws on a long history of mainstream Hollywood cinematic narratives about and representations of Native people in order to repudiate them, while in the process also asserting a distinct, coherent, and modern Native world rooted in a specific Native place: the Coeur d'Alene Reservation. The film generates a "virtual reservation" and practices "visual sovereignty," terms defined by Michelle Raheja, respectively, as "a space where Native American filmmakers put the long, vexed history of Indigenous representations into dialogue with epistemic Indigenous knowledges" and a way of thinking about "the space between resistance and compliance wherein Indigenous filmmakers and actors revisit, contribute to, borrow from, critique, and reconfigure ethnographic film conventions, while at the same time operating within and stretching the boundaries created by these conventions" (147, 193). It models, Hearne argues, "a form of activist pedagogy" and emphasizes "Indigenous political sovereignty" (*Smoke Signals,* xviii).[1] In much the same way that to many literary critics the politics of *House Made of Dawn* diverge from rather than cohere with the American Indian literary politics of the early and mid-twentieth century, the cinematic politics of self-representation and tribal-nation-specific location shooting in *Smoke Signals* appear so new and groundbreaking that *Reel Injun* presents the film as inaugurating a Renaissance in Native film precisely thirty years after Momaday's novel inaugurated one in literature.

Yet as the previous chapters argue, the decades preceding the civil rights era hold many surprises, both artistic and political. Cherokee dramatist and poet Lynn Riggs, who made a film in 1931 and screened it in the first week of 1932, had a career in the arts with several notable parallels to Alexie's. They both earned reputations as poets in their midtwenties before shifting their attention to other genres. While Alexie continued to write poetry as he began publishing short fiction and novels, Riggs almost entirely abandoned poetry for drama, despite the recognition of his early work by establishment poets and editors. Riggs made his mark in drama as well, with his 1930 play *Green Grow the Lilacs* earning Pulitzer Prize buzz. At almost the same age that *Green Grow the Lilacs* cemented Riggs's status as a star playwright, Alexie won an American Book Award for his first novel, *Reservation Blues* (1995). He eventually also received a National Book Award in the Young People's Literature category for *The Absolutely True Diary of a Part-Time Indian* (2007) and a PEN/Faulkner Award for *War Dances* (2009). Their success as writers opened doors in Hollywood, where they both spent remunerative but deeply unrewarding time working for major film studios.[2]

Riggs and Alexie also both made independent films informed by their poetry. Riggs's *A Day in Santa Fe* contains a series of intertitles with lines from his poem "Santo Domingo Corn Dance," which first appeared in the April 14, 1926, issue of the *Nation*. In the film, he intersperses lines from the poem throughout a scene of a harvest dance at Santa Clara Pueblo. Alexie drew the title of his film *The Business of Fancydancing* (2002) from a book of poems published in 1992. It follows the story of a character remarkably similar to Riggs: Seymour Polatkin (Evan Adams), a young, gay Spokane poet trying to find a sense of belonging on the reservation and in Seattle. Riggs left the University of Oklahoma in the fall of 1923 for Santa Fe, gained fame as a writer, and lived more openly as gay than generally acknowledged, but he remained "constantly wary of Oklahoma's judgments, and [was] never quite so full of self-esteem" as his openly gay friend, Witter "Hal" Bynner (Braunlich, *Haunted by Home*, 13). Alexie also incorporated some of his own poems into the film, in some cases in revised form, including "How to Write the Great American Indian Novel," "Memorial Day, 1972," "Giving Blood," "The Unauthorized Autobiography of Me," "Influences," and "The Alcoholic Love Poems."[3] Dean Rader argues that American Indian writers and artists simultaneously use text and image "to replicate the immersive experience of the oratory and the visual experience of ritual and performance" and "to create an aesthetic landscape of dialogue and collaboration that underscores Native autonomy and collectivity" ("Reading the Visual," 300, 301). Riggs's and Alexie's films work within this tradition of formal experimentation, a tradition that includes, for example, Momaday's *The Way to Rainy Mountain* (1969), Silko's *Storyteller* (1981), and Diné writer Laura Tohe's *No Parole Today* (1999).

While their career trajectories generate a moderately curious historical array of shared experiences between pre-Renaissance and post-Renaissance Native authors, Riggs's experimental film, Alexie's experimental and mainstream films, and the cultural, gender, and sexual politics of their lives and art form a fantastically diverse array of Indigenous political positions with some surprising continuities. In its treatment of the Native past and present and its representation of the opposition though not incommensurability between non-Native and Native spaces, *A Day in Santa Fe* also anticipates contemporary films such as Diné filmmaker Arlene Bowman's *Navajo Talking Picture* (1986), Bay of Quinte Mohawk filmmaker Shelley Niro's *Tree* (2005), and White Mountain Apache filmmaker Dustinn Craig's *4wheelwarpony* (2008). Along with Chickasaw director Edwin Carewe's mainstream film *Ramona* (1928), *A Day in Santa Fe* is one of the single most significant contributions to Native cinema and Native art before the Renaissance.[4] By most scholarly accounts, Alexie's film immediately fulfilled its "revolutionary" potential. Riggs's film had similar potential, despite his own modest assessment of his accomplishment. This potential will remain latent until more viewers see it, talk about it, and place it in a prominent place in American Indian literary and cinematic history.[5]

The Cross and the Harvest Dance: Lynn Riggs's and James Hughes's *A Day in Santa Fe*

In the first week of 1932, as multimedia star and international celebrity Will Rogers traveled through Southeast Asia on a very long journey home, fellow Cherokee and Rogers family friend Lynn Riggs introduced the public to his first venture into film. On Wednesday, January 6, in a room at La Fonda Hotel on the plaza in Santa Fe, New Mexico, Riggs, with cowriter, codirector, and cameraman James Hughes, hosted the premiere of their silent black-and-white "city symphony film" *A Day in Santa Fe* (1931). Riggs had arrived in Santa Fe in the fall of 1923, when the town was in the middle of a growth spurt that saw its population double from about five thousand in 1910 to just over eleven thousand in 1930. Some of the new residents, such as Bynner, Alice Corbin Henderson, and Mary Austin, were writers.[6] Many other celebrated writers, including Willa Cather, Robert Frost, John Galsworthy, D. H. Lawrence, Sinclair Lewis, Vachel Lindsay, and Carl Sandburg, visited Santa Fe in the 1920s and 1930s. As J. J. Brody notes, Santa Fe was also the "activating center" of a Pueblo art movement (6), and many non-Native artists, including Los Cincos Pintores, or "the five nuts in mud huts," came to paint the landscape and the Indigenous people of the region.[7] Social reformers and patrons of the arts, such as sisters Amelia Elizabeth White and

Martha White, came to stay as well.[8] Of the White sisters, art historian Elizabeth Hutchinson observes, "Experienced in urban philanthropic work, they were familiar with the progressivist notion that art could be the site of economic and cultural revitalization for Indian people as well as a meaningful medium of cross-cultural contact, and they saw the patronage of art as a means of social activism" (224). The White sisters, reformer and eventual commissioner of Indian affairs John Collier, and residents of all nineteen Pueblos, among many others, contributed in 1923 to the defeat of the Bursum Bill, which if implemented would have dispossessed the Pueblos of land, deprived them of water rights, and undermined their right to self-government.[9] The Pueblo people, American Indians across the United States, and non-Native activists like Mary Austin also fought in the early 1920s against attempts by the Office of Indian Affairs to regulate traditional dances.[10] Riggs embraced this dynamic mix of modernism, Pueblo art and religion, and political activism that shaped daily life in Santa Fe and the surrounding area.

Riggs also quickly established a friendship with Levi and Christine Hughes and their children, Mary Christine and James.[11] In early 1932, James Hughes was a twenty-one-year-old aspiring filmmaker, and his thirty-two-year-old friend was in the middle of a productive and successful artistic period. Riggs had published *The Iron Dish* (1930), a collection of poetry that earned a critical though encouraging review by Robert Liddell Lowe in the March 1931 issue of *Poetry*. *Green Grow the Lilacs*, which Riggs wrote while on a Guggenheim Fellowship in France, debuted on January 26, 1931, at the Guild Theater in New York. It received consideration for the Pulitzer Prize and served as the source play for Richard Rodgers and Oscar Hammerstein's musical *Oklahoma!* (1943).[12] Riggs had also started work on *The Cherokee Night*, a play he would tell Betty Kirk a month later in a letter from Santa Fe that he had finished. "As I thought, and hoped," he tells Kirk, a journalist and close friend from his Norman days, "it turns out to be my best play. It'll be a long time before I write another like it, I'm afraid" (Riggs to Kirk). Riggs was not as confident about the artistic value of the film. In the same letter, he suggests to Kirk that an article she has written about the film praises it too highly: "In the national sense," he concedes, "our movie is really not very significant." Kirk did not publish the article, and despite a New York premiere at the Julien Levy Gallery later in 1932, the film disappeared for four decades.[13]

Joseph F. Halpin, the records administrator for the New Mexico State Records Center and Archives (SRCA) in the early 1970s, saved *A Day in Santa Fe* from obscurity. Halpin wrote to James Hughes asking him to donate his copy of the film and the solo Hughes production *Last Run of the Chili Line* (1941) (Halpin to Hughes). Hughes initially expressed reluctance: "My wife and I have discussed this on several occasions but have come to no conclusions" (Hughes to Halpin). He eventually donated the film to the SRCA some time prior to January 1973. At that point, David Margolis, the film archivist at the SRCA, began to investigate the history of the film by interviewing John Dorman, who appears in *A Day in Santa Fe,* and writing to Ansel Adams, who Margolis hoped could illuminate the history of early filmmaking in Santa Fe and Taos. Dorman provides an anecdotal first-person account of the Santa Fe social world that Riggs and Hughes depict in the film, but no record of a response from Adams exists in the archives.

It took another thirty years for the film to reach a broad audience. Film historian, archivist, and curator Bruce Posner chose *A Day in Santa Fe* for the collection *Unseen Cinema: Early American Avant-Garde Film 1894–1941* (2005). This first generation of avant-garde filmmakers in the United States, explains Jan-Christopher Horak, "viewed themselves as cineastes, as lovers of cinema, as 'amateurs' willing to work in any arena furthering the cause of film art, even if it meant working for hire" (19). Posner describes the film as part of the vibrant artistic life of Santa Fe in the late 1920s and early 1930s that included Paul Strand, Robert Flaherty, and Henwar Rodakiewicz. These three filmmakers, along with Academy Award–winning cinematographer Floyd Crosby, were finding inspiration in the U.S. Southwest "outside the Hollywood regime" (Posner, 11).[14] Flaherty arrived in the region, Posner explains, intending to build on his success with *Nanook of the North* (1922) by making another film, called initially *Nanook of the Desert* and then *Ácoma*, about the Indigenous peoples of the Southwest.[15] Flaherty never completed this project. Riggs knew Rodakiewicz, who "assisted ... at the projector" during the premiere ("Santa Fe Picture at Fonda"), but he did not see Rodakiewicz's *Portrait of a Young Man* (1925–31) until February 4, 1932, a month after the screening of *A Day in Santa Fe*.[16] Posner concludes, "Riggs' and Hughes' film can be seen as the product of a very fertile germination process that swept across America during the late 1920s and into the '30s" (15). *A Day in Santa Fe* is also the product of a Cherokee dramatist's flourishing career coinciding with the rapidly developing tradition of amateur experimental film.

As a result of the film's obscurity and inaccessibility, until recently scholars have not had the opportunity to situate it within both Riggs's career and American Indian film history. Beverly Singer, Philip Deloria, Michelle Raheja, and Joanna Hearne trace the origins of American Indian cinema to the work, in the first few decades of the twentieth century, of Lillian St. Cyr / Princess Red Wing (Winnebago or Ho-Chunk); her husband, James Young Johnson / James Young Deer; and Jay John Fox / Edwin Carewe (Chickasaw).[17] Riggs joins them as a forerunner of the Indigenous filmmakers in the late twentieth century under consideration by Singer, Raheja, and Hearne in, respectively, *Wiping the War Paint Off the Lens: Native American Film and Video* (2001), *Reservation Reelism: Redfacing, Visual Sovereignty, and Representations of Native Americans in Film* (2010), and *Native Recognition: Indigenous Cinema and the Western* (2012). *A Day in Santa Fe* does not focus exclusively or primarily on Indigenous people in New Mexico. However, Riggs and Hughes position indigeneity as well as Indigenous people and ceremonies as formative of the region's life and identity.

Though they represent the cultural and socioeconomic diversity of the town, Riggs and Hughes devote more than half the film to the world of elite Anglo, Hispano, and European immigrant Santa Feans: professionals, writers, artists, and members of affluent and socially prominent families. The people of this privileged social world appear in the film and on the guest list, edited by Riggs, for the premiere (Riggs, "Private Showing").[18] Hughes's father was a banker, and Juan Sedillo, whose wife, Eva Knuth, also appears in the film, was an actor and attorney.[19] The filmmakers invited painters such as Gustave Baumann and Jozef Bakos, the latter a member of Los Cincos Pintores, and writers such as Henderson and Bynner to attend the screening. Spud Johnson, a cofounder of the literary magazine *Laughing Horse* and first Bynner's then Mabel Dodge Luhan's secretary, also received an invitation, as did Virginia Morley, the daughter of the prominent archaeologist Sylvanus Morley. In the film, Riggs and Hughes show these well-heeled locals living together in harmony in the shared space of the town.

While the pace of the film is leisurely and the tone celebratory and, at times, whimsical, *A Day in Santa Fe* is one of the most politically engaged and subversively anticolonial Native artistic productions in the years between the progressive and civil rights eras. Two of the film's most striking images—the Cross of the Martyrs (now the Old Cross of the Martyrs) and the Santa Clara harvest dance—remind viewers of the conflicts that shaped the region and the resistance of the Pueblos to Spanish colonialism and U.S. settler colonialism. The Knights of Columbus and the Historical Society of New Mexico erected the cross, which appears at the beginning and end of the film, on a hill above Santa Fe in 1920 to commemorate the twenty-one Franciscans killed in the Pueblo Revolt of 1680. The harvest dance, which predates the arrival of the Spanish, demonstrates Indigenous religious and cultural continuity despite this violent history and attempts as recently as the early 1920s to prohibit such ceremonies. As the dramatic shift in focus from Indigenous cultural productions within colonial and settler–colonial contexts in Part I to Indigenous people involved in ceremony in Part II makes explicit, the film focuses rigorously on Indigenous representation and the politics of modernist primitivism. As Gill Perry observes, primitivism, a "deeply problematic" label, assumes European superiority over the Indigenous peoples of the globe (5). In the discussion of European art and cultures, explains Perry, primitivism "has generally been used to describe a Western interest in, and/or reconstruction of, societies designated 'primitive', and their artefacts" (5). The Western interest in Indigenous American artifacts within a historical context of colonial Spanish and Catholic dominance defines much of Part I. Part II of the film, however, decenters the colonial authority and primitivist orientation of Santa Fe in Part I by asserting a specifically Pueblo way of being in and knowing the land. Indeed, like Shelley Niro's *It Starts with a Whisper* (1993) and Michael Linn's *Imprint* (2007), two films central to Raheja's study, *A Day in Santa Fe* "[foregrounds] the importance of spirituality as an enabling tool for combating colonialism and reengaging Indigenous epistemologies without attempting to explain particular aspects of specific tribal practices or inviting spectators to partake of Indigenous spirituality through commodification and consumption" (Raheja, 147).[20] As these comparisons to Niro's and Linn's films suggest, *A Day in Santa Fe* establishes within the history of independent Indigenous cinema an early node of an anticolonial political array, one with a remarkable emphasis, for this era, on cultural sovereignty.

Colonial Histories, Indigenous Commodities

Riggs and Hughes use recurring images appearing in strategic variations in Parts I and II to generate the film's richly textured political commentary on Indigenous representation and modernist primitivism. The film's two approximately equal parts have eighty-three shots and ninety-five shots, respectively, and regularly spaced poetic intertitles by Riggs. It begins at sunrise and ends at sunset and intermittently follows the progress of a burro loaded with firewood. Riggs sets Part I exclusively in Santa Fe. The filmmakers convey the city's multicultural identity with shots of residents walking down a sidewalk. They describe this scene in the shooting script: "48. CLOSE UP. A succession of different kinds of feet move along a strip of sidewalk. a. Mexican workman's feet; b. American shoes; c. Mexican guarraches; d. An Indian woman's feet in moccasins; e. A young American girl's high heeled shoes; f. Cowboy boots" (Riggs and Hughes, I-4).[21] Part I ends as several people begin an afternoon siesta, after which the filmmakers shift the scene about twenty-five miles north-northwest of Santa Fe to Santa Clara Pueblo for Part II, which opens with another shot of feet, this time belonging to harvest dancers. The film then moves among the dancers, the sleeping figures back in town, and an increasingly stormy sky before returning to a Santa Fe afternoon filled with swimming at the White Estate, or El Delirio, and the drinking of cocktails.[22] Once a steam whistle announces the end of the workday—for the men and women not already relaxing—Riggs and Hughes show the townspeople gathering in the plaza for a performance by what they call "a Mexican orchestra" (Riggs and Hughes, II-5). The *Santa Fe New Mexican* identifies the musicians as the Mariachi Jalisco players ("Santa Fe Picture at Fonda"). The final scenes show the burro finding a customer who purchases the wood and builds a fire that begins to blaze as the sun sets.

By beginning the film with a fade-in from darkness to a long, slow pan of the eastern mountains at sunrise followed by a stationary shot of the concrete cross from a camera set near its base, Riggs and Hughes establish the religious and social authority of the Catholic Church in Santa Fe but position the city within or even surrounded by the Indigenous landscape of the Pueblos and foreshadow, with the movement of the camera across the mountains, the ceremonial motion of the dancers at Santa Clara in Part II. Mary Ann Anders, who worked during her career as an architectural historian for the New Mexico State Historic Preservation Division, sees the cross as part of a long history in the town of remembering the Pueblo Revolt and commemorating the return of Spanish control in 1692. "The dedication ceremonies began in front of the Palace of the Governors with about 500 spectators in attendance," Anders begins. "Former Governor L. Bradford Prince, president of the historical society, gave a brief history of the rebellion that led to the friars' deaths and characterized the event as a sad blow to the Franciscan Order. He went on to speak of the martyrdom of the friars and the military achievements of Don Diego de Vargas's reconquest and occupation of Santa Fe" (2–3). Santa Feans continued to use the area around the cross during the fiesta until the area developed into a well-populated neighborhood. The cross, which stands twenty-five feet tall and weighs seventy-six tons, looms over the camera in *A Day in Santa Fe* just as it looms over the town as a reminder of colonial invasion and occupation as well as Indigenous resistance.

The following scenes build upon the film's second shot of the cross by continuing to represent Santa Fe as a colonial space. Riggs and Hughes cut from the cross to a long shot of the Cathedral Basilica of St. Francis of Assisi and a medium shot of one of the cathedral's towers. The cathedral was completed in 1887 one block east of the plaza on a site where three other churches once stood. Pueblo freedom fighters destroyed the second church, built in 1630, in the Pueblo Revolt, and a chapel from the third church, built in 1714, remains attached to the Cathedral ("Our Parish History"). In the medium shot, the camera looks up at the tower and nearby trees, including one partially obscuring the tower and another filling the left side of the frame, while the sky behind it glows with the morning sun. The cross and the cathedral assert the sacred authority of Catholicism; they are concomitant with the coming of the light. The next shot, a view from the front of the Palace of the Governors looking into the plaza, establishes the secular authority of colonial Spain, settler–colonial Mexico, and both the colonial and settler–colonial United States. Spain built the palace in the second decade of the seventeenth century as the center of its government in the region. After the end of the War for Mexican Independence in 1821, the building became the capital of the Mexican federal Territory of New Mexico. It continued as the capital of the U.S. Territory of New Mexico after the U.S.–Mexican War (1846–48) until New Mexico became a state in 1912.[23] Riggs and Hughes position the camera near the southeastern corner of the building underneath the colonnade and facing the plaza through the columns holding up the roof. The Museum of New Mexico has reserved this part of the building—the front porch or portal—for American Indian vendors, primarily of pottery and jewelry, beginning with weekend markets in 1936.[24] This development, five years after Riggs and Hughes shot their film, affirmed the control of settler–colonial institutions over the trade in American Indian arts in the plaza.

As they continue to build the groundwork for the full realization of the film's anticolonial politics in Part II, the filmmakers isolate indigeneity in the public space of the plaza in Part I. The first and only appearance of an Indigenous person in Part I occurs within a carefully planned movement from a panoramic shot to a series of close-ups of residents' hands. A thirty-five-second shot from Bynner's roof of the mountains and large clouds in early morning sun followed by shots of flowers (identified in the shooting script as daisies, hollyhocks, willows, and morning glories) and the introduction of the burro anticipate signs of the town awakening: a cow swishes its tail and turns to look at the camera; a boy at a small stream fills a bucket of water and walks along the edge of a cornfield; a hand delivers bottles of milk; a lawn sprinkler sprays water; hands unlock and open shop doors. Riggs and Hughes accelerate the cuts to suggest the increased human motion in the town, and machines begin spinning. As Riggs explains in his short article on the film in *Cine-Kodak News*, "Up to this point, we thought, all action should be quiet, slow. But now it should be speeded up—naturalistically, of course, for at this time the day has really begun. And it must be speeded up *visually*, too, on the film. The eye must be assailed, hurt if necessary, to project the idea of swiftness" (Riggs, "A Day in Santa Fe," 5). Santa Fe has both an agricultural and an industrial economy, the filmmakers suggest, though the images of gears and belts and a single automobile appear modest in comparison to the machines at work in New York in Charles Sheeler and Paul Strand's *Manhatta* (1921) and Robert Flaherty's *24 Dollar Island* (1926). The strains of antimodernism and romanticism in *A Day in Santa Fe* are typical, Jan-Christopher Horak observes, of the first American avant-garde. Yet Riggs and Hughes resist the opportunity, made possible by large populations of Indigenous people in the region and the popularity in the era of Indigenous-made commodities from the Southwest, to draw on indigeneity as a marker of this antimodernity.

The recurring images of hands, like the contrast among the feet of walkers in Santa Fe and dancers at Santa Clara, draw attention to national and ethnic divisions in a world in which harmonious social interaction otherwise appears to prevail. "Mexican hands smear adobe mud on a wall," the shooting script reads, though viewers cannot identify the nationality or ethnicity of the *adobero* from what they see on screen (Riggs and Hughes, I-3). While "Mexican hands" make an adobe wall, the people whom Riggs and Hughes do not identify or mark as ethnic paint, sharpen pencils, and write poems before taking siestas. They show Jozef Bakos at work in his studio and position the camera over Alice Corbin Henderson's shoulder as she writes the poem "Cundiyo." Viewers see her left hand holding the notebook, her right hand holding the pencil over the paper, and the title and first line of the poem. Henderson published "Cundiyo," which describes an encounter with three grieving women on their way to visit a dying young man, in the August 1920 issue of *Poetry* in a section entitled "New Mexico Folk-Songs" and then again in *Red Earth: Poems of New Mexico* (1920). The poem would have helped viewers identify one of the nationally known people who make an appearance in the film.

These close-ups of individual hands at work set the stage for the fraught meeting of Anglo and Indigenous hands in the plaza. While Riggs and Hughes reserve artistic labor almost exclusively for Americans of European ancestry, in Part I a man, remembered by Dorman as "Indian Joe," appears in the plaza to sell jewelry presumably of his own making (Margolis, 4). While Bakos works on a landscape in his studio, "a Mexican man comes out of his house and leans lazily against the wall in the sun" (Riggs and Hughes, I-3). This image of a Mexican man standing in the sun, "a habit of elderly Mexicans" (Riggs, "A Day in Santa Fe," 5), serves as an ethnic transition between Bakos's studio and the plaza, where the jewelry maker, dressed in a headband, striped shirt, and jeans, examines a piece of jewelry he holds in his hands. Another man, apparently Anglo and dressed in a white suit, approaches from the right and looks at the piece of jewelry and the long, elaborate necklace.[25] His appearance activates a familiar colonial encounter: as Hutchinson observes, "Collectors of Native American art often relate the story of acquisition as a kind of conquest" (26).[26] After he asks to see a ring on one of the jewelry maker's fingers, a close up of their hands shows the customer holding the fingers of the jewelry maker's right hand and pointing at the ring before removing the ring from the jewelry maker's finger and putting it on his own. The camera returns to a medium shot as the men negotiate. They agree on a price, after which the customer gives a bill to the jewelry maker. They shake hands, and the customer exits the screen to the left.

The following scenes also position both Santa Fe residents and viewers as voyeurs of American Indians and consumers of their cultural productions. As automobile traffic grows in the plaza, six shoppers, including James Hughes's sister, Mary, approach a store. Viewers see them first in a reflection in the store window displaying kachina dolls. After they enter the screen door of the store, Riggs and Hughes show three drawings of Pueblo dancers by Velino Shije Herrera / Ma-Pe-Wi from Zia Pueblo. Herrera was a prominent figure in what J. J. Brody calls a "new tradition" of Pueblo painting in which artists "depicted public religious and social dances of the Pueblo people or, much less often, activities of daily life" (3). He explains, "These were rare subjects in any earlier Pueblo art, and they required new ways of seeing and thinking about art" (4). This tradition was the primary force in Pueblo art from 1900 to 1930. The drawings sit on an easel, and a hand emerges in the upper-right-hand corner of the screen to take one and reveal the next beneath it. The filmmakers next show two kachina dolls positioned in a chair and a stylized burro with long legs casting a shadow on the wall. In a mainstream modernist context, they have put "the primitive" on display. The staging obscures the Indigenous artists and removes the works of art from Indigenous cultural contexts. In the description of this scene in his short article on the film, Riggs emphasizes the objects as exotic: "Tourists examine strange Indian paintings and Katchina dolls" ("A Day in Santa Fe"). Yet Riggs and Hughes cut from the burro carved from wood to the burro carrying the firewood through the streets of the town. The juxtaposition of the carving and the animal on which the artist based it startles viewers out of the objectifying process and prepares them for the shift from the decontextualized work of Indigenous artists to the ceremonies of Indigenous people in Part II.

Riggs and Hughes contain indigeneity in the plaza and represent it primarily as a cultural object in Part I. The American Indian man trading his jewelry flashes a brief smile during the scene, but the encounter appears uncomfortably invasive. The Anglo man lifts the necklace off the jewelry dealer's chest, then holds the dealer's hand and moves his fingers so he can remove the ring he wants. The creators of the drawings, kachina dolls, and burro carving do not appear. At the end of Part I, a cowboy, a young woman, and a young man lie down to sleep. The young man, Dorman, the stepson of Bakos, falls asleep at his stepfather's house beneath a small shrine holding a statue of the Virgin Mary.[27] The shooting script reads, "The camera PANS to a beautiful Madonna in a niche, in a sun-flecked wall" (Riggs and Hughes, I-6). Riggs and Hughes fix the camera on a window as someone inside the home closes the curtains. The intertitle, subtitle 10 in the shooting script, reads, "The curtains close against the day" (Riggs and Hughes, I-6). The filmmakers position the Madonna, the final image of Catholicism in Part I, as Dorman's protector, but she represents a less imposing symbol of church authority than the cross and cathedral that open the film.

Indigenous Ceremony

In Part II, the filmmakers begin resisting the politics of modernist primitivism by shifting the focus from decontextualized, static artifacts for sale and on display to a culturally specific, dynamic ceremony in a specifically Indigenous space. The setting shifts in Part II to what Riggs and Hughes call "the Indian pueblo" and what Riggs identifies as "a nearby pueblo" (Riggs, "A Day in Santa Fe," 5). At the pueblo, the filmmakers focus their camera on a familiar event in early American film, beginning with actualities produced by Edison Studios in the late nineteenth century: Indigenous dance.[28] They replace the dancers in the Herrera drawings with dancers in an actual ceremony and the parade of feet on the Santa Fe sidewalk with the feet of participants in the ceremony. The first shot in the pueblo is a low-angle close-up from behind a line of dancers. The sun shines brightly, and the shadows suggest that it sits almost directly overhead. The feet of three dancers are visible in the foreground. In the background, a second line of dancers faces the camera, but only the feet of several dancers are visible. Riggs and Hughes cut to another low-angle shot with a large drum in the center foreground. To the left and in the background, a line of dancers faces away from the camera. The drummer's body occupies most of the right side of the frame. He wears slacks and a white shirt. As he drums with his right hand, a man in slacks, white shirt, and suspenders dances into the frame. These shots emphasize the movement and rhythm of the dance. The contrast that Riggs and Hughes establish between the dancers in formal regalia, the drummer in "modern" and "European American" clothes, and the man dressed like the drummer who dances beside him, disrupts the conventional use of costuming to mark racial identity in Indian dramas.[29]

Riggs and Hughes use the intertitles to reinforce the dramatic political reorientation of the film from the oppressive colonial and settler-colonial space of Santa Fe to a vibrant and, in the context of enduring hostility toward Indigenous religions, implicitly defiant Indigenous world. Following two more shots of the feet and one of the drummer, an intertitle explains that the dancers perform to bring rain. This intertitle and two more come from Riggs's poem "Santo Domingo Corn Dance":

> Bring rain,
> As we bring now
> Our gift of dance and song—. (Riggs and Hughes, II-1)[30]

The subsequent shot, "LONG SHOT of Indians dancing for rain" in the shooting script, is an overhead with the drummer, a bandanna tied around his head now visible, in the middle of the frame (Riggs and Hughes, II-1). The line of dancers performs in the foreground, while behind the drummer men dressed in slacks, white shirts, and wide-brimmed hats stand in a circle, perhaps around another drum. Viewers see tourists, some using umbrellas as protection from the sun, in the background. Riggs and Hughes hint in the intertitle, though, that the tourists will soon need the umbrellas to keep dry rather than stay cool.

By linking the dancers to the sky in the following shots, Riggs and Hughes establish a contrast between the motionless and somber-looking cross and cathedral in early-morning shadow in Part I and the serious yet joyful expression of active Indigenous religious practice under the bright sun in Part II while also preparing viewers for the response of the spiritual world, in the form of a rainstorm, to the devotion of the dancers. In the shooting script, which Riggs and Hughes follow exactly, the sequence of nine shots reads:

    7. The feet pound.
    8. A small cloud comes into the sky.
    9. The feet pound.
    10. MEDIUM SHOT. A long line of dancers like a row of corn.
    11. A tree tosses in the wind. The cloud is growing.
    12. MEDIUM SHOT of the dance.
    13. Two great clouds combine in the sky.
    14. MEDIUM SHOT of the dance.
    15. A tree tosses wildly in the wind. (Riggs and Hughes, II-1)

Within this sequence of shots, in which the camera, the dancers, the trees, and the clouds are all in motion, Riggs and Hughes raise the camera not only from the dancers to the sky but also slowly up the dancers' bodies from their feet until their entire bodies come into view. They double the ascending motion.

Riggs and Hughes continue to reverse the objectifying, condescending primitivist gaze of Part I by reminding viewers of the temporarily suspended activity in town. During the ceremony, they cut to the young woman, the statue of the Virgin Mary, John Dorman, the burro, and the Mexican man standing by the wall of the house. The young woman and Dorman sleep with their arms limp. The shadows of the trees move restlessly over Dorman as the wind from the approaching storm gathers force. The burro swishes its tail, and the Mexican man stands completely still, his face in almost complete shadow from his hat. These cuts might lead some viewers to interpret the scene at the pueblo as a collective dream of the sleeping Santa Feans. However, the increasingly anticolonial politics of the narrative suggest Riggs and Hughes use the cuts to put on display the non-Native residents of Santa Fe and a single Catholic artifact.

Riggs and Hughes eventually complete the transfer of cultural, and implicitly political, authority from Europe to Indigenous America in Part II. At the pueblo, they continue the slow upward movement of the camera from the dancers to the cloud-covered sky and the entire plaza of the pueblo as seen from a roof. From the roof, they pan from the dancers to the tourists on the ground and up to the people on the roofs of one- and two-story homes. Eventually the dancers, a wall of the pueblo, and the sky share the screen. The camera work joins the dancers to the pueblo and the sky, which quickly responds to the dancers' supplications. The rain begins to fall in what Riggs and Hughes call "a tiny bowl" sitting on the ground, apparently in Santa Fe. The cowboy, the young woman, and the Mexican man hurry inside, and Dorman awakens beneath the shrine. In the interview with Margolis, Dorman explains, "As I recall, it was sort of a warm day, possibly a summer day, I think they had to simulate rain with hoses" (Margolis, 1). Beneath this simulated rain, Dorman runs off camera to escape the storm. Riggs and Hughes finally found real rain, as the next scene shows a downpour on a Santa Fe street, on a sidewalk, and in the trees. The water flows in the street and in a stream. Through the medium of the rain, requested by the dancers, the Pueblo world asserts authority over Santa Fe.

Part II of the film depicts a powerful Indigenous religion at work: sacred forces reward the ceremonial effort of the Pueblo dancers and interrupt the restful sleep of the residents of Santa Fe. While images of Catholic authority dominate the first section of the film, Riggs and Hughes show another vibrant religious tradition in the region. Indeed, the contrast between the looming cross and cathedral in Santa Fe and the dancers at Santa Clara conveys several stark distinctions between the two traditions. Catholicism in the film is grim and aloof, impersonal, and even menacing; Pueblo religion is public and communal, as both men and women dance in long lines to the rhythm established by the drummers. It is also physically active and, in the case of the particularly expressive man who dances beside the drummer, explicitly joyful.[31] While the cross and cathedral tower stretch toward the sky, the chants of the Pueblo dancers actually reach the sky and receive an immediate response. Catholic authority, at least as represented by the filmmakers, does not extend beyond the boundaries of the town. Indigenous sacred power does not stop at the walls of the Pueblo, however. Dorman does not find himself in any danger, but the image of him fleeing the protection of the Virgin Mary to escape the rain destabilizes the Catholic authority so prominent in Part I.[32]

The filmmakers do not include an equivalent representation of Catholic religious practice, and they do not mark people in Santa Fe as Catholic, unless the five women in black rebozos that viewers see early in the film are on their way to morning mass. Riggs describes this scene: "Black-shawled *señoras* pass along lovely streets at the ringing of the cathedral bell" (Riggs, "A Day in Santa Fe," 5). While the filmmakers structure the film to subvert the type of primitivism that appropriates and decontextualizes Indigenous material culture and dehumanizes Indigenous people, the reductive contrast Riggs and Hughes establish between Catholicism and Pueblo religion functions as another form of primitivism. As Gill Perry notes, within a "European frame of reference, concepts of the 'primitive' have been used *both* pejoratively *and* as a measure of positive value" (5). This observation applies in a U.S. frame of reference as well. The artists and reformers promoting these "more positive views" recognized "the essential purity and goodness of 'primitive' life, by contrast with the decadence of over-civilized Western societies" (6). Perry continues, "Such views were influenced both by notions of the 'noble savage' (derived, often in distorted form, from the writings of the eighteenth-century philosopher Jean-Jacques Rousseau) and by well-established traditions of pastoralism in art and literature" (6). John Collier and other influential reformers, including those based in Santa Fe, held U.S. variations of these views. They informed the shift in federal Indian policy under Collier from assimilation to the limited self-government made possible by the 1934 Indian Reorganization Act.

The tensions between antiprimitivism and reform-minded, but romanticizing, primitivism remain unresolved at the end of the film. Riggs and Hughes include another shot of the cross near the end of the film. They position the camera to one side rather than directly in front of one of its faces. As a result, damage to one corner at the top of the cross becomes visible. Dark clouds, the remnants of the rain summoned by the dancers, sit in the sky behind the cross. Some viewers of the film, especially ones from a Tewa-speaking pueblo like Santa Clara, might see these *okhúwá*, "clouds," as *ókhùwà*, "cloud-beings," the "ancestral spirits that leave the bodies of the deceased, travel up to the mountains, and then return to the village in the form of rain and male impersonators" (Ortman, 92).[33] These ancestral spirits loom over and entirely envelop the cross, thereby demonstrating the enduring vitality of Pueblo religion despite the incursion of Catholicism. Following the events at the pueblo, the cross no longer appears powerful or imposing. It reaches mute toward a sky now linked to the Pueblo dancers and their ancestors. After a cat yawns, Riggs and Hughes focus in the final scene on a fire, made by a local resident in her fireplace with wood purchased from the burro, before fading to dark.

"I'm Not Going to Hollywood!": The Cherokee Avant-Garde

Riggs and Hughes work self-consciously in the city symphony tradition both to represent and celebrate an Indigenous American urban space and to draw sharp contrasts between life there and in the colonial, if multicultural, urban space of Santa Fe. Riggs opens his short article on the film in *Cine-Kodak News* by explaining, "In making plans for our movie, 'A Day in Santa Fe,' Mr. Hughes and I both agreed to think of the picture as a symphony, with movements, with recurring themes and rhythms, with variety, with humor, and with a conclusion prepared for and demanded by everything that preceded it" (Riggs, "A Day in Santa Fe," 5). It is a "symphonic picture," Betty Kirk affirms.[34] To establish the symphonic rhythm of the film, Riggs and Hughes shift the focus back and forth between two distinct cities in visual, historical, and cultural tension, with Santa Clara Pueblo representing all Pueblo life in New Mexico. They do not identify the pueblo either in the film or the shooting script, and Riggs's use of his poem "Santo Domingo Corn Dance" even suggests Santo Domingo Pueblo as the setting.[35] However, Santo Domingo has long enforced a strict prohibition on photography, still or moving. Angie Owens, a renowned jewelry maker from Santo Domingo, confidently identified the pueblo in the film as Santa Clara based on the regalia of the dancers.[36] After viewing stills from the film, Fred Martinez, who runs the Santa Clara Tewa Language Program, said, "I immediately knew they were from here in Santa Clara Pueblo." Santa Clarans perform a harvest dance, Martinez explained, rather than a Corn Dance.[37]

By not identifying the pueblo as Santa Clara, Riggs and Hughes risked perpetuating generalizations about Indigenous people and romanticizing them in much the same way as did the many writers and artists who had converged on northern New Mexico in the 1920s and 1930s. Jan-Christopher Horak asserts:

> The first American avant-garde—like the second, and unlike the European avant-garde—seems to have had an extremely contradictory relationship to the modernist project. Its utilization of modernist form in connection with expressions of highly romantic, even anti-modernist, sentiments is symptomatic of this ambivalence

toward modernism. A particularly American romanticism, which manifests itself in a longing for (wo)man's reunification with nature, informs the early American avant-garde's visualization of the natural environment and the urban sprawl. (27)

While viewers could read the scene at Santa Clara Pueblo as an expression of this American longing for "reunification with nature," it is also a longing with specifically Cherokee roots. At the same time, the harvest dance involves the human unification with nature experienced by the Santa Clarans through the ceremony. After all, the Santa Clarans do not need to reunify with a nature from which they have not experienced separation.

A Day in Santa Fe thus offers a significant variation on the romantic strain in American avant-garde film. As Horak explains, American avant-garde films such as Flaherty's *24 Dollar Island* "[present] urban civilization as completely overpowering and destructive of nature, as when a lone tree is seen against a backdrop of the concrete jungle" (29). *A Day in Santa Fe* narrows the gap between that "lone tree" and "concrete jungle" by focusing on the smaller, less industrial urban site of Santa Fe and contrasting it to an older and even less industrial urban site, the Santa Clara Pueblo. The unification with nature that viewers see in the Riggs and Hughes film occurs in a town rather than in the country. Shelley Niro achieves a similar effect in her short film *Tree* (2005), which opens with quick cuts between a young Native woman walking off a rock in the water and up a rocky shoreline with scenes of skyscrapers and urban streets.[38] As the woman walks through a grove of leafless trees and into the city streets, Niro superimposes her ghostly image onto city scenes, including final dystopic ones of a ruined building and a fiery explosion. In the next scene, the woman stands again on the rock in the water, and Niro uses time-lapse photography to show either a tree growing out of her or her transformation into a tree. She cuts to a clump of grass superimposed over billows of dark gray smoke, after which the young woman appears again and looks to the sky before the film fades to black as viewers hear the sound of water hitting the shore. Niro's film, while much more ominous than *A Day in Santa Fe* in its depiction of urban life, dramatizes the same coherence between the natural world and indigeneity, on the one hand, and, on the other, the same opposition between the natural world and the built environment of a city. In addition, Riggs and Hughes's repeating and lingering focus on flowers, trees, and rainfall mirrors Niro's on the trees, grass, and water. In both films, finally, sacred authority and power reside with the natural world, especially with water, and Indigenous people.

Riggs's plays provide additional insight into his critical views of the politics of Indigenous representation in the 1920s and 1930s. Throughout his career as a dramatist, he remained consistently attuned to specific Indigenous histories and concerned with the representation of Indigenous people. *The Cherokee Night* (1936) follows a young generation of Cherokees struggling to make sense of their historical, cultural, and biological identities, while in *The Cream in the Well* (1947) Riggs tells the story of the Sawters, a troubled Cherokee family trying to come to terms with the dispossession of allotment and imminent Oklahoma statehood. Clabe, the middle of three Sawter children, returns from a stint in the U.S. Navy disgusted with U.S. imperialism. Riggs's two plays set in Mexico, *The Year of Pilár* (1947) and *A World Elsewhere* (1947), stage, respectively, an Indigenous revolution in Yucatán and a failed counterrevolution by the hacendados and military elites in Mexico City.

Riggs also returned to Santa Fe as a setting for a play in which he mocks the class and racial politics of the city's Anglo elite. *Russet Mantle* (1936), a Depression-era social satire dedicated to the actor, lawyer, and women's rights activist Ida Rauh, centers on Horace and Susanna Kincaid and the guests at their Santa Fe ranch.[39] After retiring, the Kincaids lost much of the money Horace had made in real estate. They are self-absorbed and casually oblivious to the difficult lives of the working classes and young people. Horace worries about the stock market, which, speaking like a "martyr," he calls "my cross" (Riggs, *Russet Mantle and The Cherokee Night*, 8). Susanna worries about her chickens not producing enough eggs. Riggs aligns both characters culturally with the region's first European colonial presence. When Susanna hears the bells of the cathedral featured at the beginning of *A Day in Santa Fe*, she comments, "They're so peaceful, so Old World" (Riggs, *Russet Mantle and The Cherokee Night*, 10). Horace observes to John Galt, a disaffected young man visiting their ranch, that "New Mexico is Spain, my boy—the same hills, the same sun, the same arid and cruel earth" (83). While they appreciate Santa Fe as European or Old World, they have a shallow, ostensibly benign, and condescending relationship with the residents of the pueblos, including their friend Salvador from San Ildefonso Pueblo.

Susanna's sister Effie, with her "mindless cheerfulness," has a more malevolent view of American Indians. When Effie appears, she inquires in her Kentucky accent, "Will I see any Indians while I'm here on my visit?" Susanna explains to Effie that she will see Indians from the local pueblos. Effie responds, "In towns! I thought they lived on the plains! History says that the Indians are inhabitants of the Great Plains region west of the—." Her sister's ignorance amuses Susanna: "Effie! There aren't any plains here. These are a different kind of Indian. They're Pueblos." Effie rejects any distinctions between Indigenous peoples: "Oh, Indians are all alike. Red and bloodthirsty!" (13). This view of Indigenous people informs her reaction to the news that her daughter, Kay, is pregnant. She requests a "lynchin' party" and adds, "It must have been one of those natives. Oh! It must have been one of those savage Indians—maybe one from Ildefonso" (109). Effie expresses multiple dominant, reductive views of Indigenous people: they live on the plains; they are all alike; they are a sexual threat to white women. Riggs explicitly satirizes rather than perpetuates these views. By ascribing these views to such an unpalatable character, he encourages his audience to reject them.

Discourses of the incommensurability of European and Indigenous American ways of being and knowing are common, including during the 1920s and 1930s, but this incommensurability is as much an invention in *A Day in Santa Fe* as it is in the art and literature of Riggs's and Hughes's predecessors and contemporaries. Significant distinctions exist between life in Santa Fe and life at Santa Clara Pueblo, but Riggs and Hughes stress the differences and obscure the similarities. Though the Pueblo harvest dances and Corn Dances predate the arrival of the Spanish, they now occur on the feast day of each pueblo's patron saint. The shrine at Santa Clara even appears during the scenes Riggs and Hughes shot there. Many Pueblo people are practicing Catholics, though many also still participate in the traditional ceremonies of their home communities. Their Catholicism also differs from the religion practiced in primarily Spanish-descended or other Indigenous Mexican and American Indian communities. In his essay "Towards a National Indian Literature: Cultural Authenticity in Nationalism," Acoma Pueblo poet Simon Ortiz explains, "Many Christian religious rituals brought to the Southwest ... are no longer Spanish. They are now Indian because of the creative development that the native people applied to them" (254).

Fred Martinez also emphasizes that the coincidence of the dances on the saints' days does not necessarily make the ceremonies Catholic.[40]

Despite the various possible interpretations of the politics of Riggs's and Hughes's representations of Indigenous people, in 2013 those representations became a historical archive and pedagogical tool for the people of Santa Clara. Martinez requested a copy of the film to teach the young people of Santa Clara about their history and religious traditions. Riggs's characters in *The Cherokee Night* had nearly debilitating and frequently self-destructive anxiety about their severely compromised connections to an older Cherokee world and their lack of access to historical, political, and cultural Cherokeeness. Riggs thus admired Indigenous peoples, especially the Pueblos of New Mexico and the Mayans of Yucatán, who had maintained what he perceived as stronger ties to their traditions and histories than the Cherokees. This admiration led him to film the Santa Clara harvest dance, which, in turn, now provides the younger generations at Santa Clara with documentation of a ceremony that has endured into the present.

Hollywood recruited Riggs soon after he completed *A Day in Santa Fe,* but he expressed reluctance about going to Southern California. He ends a March 1932 letter to Alice Corbin Henderson with the following emphatic lines:

> I'm not going to Hollywood!
> I'm not going to Hollywood!
> I'm not going ——— (Riggs to Henderson)

The assumption in this era's avant-garde film circles that "professionalism was equated with commercialism, while amateurism connoted artistic integrity" might have motivated this anxiety (Horak, 22). Riggs eventually went to Hollywood, where he lived in the Montecito Apartments on Franklin Avenue. He shared his thoughts on his work there with Santa Fe resident Ann Webster, who provided Riggs with local help purchasing land and building a house in his adopted hometown. He refers to his work at Universal Studios, which hired him to write an adaptation of Charles Dickens's *The Mystery of Edwin Drood,* as "servitude" (Riggs to Webster, April 26, 1934). While working for MGM the following month, he sounded a little more sanguine about the film industry: "I've agreed to do a picture for MGM and, as I told you in a telegram, the money is pouring in like a river, at the moment (and like the rivers of New Mexico, it stops with a bang when the cloud burst is over)" (Riggs to Webster, May 17, 1934). In October, he exclaims, "I ought to thank God for the pictures. Sammie Goldwyn is supplying me a place to sleep!" (Riggs to Webster, October 25, 1934). Financial security and the promise of more time to write plays overrode his initial reluctance to accede to Hollywood's offer of employment.

The film industry appreciated Riggs's talents. During World War II, as the military tried to decide where to place Riggs, several of his former employers wrote letters of recommendation on his behalf. David O. Selznick writes, "Lynn Riggs worked under my supervision as a scenario writer. I found him to be the possessor of an extraordinary and very sensitive talent. I also found him to be extremely conscientious, hard-working and in every way of admirable character" (Selznick to U.S. Coast Guard Auxiliary). Marshall Grant, a producer at Universal, observes, "As a writer of both the screenplay and other writing mediums, I judge him to be one of the most competent writers with whom I have ever been associated. He has been spoken of as the greatest living writer of the American Scene. In this belief I unreservedly concur" (Grant "To Whom It May Concern"). In the mid-1940s, Twentieth Century Fox continued to request his services, including for help with an adaptation of playwright Richard Walton Tully's *The Bird of Paradise* (1912) and a film by Otto Preminger (Langdon to Riggs, November 14, 1944, and December 8, 1944).[41] After developing a friendship with Sidney Lumet, who expresses his "total love" for Riggs's play *Roadside (Borned in Texas)*, the future four-time Academy Award–nominated director asked Riggs to help adapt Ambrose Bierce's "An Occurrence at Owl Creek Bridge," Katherine Anne Porter's "Noon Wine," and Willa Cather's "Paul's Case" into a film about what Lumet calls "a story of destruction, from outside to inside in 70 short years" (Lumet to Riggs, May 14, 1951, and June 11, 1952). Lumet envisioned "literal reproductions of the stories themselves" and specifically requested Riggs's help with "the heart" of the project, the screenplay for "Noon Wine." Lumet writes, "You're the best person to do it. . . . Your name would probably help in money raising too" (Lumet to Riggs, June 11, 1952). Riggs, whose health began to deteriorate quickly in 1952 as the result of a stomach ulcer that eventually became cancerous, does not appear to have accepted the offer, and Lumet did not complete this project. Riggs received credit as a screenwriter on seven scripts, including *The Garden of Allah* (1936), *The Plainsman* (1936), and two Sherlock Holmes films. A year after Riggs's death, too late to help make him a household name, Twentieth Century Fox released Fred Zinnemann's *Oklahoma!* (1955) to wide acclaim. Now that this seminal work of the Cherokee avant-garde is accessible to a wide audience, *A Day in Santa Fe* could become the more enduring part of his contribution to the history of American Indian and U.S. cinema.

Lynn Riggs and Contemporary Native Film

A Day in Santa Fe anticipates, thematically and formally, a wide range of Indigenous films in the Renaissance and post-Renaissance eras and serves as one point of origin in a cinematic political array composed of both challenges to dominant representations of and narratives about Indigenous American peoples and expressions of Indigenous cultural sovereignty. *House Made of Dawn* (1972), adapted from the urtext of the Renaissance and directed by Richardson Morse from a screenplay by Morse and Momaday, includes scenes at the Pueblos of Isleta and Sandia and a cast with several members of a family from the Pueblos of Laguna and Santo Domingo.[42] Hearne places Morse's film in a group that "[represents] an emerging experimentalism in representations of Native peoples on screen" (*Native Recognition*, 222). Indeed, Morse's formal approach suggests more remarkable links between *A Day in Santa Fe* and *House Made of Dawn* than the coincidence of their setting. Morse used "montage, superimposition, and flashbacks," Hearne observes before adding, "These modernist, avant-garde filmmaking techniques counter primitivist readings of Pueblo culture with technologically and aesthetically dynamic methods and an urban setting" (240). Morse took an experimental formal approach similar to Riggs's and Hughes's to achieve precisely the same goal: overturning primitivist representations and narratives of Pueblo peoples and cultures.

The generative political contrasts between non-Indigenous and Indigenous spaces so central to *A Day in Santa Fe* also structure some Renaissance and post-Renaissance films, especially experimental films, such as Niro's aforementioned *Tree,* and documentaries. In *Navajo Talking Picture,* which begins, like *A Day in Santa Fe,* with a sunrise, Arlene Bowman develops a tense contrast between life in what she calls in voice-over "the big city," Phoenix and Los Angeles, and Lower Greasewood and the "small town" of Holbrook in the Navajo Nation. Bowman attempts to make a film about her grandmother, who does not want her image recorded and therefore does not cooperate with the production of the film, but she finishes with a documentary about Indigenous representation and self-representation, much like *A Day in Santa Fe*. Though she is a Navajo, Bowman, like Riggs, is an outsider, geographically and linguistically if not genealogically, to the Indigenous community that she films. By not addressing the issue of his responsibility to the Indigenous community at Santa Clara, however, as well as by positioning the camera in the audience watching the harvest dance rather than entering residents' homes, Riggs avoided the conflict so central to Bowman's film. Nevertheless, both films examine the cultural and political risks and rewards of cinematic representations for Indigenous people.

A Day in Santa Fe also shares formal features and political commitments with Dustinn Craig's kinetic *4wheelwarpony*, an eight-minute film that celebrates late-twentieth- and early-twenty-first-century White Mountain Apache skateboarding culture. While Riggs and Hughes drew a contrast between static art objects in Part I of their film and dynamic ceremonial dancers in Part II in order to reject the objectification and commodification of indigeneity, Craig, as Joanna Hearne explains, uses the mobility of both skateboard and camera as a "repudiation of the stasis implied by many Euro-American images of Indians" ("This Is Our Playground," 60). Like Riggs, Craig includes one of his own poems in the film. The poem, Hearne observes, "functions as [the film's] primary text" in its assertion of the playground, or the skatepark, as their sanctuary from a dreary world and a place in which to feel young and alive (67). In one of six screens playing simultaneously, the words scroll over a flower blowing in the wind, a recurring image in Riggs's and Hughes's film. This image suggests that the entire region depicted in the film also serves as a playground for the White Mountain Apaches. Craig's early-twenty-first century independent and experimental film appears to have a more emphatic political message than Riggs's interwar avant-garde effort. Hearne describes *4wheelwarpony* as "[combining] the punk and do-it-yourself (DIY) aesthetics of skateboarding with family and tribal history to assert an expressive politics of Apache resilience" (47). This resilience occurs in a cinematic world composed of photographs and moving images appearing on multiple screens and evoking continuities between nineteenth-century and contemporary White Mountain Apache life. Indeed, the young Apache men dressed as their nineteenth-century male forebears ride their way into the present after rapid editing suggests an equivalence between skateboards and rifles. Yet Riggs's film conveys an equally explicit political statement about Indigenous resilience within the context in which he produced it, in the moment a few years before the reform of federal Indian policy culminated in the passage in 1934 of the Indian New Deal in the form of the Indian Reorganization Act.

In addition to linking Indigenous literary and cinematic production by featuring their own poems in *A Day in Santa Fe* and *The Business of Fancydancing* and depicting the act of writing poems (Alice Corbin Henderson on a porch in the former; Seymour Polatkin in bed in the latter), Riggs's and Alexie's films share a narrative structure that shapes their political commentary on colonialism and settler–colonialism. They begin in a city (Santa Fe; Seattle) represented as predominantly non-Native and vexed or even hostile terrain for Indigenous people and with skylines marked by monuments to colonialism and settler–colonialism (the Cross of the Martyrs and the Cathedral Basilica of St. Francis of Assisi; the Space Needle, built for the 1962 World's Fair, which appears immediately after the opening credits and several other times during the day and at night). Riggs and Alexie then move their narratives to Native spaces (Santa Clara Pueblo; the Spokane Indian Reservation) defined by Native cultural practices (dance, food preparation, mourning rituals, 49s).[43] The filmmakers return their narratives to the city for the concluding scenes, as if to suggest the necessity of continuing to confront the anti-Indigenous forces there. Indigenous dance plays a central role in both films, with the Santa Clara harvest dance asserting Indigenous religious authority and the regularly spaced scenes of a fancy dancer in full regalia rooting Alexie's film in the intertribal, secular ceremonies of powwows.[44] Agnes Roth (Michelle St. John), Seymour Polatkin's friend and former lover, replaces the fancy dancer several times, once with Seymour, though they dance with colorful blankets over their shoulders rather than in regalia. In the final sequence, Alexie cuts from Seymour backing out of a driveway to Agnes singing to Seymour kneeling and removing the regalia as if he had just completed a performance. Eventually, as he leaves the reservation, Seymour passes Aristotle Joseph (played by Cherokee, Tlingit, and

Filipino storyteller Gene Tagaban). He looks in the rearview mirror and sees Aristotle starting to dance. The fancy dancing will continue, even as Polatkin ends the film in Seattle with his partner.

Finally, Riggs's and Alexie's use of intertitles doubles the level of Indigenous diegesis in their films.[45] In *The Business of Fancydancing*, intertitles include, for example, blurbs from reviews of Polatkin's poetry, short poems identified as authored by Polatkin, phrases (such as "How many funerals have you been to?" and "How to make a bathroom cleaner sandwich") that explain the forthcoming scene, and settings ("St. Jerome the Second University, Seattle, Washington, 1985"; "The First Annual All Spokane Indian Mouse Memorial Urban-Skin vs. Rez-Skin Half Assed Football Game"; "Colonial Aptitude Testing Service, Seattle, WA, 1985"). While viewers see Henderson handwrite her poem "Cundiyo," Riggs saves his own poem, which conveys the significance of the harvest dance to the film's politics, for the intertitles. When Alexie includes an intertitle with one of Polatkin's poems, the diegesis works at the level of the main plot, written and directed by Alexie, and at the level of the intertitles, written by Seymour Polatkin, but it also directs viewers back to scenes of Polatkin reading poems from his book, *All My Relations*. This book, too, appears on display with Alexie's own publications in the window of the bookstore in which Polatkin reads in *The Business of Fancydancing*'s opening scene. Alexie, more vigorously and consistently than Riggs, reminds viewers of Indigenous authorship, as well as Indigenous filmmaking, since Aristotle Joseph and Mouse (played by Lummi violinist, storyteller, and actor Swil Kanim) record themselves on a handheld camera. Riggs, in his film, nevertheless uses the same formal strategy to center indigeneity, specifically Indigenous ceremonial dance but also his own Indigenous authorship.

The continuities between *A Day in Santa Fe* and *The Business of Fancydancing*, as well as among them and the films by Niro, Bowman, and Craig, link the pre-Renaissance, Renaissance, and post-Renaissance eras formally, thematically, and politically. While *A Day in Santa Fe* is not, like the other four, Indigenous-centric, the film makes an emphatic political statement about Indigenous resilience, as well as cultural authority, near the end of the era of assimilation as official federal policy. Its emphasis on religious ceremonialism as the center of Indigenous life and identity speaks directly to many Renaissance-era works of literary art, including and perhaps especially Momaday's *House Made of*

Dawn and Silko's *Ceremony*. Indeed, Ortiz's "Towards a National Indian Literature," a seminal text of American Indian literary nationalism, foregrounds participation by the author's Uncle Steve/Dzeerlai in the summer fiesta days at Acoma Pueblo as "a celebration of the human spirit and the Indian struggle for liberation" (254). The film's respectful depiction of the dynamic, joyful dance and the immediate response to it by the spirit world conveys that Riggs saw the dance as a celebration of the human spirit. The images of the fancy dancer in *The Business of Fancydancing*, as well as Agnes Roth's singing at Mouse's funeral of "Amazing Grace" and "Osinilshatin" (written by St. John and translated into Spokane by Lillian Alexie, Sherman Alexie's mother), similarly celebrate the human spirit in the face of a violent, traumatic history.[46] The political context in which Riggs produced *A Day in Santa Fe*, too, suggests that he saw the dance as part of the struggle for liberation from the Spanish colonial and U.S. settler–colonial worlds. As he does in his dramatic work, and as Momaday and Silko do in their novels, in *A Day in Santa Fe*, Riggs imbues Indigenous ceremony with explicit political meaning in an avant-garde narrative about colonialism and enduring resistance to it.

CHAPTER 4

Academic Networks

John Joseph Mathews and the Politics of Indigenous Correspondence

The private correspondence of American Indian writers navigates on an intimate scale the same tribal national and settler–colonial contexts as newspaper columns, short stories, poems, plays, films, and novels. As Abenaki scholar Lisa Brooks explains, American Indian letters, which in the Indigenous Northeast originated in birchbark messages, also emerge as a significant form of communication "long before Indian people began writing poetry and fiction" and, in addition to various other genres prevalent in this period, "represent an indigenous American literary tradition" (13). When a Native author such as Samson Occom participates in this tradition but chooses not to discuss Mohegan politics in his letters, those letters nevertheless enter the world as documents implicated in the struggle for and conflict over power. Joanna Brooks identifies "the virtual absence of letters pertaining to the internal affairs of the Mohegan tribe" in Occom's archive and observes:

> This gap suggests that either a significant body of such letters was lost or destroyed, or that tribal business was not conducted by correspondence. Even as they became literate in English and versed in the legal and governmental discourses of colonial and early national Connecticut, Occom and other Mohegan tribal leaders continued to observe the political protocols essential to and constitutive of tribal life: meeting together on traditional territorial grounds, sharing meals, and affirming relationships of status and kinship. They may have rightly feared, as well, the interception and manipulation of correspondence by colonial officials. (63–64)

Indeed, the deep incursion of various colonial and settler–colonial forces into Indigenous lives makes apolitical spaces elusive. Following the policy shift by the federal government in the late nineteenth century from military action to assimilation, Nez Perce scholar Beth Piatote asserts, "Indian economies, lands, kinship systems, languages, cultural practices, and family relations—in short, all that constituted the Indian home—became the primary site of struggle. The battle, although not the stakes, moved from the indigenous homeland, what I call the tribal-national domestic, to the familial space of the Indian home, or the intimate domestic" (*Domestic Subjects,* 2). Letters composed in American Indian homes leave these "intimate domestic" and familial spaces as politically charged documents.

When non-Natives, especially ones with settler–colonial male privilege and other forms of unearned social and cultural power, receive and open letters from American Indian authors, they activate additional settler–colonial political contexts of which they might or might not be aware. The exchange of private letters between Natives and non-Natives, therefore, generates new, and contributes to existing, political arrays rooted in both Indigenous and settler–colonial communities, histories, and literary histories while establishing local, intimate links among them all. From the 1930s through the 1950s, John Joseph Mathews and Lynn Riggs were members of primarily, though not exclusively, Anglo male literary and academic networks that promoted the work of individual Native writers, if not Native American literature as a field or movement. Both authors corresponded with Walter S. Campbell, an English professor at the University of Oklahoma and a prolific writer under the pen name Stanley Vestal of books on western and southwestern themes, and Campbell and Mathews, in turn, had a mutual friend in legendary Texas folklorist J. Frank Dobie. Campbell and Dobie particularly influenced the development of a field of southwestern literary studies inclusive from its inception of Native American writers. The evidence of their efforts survives in their correspondence and the bibliographies and anthologies of southwestern literature to which they devoted years of labor during the first decades of English as "a serious discipline" (Eagleton, 27).[1] These letters, as well as the bibliographies and anthologies, express political positions, sometimes implicitly, sometimes stridently, about the role of the literary arts in a democracy as well as on education, family, and race, for example.[2] They also show Native writers shrewdly negotiating anti-Indigenous settler–colonial structures, especially the academy and print media, in the late assimilation era, through the brief reform period during John Collier's tenure at the OIA and into the early years of termination and relocation after World War II, as well as throughout the middle to late decades of Jim Crow. The documents produced by this network constitute a pre-Renaissance era, institutional American Indian literary history: Native authors in conversation about their writing with university professors who, in turn, promoted these authors in their roles both as scholars and as public intellectuals. This pre-Renaissance American Indian literary history also has remarkably direct links to the early moments of the Renaissance.

This chapter focuses on Mathews's relationship with Dobie before considering the impact of Riggs's correspondence on our understanding of his life, art, and, especially, politics. Dobie's friendship and correspondence with Mathews comprise one of the most intimate, generative, and vexed pre-Renaissance alliances between a representative of the academy and a Native writer and, in this case, respected independent scholar. Mathews earned the appreciation of this nationally known author in an era still widely viewed as a fallow precursor to the Native American Renaissance, despite more than twenty years of work by scholars recovering the many Native authors of the period and putting critical pressure on the well-deserved but outsized role literary critics such as Louis Owens gave "the dreadnaught Momaday" in "trigger[ing] a long-dormant need among Indian writers" and generating the Renaissance by winning the Pulitzer Prize for his 1968 novel *House Made of Dawn* (Weaver, Foreword, ix; Owens, 24).[3] Indeed, Dobie's advocacy for Mathews demonstrates a mid-twentieth-century commitment to an author at the center of a significant political and archival turn in Native literary studies beginning in the mid-1990s.[4] At the same time, their personal and professional relationship developed within social, cultural, and political contexts dramatically more advantageous to the career of the Anglo Texan as well as more favorable to Native men than Native women.

Dobie exerted his considerable influence nationally in books, periodicals, and newspapers as well as on television and, in several cases, film. His numerous correspondents included many writers, some with enduring reputations, such as Frances Densmore, John Lomax, and Henry Nash Smith, who acknowledges in the preface to the first edition of *Virgin Land* (1950) an "intellectual debt" to Southern Methodist University English professor John H. McGinnis and Dobie for "open[ing] my eyes to the significance of the West within American society"

(Smith, xi). Others, such as Mary Tucker, Mabel Major, T. M. Pearce, and Rebecca Smith, made in some cases equally significant but now nearly forgotten contributions to American literary studies, which during this era faced "disparagement" and "hostility" within many university English departments and was associated with "lower levels of schooling [that] hampered the professionalization of the field" (Renker, 23, 26). Dobie had only a brief correspondence with Tucker, an Indian detour courier for the Santa Fe Railway and the author of *Books of the Southwest: A General Bibliography* (1937). It began in November 1936, when, at Tucker's request, Dobie shared with her the reading list for his "Life and Literature of the Southwest" course. His correspondence with Major, Smith, and Pearce, the coauthors of *Southwest Heritage: A Literary History with Bibliography* (1938) and professors of English at Texas Christian University (Major and Smith) and the University of New Mexico (Pearce), endured for decades and, in the case of Major and Pearce, until Dobie's death. Campbell also shared a decades-long friendship in person and on paper with Dobie. The members of this academic network discussed many topics, both personal and professional, in their letters, though the focus often fell on their writing projects, such as Campbell's *The Book Lover's Southwest: A Guide to Good Reading* (1955), and their southwestern literature courses. They even engaged in friendly competition by boasting about the number of students enrolled in them.[5] While these scholars rarely mention Native writers in their letters, they researched Native American history and culture and included Native writers in their bibliographies and anthologies. The consistent attention of these scholars to Native writers constitutes an unrecognized intellectual and institutional component of a still curiously understudied mid-twentieth-century American Indian literary history.

The May 16, 1942, issue of the *Saturday Review of Literature*, edited by McGinnis and fellow Southern Methodist University English professor Lon Tinkle, demonstrates the national influence of the network on which Mathews exerted cultural and political pressure as an Osage writer actively engaged in tribal national life. As one of the editors of the *Southwest Review,* a journal founded in 1915 as the *Texas Review* by faculty at the University of Texas at Austin but published at Southern Methodist University beginning in 1924, McGinnis occupied an important position in the region's literary circles.[6] In this *Saturday Review* issue, an article by Mathews on the University of Oklahoma Press appears alongside contributions by Dobie and Campbell, writing as Vestal; Henry Nash Smith, John Lomax, and Rebecca Smith; and Riggs's Santa Fe friends Witter Bynner and Paul Horgan. In the middle pages of the issue, an illustrated, two-page literary map of the U.S. Southwest and northern Mexico borderlands by artist and cartographer Fanita Lanier points readers to Mathews (*Wah'kon-tah*), Riggs (*Green Grow the Lilacs*), and John Milton Oskison (*Brothers Three*) as "well-beloved and remembered" southwestern writers ("A Literary Map of the Southwest," 23).[7] By this time, Mathews had been friends with Campbell for nearly two decades, but he did not meet and begin corresponding with Dobie until the late 1940s. Their meeting set in motion a close friendship distinct for the way its archival evidence shows a Native writer operating on an intimate scale to infiltrate a settler–colonial network of academics.

Mathews was born in 1894 at Pawhuska in the Osage Nation in Indian Territory to parents with Osage, French, English, and Welsh ancestry. Robert Warrior, who in *Tribal Secrets* (1995) situates Mathews's *Talking to the Moon* at the center of his recovery of an American Indian intellectual tradition, observes, "Mathews's bicultural existence as a youngster did not fit into any of the typical patterns of reservation life at the time" (15). "His life," Warrior continues, "was a combination of upper-class luxury and contact with traditional Osage culture" (17).[8] Mathews was Osage through his great-grandmother, A-Ci'n-Ga, who married William "Old Bill" Sherley Williams, a trapper, guide, and Indian fighter and a figure known to Dobie before he met Mathews. In the opening pages of *Twenty Thousand Mornings* (2012), his posthumously published autobiography, Mathews identifies as a formative experience the sound of Osage men chanting as dawn approached. He explains:

> The prayer chant that disturbed my little boy's soul to the depths was Neolithic man talking to God. These Neolithic men, the Osages, were profoundly urged to communicate with their god each pre-dawn, embodying him in the morning star. They arose from their bear skin beds, wrapped their robes about them, and strode out into the darkness, and raising their faces to the morning star, they chanted and wept in frustration. (4)

The autobiography contains rich descriptions of life in the Osage Nation and on the Great Plains in the first two decades of the twentieth century. He describes his early education, including a memory of listening to Mrs. Tucker, his teacher, read Jack London's *The Call of the Wild,* and the family's Thanksgiving celebrations at his Aunt Sue and Uncle Jim's, where he recalls a leather-bound copy of either *Vanity Fair* or *David Copperfield* (55). He played soccer, or what he called "association football," as well as American football and basketball in high school, and he worked as a soda jerk before enrolling at the University of Oklahoma in 1914. During World War I, Mathews joined the U.S. Army Air Service, then in its infancy. He completed ground school in Austin, Texas, in 1917 before going to Kelly Field in San Antonio for flight training. He returned to Oklahoma after the war and finished his BA in 1920, then earned another BA while attending Oxford from 1921 to 1924 before beginning his career as a writer. His service to the Osage Nation included two terms on the Osage Tribal Council, from 1934 to 1942, and successful efforts to establish the Osage Tribal Museum in 1938.[9]

Yet his advocacy for the Osages does not imply a commitment to the kind of progressive politics that motivated the civil rights movement and shaped late-twentieth-century Native literary studies. Mathews was a social conservative. According to Susan Kalter, he was anti-Semitic and "hated male homosexuality and viewed it as degenerate" ("Introduction," xxxvii, xxxvii). She warns, "Although we might wish to associate Mathews with civil rights, his reactions toward blacks in general and the leaders of the civil rights movement were ambivalent at best" (xxxviii). Mathews also had a tendency to severely judge other people. Robert Dale Parker identifies "Mathews's disgust with his generation's aimless dissipation" in a letter to Campbell (*The Invention of Native American Literature,* 200). The "few flaming youths" among whom the thirty-six-year-old Mathews spent a weekend are "lost, poor little disillusioned nit-wits." The rant continues: "Graceless and clumbsy, without the charm of youth, they are often bestial in their drinking and sordidly carnal in their new found relationships; completely without the beauty of youth and romance" (Mathews to Campbell, December 3, 1930). His observations on the behavior of a "girl of about eighteen" who "fondled me for a few minutes like some half hearted kitten" also hint at the male chauvinism that runs throughout his autobiography.

Mathews met the slightly older Dobie in the late 1940s. Don Graham, the foremost contemporary authority on Texas life, literature, and culture, describes Dobie as a man that "old-time Texans would call a 'character'" (108). Dobie was born in 1888 on a ranch in Live Oak County in southeast Texas between San Antonio and Corpus Christi.[10] His mother encouraged him and his siblings to read by procuring a reading list "chosen by educators" and buying the books: *Pilgrim's Progress, Robinson Crusoe,* and *Ivanhoe,* for example, as well as *David Copperfield* and *Idylls of the King* (Tinkle, 6). His grandparents also had books by Mark Twain and Henry Wadsworth Longfellow in their home. He graduated in 1910 with a BA from Southwestern University in Georgetown, Texas, and earned an MA at Columbia University in 1914. After two years of army service during World War I as uneventful as Mathews's own, indecision about academic life led Dobie to consider a career as either a rancher or a journalist. He eventually settled into a position at the University of Texas at Austin, where he began publishing the books that established his reputation as "Mr. Texas." The racial politics of Dobie's views on Texas life and culture were already explicit when, during the planning stages for the Texas Centennial celebrations in 1936, he encouraged the construction of monuments "not merely to great men but to the genius of a great race that created Texas during the course of a century-long struggle with nonwhite races" (J. González, *Border Renaissance,* 75). Yet Tinkle, one of Dobie's biographers, claims, "By the early forties, Dobie was widely regarded as a subversive, a traitor to Texas tradition and values" (176). He became "an outspoken New Dealer and civil libertarian" (Graham, 109), and, as an illustration of Dobie's politics, Graham notes, "In 1945 Dobie had the gall to argue, in print, that blacks should be given full voting rights, and in a speech in Fort Worth, he declared that he would welcome qualified black students to the University of Texas" (109). In a more recent biography of Dobie, Steven Davis confirms and documents in detail this trajectory from young conservative to middle-aged liberal publicly supporting, often with relish, organized labor and protesting McCarthyism.

Dobie's evolving relationship with Américo Paredes, a seminal figure in Mexican American, borderlands, and transnational American studies, suggests how this political transformation resonated in his personal and professional lives. After angering a young Paredes by neglecting and stereotyping Mexican Americans in his work, Dobie developed "a modest friendship" with him (Davis, 209). Dobie valued Paredes's scholarship, and, once the University of Texas Press published

Paredes's dissertation, as *"With His Pistol in His Hand"* (1958), Dobie and Mody Boatright, his colleague in the University of Texas at Austin's Department of English, "helped to keep the book in print by distributing copies to some four hundred members of the Texas Folklore Society" (Davis, 211).[11] When the governor-appointed board of regents of the University of Texas told President Homer Rainey to fire four economics professors perceived by the board as radical, Rainey refused. The board, in Tinkle's words comprised primarily of "conservative men of wealth and power, haters of Roosevelt and the New Deal, fearful and resentful of intellectuals" (175), fired Rainey. Dobie's defense of Rainey led Governor Coke Stevenson to express his desire that the university fire Dobie, too. The regents, with the help of new University of Texas president Theophilus Painter, eventually found a way to relieve Dobie of his faculty position in 1947 by denying him one of the annual leaves of absence to which he had become accustomed.[12]

Dobie's long friendship with Mathews began after Dobie's political transformation and was the product of mutual and genuine admiration. They exchanged letters for more than a decade and went on annual hunting trips together. When Dobie published the revised and expanded edition of his *Guide to Life and Literature of the Southwest* in 1952, nine years after the first edition, he added the Book-of-the-Month Club selection *Wah'Kon-tah: The Osage and the White Man's Road* (1932), *Sundown* (1934), *Life and Death of an Oilman: The Career of E. W. Marland* (1941), and *Talking to the Moon* (1945) by Mathews. Dobie effusively praised both *The Osages* and *Talking to the Moon*, and he consulted with Mathews while he worked on his last book, *Cow People* (1964), specifically about Les Claypoole, a cowboy to whom Mathews had introduced him. Their letters show a quickly developing friendship based on their passion for both literature and the land and a shared belief that modern life alienated people from the latter, while Dobie's responses to *The Osages* in one letter and in the marginalia in the copy Mathews sent him also evince a mutual regard for—accompanied by a tendency to romanticize—an older generation of American Indian men. Their correspondence marks one particularly vibrant point of many in the emergence of a mid-twentieth-century academic network inclusive of American Indian writers in the decades before the Native American Renaissance.[13] As nodes in multiple political arrays, Mathews's letters represent, following Piatote, intimately political Indigenous writing not intended for publication. Instead, these letters record the private expressions of an American Indian author working behind the scenes, yet still within tribal national and settler–colonial contexts, to make his voice, and the voices of other Osages, heard.

Tribal Secrets in the Settler Borderlands

The extant documents suggest that Mathews had more interest in Dobie as a hunting companion than as a writer or progressive public intellectual, perhaps due in part to the strikingly divergent approaches that each author took to writing about Native peoples and communities as well as the colonial and settler–colonial history of the West and Southwest. As an author focused on tribal-nation history and contemporary Osage life in books such as *Wah'Kon-tah, Sundown, Talking to the Moon,* and *The Osages,* Mathews must have seriously challenged Dobie's far narrower, reductive conception of Indigenous America. The archival record of their friendship, in fact, shows Dobie reading Mathews carefully and expressing admiration for his friend's writing. This attentive, active reading and private praise form the roots, or the rough drafts, of Dobie's public acclaim for Mathews. In this private communication, we see an Indigenous author challenging a reader to develop new perspectives on indigeneity, and, in the marginalia, the precise moments Mathews elicits responses from Dobie. While these moments did not produce a movement like the Renaissance, they did produce motion— intellectual, emotional, institutional—originating in Mathews's labor as a writer. As Piatote demonstrates, the "intimate domestic"—Mathews's writing space in his home, for example—pulsed with Indigenous political energy. In his often endearing missives to Dobie, Mathews put pressure on his friend to hear and see Indigenous life in a way that contrasted with the lamentably stereotypical views in which Dobie trafficked in his early career.

Dobie published approximately twenty books, most of them about Texas, the Southwest, and the United States–Mexico borderlands, and he was one of the founders of western and southwestern literary studies. These books offer a mixed literary historical and political legacy. In early publications such as *Coronado's Children* (1930) and *Apache Gold and Yaqui Silver* (1939), both collections of stories about primarily, though not exclusively, Anglo treasure hunters, Dobie and his informants perpetuate familiar colonial and settler–colonial discourses of what Roy Harvey Pearce, who began his career as Dobie's entered its final phase, called "savagism and civilization."[14] Indigenous people are frequently "savage," and prospectors and other settlers face perpetual attack. Nearly every quest for treasure in both books involves either the threat of violence or an actual slaughter of prospectors by Indigenous people trying to keep hidden what Dobie consistently calls their "tribal secrets," hordes of gold and other valuables. While Dobie uses the perpetual fear of attacks by Indigenous people to generate suspenseful narratives, he treats the violence committed by Texas Rangers and scalp hunters flippantly. He shares, in an apparent attempt at humor, the Ranger euphemism for killing a target, "naturalizing," and observes that the scalp hunters on occasion are "not fairly paid" for chores such as clearing an "Indian-infested desert" (*Coronado's Children*, 97; *Apache Gold*, 265, 276). When a prospector joins the scalp hunters, who make a dramatic return to American literary history in Cormac McCarthy's *Blood Meridian* (1985), he does so in an effort to "collect a little expense money" (*Apache Gold*, 269).[15] In Gerald Vizenor's words, Dobie contributes to a long history "of the surveillance and dominance of the tribes in literature" (*Manifest Manners*, 4). At this early stage of his career as a writer, Dobie neither challenged what Vizenor calls the "manifest manners" of settler–colonial narratives about American Indians as intractable obstacles to Anglo progress and modernity nor made efforts to advocate for their rights, as writers such as Riggs's friend Mary Austin, whose work Dobie admired, had started to do.

Only a few, generally insignificant fissures appear in Dobie's almost entirely monolithic assumption of settler–colonial supremacy. General John R. Baylor earned Dobie's condemnation for attacking a group of Comanches, taking nine scalps, and celebrating in a "fervid orgy of vengeance" (*Coronado's Children*, 64), while the Aravaipa Apaches, Dobie notes, "killed their white enemies" because "they wanted to keep their homeland" (*Coronado's Children*, 215).[16] A wide range of Indigenous peoples, such as Lipan and Mescalero Apaches, Black Seminoles, Comanches, Karankawas, Paiutes, Papagos (Tohono O'odhams), Tarahumaras (Rarámuris), Tonkawas, Yaquis, and Yumas (Quechans), also populate Dobie's U.S. Southwest and northern Mexico. He thus configures diverse Indigenous borderlands, though always in the service of a settler–colonial politics of representation that situate

Indigenous people as a threatening presence in the margins of Anglocentric stories.

In the first edition of his *Guide to Life and Literature of the Southwest*, published in 1943 prior to the beginning of his friendship with Mathews, Dobie's settler–colonial politics shape his presentation of southwestern literature. The first edition of the *Guide*, a book that Larry McMurtry calls one of his two favorites by Dobie in an otherwise unflattering portrayal of Dobie's work, appeared around the time Dobie told his friend Tom Lea that he had lost patience with "Texas bragging and nationalism fever" (quoted in Tinkle, 190).[17] The *Guide*, based on a class that Dobie calls "my only academic love" in the first chapter, "A Declaration," draws on the legacy of Dobie's earlier books but reflects a broader interest in the region's many voices (*Guide*, 1st ed., 7). "No informed person would hold that the Southwest can claim any considerable body of *pure literature* as its own," Dobie observes, though "the region has a distinct cultural inheritance, full of life and drama, told variously in books so numerous that their very existence would surprise many people who depend on the Book-of-the-Month Club for literary guidance" (9). Southwestern literature thus stands in a cultural space apart from "*pure literature*"—presumably works by authors receiving his praise on the previous page: Percy Bysshe Shelley, John Keats, Edmond Rostand, William Wordsworth, Robert Louis Stevenson, Charles Lamb, William Hazlitt, Joseph Conrad, J. M. Barrie, Sir Thomas Browne, and William Shakespeare—and "middlebrow" selections for the Book-of-the-Month Club, a "recognition," explains Gordon Hutner, "that once would have probably guaranteed their debased status among critics anxious about the incursions made against elite culture by such institutions" (7).[18] For good measure, Dobie distinguishes southwestern literature from the "dreary creatures of colonial New England who are utterly foreign to the genius of the Southwest" (*Guide*, 1st ed., 9). He makes a case, too, for a particular methodological approach to literary study: "The attempt to study a people's literature apart from their social and, to a lesser extent, their political history is as illogical as the lady who said she had read Romeo but had not yet got to Juliet" (9). This attention to social and political history must begin, Dobie argues, with "the aborigenes," though they have not "left any records, other than hieroglyphic" (10). In a sentence reminiscent of an oft-cited passage from Momaday's *House Made of Dawn* about "latecoming things," Dobie claims that readers must consult "late-coming men [who] have written about them" (10).[19] To emphasize the inaccessibility of an Indigenous perspective, Dobie notes that the Indigenous people of the Texas coast have "vanished" (13). The intellectual dictum—to know Indigenous history—conflicts with the settler–colonial ideological imperative to ignore the modern Indigenous presence and accentuate Indigenous absence.

The first edition of the *Guide* generally fulfills this imperative. In Chapter 3, "Indian Culture (Pueblo and General)," Dobie remarks, "The literature on the subject of Indians is so extensive and ubiquitous that, unless a student of Americana is pursuing it, he may find it more troublesome to avoid than to get hold of" (*Guide*, 1st ed., 19). At the same time, "In all this lore and tabulation of facts, the Indian folk themselves have generally been dried out" (19). While he acknowledges "the vaunted Indian blood of such individuals as Will Rogers" (21), one of the most famous men in the world in the 1920s and 1930s and certainly the most famous American Indian, Dobie does not read this "Indian blood" as a marker either of a specific Cherokee past or of a modern present.[20] When he affirms an Indigenous presence, such as the residents of the pueblos in New Mexico, he evinces concern primarily for their influence on Mexicans and Anglo Americans, especially "arty" ones (21). A reference to "a renaissance of Indian pottery, weaving, and painting" provides an opportunity to refer readers to contemporary Native artists such as Velino Shije Herrera/Ma-Pe-Wi from Zia Pueblo, Hopi painter Fred Kabotie, or the Kiowa Six, but Dobie focuses instead on the "outsiders" who buy and appreciate the art rather than the Indigenous producers. He confirms this focus with his comments on Mary Austin, who in her own observations of how "the tribal people . . . attuned themselves to the rhythms of their own land," Dobie asserts, demonstrates "how we newcomers who would achieve harmony with the land will adopt the principles of these Amerind rhythms" (22). In the following chapter, "Apaches and Comanches," Dobie identifies and asserts as intellectually productive the settler–colonial bias at work in, or the manifest manners of, the literature about American Indians. He remarks, "It is unfortunate that most of the literature about them is from their enemies. Yet an enemy often teaches a man more than his friends and makes him work harder" (24). In these two chapters, he includes one work by an Indigenous author, the autobiography of the triracial Chief Buffalo Child Long Lance, a graduate of Carlisle Indian Industrial School.[21] He includes a second Indigenous author, Lynn Riggs, in the "Poetry and Drama" chapter and observes that Riggs "has so far been the most successful dramatist" in the Southwest (103). Dobie bases this assessment on *Green Grow the Lilacs* (1930), though by 1943 Riggs had also produced and published other Indian Territory and southwestern plays, such as *Roadside* (1930), later renamed *Borned in Texas* after the repeated boast of Texas, the play's folk hero; *Russet Mantle* (1936), a satire of the "arty" Anglo Americans in Santa Fe who earned Dobie's disdain; and *The Cherokee Night* (1936), with the same Indian Territory and early Oklahoma setting as *Green Grow the Lilacs*.[22] Dobie appears unaware that Riggs, like Rogers, was Cherokee.

American Indians occupy a conventionally second-class social and historical place in Dobie's settler–colonial, southwestern U.S. imaginary. In the headnote to the third chapter, "Indian Culture (Pueblo and General)," he observes, "The Anglo-American's policy towards the Indian was to kill him and take his land, perhaps make a razor-strop out of his hide. The Spaniard's policy was to baptize him, take his land and enslave him. Any English speaking frontiersman who took up with the Indians was dubbed a 'squaw man'—a term of sinister connotations" (*Guide*, 1st ed., 21).[23] He undermines any attempt to interpret these remarks as critical, though, by referring throughout the guide to Indigenous people as "savages" and identifying a figure such as Stephen F. Austin as a "great Anglo-American colonizer" (35). While he observes that "the modern Indian hardly enters into Texas life at all" (95), Dobie does not explain which Texas and United States policies, from strategic military and police actions to removal legislation, led to the ostensible absence of Indigenous people in Texas.[24] Instead, his observation that "the whole plains area" was "denuded of buffalo and secured from Indian domination" conveys relief at an inevitability rather than concern or critical self-reflection (58).

However, Dobie builds explicit intellectual and political challenges to settler–colonial discourses into the second, post–World War II and postpolitical transformation edition of the *Guide,* which appeared in print as American literary studies "achieved institutional maturity" (Renker, 38). He announced this new perspective in "A Preface with Some Revised Ideas." After invoking Walt Whitman's oft-quoted embrace of contradiction, Dobie asserts, "I have heard so much silly bragging by Texans that I now think it would be a blessing to themselves—

and a relief to others—if the braggers did not know that they lived in Texas" (*Guide*, 2nd ed., 1). Thus begins a statement of Dobie's new cosmopolitan outlook: "Nobody should specialize on provincial writings before he has the perspective that only a good deal of good literature and wide history can give. I think it more important that a dweller in the Southwest read *The Trial and Death of Socrates* than all the books extant on killings by Billy the Kid" (1–2). He never, he says, viewed the books in the first guide as a "substitute" for the aforementioned "good literature" (2). In fact, "to reread most of them would be boresome, though *Hamlet*, Boswell's *Johnson*, Lamb's *Essays*, and other genuine literature remain as quickening as ever" (2). He makes clear that his new perspective has political roots. He imagines a book entitled *Emancipators of the Human Mind* and notes, "When I reflect how few writings connected with the wide open spaces of the West and Southwest are wide enough to enter into such a volume, I realize acutely how desirable perspective is in patriotism" (3). Southwesterners, he argues, must have an "awareness of other times and other wheres"; they must learn to see that "despite all gulfs, canyons, and curtains that separate nations, those nations and their provinces are all increasingly interrelated" (6). Despite these assertions, the second edition of the *Guide* provides readers with nearly twice as many works about the Southwest as the first.

A decade following the publication of the first edition of the *Guide*, and after Dobie and Mathews meet, begin their correspondence, and join each other to hunt at Houston oilman Ralph Johnston's Rancho Seco in southwest Texas, Dobie also included four of Mathews's books in the second edition. These additions neither dramatically reshape nor indigenize the volume's representation of southwestern literature. However, they illustrate Dobie's appreciation of Mathews's talents and a desire to build and diversify the field Dobie helped invent. In the headnote to a new chapter, "Interpreters of the Land," Dobie reveals how this new perspective shapes his view of southwestern literary history: "In the multitudinous studies on Spanish-American history all padres are 'good' and all conquistadores are 'intrepid,' and that is about as far as interpretation goes" (*Guide*, 2nd ed., 18–19). He uses Mathews's *Talking to the Moon* as an example of the best writing the Southwest produces: "This Oxford scholar of Osage blood built his ranch house around a fireplace, flanked by shelves of books. His observations are of the outside, but they are informed by reflection made beside a fire. They are not bookish at all, but the spirits of great writers mingle with echoes of coyote wailing and wood-thrush singing" (21). He places *Talking to the Moon* in "Coyotes, Lobos, and Panthers" and describes the memoir as "a wise and spiritual interpretation of the black-jack country of eastern Oklahoma, close to the Osages, in which John Joseph Mathews lived. Not primarily about coyotes," he continues, "the book illuminates them more than numerous books on particular animals illuminate their subjects" (167). *Coyote Stories* (1933) by Okanogan author Mourning Dove (Christine Quintasket) also appears in this section. Along with *Black Elk Speaks* (1932), Dobie adds *Wah'Kon-Tah*, which he calls "a book of essays" with "profound spiritual qualities" (35), to the chapter now called "Apaches, Comanches, and Other Plains Indians."[25] He selects *Life and Death of an Oilman*, which he reviewed favorably while also praising Mathews's other books in the *New York Times*, for the section on "Mining and Oil," and *Sundown* appears in "Fiction, Including Folk Tales." The novel, claims Dobie, "goes more profoundly than *Laughing Boy* into the soul of a young Indian (an Osage) and his people." In addition to this favorable comparison to Oliver La Farge's Pulitzer Prize–winning novel, Dobie concludes that *Sundown* is an example of "superb writing" (181–82).

The revisions to "Indian Culture; Pueblos and Navajos" also indicate that Dobie gave careful consideration to his own earlier representations of the Indigenous Southwest. He revises his criticism of the privileged classes of Santa Fe to read, "The special groups incline to be arty and worshipful, but they express a salutary revolt against machined existence and they have done much to revive dignity in Indian life" (*Guide*, 2nd ed., 27). He deletes the sentence about the renaissance in Native arts and inserts a passage from "Navajo Holy Song" as interpreted by the poet Edith Hart Mason. "It expresses," Dobie claims, in a voice that sounds much like Mathews's in *Talking to the Moon*, "a spiritual content in Indian life far removed from the We and God, Incorporated form of religion ordained by the National Association of Manufacturers" (28). Other entries include references to the "dignity and beauty" and "spiritual qualities" of Indigenous literary arts (28–29). Of John Louw Nelson's *Rhythm for Rain*, Dobie observes, "Based on ten years spent with the Hopi Indians, this study of their life is a moving story of humanity" (30). In the revised "Apaches, Comanches, and Other Plains Indians" section, Dobie updates the Long Lance entry to account for new information about his biography, and Riggs remains "the most successful dramatist" in the Southwest (186).[26] Of "the history of art in the Southwest," Dobie adds, "it will begin with clay (Indian pottery), horse hair (vaquero weaving), hide (vaquero plaiting), and horn (backwoods carving). It will note Navajo sand painting and designs in blankets" (187). The second edition places Dobie more in line culturally and politically with the American Indian policy reformers of the interwar era. While it accords non-Native writers like Mason and Nelson authority over representations of Indigenous life and culture, it also asserts dignity in contemporary Indigenous life, acknowledges Indigenous cultural producers, and celebrates Indigenous material productions. By the time he published the second edition, however, federal policy had taken a reactionary turn against supporting political and cultural self-determination under Office of Indian Affairs commissioner John Collier to pursuing, under Collier's successors, the termination of the relationship between tribal nations and the federal government and the relocation of Native peoples to urban centers.[27]

Dobie also promotes Mathews as a talented naturalist in one other book. He cites *Wah'Kon-Tah, Sundown,* and *Talking to the Moon* in *The Voice of the Coyote* (1949), the postpolitical transformation book in which Dobie most extensively engages American Indian cultural productions. A work of natural history and folklore, *The Voice of the Coyote* contains two chapters devoted to American Indian coyote stories and many others that compare them to ostensibly similar European and European settler–colonial stories. However, Dobie remains unwilling to acknowledge either an intellectual or a serious social component to these stories. In the introduction, for example, he observes, "The American Indian's sympathy for fellow animals was not sentiment or superstition; nor was it an expression of intellectual curiosity; it was part of his harmony with nature" (xii–xiii). He maintains this patronizing view of American Indians throughout the book. Yet Mathews calls *The Voice of the Coyote* "one of my mood books to be dipped into several times a month" (Mathews to Dobie, January 3, 1951), and he thanks Dobie for the gift of an autographed copy of it for his grandson (Mathews to Dobie, April 18, 1963). As the acknowledgments section at the end of *The Voice of the Coyote* makes clear, Mathews's writing deeply and sincerely moved Dobie. In this final section, entitled "My Creditors: Books and People," Dobie writes, "Of recent books, there is in *Talking to the*

Moon, by John Joseph Mathews, from whom I have quoted extensively, more comprehension of the coyote as a living creature of the earth than can be found in some of the scientific treatises that regard the coyote as nothing more than a stomach, as unanimated as a pipeline" (371). Dobie also cites Mourning Dove's *Coyote Stories,* which illustrates "especially well," he asserts, that Coyote fails to learn from his experiences (367). He treats American Indian writers respectfully as intellectuals and writers, as evident also in his deference to Mathews in an article on coyotes, "Can a Coyote Raise His Tail?," in the March 11, 1951, edition of the *Oklahoman,* but he does not extend this view to Mathews's fellow Osages, Mourning Dove's fellow Okanogans, or other American Indians and their communities. As the revisions to the *Guide* and Dobie's effusive expressions of regard for Mathews's talents as a writer demonstrate, Mathews clearly influenced Dobie's views and representations of Indigenous peoples, cultures, and histories.

When Our Trails Crossed

The letters exchanged by Mathews and Dobie move within various established networks of tribal national and settler–colonial cultural, social, and political power. At the same time, they exert political pressure on those networks. Mathews and Dobie had ongoing relationships with university presses, for example, while Dobie also had strong ties to scholarly journals, national periodicals, and Little, Brown, his New York publisher. While Mathews worked to secure a place for himself within these networks, praise for or defense of Mathews by Dobie also resonated within them. Indeed, university presses and scholarly journals played a significant role in the Native American literary history of the decades prior to the officially recognized beginning of the Renaissance, and Native writers such as Momaday and Silko began their careers in the 1960s by gaining access to the same institutional networks in which both Mathews and Riggs circulated. That this potential materialized more modestly for Mathews than it did for Momaday and Silko does not diminish either the literary historical and political significance of his efforts or the role his personal correspondence played in them.

The letters generate moments of political potential in multiple ways: they convey, for example, the intellectual seriousness of Dobie's engagement with Mathews as a writer as well as the emotional intensity of their friendship. The correspondence begins with a telegram dated December 15, 1949, from Mathews to Dobie telling Dobie he will not be able to meet him at the Tulsa Farm Club, which had invited Dobie to give a talk. Dobie, in turn, asked the club's Executive Secretary to extend an invitation to Mathews: "My last book, The Voice of the Coyote came out last spring. . . . In it I quote extensively from John Joseph Mathews of Pawhuska. He has a small ranch in that country, I understand. Not many people have written of the land and of its wildlife with more sympathy. If you don't mind, I wish you would invite him to come to the meeting" (Dobie to Lester).[28] Founded in 1939 during the fiftieth anniversary of the large-scale settlement on Indigenous land known as the Land Rush, the Tulsa Farm Club had a "partly social, partly educational, and partly economic development" agenda and bylaws prohibiting politics. It also welcomed its first woman member in 1950 (Lee). The political promise of Dobie's invitation into the settler–colonial network represented by this social club remained unfulfilled. However, Gertrude Bonnin's work with the General Federation of Women's Clubs (GFWC), which sponsored some of her lectures and investigations into the living conditions in Native communities, represents one approach by a contemporary of Mathews to leveraging the political power of a predominantly non-Native social organization for the benefit of Indigenous people.[29]

The letters scattered over the course of the next fourteen years include discussions of their writing projects, suggestions for reading, and plans for their hunting trips. The evidence in the extant letters suggests that Dobie appreciated Mathews's writing more than Mathews appreciated Dobie's. Dobie consistently offers effusive praise of Mathews. He even defends Mathews in response to criticism by Elizabeth Hunt, Mathews's wife. Hunt, Mathews tells Dobie in one letter, views Dobie as the superior writer: "He seems to have confidence in words to express what he feels, and this gives his reader confidence." She follows with a harsher assessment of Mathews: "You seem to make your reader restless by your lack of confidence in words to express what you feel." Dobie writes in pencil in the margins: "not true about Mathews" (Mathews to Dobie, January 3, 1951). He shares this private defense with Mathews in a letter dated nine days later: "I don't agree with Miss Elizabeth in her saying that you make your readers restless through 'lack of self-confidence in words to express what you feel.' It seems to me that you write about some things very precisely and illuminate life out of which those things come" (Dobie to Mathews, January 12, 1951). A month later, he sent his own review of *Life and Death of an Oilman*, the biography of E. W. Marland, to Mathews (Dobie to Mathews, February 28, 1951). When the *Atlantic* asked Mathews to write a piece on Dobie (Mathews to Dobie, May 9, 1960), Mathews expressed reluctance. Dobie responded, "It's news to me that Little, Brown & Company is promoting a piece on me for the Atlantic Monthly. I can't think of anybody who would do it more understandingly or skillfully, and if you want to know what my reaction is—it's that you go ahead and do it" (Dobie to Mathews, May 14, 1960). Ralph Johnston had a different response: "If you include any of the conversation you taped in the article for the Atlantic Monthly, you are DEAD. Since I did not hear anything more about the 16 MM film, I am sure they got rid of it" (Johnston to Mathews, November 17, 1960).[30] Johnston's threat suggests the public revelation of the content of the audio tapes would embarrass some of the men.[31] Mathews did not write the article, though a publication in the *Atlantic*, which featured articles by Bonnin writing as Zitkala-Ša in 1900 and 1902, would have provided significant exposure for a man who struggled his entire life, including through some dire financial times in the late 1940s and early 1950s, to earn the attention of readers.[32] After receiving a copy of *The Osages*, Dobie also wrote quickly back to Mathews, "I've read far enough in it to recognize its majesty as an earth book" (Dobie to Mathews, November 6, 1961). Evidence in Dobie's marginalia suggests that Mathews's evocative descriptions of the land and its residents, including an older generation of Osages represented by Mathews as deeply connected to it, elicited this generous compliment.

In contrast, Mathews's more measured praise of Dobie's writing illuminates a curious dynamic in their friendship, one with roots in the settler–colonial politics of white privilege: their correspondence implies that they shared an awareness of Mathews's superiority as a writer, even if Dobie's national celebrity eclipsed Mathews's more modest reputation. In a letter dated "late 1959 or early 1960" by Dobie after he received it, Mathews tells him, "I wrote to Ralph that I knew you through your books, and upon meeting you every brush stroke of my imagined picture of you was there, with delightful supplementary highlights of personality. I can still smell the cedar and mesquite smoke from your ranch chinmey" (Mathews to Dobie, late 1959 or early 1960).[33] After Dobie sent Mathews the Romany-themed 1851 novel *Lavengro* by British author George Borrow, Mathews says, "I am not sure when I shall be able to read Lavengro, which you so thoughtfully sent me. The inscription was gracious, and I liked it very much. The strange thing about it is, that you 'linger' with me also." Mathews adds, "I have never made the least attempt to meet the people whose books I have liked. Afraid, I suppose. Your personality is even more attractive than your Tongues Of The Monte" (Mathews to Dobie, May 9, 1960). Mathews conveys only that he has read some of Dobie's books and "liked" them and that he appreciates Dobie more as a friend than as a writer—Dobie, not his books, "lingers" with Mathews; he prefers Dobie's personality to his publications.

Their friendship grew increasingly intimate after Mathews finished his magnum opus and as Dobie neared the end of his life.[34] After an illness kept Dobie from hunting in 1962, Mathews wrote to him:

> You were missed, Frank. It was more than the absence of a very attractive and dominating personality, but the very atmosphere of the 'fireplace blind' in some way, seemed to want something; a very important ingredient, to make it whole.... The day I left [seemed strange not having you as a companion] Hal was preparing to go out in the pick-up and 'road shoot' a gobbler for you. I hope he did and you had a wild turkey Thanksgiving and a pleasant Season. I hope you recover completely from your mischance, and we may look forward to hunts in the future. (January 7, 1963)

Their literary interests shaped the atmosphere of this "fireplace blind," too, as the men told stories over drinks in the evening. Dobie repeated one, for example, that he had heard from Carl Sandburg, also a friend of Lynn Riggs and Will Rogers, about Abraham Lincoln's sense of humor.[35] Mathews sat at the center of this storytelling event as a revered chronicler of the Osages.

Dobie surely missed the "fireplace blind" as well, for on one point he and Mathews always agreed: the life of the rancher, cowboy, and hunter was far superior to any other option. In one letter, Mathews laments what he viewed as the increasing alienation of the younger generations from the land: "There are thousands of young men who, brought up on ranches and farms, will know 'querencia,' but I suppose I feel that the roar of jets, the pitchman's inanities, will interfer with their complete understanding of the earth, their receptive souls notwithstanding"

(Mathews to Dobie, January 21, 1954).[36] Like Will Rogers, Mathews was involved in the earliest age of aviation, and he expressed in his autobiography the joy of becoming "at last brother to the golden eagle" (*Twenty Thousand Mornings*, 183). However, rather than expressing admiration for men like Charles Lindbergh or Wiley Post, both larger-than-life figures of early aviation and both good friends of Will Rogers, Mathews and Dobie tended to appreciate the lives of men like Les Claypoole, the cowboy about whom Mathews wrote in *Talking to the Moon* and *Twenty Thousand Mornings*. Claypoole rented land from the Mathews family and worked the big cattle drives to Dodge City, Kansas, Mathews recalls, "during the days when a cowboy slept in his wet clothes and used his saddle for a pillow" (*Talking*, 44). Mathews describes Claypoole thus:

> His face was weathered granite, and his steel grey eyes and his silence, as he looked at his great gold watch with the hunting case, caused me to feel like a guilty schoolboy when I was late for a meeting with him. He wore a big black hat of the early days, and it was the first thing he put on as he sat on the edge of his bed at four o'clock each morning, catching it behind and not in front. Then he took a chew of tobacco. (44–45)

Claypoole also shared Mathews's and Dobie's distaste for modernization. A neighbor's use of a tractor to destroy good prairie grass disrupted Claypoole's normal "down-to-earth reasonableness" (46). Claypoole called the neighbor and his ilk "the sorriest set of goddam road lizzards in this world" (46). Mathews had a large picture of Claypoole in his home and sent it to Dobie in 1951. Dobie misplaced it for more than a decade before finding it during the summer of 1963 (Dobie to Mathews, June 5, 1963). Dobie planned to include Claypoole in *Cow People,* which he dedicated to Walker Stone and Ralph Johnston. However, the Oklahoma cowboy does not make an appearance in the book. Dobie received a copy of *Cow People* in the mail on the morning of September 19, 1964. He died in his sleep that afternoon.

The expression of mutual admiration reached a crescendo in Mathews's inscription to Dobie in *The Osages*. Mathews presented Dobie with the book at Dobie's Paisano Ranch in southwest Austin, where the two were preparing for their annual fall hunting expedition. Mathews writes:

Austin, Texas
November [Day Before the Hunt at Rancho Seco] 15 1961

For J. Frank Dobie, the most interesting man I have ever met. He is half Texan and half Spiritual, and I shall forever know that I was fortunate when our trails crossed.

Jo
John Joseph Mathews

Dobie wrote the following beneath the inscription:

I have not read all of this tome, but have read far enough to realize that it is as noble a representation as well as ample ~~representation~~ of people of the earth—I doubt if I could enjoy it as much as I enjoyed Talking to the Moon, from which I borrowed some of the best things put into The Voice of the Coyote.

When the deer hunting season comes Jo Mathews comes to Austin, sometimes driving hundreds of miles out of his way, to drive me to Medina County, where we are guests of our longtime friend Walker Stone. No other writer has written in his book an inscription that I value more highly than this.

Frank Dobie[37]

Dobie appears to have finished reading the book, as his scattered marginalia, in pencil, appears as late in the book as within sixty pages from the end.[38] These notes indicate that he read the book critically and lovingly. Question marks and checkmarks appear, and Dobie, an active reader, underlined passages in a shaky hand and wrote comments such as "pathetic fallacy," "style," and "vivid."[39] When Mathews describes the treatment of prisoners of war by residents of an Osage camp, he says, "[The dogs] lifted their legs against" the captives. Dobie circled the passage and revised it in the margins to read "pissed on," thereby capturing for a brief moment the bawdy tone of the conversations recorded at Rancho Seco.[40]

Mathews's references to and descriptions of animals and the rhythm and harmony of human life in the natural world elicited the most consistent interest from Dobie. "The rhythms of the earth," he writes next to a passage in which Mathews describes the Osage men praying to the sun at dawn as the rest of the camp mourns a murder victim (77).

"What description" he notes next to a passage in which Mathews describes a Tzi-Sho chief's attire (99). He pushes back against Mathews's representation of Anglos, the Heavy Eyebrows. When Mathews refers to "armpit odors" of white men, Dobie writes, "Not in Indians?" (100). When Mathews writes that the Heavy Eyebrows "seemed so eager to please" that the Osage men "wondered if they ought not be killed before they reached the *Tzi-Sho* lodge of sanctuary," Dobie challenges the logic: "Anybody eager to please should be killed?" (101). In the margins of this presentation copy of *The Osages*, Dobie engages Mathews's work both sympathetically and critically. He begins to practice the kind of scholarly work on American Indian literature that blossoms in the first generation of the Renaissance, when non-Native literary critics dominated the conversation within academic institutions.

Mathews's presence in the revised edition of Dobie's bibliography places him, along with Black Elk, Mourning Dove, and Riggs, in one of the founding documents of regional literary studies in the United States. This recognition does not occur on the same scale as Momaday's Pulitzer Prize. Yet Mathews's effort to earn Dobie's recognition of his talent and dedicated support of his career represents a significant moment in American Indian literary history. While the recovery of Mathews's importance to American Indian literary history continues as a work in progress, his friendship and correspondence with Dobie demonstrates that he has always received recognition, at least by some scholars, as an important chronicler of the Osages and late-nineteenth- and early-twentieth-century life in the Southwest. This friendship and correspondence resonate as intimately political within mid-twentieth-century tribal national and settler–colonial contexts in which Indigenous authors faced the daunting task of navigating settler–colonial institutions in order to reach audiences and have their voices heard. By contributing to the work of establishing Mathews's presence within at least three of those institutions—academy, archives, and publishing industry—Dobie and Mathews's friendship and correspondence had an explicit, documented impact on pre-civil-rights-era American Indian literary history.

The Networked Foundations of Native Literary Studies

By establishing friendships with and gaining the loyal support of writers and academics in the middle decades of the twentieth century, other

Native authors, and especially Riggs, also helped make space for Native people and Native literature in the academy and prepare the ground for the emergence of Native literary studies as a discipline. Their correspondences with academics—which they used to describe new projects; announce imminent publications or, in Riggs's case, productions; and share completed works—made their literary labor visible at universities. These epistolary efforts also anticipated the work of and shared a goal with Native students and professors of the civil-rights-era generation. Their letters, in other words, are political documents insisting on the value of Native voices and exerting pressure on the academy to accept them. Riggs skillfully cultivated his university friendships with Walter Campbell and Paul Green, among others, and spent time in classrooms as a teacher at the University of Oklahoma and Baylor University, where he taught a course called "Drama and the Playwright" while serving as a Rockefeller Professor in the fall 1941 semester.[41] That fall, Riggs corresponded with Rebecca Smith, a Texas Christian University professor of English, acquaintance of Dobie, and cofounder of the field of southwestern literary studies. As president of the Texas Institute of Letters, Smith invited Riggs to speak at Texas Christian University at the organization's annual meeting. Riggs accepted the invitation and proposed as his topic "The Dramatic Instinct and its Fulfillment (with special reference to Texas and the Southwest)" (Riggs to Smith, September 30, 1941). His letters to Campbell and Green show a young writer hyperaware of the potential benefits but also the pitfalls of using an academic network to promote his work.

In the first extant letter to Campbell, with whom he began corresponding after leaving the University of Oklahoma for Santa Fe in the fall of 1923, Riggs demonstrates his characteristic satirical wit and, in contrast to Mathews, uses the letter to draw attention to Indigenous politics in a settler–colonial context. The letter opens with Riggs telling Campbell about a visit to two pueblos with two women, including a Miss McKittrick, identified by Riggs as the secretary of the New Mexico Indian Association. "The Pueblo life must be wonderful," Riggs opines, "—the real communal life" (Riggs to Campbell, November 25, 1923). He adds a statement that parodies the view Anglo reformers held of Indigenous and Mexican people: "And to think of how they are being contaminated by the damned whites and stinking Mexicans! (You see I already speak the lingo of the Pueblo enthusiasts.)" Riggs explains that these enthusiasts, including Witter Bynner and Alice Corbin Henderson, "are trying to get a bill through Congress to settle up the land grant and prevent further encroachment on the Indians." Riggs shifts from politics to literature with observations about the literary journal *Laughing Horse*; life at Sunmount Sanatorium with other patients such as Momaday's future mentor, Yvor Winters; and comments about writers such as F. Scott Fitzgerald ("Damn Scott Fitzgerald!"), Robert Frost, and Willa Cather, his current reading interests. The letter conveys Riggs's attentiveness to the politics of federal Indian policy, his admiration for and idealization of Indigenous peoples of the Southwest, and his skepticism, made explicit in his mockery of their self-righteous prejudices against Anglo Americans and Mexicans, of the earnest reformers and Indian rights activists descending on Santa Fe during this period.

After sending Christmas greetings to Campbell and his wife in the form of six stanzas of doggerel dated "Xmas 1923," Riggs displays his acute sensitivity to stereotypes of American Indians and grows serious, or as serious as the often wonderfully daffy Riggs could be, about his literary labors. In a letter dated January 19, 1924, from Sunmount, Riggs relates his failed attempts to see Indian dances at San Ildefonso, San Felipe, and Santo Domingo Pueblos; tells Campbell the news that Alice Corbin Henderson had become a grandmother; and says of Mabel Dodge Luhan, "It is rumored that she is about to divorce Luhan, the Taos Indian, and marry a Chinaman in California" (Riggs to Campbell, January 19, 1924). He shares a humorous anecdote about "two little overalled tots" fooling his party into thinking that another dance was about to begin and another about a "tall Indian with a suitcase and a linen duster and an umbrella" who "scattered candy to the children and young ones, and cried in Spanish: 'How do you do? You nice Indians! I'm from New York and I think you're so interesting" (Riggs to Campbell, January 19, 1924). Riggs concludes the latter story: "And people are fond of believing they have no sense of humor." Riggs takes considerable enjoyment in the "tall Indian's" carefully planned performance, which mocks tourists from the East Coast.

This political commentary on the commodification and representation of indigeneity sits alongside one of Riggs's creative projects: he enclosed with the letter a self-published chapbook of twenty-seven mostly lyric poems entitled *Rhythm of Rain*. After drawing Campbell's attention to the enclosure as "a reminder that I am still alive," he adds only the brief comment "Hope you will like the 'Rhythm'" (Riggs to Campbell, January 19, 1924). These early poems, published in *Palms, Poetry,* the *Reviewer, Smart Set,* and the *University of Oklahoma Magazine,* contain often predictable rhymes and little variation in stanza form or line length.[42] Riggs must have later decided that the poems in *Rhythm of Rain* did not represent his best work. He did not publish any of them in *The Iron Dish* (1930), the only collection of his poetry to appear during his lifetime. Robert Dale Parker also does not include any of the poems that Riggs selected for *Rhythm of Rain* in *Changing Is Not Vanishing.* Yet the moving dedication to the Campbells, "For the ideal family—Mr. and Mrs. W. S. and M & D—with my love," suggests the chapbook's personal value as a gift from a young man in the process of recovering either from "consumption, severe depression, or a nervous breakdown" (Braunlich, *Haunted by Home,* 6). This recovery includes the search not only for physical and psychological health but for both a creative and a political voice. As the intimate linking of the letter with the chapbook demonstrates, Riggs worked on these projects simultaneously.

As their writing careers gained momentum at approximately the same time, this personal connection between Riggs and Campbell began to develop a sense of professional urgency. Campbell also sent a manuscript, a collection of ballads of the American West, to Riggs. Riggs explains his delayed response to the manuscript by telling Campbell that he wanted an opportunity to share it with a poetry club, perhaps similar to one held at Campbell's house from 1920 to 1923, that he had cofounded with Witter Bynner, Alice Corbin Henderson, and Haniel Long.[43] "If it can be arranged," he explains, "I am going to read the ballads, jot down all the criticism, and send it to you" (Riggs to Campbell, June 16, 1924). In the same letter, he refers to a work in progress called, all in capital letters, "SONNETS FROM A SANTA FE PRIVY." This moment of self-deprecating whimsy disguises, probably in a way that did not fool Campbell, the fact that Riggs was hard at work on both poems and plays. Later in the summer, Riggs writes again to let Campbell know that his plan to present the ballads at the poetry reading group, now identified as the Censors' Club, failed. Instead, he summarizes Long's and Bynner's criticism and encloses, separate from the letter, his own three and a half pages of comments (Riggs to Campbell, July 13, 1924). Riggs read the manuscript, eventually published as Campbell's first book, *Fandango: Ballads of the Old West* (1927), very carefully. He comments on the title and the foreword and gives detailed reflections and suggestions on individual ballads: "'Rapaho Gal" needs more "emotional content"; "Captain Gant" is "very weak"; "Little Chief" has a "very weak" line that "lessens the dramatic effect of Kit's speech"; "The Spanish Trail" has lines identified by Riggs as "not vivid and unusual enough," and the enemy in this ballad, Riggs says, "as in 'Captain Gant,' is unreal" (Riggs to Campbell, July 13, 1924). He concludes by saying "Don't like at all" of "Mistress White" and "Like enormously" of "Kit Carson's Last Smoke." Campbell, in turn, marked some of Riggs's comments in blue pen and even objected to a few of them. These exchanges between two writers still at the beginning of their careers, but with the younger, more precocious Riggs already achieving some national recognition, set the stage for Riggs to enter the same academic conversations that would soon include Mathews and other Native writers. In other words, these letters perform important literary and political labor.

Indeed, five years later Campbell found himself in a position to promote Riggs and his career. In a letter posted from Cagnes-sur-Mer, France, to Campbell in 1929, Riggs responds to a request from Campbell for information about his career for an article solicited by *Southwest Review*, by this point under the editorship of McGinnis. While Riggs feels flattered, he expresses anxiety about all his work. In response to a query about his literary approach, he tells Campbell, "I don't know where to begin. I honestly haven't any theories, any very definite aims (except to be a good dramatist), and I don't know any rules. All I am sure of is this: Drama to me, in full, is simply the effect of person upon person" (Riggs to Campbell, March 13, 1929). He discusses his work in progress, *Green Grow the Lilacs,* and why he continues to write about Oklahoma:

> The main reason, of course, is that I know more about the people I knew in childhood and youth than any others. But it so happens that I knew mostly the dark ones, the unprivileged ones, the ones with the most desolate fields, the most dismal skies. And so it isn't surprising that my plays concern themselves with poor farmers, forlorn wives, tortured youth, plow hands, pedlers, criminals, slaveys—with all the range of folk victimized by brutality, ignorance, superstition, and dread. And will it sound like an affectation (it most surely is not) if I say that I wanted to give a voice and a dignified existence to people who found themselves, most pitiably, without a voice, when there

was so much to be borne, so much to be cried out against? (Riggs to Campbell, March 13, 1929)[44]

He appends a list of twelve plays, including three destroyed and four produced, with a parenthetical note about his next one, *The Cherokee Night*, and he compliments Campbell on his Kit Carson book.[45]

Campbell, as Vestal, published the article "Lynn Riggs: Poet and Dramatist" in the Autumn 1929 issue of *Southwest Review*. The editors featured the article on the cover with stories on efforts to maintain global peace, French political life, and the history of Oxford, Mississippi. The issue also includes reviews of Frank C. Applegate's *Indian Stories from the Pueblos* and Oliver La Farge's *Laughing Boy*, as well as a poem entitled "Navajo" by University of New Mexico graduate Norman MacLeod, which appeared at the end of Campbell's contribution on Riggs. Campbell opens his article by situating Riggs in an English literary history:

> It is said that all good literature—which may be interpreted to include literary drama—is in the best sense provincial. Certainly the dramas of Lynn Riggs smack of the soil where he was born and bred with an intimacy and intensity which might do credit to Thomas Hardy or some other literary lover of an English village. In this, the work of Mr. Riggs is certainly in the best tradition of English literature. (64)

The biography that comprises the bulk of the article draws upon the notes that Riggs asked Clark to send to Campbell. While Campbell's observation that Riggs came from a line of "small ranchers or pioneer farmers" conveys only a partial truth, his neglect of Riggs's Cherokee family follows Riggs's own exclusion of it from the autobiographical notes (65). When he returns to Riggs as an artist near the end of the article, Campbell praises Riggs's lyricism, his ear for the speech of eastern Oklahoma, and his friend's increasingly mature later work. Riggs produces, Campbell argues, "genuinely fine drama" (71). It is a compelling piece of advocacy for Riggs's importance as a writer, though its racial politics (the whitewashing of Riggs) and colonial politics (the positioning of English literature as superior to American and Indigenous literatures) make it a deeply troubling document.

Riggs, apparently recognizing the professional value of having a friend in the academy, continued to update Campbell on his current projects. After informing Campbell that *Sump'n Like Wings* would probably go into production in the fall, he notes in a letter posted from Provincetown, Massachusetts:

> And the news about *Green Grow the Lilacs* is no further along. (I judge Ben has told you about it). The Theatre Guild has until Oct 1 to make up their minds. They may not take it. So please say nothing about it, unless you wish to intimate that a production is possibly in the offing. But please leave the Guild out of it. Such things get around, and as I say, they have a perfect right to refuse it even now. (Riggs to Campbell, September 16, 1929)

Riggs assumes gossip has taken place ("Ben has told you about it") and both discourages ("please say nothing") and encourages ("intimate that a production is possibly in the offing") it. After commenting on *Roadside* and *The Cherokee Night*, he returns to the topic of gossip by asking Campbell, cryptically, to "please leave Witter Bynner out of the story." By observing "things get around" and asking Campbell to help squash the "slightly embarrassing" tales of his departure from Norman in 1923, Riggs makes transparent the power of these networks to support, though also to undermine, Native writers.[46]

Riggs and Paul Green, a Pulitzer Prize–winning dramatist and professor at the University of North Carolina at Chapel Hill, also had a close personal and professional relationship animated by their literary aspirations and political commitments. Riggs once sent Green a "crime story," and Green forwarded it to Darryl Zanuck at Twentieth Century Pictures and shared it with his own story editor at Fox Film (Green to Riggs, May 25, 1933). Riggs also sent Green "Hamlet Not the Only," a manuscript of poems previously called "Of Oak and Innocence," on August 27, 1952. Green responded in a letter on September 4, 1952, to say he had contacted the University of North Carolina Press on behalf of Riggs. In a seventeen-page letter dated March 5, 1939, Riggs even entrusted Green with his manifesto "The Vine Theatre," which he conceived with Ramon Naya, his professional and romantic partner; Mary Hunter, a director and Mary Austin's niece; and Andrius Jilinsky, an acting teacher who had immigrated from Russia. In the letter, Riggs announces, "I am writing you now on a matter of great moment and importance to me" (275). After lamenting the state of a contemporary theater that constrains and destroys its artists, Riggs explains that creating a new theater will require "a clear and exact body of theory—in the way revolutions are made" (276). A draft of such a revolutionary theory follows this declaration in the form of thirty-five numbered points. Riggs and his cotheorists imagine a theater that "must change the cells of the people who come within its doors" (276). The Vine Theatre will be a "place of creation, not of destruction. The way to combat destructive forces is not by destruction. Rather our action will always be on creation" (277). Riggs shifts here to a more concrete statement of their concerns about both art and politics:

> In the world today, forces in opposition to the triumphant, arrogant state are demolished by pogrom, by discriminatory laws—and the other tools of inhumanity and cruelty. We do not believe that those forces really achieve their ends. We believe that the way to destroy is not to destroy. The way to change the world is to offer such a living and singing force that all people in whom the germ of truth resides, however deeply, will be drawn and changed by an instinctive need to ally themselves with life instead of death. (277)

The rest of the letter adheres to the hopeful idealism at the end of this passage: "The Vine Theatre, among other things, will remind human beings of the dignity of man" (283). Before providing a biography of Hunter, Jilinsky, and Naya, Riggs points to the significance of their diversity, calling Hunter "our Irish-American"; Jilinsky, "our Russian"; Naya, "our Mexican"; Green, "our white man in the south"; and himself, "our red Cherokee" (285). This last detail appears particularly significant, especially in the way that Riggs plays with "red" as a marker of radical interwar politics and indigeneity.

Riggs's references to the "triumphant, arrogant state" and its "tools of inhumanity and cruelty" evoke some of the events that shaped the decades to either side of his birth: allotment, statehood, and the attendant dismantling of tribal-nation governments. His self-identification in the document as Cherokee suggests that he had this tribal-nation history on his mind. However, Riggs was possibly also thinking about violence in the United States against striking laborers as well as Kristallnacht, which had occurred four months before he posted the letter. Six months later, on the day England and France declared war on Germany, he wrote to Green, "This is a terrible day for the world and we know that wherever we are the darkness hangs over us all" (Riggs to Green, September 3, 1939). Riggs, like the older Mathews and Dobie, eventually served in the army at Wright Field in Dayton, Ohio. This letter ends with Riggs stating his determination to continue with the Vine Theatre; "Yours in the Vine," he writes in the valediction, with Naya's signature next to his.

After Riggs's death, and with the Native American Renaissance on the horizon, Green worked to promote his legacy. His correspondence includes discussions in 1965 with Lucy Kroll, Riggs's agent, about Riggs's unfinished novel *An Affair at Easter* and "Hamlet Not the Only." He also gave advice in the spring and summer of 1955 to a University of Pennsylvania graduate student, Eloise Wilson, who was writing a dissertation on Riggs's use of folk materials; Barrett Clark found himself in a similar position at a drama conference in 1935, when he advised a University of Washington graduate student writing a master's thesis on "the American-stage Indian" to contact Riggs about her interest in the not-yet-published *Cherokee Night*.[47] Kroll had Macmillan interested in the novel, but Green said that the manuscript required too much work to prepare for publication. Instead, he suggests the "unpublished little collection of Lynn's poetry" (Green to Kroll, March 15, 1965). Kroll wrote back to say she has another writer for the novel project and asks about the poetry manuscript (Kroll to Green, April 21, 1965). Green responds:

> I don't know where the manuscript of Lynn's last collection of poems is. I thought you had it there in your office. It was returned to Lynn by the University of North Carolina Press before he died. Isn't there a sister or a brother in Oklahoma I could write to? If you have any information as to who might know about these poems I wish you would let me know. The poems, I think, would do more for Lynn's posthumous reputation than the novel. (Green to Kroll, April 21, 1965)[48]

Green's and Kroll's efforts on behalf of Riggs had even less impact on American Indian literary history than Dobie's support of Mathews: they did not succeed in publishing either the novel or the book of poems.

Green's and Kroll's enduring concern for Riggs's posthumous reputation parallels Campbell's for Mathews's and helps prepare the ground for scholars and activists in the next generation, when cultural and political shifts reactivated preexisting sites of literary and political interest in Native writers and created even more powerful new ones. Campbell, in fact, serves as an intellectual and political link between Riggs and Green, on one hand, and Mathews and Dobie, as well as other Native authors, on the other. In his correspondence with Mathews, Campbell mentions spending time at Yaddo with Riggs, and Mathews forwards a letter to Campbell from Ella Deloria, who had written to Mathews with a request for funds to support her research. Campbell and Mathews discussed their writing projects (Campbell's book of ballads, which Campbell had sent in manuscript form to Riggs, and his biographies of Sitting Bull and Kit Carson; Mathews's short stories and *Wah'Kon Tah*) as well as their personal lives: Campbell's frequently dire financial situation; Mathews's separation from his first wife. In a letter dated January 7, 1933, Campbell makes an assertion that sounds modest to Native literary studies scholars in the early-twenty-first century but that in the mid-twentieth century might have sounded revelatory: "I think we should make a concerted effort, you and I, to impress upon reviewers and editors the fact that Indians are people and that books about them may conceivably be literature" (Campbell to Mathews). Lamentable representations of American Indians even compelled Cherokee writer Ruth Muskrat Bronson a decade later to title her 1944 book *Indians Are People, Too*. Campbell's correspondence with Gertrude Bonnin and Luther Standing Bear, as well as N. Scott Momaday's mother, Natachee Scott Momaday, points to an even broader and unexamined network of literary scholars and American Indian writers in the immediate pre-Renaissance era. In January 1954, Natachee Scott Momaday sent Campbell a draft of her book *Owl in the Cedar Tree*. Posted from Jemez Pueblo, the setting of most of her son's novel *House Made of Dawn*, the letter conveys a sense of excitement and some urgency about the book, which the University of New Mexico Press had rejected. Momaday writes as "a former student and loyal friend" with a plea that Campbell help get the book published (Natachee Scott Momaday to Campbell, January 27, 1954). Campbell took *Owl* to the University of Oklahoma Press, but they rejected it, too. He suggests trying the University of New Mexico Press again and offers to send his own comments on it (Campbell to Natachee Scott Momaday, June 18, 1954). In a letter dated a week later, he provides detailed suggestions while calling the book "sweet, wholesome and charming" (Campbell to Natachee Scott Momaday, June 22, 1954). The book did not reach print until 1965.

The private correspondence between Native writers and their friends and fellow writers employed in university English departments reveals a more extensive record of and interest in Native writing by academics in the mid-twentieth century than post-Renaissance scholarship acknowledges. In addition to the presence of Native writers in Dobie's bibliographies, Campbell included Mathews and Francis La Flesche, D'Arcy McNickle, Riggs, and Rogers, as well as Choctaw historian Muriel Wright, in *The Book Lover's Southwest: A Guide to Good Reading* (1955).[49] Mary Tucker's *Books of the Southwest* has entries for Mathews's *Sundown* as well as works by Edmund Nequatewa, James Paytiamo, and Arthur C. Parker. Mabel Major, Rebecca Smith, and T. M. Pearce begin the first edition of *Southwest Heritage* with "Myth, Legend, and Song of the Indian" and later list *Sundown* and *Wah'Kon-Tah* by Mathews, as well as the novel *Brother's Three* by John Milton Oskison, poems by Alexander Posey, poems and seven plays by Lynn Riggs, newspaper columns by Will Rogers, and works by Paytiamo and Standing Bear. The second edition, published in 1948, contains a revised opening section, "Poetry and Prose of the Indian," and includes Isleta Pueblo author Louise Abeita's *I Am a Pueblo Indian Girl* (1939) in a new section called "Literature for Children." Major and Pearce's *Signature of the Sun: Southwest Verse, 1900–1950* (1950) includes poems by Abeita, Posey, and Riggs and, in the introduction to "Part I: Pueblo, Hogan and Tepee," one reference to Cherokee novelist and poet John Rollin Ridge. This first section of *Signature of the Sun* opens with Washington Matthews's translation of a prayer from the Navajo Night Chant, from which N. Scott Momaday drew the title and part of the structure of his award-winning novel.[50] Charles Hamilton's *Cry of the Thunderbird* (1950) provides an even starker reminder of the daunting intellectual and political boundary formed by the civil rights and Renaissance era between American Indian literary history pre- and post-1968. Hamilton's collection covers an impressive number of American Indian writers, including the subjects of recovery efforts, such as William Apess, Joseph Nicolar, and Samson Occom, in the 1990s and the first decade of the twenty-first century. Andrew Blackbird, George Copway, David Cusick, Ella Deloria, Charles Alexander Eastman, E. Pauline Johnson, Peter Jones, Francis La Flesche, Mourning Dove, Narcissa Owen, Simon Pokagon,

Alexander Posey, John Rollin Ridge, William Warren, among others, also appear. Surprisingly, Mathews does not; nor do Todd Downing, D'Arcy McNickle, Oskison, or Riggs, for example.

One particular characteristic of this academic network, however, also makes plain the deeply embedded social, cultural, and political barriers all Indigenous authors faced: when they wrote a letter to a friend employed by a university, this correspondence always went to a non-Native. Settler–colonial racial politics shaped all their communications. In the end, too, neither Dobie nor Campbell drew cultural, historical, or political connections between Mathews, Riggs, and other American Indian writers, and they did not see Mathews or Riggs as part of a group of Native American writers or a movement with shared aesthetic, cultural, or political goals. Satisfactory intellectual engagement also does not necessarily accompany inclusion in a scholarly conversation. However, Mathews and Riggs gained access through Dobie and Campbell to an influential academic network and a broader reading public. Dobie in particular made a case, mostly unheard until Warrior's book, for the importance of reading Mathews.

The many early- and mid-twentieth-century Native writers and their correspondents and acquaintances in the academy helped prepare the political, intellectual, and institutional ground for the Native American Renaissance. This ground included the *New Mexico Quarterly,* the journal founded by Pearce and modeled on the *Southwest Review,* in which Campbell's laudatory piece on Riggs appeared in 1929. N. Scott Momaday's first publication, the poem "Earth and I Gave You Turquoise," appeared in the Summer 1959 issue of the *New Mexico Quarterly.* In its evocation of a southwestern landscape, it recalls poems such as "Spring Morning—Santa Fe," "Santo Domingo Corn Dance," and "Morning Walk—Santa Fe" by Riggs, Yvor Winters's old acquaintance. Momaday, had he read "Spring Morning—Santa Fe," might have paused with some pleasure at the sonnet's first line: "The first hour was a word the color of dawn" (Riggs, *Iron Dish,* 6). The *New Mexico Quarterly* also published two selections from *House Made of Dawn* in the Summer 1967 issue to promote the forthcoming novel and Silko's first work of fiction, "The Man to Send Rain Clouds," in Winter 1968.[51] This recovery of the private (letters) and public (bibliographies and journal publications) American Indian literary history of the mid-twentieth century situates the Renaissance in new contexts and links it to a new set of nuanced and vexed political arrays.

CHAPTER 5

Crimes against Indigeneity

The Politics of Native American Detective Fiction

The American Indians are "unemotional" and exhibit their "accustomed stoicism" in Sir Arthur Conan Doyle's first Sherlock Holmes mystery, *A Study in Scarlet* (1887), in which the murderer "possessed also a power of sustained vindictiveness, which he may have learned from the Indians amongst whom he had lived" (82, 105). Conan Doyle, who had a strong but imperfectly informed interest in Native Americans and the U.S. West, equivocally suggests Native Americans as one possible stimulus for the crimes in the novel that introduced readers to the world's most famous detective.[1] Part 2 of the novel, set during the settler–colonial occupation of the land that became Utah, situates the homicides under Holmes's investigation in the history of Mormon immigration to and assertion of control over the region. Settler–colonial development of the U.S. West was a bloody business indeed, and as the Mormons in *A Study in Scarlet* begin to build Salt Lake City, the enforcement of church rules by its fundamentalist leaders generates the acts of violence and retribution that drive the plot. The dispossession of Paiutes, Utes, and Shoshones (and, to the east and north, the Pawnees and Blackfeet mentioned by Conan Doyle) remains obscured by Conan Doyle's descriptions of an uninhabited wasteland into which the Mormons journeyed, a small part of the North American world that historian Roxanne Dunbar-Ortiz calls a "crime scene" (228). Yet Conan Doyle's obfuscation of this history of dispossession is not so much a mystery as a familiar narrative convention as well as a tacit acknowledgment of the daunting task facing anyone investigating colonial crimes. He imagined some truly baffling cases for Sherlock Holmes to solve, but he could not come to terms with the crimes—local, regional, continental, hemispheric, global—committed by European colonial powers and settler–colonial states.

Writing by American Indians has always focused on colonial and settler–colonial crime: homicide and mass murder; sexual assault; the theft of land, cultural property, and human remains; the violation of treaties; police brutality. While these crimes appear in all genres, Native novelists have produced an especially extensive and coherent tradition of dramatizing them. Cherokee author John Rollin Ridge published *The Life and Adventures of Joaquín Murieta, the Celebrated California Bandit*, the first novel by a Native author, in 1854. Murieta, the Mexican protagonist, and his wife face many of the same violent outrages that Native Americans had long endured during the settler–colonial expansion of the United States. Throughout the novel, Murieta fights desperately but futilely against the California legal authorities hunting him. Though Murieta is Mexican rather than Native American, Ridge introduces what became a familiar feature of plots in novels by Native authors: protagonists unprotected and often explicitly targeted by agents of state and federal law and other settler–colonial institutions. This focus on settler–colonial crime in Indian Country can be traced consistently in Native literary history, both pre- and post-Renaissance, from *Murieta* through many other novels, such as John Milton Oskison's *Black Jack Davy* (1926), Mourning Dove's *Cogewea* (1927), D'Arcy McNickle's *Wind from an Enemy Sky* (1978), Linda Hogan's *Mean Spirit* (1990), Gerald Vizenor's *The Heirs of Columbus* (1991), Thomas King's *Green Grass, Running Water* (1993), and Louise Erdrich's *The Round House* (2012). For the debut of Sherlock Holmes, in fact, Conan Doyle drew upon a context, settler–colonial development in the United States, in which Native authors also frequently situate their crime narratives: the oil industry in *Mean Spirit*, for example, and hydroelectric dams in *Wind from an Enemy Sky* and *Green Grass, Running Water*.

By the time Choctaw author Todd Downing published *Murder on Tour* (1933), the first detective novel by a Native American writer, Native writers had already adopted fiction to publicize and condemn the criminal acts committed against Native people and expose a legal system indifferent or antagonistic to them. Downing introduced to Native literary history a genre that allowed authors to focus on settler–colonial crime in a popular and predictable form. The authors under consideration in this chapter, Downing included, hew closely to the murder mystery type of detective novel, which has as its three major components, Charles Rzepka explains, "detective, mystery, investigation" as well as, in some cases, a "puzzle-element" providing readers the opportunity to try to solve the crime along with the detective (*Detective*

Fiction, 10). Native authors reveal detective fiction as particularly well-suited to investigating the settler–colonial context that Glen Coulthard describes as "characterized by a particular form of *domination*; that is, it is a relationship where power ... has been structured into a relatively secure or sedimented set of hierarchal social relations that continue to facilitate the *dispossession* of Indigenous peoples of their lands and self-determining authority" (6–7; emphasis in the original). In most of Downing's nine novels and one novella, Anglo citizens of the United States commit crimes in Mexico and, in some cases, against Indigenous Mexicans. Hugh Rennert, a retired customs officer and the detective figure in the first seven novels, relentlessly follows the clues to catch the perpetrators and bring justice to the victims. While Downing did not maximize the genre's possibilities for deeply engaging the legacies of settler colonialism, his work anticipates post-civil-rights-era detective novels, examples of what Rzepka calls "alternative detection" (*Detective Fiction*, 235), by Native authors, such as Thomas King, Carole laFavor, Sara Sue Hoklotubbe, Louis Owens, and Ron Querry. Rzepka observes, "Alternative detective writers seek to challenge traditional assumptions about the nationality, race, and gender of investigative authority by placing a culturally non-conforming protagonist in the position of primary investigator. Typically, this person will bring to the task of investigation skills and abilities not ordinarily attributed to Western, white, male detectives, and face obstacles that his or her traditional counterparts need never face" (235–36). King, laFavor, and Hoklotubbe use detective fiction to expose the historical and contemporary crimes that emerge from and sustain settler–colonial states and, in some cases, to imagine worlds in which Native people have the opportunity to enforce, rather than face the coercive force of, the law. The political arrays in their detective novels include expressions of moderate to more vehement prosovereignty and anticolonial positions, while the divergent gender and sexual politics of laFavor's and Hoklotubbe's novels also discourage ascribing to these works a single, narrow political perspective.

The Golden Age Roots of Native American Detective Fiction

The mass murder of Indigenous people and the theft of land and property, the criminal acts that precede settler–colonial development, occupy a central role in Native literary history. In *Murieta*, "a band of lawless men" sexually assault Murieta's mistress and drive him from his land before a "company of unprincipled Americans" dispossesses him a second time (10). Several additional outrages send Murieta on a mission of revenge that ends with his death and postmortem decapitation. The protagonist of Mourning Dove's *Cogewea*, the young "half-blood" Okanogan woman of the title, finds herself bound to a tree by Alfred Densmore, the easterner who schemes to dispossess her of the cattle and "vast tracts of land" that he mistakenly believes she owns (262).[2] He assaults Cogewea and robs her of one thousand dollars, but, claiming that she has participated in the deception that led him to believe in her affluence, he says, "I am tempted to turn you over to the proper authorities to be dealt with according to the just laws of our land!" (263). As Densmore accurately observes, "The law is of the white man's make, interpreted by the white man, made to talk by the white man's money. . . . You have no witnesses! It would be my word against yours; a white gentlemen's against an Injun squaw's" (264). Both of these early Native novelists depict the U.S. legal system as an enabler of settler–colonial crime, specifically the theft of land and property, and a force that protects rather than punishes settler–colonial criminals.

John Milton Oskison's *Black Jack Davy*, his 1926 novel set in the Cherokee Nation in Indian Territory a few years prior to Oklahoma statehood in 1907, tells the dramatic story of successful efforts to foil a plot to steal Native land. "Black Jack" Davy Dawes and his foster parents arrive in Indian Territory and lease land from Ned Warrior. They learn immediately that Jerry Boyd, another non-Native immigrant to the Cherokee Nation, "wants to get hold of all this land between the river and Horsepen creek—more than three thousand acres" (19). Boyd, "the deliberately scheming, merciless and powerful enemy" (97), spends the novel devising plans to gain ownership of Warrior's land and eventually joins forces with the outlaw Jack Kitchin and his gang to attack Warrior. Warrior successfully defends his land, though, and, as the novel ends, makes plans to partner with Davy. Boyd, the narrator tells us, "was sure to be convicted and sent to prison for a long term," along with his allies (307). Oskison draws clear distinctions between settlers like the Dawes family, who abide by the laws of the Cherokee Nation and the United States, and those like Boyd, who break the law and try to use both legal systems to their advantage. At the same time, the Dawes family ominously carries the surname of the politician who sponsored one of the most destructive pieces of legislation for American Indians in U.S. history: the 1887 General Allotment Act, or the Dawes Act. By making Ned Warrior a fictionalized version of the Cherokee leader and cultural hero Ned Christie, who was falsely accused of murdering a U.S. marshal and killed during a posse's assault on his home with a cannon and dynamite, Oskison also highlights the capriciousness of law enforcement in a settler–colonial context.

Other authors from this era also incorporate local battles between Native Americans and legal authorities into their novels. In *The Surrounded,* D'Arcy McNickle (Confederated Salish and Kootenai), as Robert Dale Parker explains, draws on a fatal encounter in 1908 in which "a white game warden and deputy shot and killed four Flathead hunters, three men and a boy, who shot and killed the warden and wounded the deputy" (*The Invention of Native American Literature,* 60). *Sundown* by John Joseph Mathews briefly considers the Osage oil boom in the early 1920s, when, within the same context of corruption in Oklahoma's legal and financial institutions under investigation by Bonnin and her coauthors in *Oklahoma's Poor Rich Indians,* white men killed Osages to gain control of their headrights and the oil royalties that came with them (Mathews, *Sundown,* 305). Dennis McAuliffe Jr., in *Bloodland,* the narrative of his attempt to discover if his white grandfather had killed his Osage grandmother, observes that the discovery of oil on Osage land made them "the richest people, per capita, in the world" (42). Following this discovery, a shocking increase in the number of homicides in the Osage Nation led the FBI in 1923 to begin investigating what it called the "Osage Indian Murders." They counted twenty-four murders, though, McAuliffe notes, "Other counts went as high as 45 to 60 by that time" (250). The evidence, he discovered, indicates an even higher number. He quotes an FBI document from July 24, 1925, that refers to "hundreds and hundreds" of murder cases. Even the lowest number made the Osages "the most-murdered people per capita in the world" (251). Linda Hogan (Chickasaw) made these murders the centerpiece of the aforementioned novel *Mean Spirit.*

A criminal act by local police also made international news the summer Todd Downing began writing the first American Indian detective novel in the middle of detective fiction's Golden Age. Deputy sheriffs in Ardmore, Oklahoma, about seventy miles from his home in Atoka, murdered Emilio Cortes Rubio and Manuel Gomez on June 8, 1931. Salvatore

Cortes Rubio, who survived the shooting, was, like Emilio Cortes Rubio, a cousin of Pascual Ortiz Rubio, president of Mexico from 1930 to 1932. The deputy sheriffs were tried and acquitted; the U.S. government sent the Cortes Rubio and Gomez families fifteen thousand dollars each. The diplomatic crisis resulted in the cancellation of the summer tour that Downing had planned to lead in Mexico. Instead, he started writing detective fiction. The murder of Mexican citizens by U.S. law enforcement in 1931 provides a circumstantial though tragic link in Native literary history to Ridge's novel about Joaquín Murieta. Rather than writing novels about settler–colonial crimes, however, Downing adopted the detective novel form in order to stage crimes against indigeneity with the express purpose of solving them and exposing and punishing the criminals. He claims the detective, "the defender of hegemonic norms and self-perpetuating cultural value systems" (Rzepka, *Detective Fiction*, 22), or the defender of settler–colonial norms and cultural value systems, as a potential ally to Indigenous people, even if one still constrained by settler–colonial law and custom.

Downing devotes portions of the main plots of two novels to a common settler–colonial crime, the theft of and trade in Indigenous remains and artifacts, which tribal nations have expended considerable political energy fighting. In his first novel, *Murder on Tour*, the criminals use a tour group as cover for smuggling stolen goods out of Mexico and into the United States. Hugh Rennert describes the crime to a colleague as "a new racket—or rather an old, old one conducted on a business-like, wholesale basis" (223). Following this observation, he condemns public museums and private collectors as well as "artists and explorers resident in Mexico" for participating in the illegal trade. While the trade in remains and artifacts in Downing's fifth novel, *The Case of the Unconquered Sisters* (1936), has official sanction, an inspector for the Mexican Department of Archaeology gives his legal authorization for it only after requesting bribes and sending forgeries to U.S. museums in order to make the originals available for illegal sale. The inspector's partner in the offense, a former university professor, explains to Rennert that he had agreed readily to pay the bribes to help his new employer, a small San Antonio museum, quickly increase the size of its collections. Together, these novels indict the bureaucracies, institutions, and tourist economies of settler–colonial states for enabling these crimes against Indigenous peoples.

Downing's fourth novel, *Murder on the Tropic* (December 1935), takes a stand against settler–colonial dispossession and development within the specific political context of federal Indian policy reform in Mexico. The novel begins in San Antonio in the office of Edward Solier, a venture capitalist who tells Rennert that he purchased a hacienda and sold shares in his company to raise funds to build a hotel near the still uncompleted Pan-American Highway. When he discovers the inside information on the route of the highway is inaccurate, Solier attempts to buy back the shares. One shareholder, Bertha Fahn, "an old maid from Austin," refuses to sell her interest (6), and Solier hires Rennert to persuade her and solve an ostensibly minor mystery: the disappearance of the hacienda's drinking water. On his arrival at the hacienda, Rennert meets the new co-owners; the employees, including Maria and Miguel Montemayor; and Esteban Flores, the son of the former owners and, like Emilio Cortes Rubio and Manuel Gomez, a student at a Kansas college (76). Flores explains that his father sold the hacienda because "under this government it is impossible for an *hacendado* to live" (104–5), a reference to the agrarian land reform under President Lázaro Cárdenas's administration (1934–1940). Historian Ben Fallaw calls agrarian reform "the keystone of Cardenista state formation" (37). Global economic issues and political opposition from a wide variety of groups within Mexico challenged Cárdenas at every turn. By mid-1936, Fallaw asserts, the program "was a near-disaster" (161). In 1935, though, supporters of agrarian reform, including foreign visitors like Downing, still optimistically envisioned the Mexican government returning some economic and political autonomy to Indigenous people.

Downing's optimism about the future for Indigenous people in Mexico informs his representation in *Murder on the Tropic* of Maria Montemayor, whose self-sufficiency and devotion to her family show her activating the "intimate domestic," to draw once again on Piatote, as a site of political struggle.[3] Maria, "a pure Mexican aborigine" with a last name suggesting immense power (36), has lost a son prior to Rennert's arrival.[4] Her husband has also contracted an illness, and she gathers plants in the mountains to treat him (41). Downing reinforces Maria's links to plants and the earth when Esteban Flores, whose surname translates into English as "flowers," tells Rennert, "Since her own son died she spends all her time with her flowers. I think ... that she feels that he is living again in them" (103). Downing's romanticizing of Maria reaches a climax after Rennert learns that the local doctor had failed to save her son from helminthiasis, an infestation of parasitic worms, an affliction Rennert connects to another doctor's passing comments about a "terrible fatality among native children" in a small Gulf town (139).[5] In an act of mourning that initially drew the attention of Flores and finally reveals to Rennert the solution to the mystery of the missing water, Maria has been watering the flowers over her son's grave in the courtyard. After his discovery, Rennert muses:

> She stood, the embodiment of the Mexico that stands self-sufficient by the side of the road while conquering armies march by, to be replaced in days or years or centuries (it doesn't matter) by other armies under other banners. *Along the paved highway to the east,* Rennert thought, *will come another, more dreadful army with billboards and refreshment stands and blatant automobile horns, but Maria and her kind will stand when they have passed by.* (191–92; italics in the original)

Downing identifies multiple layers of colonial and settler–colonial invasion and development, from the Spanish and Mexican militaries—the "conquering armies"—to the emergent settler colonials from the United States seeking to exploit new markets and, in the case of Solier, evade U.S. and Mexican laws prohibiting casinos.

Maria's primary character traits distinguish her from the novel's avaricious Mexican and U.S. settler–colonial antagonists: Flores, who has returned to the hacienda to search for the "family plate and jewels" hidden by his grandfather (234), and the new owners, who have in fact purchased the hacienda in order to build an illegal casino. "A great opportunity, you'll admit," Solier says to Rennert, before continuing, "We rigged up this scheme among us—to form a company and sell shares for a hotel before it was known generally just where the highway would go" (258). Solier adds that he always knew the planned route of the highway but lied to investors, who felt relief when he offered to buy back the shares for an apparently doomed project. The large-scale fraud then leads to multiple murders. In addition, after Maria's remedies do not cure her husband, Rennert's investigation reveals his death as the consequence, though unintended, of Solier's scheme. Maria stands alone at the novel's end as the embodiment of an Indigenous moral center opposed to Flores and Solier while also complementing, from a socially, culturally, and politically much less powerful position, Rennert's legal authority and white male privilege.

Rennert's lyrical pronouncements on romanticized Indigenous worlds stoically enduring waves of invasion do not represent a satisfying substitute for real political programs. The novel more forcefully challenges the threat posed by the opening of rural Mexican life to U.S. business interests than Mexican settler colonialism or even Rennert's own participation in the U.S. settler–colonial history that made possible his life in retirement as the owner of a citrus farm in the lower Rio Grande Valley. Yet in the 1930s, as reform attempts by Roosevelt's Office of Indian Affairs under Collier paralleled the work of the Cárdenas administration in Mexico, Downing gives readers a tentatively optimistic view of Indigenous survival and endurance. From within Native American literary history, too, the novel consolidates and more narrowly focuses the deep suspicion of exploitative settler–colonial economic systems already apparent in the few novels published by Native authors before Downing. Within and among his detective novels, Downing develops arrays of political positions, for example, on settler colonialism, Indigenous cultural practices and property, and gendered modes of resistance. Linking them explicitly to arrays in preceding and succeeding eras of American Indian literary history reveals political convergences and divergences, either unexpected or anticipated, depending on the reader, but in each case necessary to efforts to map how Native authors throughout that literary history bring their politics to the page.

Contemporary Native Detective Fiction

Detective fiction reemerged in the second generation of the Renaissance in the 1990s, a decade in which Native authors such as laFavor, Owens, and Querry turned to the genre that Downing so effectively used to expose and condemn settler–colonial crimes. King and Hoklotubbe, as well as D. L. Birchfield (Choctaw) and Marcie Rendon (White Earth Anishinabe), joined them after the turn of the century. The detective novel's focus on crime and the investigation of and punishment for it allows these authors to devote their imaginative efforts to exposing historical and contemporary crimes against Indigenous people and communities. Some of these novels contain the most compelling condemnations of enduring settler–colonial depredations and the most unambiguous demonstrations of Native sovereign acts in the Native novel tradition. They also reclaim legal authority for Indigenous people and, in laFavor's and Hoklotubbe's novels, invest Native women with social and political, rather than religious and often primarily symbolic, authority. While moderately to more radically progressive within the post-civil-rights and reactionary 1994 "Republican Revolution" context in which the earliest of these novels emerged, their narratives contain richly textured political arrays produced as the authors represent the romantic, legal, and cultural bonds and conflicts among their characters. Yet these novels remain overlooked as significant contributions, both literarily and politically, to American Indian literary history.

Ojibwa author Carole laFavor represents one of the more unfortunate oversights by scholars, myself included.[6] Lisa Tatonetti describes her as "a powerful voice for social justice and Indigenous health sovereignty in Minnesota and the nation" but "best known for serving as an influential voice for Indigenous people with HIV/AIDS" ("Detecting," 272).[7] Her 1996 novel *Along the Journey River* follows former American Indian Movement activist and current part-time teacher, beadworker, and basket maker Renee LaRoche of the Red Earth Reservation in Minnesota as she investigates the theft of religious items and ancient human remains.[8] By imagining the life of an AIM member many years after she joined her fellow activists at Alcatraz and in Washington, D.C., and gave birth to a daughter with an activist father still on the run from the FBI, laFavor positions her novel in the activist history central to the literary scholarship on the Native American Renaissance while also encouraging critical reflection on that history.[9] By making the former activist a "tribal dreamer" and a "traditional artist" invested in multiple revitalization projects, laFavor gives her protagonist additional political credibility as a fierce defender of Ojibwa cultural sovereignty (80, 108).[10] As a lesbian, or two-spirit, raising her fourteen-year-old daughter, Jenny, a powwow dancer, with her white partner, Samantha Salisbury, LaRoche also occupies an explicitly feminist political position in an era in which "Don't ask, don't tell" and the 1996 Defense of Marriage Act were federal policy.[11] Finally, as the novel's amateur detective entrusted by the tribal police with investigative powers, LaRoche occupies a position of civil and legal authority but without the constraints under which those Ojibwas wearing badges must operate.[12] The novel adopts left-of-center politics on Indigenous cultural and environmental issues and, more implicitly, on gay and lesbian rights, though it also suggests that working with the settler–colonial legal apparatus, including AIM's nemesis, the FBI, can lead to justice for Native people.

LaFavor follows Downing by focusing on the theft of Indigenous remains and artifacts in her first novel, which she published after the federal government passed the Archaeological Resources Protection Act (ARPA) in 1979 and, in 1990, the Native American Graves Protection and Repatriation Act (NAGPRA). ARPA regulates, through an official permit process, excavations on public and Native lands and prohibits selling or purchasing any artifacts discovered by people not in compliance with the new rules. NAGPRA provides for the return of cultural objects and human remains from federal institutions to tribal nations and requires the repatriation of items discovered on tribal-nation or federal land. Like Downing in *Murder on Tour* and *The Case of the Unconquered Sisters* but with greater specificity and more sustained outrage, laFavor situates this illegal trade in a broad pattern of criminal acts committed against the people of Red Earth—the destruction of burial grounds by farmers, for example, as well as sexual assault and land theft by railroad and lumber companies. She also links the thefts on Red Earth to a crime wave at Indigenous sites across the United States and to what LaRoche calls an "international conspiracy" (103). Deputy Jesse Johnson, a crime scene investigator for the Red Earth Tribal Police, shares with LaRoche a phone conversation with Dr. Laura Begay, a Navajo archaeologist, in which Begay discusses the systematic "illegal looting of Indian sites" for "collectors in Germany and Japan" (104). Near the end of the novel, LaRoche speaks to Begay directly. Begay tells her, "Well, Renee, the markets of Paris, Tokyo, Hong Kong, and Germany claim thousands of artifacts a year. There are no laws to protect archaeological ruins except the one passed in 1979 making it illegal to buy, sell, or transport items of, quote, 'interest that were wrongly obtained, such as relics taken by trespassers'" (175). She explains that developers and excavators must tell authorities if they uncover a site, but they sometimes do not comply with the law.[13]

The criminals in the novel subvert these laws. Two tribal-nation citizens, the thoroughly villainous chairman and a young man lured into the scheme by the promise of easy money, join various non-Native locals in the criminal enterprise, though a non-Native resident scholar at a "conservative think tank" at Stanford University serves as the key player in the United States (161). A non-Native professor at Columbia, readers learn late in the novel, operates the East Coast wing of the illegal trade. A powerful sense of settler–colonial entitlement informs the think tank's vehement opposition to the repatriation of artifacts required by NAGPRA. By making the main criminals professors at two of the most prestigious educational institutions in the United States, laFavor replicates one of Downing's favorite narrative strategies—professors appear regularly as criminals in his novels—and confirms Native writers' and activists' enduring suspicion of university-based scholars.

LaFavor positions women as the cultural and political center of Red Earth in the opening pages, which find Renee on her way to see her grandmother and share information about the theft of a "pipe, cradleboard, eagle bone whistle, flute, [and] rattle" from a display case in the local high school (10). Throughout the novel, laFavor situates this crime as a representative one of many. LaRoche recalls the theft of artifacts discovered in a cave seventy-five miles from Red Earth with a nine-thousand-year-old skeleton called Browns Valley Man, and readers learn that authorities caught a reservation priest, Father Ambrose, "selling tribal goods back East" in the early 1930s (25, 34). LaRoche also hears a radio report about grave robbers targeting "burial sites of the Navajo, Zuni, and Lakota people" (52), and she reads an article in a Minneapolis newspaper with "a Native American perspective" about the recovery of stolen Zuni artifacts (94–95). In her efforts to solve the crime and, in the end, expose an international conspiracy, she relies almost exclusively for support on women: her partner, who works as a writer and professor; her daughter and grandmother, the latter a source of stories about Anishinabe origins and Nanabozho; and Jesse Johnson, the young deputy on the tribal police force.[14] LaFavor puts into literary practice what Cheryl Suzack identifies as the intellectual work of American Indian feminist critics: these critics, and laFavor in her novels, "[theorize] a relationship between community identity, tribal history, and women's collective agency in order to create an oppositional space from which to restore gender identity as an analytical category in discussions of tribal politics and community values" (171). LaFavor imagines a robust Indigenous feminism in the tradition outlined by Suzack and Shari Huhndorf in their coauthored introduction to *Indigenous Women and Feminism* and practiced artistically by many Native women, including, alongside laFavor in the 1990s, Susan Power (Standing Rock Dakota) in *The Grass Dancer* (1994), Winona LaDuke (Anishinabe) in *Last Standing Woman* (1997), and Linda Hogan (Chickasaw) in *Solar Storms* (1995) and *Power* (1998).[15]

Despite her suspicion of police authorities resulting from her history in AIM, the false accusation leveled against Jenny's father, and the beating and imprisonment of her brother, Ben, after a "trumped-up possession of heroin charge" (29), LaRoche works to solve the crime with the tribal police, led by Chief Hobert "Hobey" Bulieau. The omniscient narrator hints at LaRoche's anxiety about joining forces with the police: "She knew how different tribal police departments could be from one another. Some were as corrupt as the U.S. government—harassing people, using public funds for private enjoyment, aligning themselves with Feds against their own. Others were ineffective, made up of drunks and losers and deputies who understood little or nothing about keeping the peace" (29). Other tribal police departments, however, envisioned their goal as "keeping the peace . . . in the traditional way of providing safety, honor, and respect" (29). Bulieau practices this latter kind of police work; he "had restored the old ways to the Red Earth tribal police" (30). In *Along the Journey River*, Ojibwas like Bulieau, informed by Ojibwa tradition, or "the old ways," can make a police institution built on settler–colonial models both effective and honorable in a Native community. The novel, therefore, conveys trust in a particular kind of police authority that would probably concern some activists and that, during the most active years of AIM, might have led to accusations of collaboration with the enemy.

LaRoche even loses her initial suspicion of federal agents. In free indirect discourse aligned with LaRoche, laFavor opines, "Feds were not a welcome species on the rez, especially with the elders. They were just another invader's face: starting with the missionaries, evolving into the cavalry, becoming the pioneers, who turned into immigrants to railroad barons to the FBI" (46). When FBI agents Lawton and Lancaster arrive, they request an interview with Walter Leaper, a Red Earth resident who discovered the gun used to kill the chief, Jed Morriseau. To LaRoche's amusement, Leaper pretends to speak only Anishinabemowin. "The Feds finally gave up on Walter," laFavor explains, "recording once again the 'total lack of cooperation' they received on the reservation" (48). Their appearance at the tribal police station elicits an even more antagonistic response from Chief Bulieau, who "stared down the two agents. Stared down five hundred years of disrespect and lies, of arrogance and murder. Stared them down for all the times as a little boy, clutching his BIA ID card, he would line up for commodities for the family, load them into his rickety wagon, and before he'd be allowed to leave with the month's food allotment, have to 'dance like an Indian' for the Federals" (57). After requesting some help with the case from the FBI, Bulieau reports, "Lawton called D.C. after I talked to him last Thursday. The good ol' boy came through for us. Did it in a friendly manner, too, which surprised me even more" (143). As the case draws to a close, LaRoche, the tribal police, and officers from the Chippewa County Sheriff's Department look for evidence together. The narrator observes, "The irony of Indians and *chimooks* coming to understand and even to like each other a little better in Peterson's office was not lost on either the Ojibwa woman or the others. It turned out that Deputy Ewald was dating a Red Earther and had just received a belt buckle from her, made by Renee, for his birthday" (172). The novel, therefore, represents a détente between Indigenous people and local and federal authorities, even though it rigorously foregrounds left-leaning grassroots activism as its primary political orientation.

This network of women, with the help of Bulieau and Lawton, works against an almost exclusively white male criminal enterprise, a rogue's gallery of settler–colonial villains: Dr. Lawrence Toole, head of the Hoover Scholastic Institute at Stanford and one of the U.S.-based masterminds; Gerald Peterson, the county medical examiner; Lou Blank, the county coroner and Peterson's coworker; half-brothers John Anderson, an employee of the family excavation company, and Peter Thompson, a parolee from Attica. As a group, these men express contempt for Indigenous people and, in Lou Blank's case, commit hate crimes against them. The narrator notes, "During high school, Blank and the other jack-booted thugs liquored up, piled into trucks, and raided pow wows to bash heads" (15). They also exhibit a bitter white male privilege that informs their resentment of laws that protect American Indian cultural patrimony.

Two citizens of Red Earth, tribal chairman Jed Morriseau and Billy Walking Bear, give this criminal network access to the community. Morriseau was "a mean and vicious man" who brutally and repeatedly beat and sexually assaulted his sister (44, 59). One reservation resident calls him "Windigo," a reference to a powerful, frightening manitou and a kind of sickness that leads one to act like it (55).[16] An anonymous call leads Bulieau to Morriseau's corpse near the beginning of the novel. His shooter remains a mystery until the end of the novel, when laFavor suggests that his sister hired a man to kill him. Billy Walking Bear, in contrast to Morriseau, lost his grandfather before his vision quest and then lost his way.[17] Enticed to join the thieves by the promise of money, he regrets the decision and comes to LaRoche for help. This representation of a tribal government leader recalls what Paul Chaat Smith and Robert Warrior call "arguably, the finest moment in AIM's brief and often troubled history" (200): their decision in 1973 to intervene in the "political emergency" at Pine Ridge Reservation, where citizens were protesting Tribal Chairman Dick Wilson's authoritarian rule. In laFavor's loose adaptation of this activist event, the tribal police and tribal nation citizens become the defenders of Red Earth. In comparison to AIM's militant activism, LaRoche's alliance with the tribal police, and eventually with county officials and the FBI, looks much more moderate if not conservative politically. In *Evil Dead Center,* the second and last LaRoche novel, LaRoche even comments to Chief Bulieau that working with him would probably make one of her old activist friends suspicious of her.

The politics of the novel, nevertheless, consistently lean explicitly anti-settler-colonial and feminist. In addition to drawing the reader's attention to race-based prejudices, from Blank's hate crimes to a World War II statue with only the names of white men (137), laFavor also points to gender-based prejudices (for example, the resistance to women's drum groups, 136) and crimes against women (such as "a rash of rapes on the reservation the year before," 75) within Native communities. An unambiguously anti-settler-colonial novel with a loving Native family living in a Native community undergoing dramatic cultural revitalization, *Along the Journey River* stands as one of only a few novels that explicitly embraces but also builds upon the promises of Red Power. As Dr. Begay says to LaRoche in a discussion during the final stages of the investigation, "They've already stolen our land, as much of our identity as they could, our ceremonies. Can't they leave us be now?" (177). Indeed, laFavor's characterization of Begay and her political commitments—we learn that she helped mobilize a protest of a residential development on an ancient Native townsite (176)—suggests that just as Indigenous people can use settler–colonial law enforcement institutions to serve

Native communities, they can use settler-colonial educational institutions to do the same.

Thomas King, already the author of three other novels, began a mystery series in 2002 with Cherokee ex-cop and photographer Thumps DreadfulWater investigating multiple homicides related to an economic development project that politically divides a First Nations band. As in *Murder on the Tropic*, the crimes in *DreadfulWater Shows Up* occur during the construction of a casino, a legal one in this case, operating as part of a resort with luxury condominiums. Some members of the band hope that the resort will bring a steady flow of money into the community. However, the construction of the resort creates conflict, as the head of the band council, Claire Merchant, faces protests by the Red Hawk Society, a "mildly militant organization" formed by her son, Stanley "Stick" Merchant (2). Though King sets the novel in a First Nations community, Cherokee traditions appear to inform the Red Hawk Society's name: the color red associates the organization with the war sphere of Cherokee sociopolitical life.[18]

King explains the organization's objections to the resort and casino: "While the Red Hawks had opposed the resort as a whole, arguing that it pandered to rich whites, their main complaint was with the casino and the potential problems that recreational gambling seemed to drag along in its wake. Drugs, alcohol, violence" (182). The Red Hawk Society, which practices, DreadfulWater says, "Guerilla warfare. Civil disobedience" (182), speaks for a large contingent in their community. DreadfulWater observes to Sheriff Benjamin "Duke" Hockney, whose nickname derives from his resemblance to John Wayne, "Lot of people on the reserve have problems with the casino" (218). DreadfulWater's comments about the Red Hawk Society and casino contribute to political arrays within the novel around the issues of gambling and economic development. Stick's activism establishes him as one of the main nodes in these arrays, which work within the band as well as among band members and settler-colonial developers and law enforcement officials, but it also makes him one of the prime suspects in the murders.

Various financial crimes confirm Stick's and the Red Hawk Society's suspicions about the casino, while the pursuit and eventual shooting of the unarmed Stick by a local deputy attest to the settler-colonial law enforcement context so familiar in novels by Native authors: the burden of proof of innocence falls disproportionally on Native people, while whiteness and the settler–colonial economic system protects non-Native people committing white collar and violent crimes. Indeed, gaming brings organized crime to Native communities in other novels, such as Choctaw author LeAnne Howe's *Shell Shaker* (2001), as well as in the real world of Native politics and economic development. While working in the late 1990s and early part of the twenty-first century as a lobbyist for several tribal nations, Jack Abramoff and his associates committed various acts of bribery, conspiracy, fraud, and tax evasion while also lobbying against their own clients. His crimes earned him the name Casino Jack.

Both laFavor and King situate their second novels, *Evil Dead Center* (1997) and *The Red Power Murders* (2006), respectively, in a history of Native activism during the civil rights era, when law enforcement agents, including the FBI, infiltrated Native organizations and at times engaged in armed battles with them.[19] Like Sherman Alexie in *Indian Killer* (1996), a grim serial killer mystery that satirizes Tony Hillerman's conventional "colonial literature" about Native Americans (Alexie, "Introduction to *Watershed*," ix), laFavor draws on the 1978 Indian Child Welfare Act (ICWA) for the specific legal context of her story about a child pornography ring using children sent off the reservation into non-Native foster families. As in *Along the Journey River*, a non-Native academic drives the criminal enterprise, and a reservation bureaucrat, local law enforcement officer, and several traumatized Native people contribute. LaFavor presents a more flattering picture of Native activism than King in *The Red Power Murders*, though laFavor's and King's novels, in addition to Alexie's *Flight* (2007), share distrust of the FBI and contempt for Native activists turned informants. Indeed, laFavor reimagines activists as amateur detectives: in *Evil Dead Center*, their commitment to defending the sovereign rights of Indigenous peoples fits almost seamlessly with LaRoche's efforts, in partnership with the tribal police and the FBI, to bring child pornographers to justice.

Evil Dead Center, which features many of the main characters from *Along the Journey River*, opens with the discovery on land bordering the Red Earth reservation of the body of a Cree woman, Rosa Mae Two Thunder. The first part of the victim's name recalls Anna Mae Aquash, a Mi'kmaq activist murdered in 1975 by her fellow AIM activists. The allusion to Aquash fits a pattern of references to violence against women in laFavor's work.[20] However, in contrast to Indigenous dramatists in the 1990s such as Tomson Highway, Bruce King, Yvette Nolan, and E. Donald Two-Rivers, she does not develop the allusion into a full-blown assessment of misogyny within AIM.[21] LaRoche receives a call about Two Thunder's death from Caroline Beltrain, an Ojibwa from a reservation near Red Earth and a romantic partner during their days in AIM. While both LaRoche and Beltrain fled "from BIA police and the FBI," an FBI informant tried unsuccessfully to kill Beltrain by slitting her throat (10). By telling LaRoche that the authorities are hiding the real cause of Two Thunder's death, Beltrain initiates the investigation that reveals the child pornography ring.

Her call also initiates a thoughtful and politically delicate consideration throughout the novel of the conflict between activists and law enforcement officers. Beltrain, still deeply involved in activist work and a convicted criminal currently wanted by the FBI for questioning about a bombing at a nuclear power plant, does not know that LaRoche's post-AIM life includes helping the tribal police solve crimes. LaRoche, who takes Beltrain's suspicions about Two Thunder's death to Chief Bulieau, tells him, "If she hears I've been working with the tribal fuzz . . . there's no tellin' what suspicions'll be runnin' around in that head of hers" (13). When she meets with her old friend, Beltrain confirms LaRoche's fears by asking her, "So, workin' with the cops now, eh?" (25). LaRoche responds, "It just isn't always easy to fit the old ways in with all the *chimook* ways" (25). LaRoche's response to Beltrain's tense query contains some ambiguity. By "old ways," does she mean the traditional Ojibwa cultural beliefs and practices that readers of both novels see her helping revitalize? Or does she mean, more narrowly within the context of the conversation, the militant activism of AIM's now distant glory years? In either case, LaRoche positions distinct Native cultural and political practices in contrast to law enforcement or her own sleuthing, which she identifies as "*chimook* ways." The narrator even notes of LaRoche: "The cops could still roil her insides" (27–28). The novel, therefore, takes as its literary and political challenge proving that the "old ways," either cultural or political, and the "*chimook* ways" can work together for the benefit of Native people, specifically the young foster children of Red Earth. In other words, laFavor uses detective novel conventions to bring a divergent array of Native political positions into difficult conversation.

The political tensions between the former activist-cum-amateur detective and the current activist still threatened by federal authorities surface throughout the novel. LaRoche must first convince Beltrain, who served a three-year prison sentence, to talk to the tribal police. Since "the Movement's had some bad run-ins with tribal cops," Beltrain expresses a justifiable reluctance (57). Memories of the movement days—the excitement of direct action and flights from authorities as well as their romance that fed on it—also intrude on the present and remind LaRoche of the antagonism she once held for all police authorities. LaRoche eventually decides that she wants to see Beltrain's rap sheet. On it, she discovers "charges with convictions for carrying a concealed weapon, possession of marijuana, inciting a riot, disorderly conduct, and auto theft. Additional charges included DWI X3, parole violations X4, plus failure to appear and flight to avoid prosecution" (61). The narrator observes, "Renee knew the rap sheet would've been another three pages if her juvenile records had been included" (61). To Jesse Johnson, the young deputy, LaRoche comments, "I can't decide if she's a criminal or a hero of the People" (62). Looking back into twentieth-century American Indian literary history as the turn to the twenty-first century looms, LaRoche's statement of indecision concisely and quite provocatively captures the political crux of so much Indigenous life in the United States: what makes a Native person a criminal, and what makes a Native person a hero? By focusing on Beltrain, too, laFavor claims this political, as well as cultural and legal, conundrum—criminal or hero?—for Native and two-spirit women. Beltrain joins the likes of Proude Cedarfair in *Darkness in Saint Louis Bearheart* (1976), Gerry Nanapush in *Love Medicine* (1984), and Stone Columbus in *The Heirs of Columbus* (1991), three Anishinabe men who provoke critical inquiry into definitions of criminality and heroism for Indigenous people in a settler–colonial world, as well as the central figure, identified in the screenplay for *Smoke Signals* as Arnold Joseph, in Sherman Alexie's "Because My Father Always Said He Was the Only Indian Who Saw Jimi Hendrix Play 'The Star-Spangled Banner' at Woodstock" and Thomas Builds-the-Fire in "The Trial of Thomas Builds-the-Fire."[22]

Evil Dead Center imagines the possibility of a productive if tenuous détente between activists and police forces. LaRoche successfully convinces Beltrain to talk with Bulieau, and she and Beltrain work together to track down both Floyd Neuterbide, a politically conservative and "boisterous, overbearing professor" at Granite Rock State College, the owner of a resort, a foster parent to many Native children, and the mastermind behind the child pornography ring, and his accomplice, a young Ojibwa man suffering from Stockholm syndrome and aiding Neuterbide's attempted escape (71). LaRoche also persuades Beltrain to meet with the FBI once the investigation concludes, and the FBI clears Beltrain's name in the bombing. Beltrain's and Two Thunder's work as activists leads not only to Neuterbide's arrest and the rescue of the Native children under his tribal and state-sanctioned supervision but to the revelation of corruption within tribal social services and efforts by the Chippewa County Sheriff's Department to undermine the letter and intent of ICWA. After Beltrain leaves for a protest over fishing rights in Washington, she sends LaRoche a letter that culminates "keep up the good work for the People" (219). The novel concludes that activists and police authorities can effectively work together; activist ways and the *chimook* ways of criminal investigation are not incommensurable. In *Evil Dead Center*, laFavor produces a left-leaning narrative with a politically nuanced, and to some readers probably controversial, contemplation of fruitful cooperation between activists and police. LaRoche's proposal to her partner at the novel's end that they marry in a traditional ceremony—an allusion, perhaps, to Anna Mae Aquash's traditional marriage to an Ojibwa activist, Nogeeshik Aquash, at Wounded Knee—also reminds readers of the political fight for same-sex marriage that received a serious setback with President Bill Clinton's signing of the Defense of Marriage Act. LaFavor keeps urgent progressive political issues in the foreground throughout both her novels, which stand as part of a small group of literary works that in twentieth-century American Indian literary history directly and provocatively engage with civil-rights-era activism.

    LaFavor's and Alexie's shared outrage over the continuing loss of Native children to non-Native families, despite the passage of ICWA, also establishes a particularly compelling link between a Native detective novel and the wider Native novel tradition. *Flight* contains an astonishing amount of violent crime, from child and sexual abuse to war crimes and terrorism, for a novel that many readers would not classify as crime fiction. In three of the five jumps in time the protagonist makes, he finds himself within explicitly settler–colonial contexts, first during the Red Power era, then at the Battle of the Little Bighorn, and finally at an attack by the United States that draws on the Sand Creek Massacre (1864) or the Battle of the Washita (1868). Even the protagonist's father's shirt, a picture of Geronimo with the caption "FIGHTING TERRORISM SINCE 1492," conveys the prevailing view of colonialism and settler colonialism in Native fiction as an organized criminal enterprise (133). The caption beneath Geronimo, who spent 1886 until his death in 1909 as a prisoner of war, positions him as a law enforcement officer for the Chiricahua Apaches rather than an enemy of the settler–colonial state.

The novels by Downing, King, and laFavor capture the way detective fiction, with its suspicion of organized police forces but faith in amateur sleuths and its distrust of powerful state and financial institutions, allow for focused commentaries on the legacy of settler colonialism. Other detective novels by Native authors only touch upon settler–colonial contexts and instead emphasize general Native or tribal-specific cultural responses to crime. Choctaw author D. L. Birchfield's *Black Silk Handkerchief* (2006), for example, features Hom-Astubby / William Mallory, a photographer and nonpracticing attorney fearful of "the alarming uncertainty of nearly everything having to do with law" (8), and his nemesis, Nelson Towers, a tremendously wealthy defense contractor and owner of mining and media companies. Birchfield draws correlations between Towers, who has purchased property and then blocked access to public land in a small Colorado town, and the settler colonials who dispossessed the Choctaws. The local sheriff observes, "He'll turn this whole county into his private estate. He'll take over the local government and make life so miserable for the remaining old landowners that he'll run them right out of here." After a shrug, the sheriff adds, "Just like we did to the Indians, I guess" (33). Cherokee author Sara Sue Hoklotubbe offers a welcome corrective to the tedious objectification of women in Birchfield's novel. She sets her three Sadie Walela mysteries in the Cherokee Nation in northeastern Oklahoma. The principal crimes include the usual homicides as well as bank robberies, embezzlement, and identity theft, and throughout the mysteries Hoklotubbe touches upon specific cultural and political markers such as the Cherokee language, traditional Cherokee food (for example, wild onions, grape dumplings), Cherokee Baptist churches, Cherokee government bureaucracy, and important people and events in Cherokee history.[23]

Even when authors like Hoklotubbe mention but do not emphasize settler–colonial contexts, such as removal and allotment in *Sinking*

Suspicions (2014), Native-centered crime novels illuminate contemporary examples of criminality as familiar rather than anomalous in the history of settler–Native relations. *Sinking Suspicions* opens with a Cherokee man and World War II veteran, Buck Skinner, expressing his hatred for the U.S. government and especially the IRS for threatening to seize his property. "Buck didn't hate all white people," the omniscient narrator explains,

> but he had spent most of his life fantasizing about what it would be like had the Spanish never tromped up through Mexico, or the English never sailed in from the east, to invade Indian country.... Now the descendants of those same pushy settlers had begun to search every historical document and cemetery they could find for some unknown relative who might have had a drop of Indian blood to which they could lay claim. (5)

This prologue establishes identity theft—stealing social security numbers in order to commit additional fraudulent acts—within the context of what Philip Deloria calls the deep settler desire to "play Indian." For Native Americans, identity theft is not a new, digital-age crime but, instead, a symptom of settler colonialism and the sustained attempt to dispossess Native people of their indigeneity.

Hoklotubbe's novels share feminist political sensibilities with laFavor's, though the former read as heteronormative. She introduces Sadie Walela in *Deception on All Accounts* (2003), which begins with a man breaking into the bank. Walela, which translates from Cherokee to English as "Hummingbird," has worked at the bank for twelve years as the assistant to the manager, Tom Duncan. In the early years, the narrator explains, "She had been a naive young woman who believed she could be the first to break the glass ceiling at this good-old-boy bank" (7). The bank manager takes off the April Fools' Day on which the novel begins, and she arrives to open the bank but breaks protocol by entering it without waiting for another employee to join her. Confronted by the thief, she opens the time-delayed vault as the other three employees enter. The single male employee lies to the thief about the number of cash drawers, and the thief shoots him. Throughout the robbery, Walela remains surprisingly calm: she focuses on the thief's voice and makes mental notes about his physical features. She frees herself from her bonds, covers her dead coworker's head, and calls 911. Following interviews with the police and FBI, Walela leaves for the day. This opening scene establishes Walela as a woman undervalued at work—in fact, her decision to break protocol derives from anxiety about her male supervisors punishing her if the bank does not open on time—but with the skills necessary to succeed as an amateur detective: attentiveness to details and calm in the face of danger. Putting an extra die pack in the bag of stolen cash even earns Walela a backhanded "gutsy broad" compliment from the crook (19). However, Walela does not become as committed a detective as LaRoche. Instead, she shares hunches, as well as research done to satisfy her curiosity, with the police; they, in turn, use her information to solve crimes.

While both Hoklotubbe and laFavor represent strong, resilient, intelligent, and independent Native women as protagonists directly challenging patriarchal settler–colonial and tribal national institutions, Walela also adheres, in comparison to LaRoche, to more conservative gender expectations and fulfills a more conventional gender role. Though she acts as a "knight in shining armor" to Jaycee Jones, a financial consultant to the bank and her love interest, after a rattlesnake bites him, Walela tends to see herself as more emotionally vulnerable than men (103); in fact, she cries so frequently in the first novel that it starts to sound parodic. Immediately after the first robbery at her bank branch, she thinks about her father: "He always knew how to handle tough situations, and Sadie wished he was here so she could revert into a little girl, crawl up on his lap, and cry on his shoulder" (23). She also feels "the tick of her biological clock" as "her childhood fantasy—a husband, two kids, and the proverbial house with a white picket fence" appears increasingly elusive at age thirty-four (91), and she tells Sheriff Charlie McCord that she had married her abusive ex-husband because "I'm such a sucker for a handsome man" (112). Indeed, she has a particular vulnerability to hommes fatales. After the bank's senior vice president fires her following a second robbery, she receives a call from Jones. During the conversation, she "giggled like a young girl" and "wanted to beg him to come over, to hold her and tell her everything was going to be all right" (119). She does not extend the invitation, though, and, at the end of the conversation, she "feels empty" and asks herself, "Why did she have to be so independent?" (119). She laments, in other words, the characteristics that many readers would find worthy of admiration.

LaRoche's conversation with her partner about "Eve's Garden's latest state-of-the-art sex toy" would probably draw a blush from Walela, for whom roses and chocolate kisses establish a desirable romantic atmosphere (laFavor, *Evil Dead Center*, 36). Hoklotubbe even shows a hair stylist, possibly coded as gay, irritating Walela. Yet when read together, Walela and LaRoche give readers of contemporary Native literature an array of Native feminist politics and gender and sexual identities made engrossing, in part, by the distinctions they allow readers to draw between these representations of Ojibwa and Cherokee life.

Walela and LaRoche also share a commitment to helping people living on the margins without a safety net. Walela, like LaRoche, feeds homeless people, specifically Happy, a traumatized, speechless Black Seminole, to whom she brings meals twice a week, and she serves Christmas dinner to the homeless community at a shelter. Happy becomes a key figure in the investigation of the first bank robbery, and Walela's defense of and active sympathy for him help solve the crimes. Walela also cuts her long hair and donates it to a young girl, Soda Pop, who has lost her own to chemotherapy treatments for leukemia. When Walela learns that Jones, fatally shot by Sheriff McCord while trying to kill Walela and linked by Happy after his death to the first bank robbery, willed her a large sum of money, she tells McCord that she will use it to start a foundation for children like Soda Pop: "You know, so little kids can have wigs to wear when the chemicals that are supposed to make them better only rob them of their hair. So they can ride a horse if that's what they want to do. And their parents won't have to go to bankers, get down on their knees, and cry and plead for money to pay for medical treatment" (210). Their active though not explicitly activist generosity and empathy, especially within the context of the differences in their politics and the tribal-nation histories that shape them, make them equally compelling Native characters.

Hoklotubbe builds the explicit antiracist and more moderate antisettler-colonial politics of *The American Café*, the second installment in the Sadie Walela series, around a story about the separation of children from their Native families. In contrast to laFavor's *Evil Dead Center*, Hoklotubbe's work only obliquely mentions ICWA, when Walela says to another character seeking to solve the mystery of her parentage, "What about the tribe? Don't they have to keep track of all tribal citizens' adoptions?" (190). These separations, too, do not constitute the central crimes in the novel; in fact, Hoklotubbe represents them as tragedies if not explicitly as crimes. Instead, greed, as in *Deception on All Accounts,* drives financial crimes as well as homicides. Hoklotubbe's decision appears motivated by a desire to allow for the possibility that a non-Native could serve as a successful parent or parental figure for a Native child. She draws the same conclusion as Alexie in *Flight,* in which Office Dave helps save Zits/Michael and delivers him to his brother, a fireman, for adoption. Lance Smith, a Cherokee policeman who plays a secondary character in *Deception,* returns in *The American Café* in a more prominent role. As a young man, Smith joined the marines to flee from abusive, alcoholic parents who later die in a car accident. After his return from Vietnam, he expresses surprise that Sheriff McCord helps him readjust to civilian life. McCord finds Smith drunk outside a bar and takes him to a diner. Smith recalls, "The officer started talking and, for the first time in his life, Lance thought he was hearing fatherly advice. Strangely enough, those words of wisdom were coming from a white guy not much older than himself. He really hated that" (15). Smith, however, follows McCord's guidance and becomes a police officer.

McCord serves as a surrogate non-Native father figure to Smith, and other non-Native characters have legal guardianship over Native children. Emmalee or Emma Singer, whose murder of her sister, Goldie Ray Singer, sets events in the novel in motion, raises Goldie Ray's daughter, Rosalee. Rosalee's father, McIntosh "Mickey" Yahola, enlisted in the army during the war in Southeast Asia and died in an attack on his helicopter as it flew above the Cambodian jungle. Emma, however, tells Rosalee that her Native mother abandoned her. Gertie, a Kiowa teenager, lives with her non-Native mother's parents. Her parents, she explains to Smith, were killed while on duty for the National Guard in Iraq. While her Kiowa grandparents wanted to raise her, "the judge said I had to live with my white grandparents" (116). Rosalee struggles with alcoholism, and Gertie dies in a shootout during a bust of a meth lab. Hoklotubbe connects their substance abuse to the conflicts between the Native and non-Native sides of their families: in Rosalee's case, Emma expresses explicit and consistent anti-Indianism; in Gertie's case, she favors her Kiowa grandparents over her non-Native grandparents and resents the judge's order that she live with the latter.

While Hoklotubbe does not make any generalizations about the essential quality of life in Native or non-Native families—Smith, after all, fled from his own abusive, alcoholic parents—she emphasizes the cultural, and the implicit political, significance of strong Native families. Walela's Cherokee Uncle Eli and Aunt Mary live (in a rural sense) next door, keep an eye on her, and provide her with another place to seek love and comfort. In all three novels, Walela also fondly recalls both her grandmother and her father while expressing only relief that her non-Native mother departed the region after her father died. Rosalee ends *The American Café* reunited with her family: her father's brother, Eto Catuce / Red Stick or Red Yahola, who helps recover evidence from Goldie Ray's murder. Rosalee immediately becomes a Creek citizen, receives her tribal identification card, changes her last name to Yahola, and, the last page of the novel suggests, begins learning to speak Mvskoke. She ends the novel happy and healthy. The courts even send Gertie's son to live with his Kiowa great-grandparents, so that family also experiences a reunion.

The American Café also contains, in comparison to *Deception on All Accounts,* a slightly more robust expression of distinct Cherokee cultural and political life. In addition to the references to Cherokee beliefs (owls as messengers of bad omens) and foodways (crawdads), a strategy she continues from the previous novel, Hoklotubbe describes Smith as spending one year working for the Cherokee Nation Marshal Service.[24] Goldie Ray's funeral at an Indian church and a "Cherokee gospel singing" also give more texture to her depiction of vibrant contemporary Cherokee communities (137). She treats the language issue more directly, too, with Smith complaining that Walela's dog "knows more Cherokee than I do" and, at the gospel singing, hearing the hymns in Cherokee and feeling "comfortable and secure" (110, 139). The narrator, in free indirect discourse aligned with Smith, observes, "The language was still alive in this place and, although his ability to speak Cherokee was limited, hearing it rejuvenated his spirit and reminded him of his mother" (139).[25] The memory of his mother singing Cherokee songs to him provides Smith with the strongest and healthiest connection to her within the context of an otherwise traumatic family history. Eto Catuce's or Red's pleasure in speaking both Mvskoke and Cherokee, as well as Rosalee's aforementioned attempt to learn Mvskoke, also foreground Indigenous language use as an important cultural and political issue, though laFavor uses comparatively more Anishinabemowin in her two novels than Hoklotubbe uses Cherokee.

The novel also includes a comic moment in which a woman wrongly accused of murdering Goldie Ray compares President George W. Bush to President Richard Nixon, but the more conservative gender and sexual politics remain. Walela tentatively begins a romantic relationship with Smith. When Smith must inform Emma that her sister has been murdered, we learn that "emotional women unnerved him" (55). He backs away from Emma, too, in this scene and hopes that "Sadie's caretaker instincts would take over" (55). The narrator explains, "To his relief, they did" (55). As Walela anticipates her first date with him, a ride on horseback to investigate trespassers on the private property of one of Smith's friends, she reviews his character:

> She liked Lance even though she thought he was a walking contradiction. He had a lot of traditional Cherokee values, but she had never heard him utter one word in the Cherokee language. He exuded strength, yet he had an air of gentle compassion that she could feel when she watched him with other people. Being a police officer gave him a position of power, yet he came across as a humble being. He seemed to be old-fashioned, almost a male chauvinist. That characteristic in anyone else would have been an insult to her as an independent woman. Instead, his mere presence made her feel safe, something she craved. (109)

He opens the door for her on their date and drives, though they go in her truck. Their date ends with Smith wounded by a rock, thrown by Gertie, and a fall from his horse, and Walela protests Smith's freeing Gertie. The narrator observes, "Sadie wanted to stay mad at him but couldn't. His wall of machismo began to fade when she started giggling" (118). Smith becomes in the next chapter a "gentleman," rather than "almost a male chauvinist," in part because he "kept a proper distance" (119). Walela thus expresses some nostalgic desire for gender roles understood by conservatives in the United States as traditional; indeed, Smith was "unlike most of the men her own age" (119). At the same time, Hoklotubbe represents Walela as an independent woman with a strong attachment to her Cherokee family, a degree in business, a career in banking cut short by prejudice against women and the coincidence of multiple crimes committed at her branch, and a small business to run. She represents Walela, in other words, as an array of political positions that would appear contradictory only from absolutist perspectives.

While Hoklotubbe depicts in her novels a vibrant contemporary Cherokee Nation and comments on important cultural and political issues—language revitalization, adoption of Native children, substance abuse—their politics are not quite as progressive as those in laFavor's novels. In the case of their gender politics, Hoklotubbe's novels even trend conservative. LaFavor's *Along the Journey River* and *Evil Dead Center*, in contrast, represent two of the most explicitly anticolonial novels since the beginning of the Native American Renaissance. She uses the detective novel genre to assert tribal-nation jurisdiction over crimes on the Red Earth Reservation but also to advocate for lesbian and gay rights. LaRoche's role as an amateur detective helps affirm what should be her self-evident value to the community. These political distinctions, however, make both sets of novels—the LaRoche and Walela mysteries—all that much more significant to American Indian literary history. They contain within and between them political arrays that animate the many approaches Native individuals and communities developed, for several examples, to work through the politics of gender, sexuality, religion, law enforcement, and Indigenous languages in the 1990s and first decade of the twenty-first century.

Writing Justice

Native American literary history overflows with fiction about crime, but this general assertion should not draw attention either from the distinct forms, such as detective novels, developed by Native writers or their efforts to illuminate the different contexts in which these crimes occur. The death of Myron Pretty Weasel at the hands of Jim Loney in James Welch's *The Death of Jim Loney* (1979), Attis McCurtain's murder of Jenna Nemi in *The Sharpest Sight* (1992) by Louis Owens, and Simon's murder of his brother Lester in David Treuer's *The Hiawatha* (1999), for example, occur within formally distinct narratives as well as different tribal-nation and settler–colonial contexts. Louise Erdrich's *The Round House*, a *New York Times* best seller and the winner of the 2012 National Book Award, exemplifies the centrality of crime to Native literature. She wrote the novel in response to the epidemic of sexual assault in Native communities, and her publisher released it as Congress debated reauthorization of the Violence against Women Act (VAWA).[26] It opens with a heinous act of violence and remains diligently focused on crime and punishment, though not justice, as well as on the law and competing jurisdictions (federal, local, and tribal) in Native communities. While the publisher calls the novel "a masterpiece of literary fiction" on the front flap of the dust jacket, *The Round House* is simultaneously a masterful work of crime fiction.

Native detective fiction has distinct formal features and cultural and political emphases, but the narrow focus on crime, detection, and the search for justice distills some of the central concerns of Native literary history. These novels draw attention to the specific settler–colonial contexts in which Native people lead their daily lives while delineating the ways that Native people often experience various crimes—financial fraud, sexual abuse, identity theft—differently than non-Natives do. Native people do not live in Dashiell Hammett's Poisonville, though Hammett's novel about a town that threatens to make the Continental Op go "blood-simple like the natives" satirically captures the apotheosis of unchecked settler–colonial entitlement and crime (154). Like no other literary form, detective fiction by Native authors rigorously centers the most urgent concerns of Native communities—for example, having the authority to determine the future of their children, to protect their tribal-nation citizens from sexual assault, and to maintain control of their land, natural resources, and cultural property. These concerns almost always have a legal context—broadly speaking, the "Indian Law" represented in Erdrich's *The Round House* by a moldy casserole stacked with sharp knives and other kitchen utensils (228)—specific to Native Americans. Detective fiction conventions easily accommodate both these concerns and contexts while demonstrating, at least in novels in which the detective figures are Native, that Native people have the most urgent investment in addressing the "scarlet thread" of settler–colonial criminality that so dramatically shapes their daily lives.[27] The undermining but then stabilizing of a Native American social order dramatized in these novels, too, captures with less cultural nuance but greater legal and political clarity than celebrated novels by Momaday, Silko, and Erdrich what Jace Weaver calls "communitism," "a proactive commitment to Native community" (*That the People Might Live*, 43) and Gerald Vizenor calls "survivance," "an active resistance and repudiation of dominance, obtrusive themes of tragedy, nihilism, and victimry"

("Aesthetics of Survivance," 11). These two influential ideas in Native literary studies find a compelling articulation in Native detective fiction, in which Native legal authorities and their amateur allies practice the proactive commitment to Native communities and the active resistance and repudiation of settler–colonial dominance. Indeed, Native authors use the conventions of detective fiction to depict the search for justice as a sovereign act of Native people and communities.

CONCLUSION

Speculative Arrays

The Political Arrays of American Indian Literary History begins with a review of the politicized literary debate from the mid-1980s to the mid-1990s between Louise Erdrich, Leslie Marmon Silko, Paula Gunn Allen, and Elizabeth Cook-Lynn. A new, provocative voice appeared as that debate ebbed. In the first half of the 1990s, Sherman Alexie published several books of poetry, the short story collection *The Lone Ranger and Tonto Fistfight in Heaven* (1993), and the novel *Reservation Blues* (1995). He soon occupied a literary and political position similar to Erdrich's: a high-profile, award-winning author eliciting exuberant praise. He also faced from the beginning of his career vigorous condemnation for his failures as a writer and as an advocate for Native people. In the late 2010s, multiple women also accused him of sexual misconduct.[1] Scholars, creative writers, journal editors, and others both invested in American Indian literature and committed to supporting victims of sexual misconduct and sexual violence immediately incorporated the accusations into conversations about his writing and his status as one of the most celebrated contemporary Native authors. The women's testimony and Alexie's responses, in other words, adhered to already existing political arrays, including ones focused on gender and sexuality, that move throughout Alexie's work, American Indian literary history, and Native families and communities. The wider and sustained recognition of the literary contributions to these arrays by Carole laFavor and Sara Sue Hoklotubbe, as well as Winona LaDuke and Susan Power, for example, becomes even more urgent as young Native women writers come forward with their stories of Alexie's sexual misconduct and abuse of power.

Alexie has occupied a prominent place in the politics of American Indian literature for more than two decades. From the early years of his career as a published author, he demonstrated a penchant for activating and often disturbing the political sensibilities of readers. In "The Exaggeration of Despair in Sherman Alexie's *Reservation Blues*," Spokane author Gloria Bird laments the representations of Spokanes and other Indigenous peoples in Alexie's first novel and unfavorably compares the prose to Momaday's and Silko's. She contends, "It is a partial portrait of a community wherein there is no evidence of Spokane culture or traditions, or anything uniquely Spokane" (49), and she observes, "There is none of the sweeping, lyrical prose of Momaday's *The House Made of Dawn*. . . . Neither is there the detail of Silko's *Ceremony* wherein description of the New Mexican landscape is dense with meaning" (50). In a later essay, "Breaking the Silence: Writing as Witness," Bird suggests the political origins of her dissatisfaction with Alexie's fiction: "By looking critically at how we have been constructed as 'Indian,' and by interrogating the ways in which we become complicit in the perpetuation of both the stereotyping and the romanticizing of Indian people, can we take the first step toward undoing the damage that colonization has wrought" (47–48). Authors complicit in the perpetuation of stereotypes, Bird implies, exacerbate rather than alleviate settler–colonial conditions.[2]

Alexie aggravated the literary and political sensibilities of other scholars and writers, such as Cook-Lynn, Louis Owens, and David Treuer. In "American Indian Intellectualism and the New Indian Story," a primer on the politics of American Indian literature in the mid-1990s, Cook-Lynn observes:

> In the 1980s, the Louise Erdrich saga of an inadequate Chippewa political establishment and a vanishing Anishinabe culture suggests the failure of tribal sovereignty and the survival of myth in the modern world. Erdrich's conclusion is an odd one, in light of the reality of Indian life in the substantial Native enclaves of places like South Dakota or Montana or Arizona or New Mexico. (67–68)

She saves more withering commentary for Alexie. Novels such as *Reservation Blues* represent "the deficit model of Indian reservation life" and "reflect little or no defense of treaty-protected reservation land bases as homelands to the indigenes, nor do they suggest a responsibility of art as an ethical endeavor or the artist as responsible social critic, a marked departure from the early renaissance works of such luminaries as N. Scott Momaday and Leslie Marmon Silko" (Cook-Lynn, "American Indian Intellectualism," 68). Owens, who wrote a glowing review for *The Lone Ranger and Tonto* that Alexie's publishers quoted on the covers of *The Lone Ranger and Tonto, Reservation Blues,* and Alexie's urban mystery *Indian Killer* (1996), says that despite his public praise for Alexie, he is "in strong agreement with Bird's and Cook-Lynn's critiques" (*Mixedblood Messages,* 76). Fiction like Alexie's, he claims, with its "self-destructive, self-deprecatory humor . . . deflects any 'lesson in morality' from the non-Native reader and allows authors to maintain an aggressive posture regarding an essential 'authentic' Indianness while simultaneously giving the commercial market and reader exactly what they want and expect in the form of stereotype and cliché: what Vizenor terms the 'absolute fake'" (76). By the mid-1990s, scholars had established the exceptionalism of the Renaissance in part by emphasizing political discontinuities between American Indian literary history before and after 1968. Cook-Lynn and Owens distinguish Alexie from Momaday, Silko, and Vizenor, first-generation Renaissance writers, and therefore begin the process of reifying this exceptionalism by drawing attention to political discontinuities between them and the writers of the post-Renaissance generation.

A decade after Bird's evisceration of Alexie's work, David Treuer took an ostensibly formalist approach to a review of *Reservation Blues* and *Indian Killer.* He argues that *The Education of Little Tree* (1976), by militant white supremacist Forrest Carter, "is a close cousin—thematically, stylistically, and structurally—to Alexie's novels" (*Native American Fiction,* 164). *Reservation Blues, Indian Killer,* and *Little Tree,* Treuer claims, "are not bildungsromans, they are culture manuals" (165). It is a curious assertion about Alexie's novels, in which he assiduously avoids making specific revelations about Spokane culture. As Bird comments in her review of *Reservation Blues,* she could not identify any specific Spokane cultural beliefs and practices in the novel. Treuer continues that Carter and Alexie "mobilize stock images that have come to inform Native American literature from European writers like Rousseau, Voltaire, Chateaubriand, and Walter Scott who crossed the Atlantic, took up residence with Americans such as James Fenimore Cooper and William Gilmore Simms, and were then channeled through Longfellow and Whitman and Washington Irving and on down the line" (173). A critic could make such a politically charged statement, one that associates Alexie with writers who perpetuate stereotypes in narratives that enable and provide justification for colonialism and settler colonialism, only by either missing or ignoring Alexie's sense of humor and explicit parodying of these "stock images." Indeed, a scholar could argue that Treuer's own grim narratives contain representations of Indigenous people much more similar than Alexie's to the tragic figures in the stories of some of the writers that Treuer mentions. Such an assertion, however, also would require ignoring the nuances, both aesthetic and political, of Treuer's work. Treuer concludes, "Worse than that, we (readers) are in danger of mistaking a dead thing—like the received ideas, stale prose, commonplace realizations, essentialist projects, and racial anxiety that make up books like *The Education of Little Tree* and *Reservation Blues*—for something alive and rich and worthy of our attention" (192). The severity of Treuer's judgment recalls Paula Gunn Allen's in her 1990 critical assault on *Ceremony*. He also traps his own readers in an interpretive dead end: they can either agree with his assessment of Alexie or mistake "a dead thing" for a work of art worthy of intellectual engagement.

Yet Alexie devotes himself as much as any other Native writer to investigations of "received ideas . . . commonplace realizations, essentialist projects, and racial anxiety." His consideration and representation of these issues suggest not uncritical approbation but critical reflection. In fact, contrary to Bird's and Treuer's assertions, Alexie's poetry and fiction contain trenchant observations on storytelling traditions in which authors assert a generalized European cultural superiority and construct "savage," stoic, subservient, and romanticized Native characters. As many Native scholars, such as Rayna Green, Vine Deloria Jr., and Gerald Vizenor, explain, these storytelling traditions form a powerful component of European colonialism and U.S. settler colonialism.[3] In *The Lone Ranger and Tonto* and *Reservation Blues,* Alexie focuses his mockery on popular-culture narratives such as Hollywood Westerns while drawing a direct correlation between them and the struggles of contemporary Indigenous people.[4] More specifically, *Indian Killer,* in repudiation of Treuer's claims about its inheritance from writers such as Cooper and Simms, contains a critical focus on the storytellers like them who produce narratives that assume and justify the domination of Indigenous peoples.[5] Alexie's resistance to and revision of non-Native storytelling traditions about Native Americans function as both the defense and the practice of Indigenous artistic and intellectual sovereignty.

Alexie, in fact, shares literary interests and political allegiances with many writers of the previous generation, especially Vizenor, despite both Owens's claim that "Gerald Vizenor and Sherman Alexie are at opposite ends of the spectrum of contemporary Indian writing" (*Mixedblood Messages*, 81) and Alexie's attempt to distinguish himself from Vizenor.[6] Alexie and Vizenor, for example, devote their literary labor to combating a long history of malicious representation of Indigenous people and to using humor—frequently unsettling—in this effort. Alexie's resistance to the overdetermination of Native identity by public political protest also recalls Vizenor's skepticism of militant activism in the late 1960s and early 1970s in his articles on AIM.[7] In Alexie's short story "One Good Man," the protagonist, whose father suffers from severe diabetes, tells a story about challenging an obnoxious professor, "a white man who wanted to be Indian," during his freshman year at Washington State University (*The Toughest Indian in the World*, 227). He brings his father to the next class, and his father asks the professor, "Are you an Indian?" The professor responds, evasively, "I was at Alcatraz during the occupation.... How about you?" (228). The protagonist's father says, "I took my wife and kids to the Pacific Ocean, just off Neah Bay. Most beautiful place in the world" (228). "What about Wounded Knee?" the professor asks. "I was at Wounded Knee. Where were you?" (229). The father recalls, "I was teaching my son here how to ride his bike. Took forever. And when he finally did it, man, I cried like a baby, I was so proud" (229). The protagonist's father's prioritization of family and fatherhood over political protest leads the professor to reject him as an Indigenous man: "What kind of Indian are you? You weren't part of the revolution" (229). Alexie does not discourage activism, though he offers an unflattering representation of the militant activists of Indigenous Rights Now (IRON) in *Flight*. Instead, he discourages using activism as the defining or most significant feature of Native life, identity, and art.

Carole laFavor and Winona LaDuke, in contrast, express optimism about the legacy of a Red Power reimagined for the 1990s. In laFavor's two novels, Renee LaRoche distances herself from but also draws upon her Red Power past while working within her tribal nation toward cultural revitalization and social justice. In *Last Standing Woman*, LaDuke depicts organized resistance by a diverse group of White Earth tribal nation citizens with both women and men in leadership roles. Their successful fight against a tribal-nation chairman in the thrall of timber corporations leads also to the homecoming and political awakening of Alanis Nordstrom, a young White Earth woman and Tony Hillerman-reading journalist. Marcie Rendon's detective novel *Murder on the Red River* looks back to the Red Power era, too, with its focus on a young White Earth woman raised in abusive foster families but on her own as the calendar turns to 1970. Like LaRoche, Cash, the protagonist of Rendon's novel, becomes an amateur detective working with local, though not tribal-nation, police authorities. At the end of the novel, Rendon suggests that Cash faces a choice: attend college to earn a degree in criminal justice or join the American Indian Movement with her new acquaintance, J. R. or Long Braids. As she walks away from Long Braids on the last page of the novel, he asks, with an eye to the future, "Where we going?" (199). By leaving his question unanswered, Rendon does not foreclose on either college, AIM, or any other option for her young Indigenous characters. The future for them instead remains a set of speculative arrays: cultural, educational, romantic, and political.

The Political Arrays of American Indian Literary History makes a case for the intellectual and political urgency of accounting for the full range of Native politics in American Indian literature. To state the obvious, Native people hold political views of all kinds: liberal and conservative, moderate and extreme, unpredictable and contradictory. American Indian literary history contains equally diverse political perspectives. Native authors explore a wide range of political positions in their work and, between and even within books, shift political positions, reject old and adopt new political alliances, and deeply satisfy and disappoint their critics. By emphasizing only explicit anticolonial resistance or prosovereignty narratives, even if we believe they constitute the most important political positions in an enduring settler–colonial world and an era in which the racist Far Right finds itself openly embraced by the ruling party in the White House, literary critics risk missing both the full artistic expression of Indigenous political life and all the intellectual, emotional, and communal labor required to navigate the politics of tribal national and settler–colonial worlds.

NOTES

Introduction

1. Following Robert Dale Parker in chapter 7 of *The Invention of Native American Literature*, I use "canonical" only once here and with caution.

2. I am indebted to political scientist Anthony Ives for this definition of politics and for bringing Dahl's essay "The Concept of Power" to my attention. For a carefully developed definition of how literature works politically, see Rancière, "The Politics of Literature." Rancière asserts, in a passage suggestive of what much Native American literature does to navigate and engage tribal national, colonial, and settler–colonial politics, "Literature does a kind of side-politics or meta-politics.... This 'politics' of literature emerges as the dismissal of the politics of orators and militants, who conceive of politics as a struggle of wills and interests" (19–20).

3. Patrice Hollrah observes, "Erdrich draws on details of the Leonard Peltier trial, and on the basis of her political stance, she creates a sympathetic cultural hero in Gerry Nanapush" (*"The Old Lady Trill, the Victory Yell,"* 163).

4. Robert Nelson observes, "It may strike some readers as ironic that Paula Gunn Allen, who at the time of her critique of Silko had just published *Spider Woman's Granddaughters* and was about to publish the patently New Age *Grandmothers of the Light*, comes off in her argument as the defender of Laguna traditionalism and privacy against Leslie Silko's brazen affronts to them both." See Nelson, "Rewriting Ethnography," 48.

5. Jace Weaver, Craig Womack, and Robert Warrior call the essay "foundational" and "a major statement from one of our major statesmen" in their preface to *American Indian Literary Nationalism* (xvi). Ortiz contributed the foreword to the book, in which the authors also reprinted Ortiz's essay.

6. See Louis Owens, *Other Destinies*, 23. Owens, who identified as Cherokee and Choctaw, returns briefly to this critique of the "psychopathic" Blue Duck in *Mixedblood Messages* in the chapter "Mapping the Mixedblood: Frontier and Territory in Native America" (25).

7. After sharing his six rules, Updike adds, "Easier said than done, of course" (*Picked-Up Pieces*, xix).

8. See Lisa Brooks, *The Common Pot*, 13–14, for the history of the petition; Round, *Removable Type*, 1–2, for the anecdote about Pablo Tac; and Lewandowski, *Red Bird, Red Power*, 59–60, for Simmons's "remarkable" letter, in which she forcefully exposes "white civilization" as a myth. Simmons later married Raymond Telephause Bonnin and became Gertrude Bonnin.

9. In an interview with Camille Adkins, Momaday says of the novel, "I wrote the very first part of it at Jemez Springs. I kept it up when I went to my first teaching post at Santa Barbara, and wrote the balance of it there in fairly quick order. Then I finished it

in Massachusetts, where I had the Guggenheim and was working on Emily Dickinson, or reading her" (Adkins, "Interview with N. Scott Momaday," 221). By his own account, therefore, Momaday finished the novel in 1966.

10. Teuton mentions the convocation briefly (*Red Land, Red Power,* 10–11, 85) and draws on Cook-Lynn's perspective of it. While Cook-Lynn might have attended, she does not appear on the list of participants in the historical record of the gathering, Rupert Costo et al., *Indian Voices: The First Convocation of American Indian Scholars.* However, she cofounded *Wičazo Ša Review* in 1985 with Medicine and another convocation participant, W. Roger Buffalohead.

11. These examples come from Rader's readings of the three novels; see *Engaged Resistance,* 76–81.

12. My coeditor Daniel Justice and I suggest the mid-1990s as the beginning of a new era in Native literature in our introduction to *The Oxford Handbook of Indigenous American Literature.* We see the shift occurring in these years with the coincidence of Native scholars consistently producing influential literary critical studies, researchers recovering a dramatic number of pre-Renaissance Native writers, scholars expanding their definition of Native literature to include writing beyond fiction and poetry, and new Native writers such as Debra Magpie Earling, LeAnne Howe, Thomas King, and Susan Power publishing remarkable and celebrated works of fiction and nonfiction and others, all born during or after the civil rights era, such as Sherman Alexie, Esther Belin, Stephen Graham Jones, Eden Robinson, and Richard Van Camp, winning awards and opening Native literature to new genres. Native dramatists (with credit for this list to Alexander Pettit), such as Marie Clements, Hanay Geiogamah, Diane Glancy, Tomson Highway, Monique Mojica, Daniel David Moses, Drew Hayden Taylor, Yvette Nolan, Bruce King, William S. Yellow Robe Jr., and E. Donald Two-Rivers, still struggle for recognition by scholars, though Pettit's contribution to the *Oxford Handbook* should help generate more scholarly attention to them. In the chapter "The New American Indian Novel: A User's Map," Rader also suggests that we have moved into a new era: "We are now post-Renaissance," he explains, "not simply because of a new millennium but also because we have passed the 'rebirth' of Native writing. In fact, we have passed adolescence and moved well into adulthood" (*Engaged Resistance,* 73).

13. While the project here has sympathy for Jameson's goal of "respecting the specificity and radical difference of the social and cultural past while disclosing the solidarity of its polemics and passions, its forms, structures, experiences, and struggles, with those of the present day" (Jameson, *The Political Unconscious,* 18), it does not concur that "only Marxism can give us an adequate account of the essential *mystery* of the cultural past" or that matters of the past "can recover their original urgency for us only if they are retold within the unity of a single great collective story" of class struggle (19).

14. King identifies as Cherokee.

15. Harkins was also Chickasaw through his mother.

16. For these biographies, see Lewandowski's *Red Bird, Red Power: The Life and Legacy of Zitkala-Ša,* Dorothy R. Parker's *Singing an Indian Song: A Biography of D'Arcy McNickle,* and Phyllis Cole Braunlich's *Haunted by Home: The Life and Letters of Lynn Riggs.* Kiara Vigil also draws substantively on letters in *Indigenous Intellectuals,* especially in the chapters on Carlos Montezuma and Gertrude Bonnin. Vigil examines the way "Montezuma used correspondence to remain actively connected to a wide array of Indian performers, activists, and political leaders" (103). His letters, in addition to his publications, Vigil explains, also illuminate "the types of political and cultural networks he accessed, created, and maintained" (103). In the chapter on Bonnin, Vigil comments on "the centrality of correspondence in creating and strengthening pan-tribal networks

throughout this decade [the 1920s] and demonstrates the leading role Bonnin played in creating and maintaining these connections through her work with white reformers" (189).

17. For a brief narrative regarding the friendship between Eastman and Garland, see Vigil, *Indigenous Intellectuals,* 62–63.

18. Riggs mentions Winters in a letter to Campbell/Vestal dated November 25, 1923.

19. See Momaday, "Online Interview with N. Scott Momaday," on the website Modern American Poetry.

20. LaFavor identified as Ojibwa in the brief author's biography on the back cover of her two novels.

21. Vizenor collected his articles on AIM in *Tribal Scenes and Ceremonies.*

1. Indigenous Editing

1. The Autumn 2011 issue of *Textual Cultures* (volume 6, number 2) contains a special section, "Indigenous Editing," with contributions by Matt Cohen, Phillip Round, Chris Teuton, and Luis Cárcamo-Huechante. Their collective intervention in textual studies, to use Cohen's words, focuses on such issues as "editing and archiving indigenous-authored literary texts, analyzing contemporary publishing practices, or telling a different story about media by studying colonial and precontact communicative objects in the Americas" ("The Codex and the Knife," 115). Editing in the context of this special section, therefore, refers to the work of a textual studies scholar with Indigenous communicative objects rather than to the work of Indigenous editors. Despite this important distinction, this chapter draws inspiration from Cohen, Round, Teuton, and Cárcamo-Huechante.

2. Lionel Larré collected much of Oskison's writing for periodicals in *Tales of the Old Indian Territory and Essays on the Indian Condition* (2012), and Daniel Littlefield Jr. and Carol A. Petty Hunter edited a volume of Posey's work called *The Fus Fixico Letters* (1993; 2002). For a well-developed discussion of Will Rogers's journalism, see Amy Ware's *The Cherokee Kid* (2015). See also Maureen Konkle, *Writing Indian Nations* (2004), for example, and Phillip Round, *Removable Type* (2010).

3. See Vigil, *Indigenous Intellectuals,* 116–27, for a discussion of the content of *Wassaja*. Vigil observes that Montezuma, its editor, "honored different representations of Indianness by including a range of Indian voices" in the newsletter (118). I argue a similar point about Bonnin and Harkins in this chapter. Rock was the founding editor of the *Tundra Times,* a biweekly newspaper that continued publication after his death in 1976.

4. Lewandowski describes Bonnin's friendship with Parker in *Red Bird, Red Power.* See 103 for the story of the beginning of their relationship in 1915. Bonnin, Lewandowski asserts, "had tremendous respect for Parker" (111).

5. See Muriel Wright, "Lee F. Harkins, Choctaw," for a short biography of Harkins.

6. Janet A McDonnell observes, "The period 1887–1934 was marked by the continuation and culmination of the forced assimilation philosophy embodied in the Dawes Act, and the dominant theme was the transfer of Indian lands into white hands" (*The Dispossession of the American Indian,* viii). McDonnell documents the bureaucratic process of dispossession following the passage of the Dawes Act of 1887, or General Allotment Act, which had the support of "every commissioner of Indian affairs who served between 1887 and 1934" (6). The Dawes Act, as well as pieces of allotment legislation focused more narrowly on individual reservations, led to the loss of 86 million acres of land (121).

7. Agnes M. Picotte (Lakota) describes *ohunkakan* as "tales regarded as having some fictional elements" in her foreword to Zitkala-Ša's *Old Indian Legends* (Picotte, xi). Dexter Fisher, in the foreword to Zitkala-Ša's *American Indian Stories,* cites a letter Bonnin wrote to Montezuma in which she explains the name change as the result of a family quarrel about Bonnin's departure from the community to receive an education at a boarding school (Fisher, x). Lewandowski calls the name change a result of Bonnin's desire "to be recognized as Indian." He continues, "Her use of the name signaled a genuine psychological and spiritual rebirth" (*Red Bird, Red Power,* 37).

8. Vigil states, for example, "I focus on these four writers [Bonnin, Eastman, Montezuma, and Luther Standing Bear] in particular because some of their political works have been understudied and they have also been criticized for advocating assimilation, despite the fact that they invariably had tribal-centered agendas, which contradicted arguments in favor of acculturation" (*Indigenous Intellectuals,* 10). See also Christopher Pexa's "More Than Talking Animals," in which he asserts that "Eastman's manner of playing Indian for white audiences reads as a complexly ambivalent but nonetheless sustained act of resistance to what Patrick Wolfe identifies as settler colonialism's logic of eliminating indigenous peoples for the sake of greater access to territory." Pexa adds, "More specifically, Eastman's children's stories invoke traditional Dakota stories and knowledge, and the literary representations of *tiospaye* (literally, 'camp circle,' meaning 'extended family') kinship networks embedded in them, as political frameworks with which to analyze and criticize the United States' dispossession of Dakota lands" (653–54).

9. I will avoid the common identification "Sioux" except in quotations from other authors and use, when available, an author's preferred identification. For a detailed explanation of the social and political organization of the Dakota-, Lakota-, and Nakota-speaking peoples, see Angela Wilson (Waziyatawin), *Remember This!,* 4–5.

10. In identifying Bonnin's affiliations, I follow P. Jane Hafen (Taos Pueblo). Hafen explains that Beatrice Medicine (Lakota) and Vine Deloria Jr. (Dakota) classify the Yanktons as Dakotas. However, Bonnin probably spoke the Nakota dialect, and her pen name is Lakota. When she wrote in a Native language, she used Dakota. As Nakota is most frequently a linguistic classification, Hafen uses the term "Yanktons" (*Dreams and Thunder,* xiv). See also Lewandowski, *Red Bird, Red Power,* 211n46.

11. See Lewandowski, *Red Bird, Red Power,* 19–22.

12. Bonnin appears to have left Yankton immediately prior to the massacre at Wounded Knee. See Lewandowski, *Red Bird, Red Power,* 21 and 206n31, where Lewandowski shares the evidence that Bonnin arrived at White's Manual Labor Institute on December 18, 1890.

13. Some scholars see evidence that Bonnin converted to Mormonism. She had a Mormon burial in Arlington, Virginia, and Hafen cites from the manuscripts of William Hanson, Bonnin's collaborator on *The Sun Dance Opera,* who writes that Bonnin was a "faithful Mormon" (Hafen, "Zitkala Ša," 41). Lewandowski asserts that while Bonnin took part in some Mormon events, she did not convert (*Red Bird, Red Power,* 68).

14. Dennis McAuliffe Jr. defines headrights as "the Osages' oil shares" (*Bloodland,* 124).

15. Deloria discusses the Meriam Report and Indian Reorganization Act in detail in chapter 9 of *Behind the Trail of Broken Treaties: An Indian Declaration of Independence* (1974). Deloria generally applauds the results of the IRA and Collier's efforts as commissioner of the OIA.

16. Hafen does not use the hyphen in Zitkala-Ša. For discussions of Zitkala-Ša's use of sentimental literary modes, see Susan Bernardin and Laura Wexler. Bernardin

views much of Zitkala-Ša's writing as using the language of domesticity to challenge "sentimental ideology's foundational role in compulsory Indian education as well as its related participation in national efforts to 'Americanize' the Indian" ("The Lessons of a Sentimental Education," 213). Wexler positions her argument in reference to the debate between Jane Tompkins and Ann Douglas on the literary value of domestic fiction, but she refocuses on "the expansive, imperial project of sentimentalism" and on the way this project fails Zitkala-Ša ("Tender Violence," 15). In "Re-visioning Women," an article she frames critically with the work of Kenneth Lincoln, Renato Rosaldo, and Eric Cheyfitz, Ruth Spack sees Zitkala-Ša's writing as subverting the boarding school education she received by using English to reconstruct Native women in positive ways. Patricia Okker, in "Native American Literatures and the Canon," a discussion of what work by Zitkala-Ša has been included in the canon, considers Zitkala-Ša's writing career in terms of European American literary modes or movements such as realism, naturalism, and modernism.

17. Of Bonnin's poems, Robert Dale Parker notes, "Some specialists have also seen the poetry of Zitkala-Ša / Gertrude Simmons Bonnin, who is well known for her prose, but poetry, it turns out, was not one of Bonnin's many talents. For that reason her poems do not appear" (*Changing Is Not Vanishing*, 6).

18. Evans provides a thorough and compelling interpretation of the politics of *The Sun Dance Opera* in "Stages of Red: Intertribal Indigenous Theater in Zitkala-Ša's *The Sun Dance Opera*," chapter 4 of her dissertation, "Staged Encounters."

19. Rayna Green writes, "The living performance of 'playing Indian' by non-Indian peoples depends upon the physical and psychological removal, even the death, of real Indians" ("Tribe Called Wannabee," 31). Philip Deloria's *Playing Indian* (1998) documents the history of non-Natives playing Indian from the Boston Tea Party to the New Age movement.

20. Yellow Robe's article appears in the January–March 1914 issue. Yellow Robe asks, "What benefit has the Indian derived from these Wild West Shows? None, but what are degrading, demoralizing and degenerating, and all their influences fall far short of accomplishing the ideals of citizenship and civilized state of affairs which we most need to know" ("The Indian and the Wild West Show," 39). In "My Boyhood Days," published in the *American Indian Magazine* in 1916, he identifies himself as "Lacota oyate" (50).

21. Womack asserts that in the discussion of Native literatures, "autonomy, self-determination, and sovereignty serve as useful literary concepts" (*Red on Red*, 11). Cook-Lynn criticizes contemporary Native authors who do not foreground in their work a defense of tribal nationhood and sovereignty.

22. Vigil observes of Standing Bear, "His texts, whether written or spoken, at times replicated dominant understandings of Indianness, while at other times criticizing practices of domination carried out by white cultural producers and political reformers" (240).

23. Zitkala-Ša's formal literary decisions offer a provocative contrast with those made by Ella Deloria, another author from Yankton. Deloria wrote an ethnographic novel, *Waterlily* (1988), and in *Dakota Texts* (1932) she translated stories from the same oral traditions as those in *Old Indian Legends*. In its entirety and in terms of content, though not literary mode, *Waterlily* reads much like the chapters "The Legends," "The Beadwork," and "The Coffee-Making" in *American Indian Stories*.

24. Hertzberg explains that Charles Eastman and his brother, the Reverend John Eastman, along with the Reverend Sherman Coolidge (Arapaho), considered founding an organization of American Indians at the beginning of the century. Simultaneously, in a letter dated June 1, 1901, Bonnin continues a discussion with Montezuma about

"organizing" and the expense—"a few million dollars to begin on!" Hafen made Bonnin's letters to Montezuma, which she transcribed, available to me. The letters are available in the Carlos Montezuma Collection at the Arizona State University Library.

25. Non-Natives with an interest in participating were nonvoting members and called associates.

26. For a biography of Parker's ancestor, see his *The Life of General Ely S. Parker*.

27. As Lewandowski documents, Bonnin's sustained antagonism to peyote use originates in the criminal activity of Samuel Lone Bear, an Oglala living at Uintah-Ouray. Lone Bear was a peyote advocate as well as a con man. See Lewandowski, *Red Bird, Red Power*, 88–92.

28. Vine Deloria explains the connection between the Department of the Interior's use of certificates of competency and the loss of Native land in *Behind the Trail of Broken Treaties*, 189–90.

29. Arthur Parker published three poems in the journal, two during his editorship under the pen name Alnoba Waubunaki and one during Bonnin's under the pen name Gawasa Wanneh. He wrote "My Race Shall Live Anew," available in Robert Dale Parker's *Changing Is Not Vanishing* (284), in a defiant progressive voice demanding, in the language of slavery and freedom, the same civil and human rights as other citizens.

30. In *Land of the Spotted Eagle* (1933), Luther Standing Bear observes, "According to the white man, the Indian, choosing to return to his tribal manners and dress, 'goes back to the blanket.' True, but 'going back to the blanket' is the factor that has saved him from, or at least stayed, his final destruction" (190).

31. Bonnin revises the Christmas letter as "A Year's Experience in Community Service Work among the Ute Tribe of Indians" one year later for the October–December 1916 issue, though she adds another section in which she locates her work in the context of other efforts at the "uplift of the race" (309–310). The tone of this revised report suggests that Christian duty motivates her efforts, yet it also emphasizes that at this point in her life, Bonnin prefers direct community activism to literary interventions or, after the demise of the SAI, to social and political activism on a national scale.

32. Hertzberg identifies Frazier and Brave as "Sioux." Frazier's specific identification remains elusive; Brave was Lower Brulé Lakota.

33. However, Parker published a history of the Senecas and collection of Seneca stories during the 1920s.

34. Edith Wilson, as Bonnin notes, claimed to be a descendant of Pocahontas. Many of the oldest European Virginian families made the same claim, perhaps to suggest that they were biological rather than colonial inheritors of the region. The article includes pictures of both women.

35. "Lo! the poor Indian" originates in eighteenth-century British writer Alexander Pope's poem "An Essay on Man" (1733–34), in which he represents Indigenous people as "untutor'd" and "simple." It became a familiar phrase in the United States, where writers used it both earnestly and satirically. In her 1927 novel *Cogewea, the Half-Blood*, Okanogan writer Mourning Dove (Christine Quintasket) mocks Pope with a chapter entitled "Lo! The Poor 'Breed.'"

36. Elizabeth Wilkinson argues that Bonnin uses "powerful rhetorical strategies of silences and silencings" in the *Atlantic Monthly* articles on her boarding school experiences and *Oklahoma's Poor Rich Indians* for "the purpose of altering her audience's sociopolitical association, moving readers from their unconsciously white, Euro-American alliance to, instead, a political alignment with Native peoples, specifically on the issues of land loss and forced boarding school attendance" ("Gertrude Bonnin's Rhetorical Strategies of Silence," 34, 35).

Notes to Chapter 1

37. Carewe was born Jay John Fox. Email correspondence with David Catlin, Carewe's grandson, July 5, 2017.

38. See Buford, *Native American Son*, 253–54.

39. See McDonnell, *The Dispossession of the American Indian*, 88–102, for a discussion of the Burke Act, which amended the Dawes Act by requiring the Interior Department to determine a Native person's competence to receive the fee patent on his or her allotted land. As McDonnell explains, the act and its implementation led to rapid and dramatic land loss: "Reports from the reservations provided overwhelming evidence that Indians who received fee patents became homeless and impoverished" (93). Some Native people resisted the competency system and "refused to apply for a fee patent," though, McDonnell explains, the Indian Office often issued the patents anyway (98). In chapter 3 of *Domestic Subjects*, Beth Piatote analyzes Native occupation and performance in *Cogewea* within the contexts of the Dawes and Burke Acts.

40. John Milton Oskison refers to Irving's visit to Oklahoma in his posthumously published novel *The Singing Bird* (2007); see 91–92 for the first reference to Irving and 104 for the brief account of Ellen Wear's meeting with him.

41. For brief biographies of all these poets except Oshkosh, see Parker, *Changing Is Not Vanishing*. Oshkosh unsuccessfully challenged her uncle, Reginald Oshkosh, for chief of the Menominee Nation after the death of her father, Ernest Oshkosh, in 1929. Her uncle, a graduate of both Carlisle and Haskell, died in 1931, and her cousin, Roy Oshkosh, successfully claimed the leadership position over Alice.

42. John M. Carroll notes in his introduction to the collected issues, "There is at least one issue missing from almost all sets in those libraries which have them. This was because one issue was withdrawn from general sales and distribution as a result of an objection lodged by an individual over alleged character defamation, an objection which eventually grew into a lawsuit, and subsequently caused the magazine's cessation as an organ for the American Indian" (introduction to *The American Indian*).

43. See Rickard, *Booming Out to NYC*, episode 6 of the *Mohawk Ironworkers* documentary series by Mushkeg Productions. The head of Mushkeg, Omuskego Cree filmmaker Paul Rickard, directed this episode.

44. See Rosalyn Lapier and David Beck, *City Indian: Native American Activism in Chicago, 1893–1934* (2015); Nicolas Rosenthal, *Reimagining Indian Country: Native American Migration and Identity in Twentieth Century Los Angeles* (2012); Coll Thrush, *Native Seattle: Histories from the Crossing-Over Place* (2007) and *Indigenous London: Native Travelers at the Heart of Empire* (2016); and Laura M. Furlan, *Indigenous Cities: Urban Indian Fiction and the Histories of Relocation* (2017).

45. Mathews writes similarly about Bacon Rind in *Wah'kon-tah: The Osage and the White Man's Road*, 323–24.

46. See Rayna Green, "The Pocahontas Perplex," for a history of the representation of Native women as queens and princesses from 1575 to the early twentieth century. Green does not discuss Native women who appropriated the colonial and settler-colonial practice of exoticizing them as princesses.

47. The Haskell Institute held the event to celebrate the opening of the new football stadium. Young and Gooding describe the gathering: "Thousands of people from dozens of different tribes filled the stadium for the ceremony, which featured Secretary of the Interior Hubert Work, Indian Affairs Commissioner Burke, and Sen. Charles Curtis, a member of the Kansa tribe." They add that Brown "was the featured dancer of the ceremony" ("The Haskell Celebration of 1926," 1013).

48. See Prucha, *Documents of United States Indian Policy*, 158–60, for the history of the origin both of the rules that forbid certain Indigenous cultural practices and of the

Courts of Indian Offenses, which the federal government established to enforce them. See also Prucha, 185, specifically section 4(a), for the description of the prohibition on dances.

49. See Wenger, "Land, Culture, and Sovereignty in the Pueblo Land Dance Controversy."

50. In the article, "woman" reads "women."

51. For comparison, see "Myths and Legends," part 2 of Bill Grantham's *Creation Myths and Legends of the Creek Indians* (2002).

52. Bruner also claims in this same article that the Creeks met Columbus, who plied them with whiskey, learned their sign language, and made peace (8).

53. Craig Womack defines *sofkee* or *sofki* as "a Creek favorite made from hominy that is allowed to sour slightly. A fairly complicated process involving filtering water through ashes, and so on, is required to make *sofki*" (*Red on Red*, 313).

54. In the article, this quotation reads ". . . there is hopes for him to live."

55. Bruner appears to exaggerate here for comedic effect: Wild Cat famously escaped from Fort Marion in Florida in November 1837.

56. This battle occurred on December 26, 1861. Bruner says a General Gans joined McIntosh in the battle. He might mean Confederate General Richard Montgomery Gano, who fought in Indian Territory later in the war but did not see his first action until July 1862 in Kentucky.

57. See "Emily Peake Student File" from Carlisle. Louise Seymour Houghton identifies Robitaille as a Carlisle teacher in *Our Debt to the Red Man* (169).

58. See Vigil, *Indigenous Intellectuals,* 108–9, where she cites a letter from Bonnin to F. P. Keppel in the War Department.

59. For Eastman, Sloan, and Lookout, see *American Indian* 1, no. 3 (December 1926): 6; for Parker, see *American Indian* 1, no. 6 (March 1927): 12; for Standing Bear, Bacon Rind, and Bruner, see *American Indian* 1, no. 7 (April 1927): 16; for Long Lance, see *American Indian* 3, no. 7 (April 1929): 11. Long Lance was born Sylvester Clark Long. For a concise summary of Long's family and professional history, see Raheja, 142–43.

60. For the comparison of Howe to Rogers, see Rader's foreword to *Choctalking on Other Realities* (iii, iv, and vi). Rogers, like Howe, traveled to Japan. He visited the country in late 1931 at the start of one of his trips around the world.

61. The British occupation of Jerusalem began in December 1917 and continued until the end of the British Mandate in 1948.

62. Below the title, in bold, Lohmann writes: "Note: I wish to give credit to the assistance I received in my writings from the Reverend James Delaney, a priest who made the pilgrimage at the same time I did" ("Nazareth—Scene of Christ's Childhood—Has Cabaret," 2).

63. See Scholtz: "The key opposition to the legislation was fiscal, as representatives feared the potential liability that a court of Indian claims would present to the public purse. Commissioner Rhoades chose not to push the legislation, and it died in committee" (*Negotiating Claims,* 172).

64. Chief Buffalo Child Long Lance was Sylvester Clark Long's professional name. He also used Sylvester Long Lance, as when he donated to the Pratt Memorial Fund. See also chapter 4, note 21.

65. Patterson served as director of the Woolaroc Museum in Bartlesville, Oklahoma.

2. Transnational Representations

1. Larré says that Oskison wrote "numerous articles on the farming economy" for *Collier's* (*Tales of the Old Indian Territory and Essays on the Indian Condition*, 53).

2. Oskison's "An Apache Problem," "Acquiring a Standard of Value," and "The New Indian Leadership" appeared in the SAI's journal. Larré includes all three in *Tales of the Old Indian Territory and Essays on the Indian Condition*, his collection of Oskison's work.

3. Gilbert G. González traces this interest to the 1880s, which saw "a virtual explosion of books and articles on Mexico" in the United States (*Culture of Empire*, 8).

4. See Starr, *History of the Cherokee Indians and Their Legends and Folk Lore*, 22.

5. See Conley, *The Cherokee Nation*, 5–6.

6. For a discussion of Fields, see Everett, *The Texas Cherokees*; for Ross and Brown, see Littlefield, "Utopian Dreams of the Cherokee Fullbloods"; and for Harris and Smith, see Conley, *The Cherokee Nation*.

7. See, for example, "Historical Sketches of the Cherokees," 71–89, in which Lucy Lowrey Hoyt Keys reports on Sequoyah's trip.

8. Kirby Brown outlines the local Cherokee contexts into which these writers were born. He notes, for example, "Both Oskison and Bronson were born to working-class farm families in the more culturally and politically conservative Delaware district while [Rachel Caroline] Eaton and Riggs hailed from prominent ranching and banking families in and around the more acculturated agricultural and financial district of Cooweescoowee" ("Citizenship, Law, and Land," 18).

9. See Cox, *The Red Land to the South*, for a discussion of Todd Downing's fiction and nonfiction about Mexico.

10. See Harvey, "Cherokee and American," 45–46, for analysis of Bronson's experience in and comments on Korea.

11. White comments that Rogers visited Hearst on his ranch in Chihuahua in March 1931 and in October of the same year played polo in Mexico City with Hal Roach, the famous Hollywood director, and Eric Pedley, a well-known polo player. See *Will Rogers*, 185–86.

12. Oskison fondly remembers Rogers several times in his posthumously published autobiography, "A Tale of the Old I.T." Oskison and his schoolmates called Rogers "Rabbit." He was, Oskison explains, "the grinning, likeable son of a Verdigris river cattleman named Clem Rogers" ("A Tale of the Old I.T.," *Tales of the Old Indian Territory and Essays on the Indian Condition*, 83).

13. In the manuscript of *A Texas Titan*, Oskison calls the book a "fictionalized biography" in a brief author's note between the title page and the table of contents.

14. See Fallaw, *Cárdenas Compromised*, for a study of Cárdenas's land reform.

15. See Ana Patricia Rodríguez for her definition and discussion of "fictions of solidarity," a term from which I have drawn inspiration in my discussion of American Indian authors writing about Mexico.

16. In the course of their examinations of American Indian or specific tribal national literary histories, Jace Weaver, Daniel Justice, Robert Warrior, Sean Teuton, Craig Womack, and Scott Lyons characterize the beginning of the twentieth century to the Renaissance and civil rights era in this way.

17. See also Cox, "Tribal Nations and Other Territories of American Indian Literary History," 360–62, for a discussion of Oskison drawing on Cherokee national hero Ned Christie for his representation of Ned Warrior.

18. Oskison might have based Tall Bear on Bear Timson. In "A Tale of the Old I.T.," he observes that Timson, a resident of "the fullblood settlement," was "beloved by every one, preached there in the Cherokee language on Sundays and worked a fertile creek-bottom farm on weekdays" (71).

19. Oskison's mother Rachel was, Oskison notes, "only a quarter Cherokee," and his father, John, was an immigrant from England who "became by Cherokee law an adopted citizen of the Nation, with all the rights and privileges of any fullblood" ("A Tale of the Old I.T.," 67).

20. This quotation and all others from "A Tale of the Old I.T." are from the collection *Tales of the Old Indian Territory and Essays on the Indian Condition.*

21. See "A Tale of the Old I.T.," 120, for the brief story of his meeting with Roosevelt.

22. See G. González, *Culture of Empire,* passim, for the post-1880s history of this dominant U.S. view of Mexico and Mexicans.

23. See Powell and Mullikin, introduction to *The Singing Bird,* xxxi–xxxii and xxxvii–xl, for a discussion of these objects.

24. Oskison appears to have based this story on the experience of his friend Dane Coolidge, who "had been commissioned by the Smithsonian Institution to trap and prepare for its collection field mice in the Naples region of Italy, in Sicily, and in southern France" ("A Tale," 109). Coolidge ignores the warnings about "ignorant and superstitious" peasants, who on two nights throw stones at Coolidge's door (110).

25. The text reads "if not my blood," though Oskison clearly meant "by."

26. This belief is common in the U.S. cultural imaginary. See Horsman, *Race and Manifest Destiny,* 210, and González, *Culture of Empire.*

27. See *Weekly Articles,* vol. 1, 1. Rogers said that the income from his columns would go "to the civilization of three young heathens, Rogers by name, and part Cherokee Indians by breeding."

28. See, for example, the two weekly articles for January 1, 1928, and February 3, 1929 (*Weekly Articles,* vol. 3, 116, 248–49). The first article mentions the term of Oklahoma governor Henry Simpson Johnston, who was impeached for incompetency in 1929. In the second, Rogers returns to the scandal following reports that Johnston was using astrology.

29. See Ware, "Will Rogers's Radio," 76–83, for a careful assessment of the Cherokee-specific contexts of this scandal.

30. One of the "gags" in *Rogers-isms: The Cowboy Philosopher on the Peace Conference* (1919) is also about Villa. As Rogers discusses President Wilson's participation in the Paris Peace Conference of 1919, he notes, "This Monroe thing the Republicans talk so much of and know so little about, Protects us against everything but VILLA. And in the whole History of America he is the only *Nation* that ever attacked us" (Rogers, *Rogers-isms,* 33).

31. Dennis McAuliffe observes that by the 1920s, "oil had made the Osage Indians the richest people, per capita, in the world" (*Bloodland,* 42). This wealth also made the Osages the targets of systematic violence called the Osage Reign of Terror. McAuliffe writes about his family's role in this era of Osage history in *Bloodland.* See also Donald L. Fixico's "The Osage Murders and Oil," chapter 2 of *The Invasion of Indian Country in the Twentieth Century* (2012), as well as Linda Hogan's *Mean Spirit* (1990), a fictionalized treatment of the murders. Fixico situates both oil exploration and extraction on the Osage Reservation and the murders specifically within the history of treaties between the Osages and the United States and allotment. He identifies Edwin B. Foster as the signer of the first oil lease with the Osages, on March 16, 1896.

32. For the comment on U.S. arms sales to Mexico, see *Weekly Articles,* vol. 1, 183; for

the reference to the recognition of a new Mexican government by the United States, see *Weekly Articles*, vol. 1, 185.

33. See chapter 5 of Cox, *The Red Land to the South*.

3. A Good Day to Film

1. In the Introduction to her book *Smoke Signals,* Hearne thoroughly examines the various political contexts, especially efforts to secure and strengthen tribal-nation sovereignty, that inform the film. In fact, she argues that the film's "primary aesthetic project is not cultural expression but rather a politicized intervention in the American mediascape" (xxi).

2. See Alexie, "Introduction: Death in Hollywood," in which he announces, "I'm quitting Hollywood" (9); Kramer, "Sherman Alexie: It's Funny That Hollywood Would Hire an Indian to Make White People More Likeable"; and "Interviews with Chris Eyre and Sherman Alexie" in Hearne's *Smoke Signals,* especially 185–87, for some representative thoughts from Alexie about working in Hollywood.

3. Alexie drew these poems, respectively, from these collections: *The Summer of Black Widows* (1996); *One Stick Song* (2000); *The Business of Fancydancing* (1992); and, again, *One Stick Song* (2000). Both "Influences" and "The Alcoholic Love Poems" come from *First Indian on the Moon* (1993).

4. See Hearne's discussion of Carewe and analysis of *Ramona* in *Native Recognition,* 156–72. Hearne observes, "Carewe was not avant-garde. Drawing on his extensive experience as an actor and later director, he was thoroughly adept at wielding the conventional dramatic idioms of the American stage and cinema. He was integrated into a well-developed, profitable system of industrial film production in 1920s Los Angeles" (157).

5. Thanks to Matt Kliewer and Joshua Nelson, respectively, *A Day in Santa Fe* screened at *Returning the Gift: Native and Indigenous Literary Festival* in Norman, Oklahoma, in October 2017 and at the *Native Crossroads Film Festival and Symposium,* also in Norman, Oklahoma, in April 2018.

6. Alice Corbin Henderson and Witter Bynner arrived in 1916 and 1922, respectively. Though she had visited the region many times previously, Austin did not move to Santa Fe until 1924. See Weigle and Fiore, *Santa Fe and Taos,* 10, 18, 21. Oliver La Farge moved to Santa Fe in 1933.

7. Visitors to Santa Fe will hear that locals used to call Jozef Bakos, Fremont Ellis, Walter Mruk, Willard Nash, and Will Shuster some version of the phrase "the five nuts in mud huts."

8. Mabel Dodge Sterne (later Luhan) belongs in this group, though she moved to Taos rather than Santa Fe.

9. Collier became the commissioner of Indian affairs from 1933 to 1945 under President Franklin Roosevelt.

10. As noted in chapter 1, in both 1921 and 1923 the Office of Indian Affairs encouraged agents to enforce regulations on traditional dances. See Tisa Wenger's "Land, Culture, and Sovereignty in the Pueblo Land Dance Controversy," where she argues that the OIA used threats of force against American Indians to coerce compliance (88). The objections to the dances included that they were pagan, immoral, obscene, and cruel.

11. James Hughes was called Jimmy as a child and either James or Jim as an adult. For consistency, I will refer to him as James.

12. See Braunlich, *Haunted by Home,* 103–4, for the discussion of *Green Grow the Lilacs* as a candidate for the Pulitzer.

13. See Horak, "The First American Film Avant-Garde," 24, for the reference to the film's New York screening. Riggs also screened the film at Northwestern University while he was there directing *Green Grow the Lilacs* in July 1932. See Braunlich, *Haunted by Home*, 120.

14. Crosby won an Oscar for *Tabu* (1931). He was also the cinematographer on *The Plow That Broke the Plains* (1936) and *High Noon* (1952).

15. Posner identifies the title of the "preliminary script" as "Nanook of the Desert" ("Where the Buffalo Roamed," 13), and *100 Years of Filmmaking in New Mexico* records the title of Flaherty's unfinished film as "Ácoma," one of the nineteen pueblos in Mexico (Cosandaey et al., 110).

16. *Portrait of a Young Man* is more patient, meditative, and innovative than *A Day in Santa Fe*. Ralph Steiner's equally meditative *H2O* (1929) influenced *Portrait*. If Rodakiewicz discussed the production of *A Day in Santa Fe* with Riggs and Hughes, viewers might see his influence, for example, in Riggs's and Hughes's attention to the clouds in the sky and the wind in the trees. Riggs or Hughes had probably not seen *Man with a Movie Camera* (1929), in which director Dziga Vertov narrates a day in the life of the Soviet Union. Riggs and Hughes did not have Vertov's technical skills.

17. Johnson / Young Deer claimed to be Winnebago or Ho-Chunk. Film scholar Angela Aleiss has confirmed that he was born to multiracial parents of African, European, and possibly Indigenous, specifically Nanticoke, ancestry. See Aleiss, "Who Was the Real James Young Deer?"

18. The guest list is in the Lynn Riggs Papers at the Beinecke Library, Yale University, so it is likely that Riggs also composed it.

19. Alice Kaplan describes Sedillo as "an elitist who had always insisted on his white, European origins" (*The Interpreter*, 49). Sedillo worked in military and international courts after World War II.

20. *It Starts with a Whisper* is an experimental film in which three spirits take a young woman on a journey. *Imprint*, produced by Chris Eyre, is a supernatural thriller. The latter begins as a conventional haunted house narrative but builds to a surprise ending that requires a different interpretation of the active spirit world in the film. Despite the generic distinctions between these two films and Riggs's city symphony, all three represent Indigenous religion as a powerful force in Native communities and worthy of awe and respect. See Raheja, *Reservation Reelism*, 160–69 and 169–82, for her discussion of *Imprint* and *It Starts With a Whisper*.

21. Riggs and Hughes numbered the pages of the shooting script by identifying the Part (I or II) and the page. When they reach Part II, they begin again with page one.

22. John Dorman identified the setting of the swimming scene in his interview with Margolis (Margolis, "An Interview with Mr. John Dorman," 2). Sisters Amelia Elizabeth White and Martha White, philanthropists and patrons of the arts, founded the White Estate, now the site of the School of American Research.

23. Riggs would have been aware of and likely interested in this history, as he had been born a citizen of the Cherokee Nation in Indian Territory eight years before the United States dissolved the governments of all American Indian nations within Oklahoma's borders in 1907. Oklahoma statehood has a significant impact on the characters' lives in several of his plays, including *Green Grow the Lilacs* and *The Cherokee Night*.

24. See "'El Portal' at the Palace of the Governors."

25. "Santa Fe Picture at Fonda" and Margolis's interview with John Dorman identify the man in the white suit as Norman McGee.

26. As Hutchinson notes, prominent cultural critics as well as consumers during the international arts and crafts movement viewed handmade objects, including those

made by American Indians, as "more 'authentic' and healthful than the machine-made bibelots of Western culture" (*The Indian Craze*, 19). "Indian corners," collections of American Indian objects, "were understood to address a variety of cultural needs arising at the turn of the century, particularly the desire for an individual and national sense of mastery in the face of the increasing alienation brought on by industrialized work, urban life, and international trade" (19). Scholars tend to identify 1920 as the end of the arts and crafts movement, but this historical context informs the recurring focus on working hands in the film.

27. Dorman identifies the house as belonging to Bakos in his interview with Margolis (Margolis, "An Interview with Mr. John Dorman," 1).

28. See, for example, Edison Studios films such as *Sioux Ghost Dance* (1894), *Wand Dances, Pueblo Indians* (1898), and *Eagle Dance, Pueblo Indians* (1898).

29. See "Reframing the Western Imaginary," chapter 1 of Joanna Hearne's *Native Recognition*, for a rich and detailed analysis of costuming in silent-era Indian dramas. Hearne suggests that the Indian drama "can be seen as antecedent to what has variously been called the 'sympathetic Western,' 'Indian Western' and 'Pro-Indian Western'" (8). She explains, "Indian dramas responded to contemporary changes in public policy by situating cinematic 'Indians' in modern and urban contexts, and in this way they sometimes counterweighted the limited historical horizons of the Western genre as a whole" (8). However, while expressing sympathy for certain Native characters, Hearne argues, these films do not imagine a future for Indigenous people. Instead, they tell the familiar story of American Indians as a vanishing race.

30. See Riggs, "Santo Domingo Corn Dance," 8. Riggs's use of "Santo Domingo Corn Dance" suggests that he conceived of this part of the film, at least, as a visual poem. Along with the Hopi Snake Dance, the Pueblo Corn Dances became popular with visitors to the region in the early twentieth century. Riggs might have known that Paul Strand and Charles Sheeler used lines from poems in Walt Whitman's *Leaves of Grass* as intertitles in *Manhatta* (1921), drawing from Whitman's "City of Ships," "A Broadway Pageant," "Mannahatta," "Chants Democratic" (revised as "A Song for Occupations"), "Song of the Exposition," "Song of the Broad-Axe," "Crossing Brooklyn Ferry," and "Sparkles from the Wheel."

31. This depiction of Indigenous religious ceremony also contrasts sharply with its representation by mainstream Hollywood in feature-length films such as *Redskin* (1929), which includes what an intertitle identifies as "an ancient ceremonial," and *The Silent Enemy* (1930). Victor Schertzinger directed *Redskin*, which stars Richard Dix as Wing Foot, a young Navajo man sent by the Indian agent to boarding school and confronted by cultural, political, and romantic tensions upon his return. The intertitle appears at 38:57 of the DVD version of Schertzinger, *Redskin*, in the *Treasures III: Social Issues in American Film, 1900–1934* collection by the National Film Preservation Foundation. The dancing, intercut with drumming and sandpainting, ends at 40:08. *Redskin* includes scenes shot on location at Acoma Pueblo. A scene in *The Silent Enemy*, directed by H. P. Carver and starring Chauncey Yellow Robe / Chief Yellow Robe and Sylvester Long / Chief Buffalo Child Long Lance, shows a medicine man in a frenzy of prayer with accompanying drumming and chanting. As he prays, the narrator explains in the voice-over, "a howling storm came up. It seemed to rock the earth." The performance by the actor Paul Benoit/Chief Akawanush begins at 39:18 of the DVD version of Carver, *The Silent Enemy*, distributed by Alpha Home Entertainment.

32. Both primitivist and social reform discourses in the 1920s and 1930s often included such contrasting representations of the European and the Indigenous. See Berkhofer, *The White Man's Indian*, 178–79, for a general history of dominant representations

of Native Americans but especially for the brief discussion of John Collier's romantic view of the Pueblo people.

33. Scott G. Ortman discusses the Tewa religious view of clouds within the context of a study of metaphors for community used by Tewa speakers. As he explains, and as the different diacritical marks indicate, the Tewa words for "cloud" and "cloud-beings" have slightly different pronunciations. See Ortman, "Bowls to Gardens," 91–92.

34. Kirk's article has no title, date, or page numbers, but the reference appears on the ninth page. Vertov filmed *Man with a Movie Camera* in three cities—Odessa, Moscow, and Kiev—over the course of three years.

35. In her unpublished article, Betty Kirk identifies the pueblo as Santa Clara. The reference appears on the seventh page.

36. Private conversation, May 23, 2013, Santa Fe.

37. Private email correspondence, May 31, 2013. Martinez's response to *A Day in Santa Fe* suggests it will resonate with early-twenty-first-century Native audiences in much the same way *The Daughter of Dawn* (1920), directed by Norbert Myles, did. See Hearne, *Native Recognition*, 113–14, for a discussion of Native responses to *The Daughter of Dawn* after its recovery in 2007. Hearne also notes that the "location shooting on the Navajo Nation and the images of ceremonial sandpainting" in *Redskin* have for some viewers significant "documentary value" (175).

38. Raheja observes, "*Tree* features a postapocalyptic world in which Sky Woman appears on Earth again to either heal the wounded environment or enact its final destruction" (*Reservation Reelism*, 182).

39. Riggs completed *Russet Mantle* in 1935, and it was first performed at the Masque Theatre in New York City on Thursday, January 16, 1936. Riggs and Rauh were close friends.

40. Private email correspondence, May 31, 2013.

41. Riggs declined the offer to adapt Tully's play. While no evidence exists in the Beinecke Library archives, it appears that he also declined to meet with Preminger about his film.

42. See Hearne, *Native Recognition*, 220–21.

43. In the title story in *The Toughest Indian in the World* (2000), Alexie defines 49s as "Indian blues . . . cross-cultural songs that combined Indian lyrics and rhythms with country-and-western and blues melodies" (23).

44. The regularly spaced scenes of Abel running in the film adaptation of *House Made of Dawn* situate Abel's story in a ritual context. The fancy dancing in *The Business of Fancydancing* serves a similar cultural and political purpose.

45. Laura Frost's article on Anita Loos's innovative intertitles inspired this idea. See Frost, "Blondes Have More Fun."

46. For the lyrics in English and a description of the writing, translating, and performance of "Osinilshatin," see Alexie, *The Business of Fancydancing: The Screenplay*, 133–34.

4. Academic Networks

1. Eagleton observes, "In the early 1920s it was desperately unclear why English was worth studying at all; by the early 1930s it had become a question of why it was worth wasting your time on anything else. English was not only a subject worth studying, but the supremely civilizing pursuit, the spiritual essence of the social formation. Far from constituting some amateur or impressionistic enterprise, English was an arena in which

the most fundamental questions of human existence—what it meant to be a person, to engage in significant relationship with others, to live from the vital centre of the most essential values—were thrown into vivid relief and made the object of the most intensive scrutiny" (*Literary Theory*, 27).

2. In *Domestics Subjects*, Beth Piatote identifies the Native home and family as a key site of political contention between Indigenous people and the settler-colonial state. Piatote observes, "Assimilation-era policies, as many scholars have established, were driven by the notion that the tribal-national polity, as a competing national sovereignty, must be destroyed. And the way to break up the tribe was to break up the Indian family and to cultivate children's allegiance to the United States rather than to the tribe" (5).

3. Of a cultural prize such as the Pulitzer, James Harris asserts, "The primary function it can be seen to serve—that of facilitating cultural 'market transactions,' enabling the various individual and institutional agents of culture, with their different assets and interests and dispositions, to engage one another in a collective project of knowledge production—is the project of cultural practice as such" (*The Economy of Prestige*, 26). Native literary studies scholars tend to give Momaday's Pulitzer Prize a prominent role in facilitating and enabling the subsequent increase in literary production by Native writers.

4. Scholars recovered and published, for example, the collected works of early Native writers such as William Apess (*On Our Own Ground: The Complete Writings of William Apess, a Pequot*, edited by Barry O'Connell, 1992), Joseph Johnson (*To Do Good to My Indian Brethren: The Writings of Joseph Johnson, 1751–1776*, edited by Laura J. Murray, 1998), Samson Occom (*The Collected Writings of Samson Occom, Mohegan*, edited by Joanna Brooks, 2006), and Jane Johnston Schoolcraft (*The Sound the Stars Make Rushing through the Sky: The Writings of Jane Johnston Schoolcraft*, edited by Robert Dale Parker, 2007) and individual works such as Bertrand Walker's *Tales of the Bark Lodges* (1995), Todd Downing's *The Mexican Earth* (1996), S. Alice Callahan's novel *Wynema* (1997), the play *Out of Dust* by Lynn Riggs (2003), Dallas Chief Eagle's novel *Winter Count* (2003), John Milton Oskison's novel *The Singing Bird* (2007), and Joseph Nicolar's *The Life and Traditions of the Red Man* (2007). Studies that draw almost exclusively on archives, including Maureen Konkle's *Writing Indian Nations* (2004), Lisa Brooks's *The Common Pot* (2008), and Phillip Round's *Removable Type* (2010), also contributed to this shift in American Indian literary studies.

5. For example, in a May 14, 1938, letter to Campbell, Dobie writes of his "Life and Literature of the Southwest" course, "It has proved to be the most popular one-man course on the campus; between 125 and 150 students enroll in it annually in the regular session and also about that many during the summer." Pearce wrote to Dobie on March 2, 1959, that his "S W Lit always runs 60 or more."

6. The *Southwest Review* had a frequently rotating cast of editors, associate editors, managing editors, and contributing editors. Henry Nash Smith served for years with McGinnis and others as a coeditor, while Mary Austin, Witter Bynner, Campbell (as Vestal), Dobie, and Tinkle served in a variety of editorial roles. Cleanth Brooks also spent time on the editorial board.

7. In his biography of Mathews, Michael Snyder makes note of a significant political moment in American Indian literary history: the tribal council presented a copy of *Wah'kon-tah* to Eleanor Roosevelt in March 1937. See Snyder, *John Joseph Mathews*, 97.

8. Susan Kalter, in the introduction to *Twenty Thousand Mornings*, concurs: "Mathews and his family were firmly embedded within the tribe, even though they were also in another sense nearly thrice-removed descendants of it" (Kalter, Introduction, xix).

9. For details regarding Mathews's work for the tribal council, see Snyder, *John Joseph Mathews*, esp. 94–97. Mathews proposed establishing an Osage museum at a tribal council meeting and wrote a proposal for funding from the Works Progress Administration. The Osage Nation opened the museum, now called the Osage Nation Museum, in 1938. See Snyder, *John Joseph Mathews*, 100–101.

10. Lon Tinkle, one of Dobie's biographers, notes that he was born the same day as T. S. Eliot (3).

11. For the specific details of the Paredes–Dobie story, including the caricature of Dobie in Paredes's novel *George Washington Gómez*, see Davis, *J. Frank Dobie*, 120–23, 208–14. When Henry Nash Smith sent Dobie a tape of Smith's son, Mayne, playing bluegrass, Dobie shared it with Paredes. Paredes, in turn, copied it for the Folklore Center Archives at the University of Texas. See Smith to Dobie, November 14, 1960.

12. See Tinkle, *An American Original*, 197–204, and Davis, *J. Frank Dobie*, 163–80, for the details of Dobie's final years as an employee of the University of Texas at Austin. Dobie also described his final months at the university in a letter dated October 3, 1947, to Smith. Dobie is memorialized along with Roy Bedichek, an educator and naturalist, and Walter Prescott Webb, a historian of the American West, in a statue of the three Texas authors called Philosopher's Rock at Barton Springs Pool in Zilker Park in Austin, Texas. Mathews uses an epigraph entitled "The New Long Knives" from Webb's *The Great Plains* in *The Osages*: "To the white man, especially to Anglo-Americans, the Indian was primarily a warrior, a fighting man, and implacable foe. The Indian's economy of life, his philosophy, his soul, were secondary and of little concern to the Anglo American" (Mathews, *The Osages*, 339).

13. Kalter identifies another way that Mathews participated in this academic network. She observes, "At a time when most imagine that American Indians were rendered nearly impotent to shape the discourses about them, Mathews was actively and meaningfully shaping the body of scholarship that would emerge about the Osages and affect their lives. From 1933 to 1967, he worked as a manuscript reviewer and consultant for the University of Oklahoma Press" (Kalter, Introduction, xxxiii).

14. Pearce titled the first edition of his book *The Savages of America: A Study of the Indian and the Idea of Civilization* (1953).

15. Davis asserts, "Cormac McCarthy's *Blood Meridian* utilizes portions of Dobie's writing on scalp hunters" (*J. Frank Dobie*, 240).

16. General Baylor was the nephew of the cofounder of Baylor University, Robert Emmett Bledsoe Baylor.

17. See McMurtry, "Southwestern Literature?," 69. Tinkle provides no source for this comment by Dobie.

18. Hutner rejects the term "middlebrow," as do I.

19. Momaday writes, "These—and the innumerable meaner creatures, the lizard and the frog, the insect and the worm—have tenure in the land. The other, latecoming things—the beasts of burden and of trade, the horse and the sheep, the dog and the cat— these have an alien and inferior aspect, a poverty of vision and instinct, by which they are estranged from the wild land, and made tentative" (*House Made of Dawn*, 57).

20. In *The Cherokee Kid*, Amy Ware has recovered much of the Cherokee context that shaped Rogers into the famous celebrity beloved by the American public.

21. On Chief Buffalo Child Long Lance, or Sylvester Clark Long, see chapter 1, note 64. In the first edition of the bibliography, Dobie treats him as a Native author, following Long's self-identification in his autobiography as a "Black Foot Indian." In the second edition, he revises the Long Lance entry to account for new revelations about his life: "He is said to have been a North Carolina mixture of Negro and Croatan Indian; he was

Notes to Chapter 4

a magnificent specimen of manhood with swart Indian complexion" (*Guide,* 2nd ed., 34). Dobie tells Campbell in a letter dated May 14, 1938, that he teaches Long's autobiography in "Life and Literature of the Southwest."

22. *Roadside,* a play that Dobie probably would have enjoyed, was staged at Baylor University in 1941 during Riggs's tenure there as a teacher and at the University of Texas at Austin in 1951.

23. Dobie revised this passage to read "to baptize him, take his land, enslave him, and appropriate his women" in the second edition (*Guide,* 2nd ed., 26).

24. In an apparent reference to the 1934 Indian Reorganization Act, Dobie observes, "Since about 1933 the United States Indian Service has not only allowed but rather encouraged the Indians to revert to their own religious ceremonies" (*Guide,* 1st ed., 42).

25. For an introduction to the vexed production and reception history of *Black Elk Speaks,* the story of Nicholas Black Elk (Oglala Lakota) as told to John G. Neihardt, see DeMallie, *The Sixth Grandfather.* Dobie's reference to *Wah'Kon-Tah* as a "book of essays" adds to the lack of consensus about the book's genre. See Kalter, "John Joseph Mathews' Reverse Ethnography."

26. Dee Brown, almost two decades before publishing *Bury My Heart at Wounded Knee,* makes an appearance as the coauthor of *Trail Driving Days* (1952).

27. See historian Donald Fixico's *Termination and Relocation,* a study of the post-Collier and post-World War II era of federal Indian policy.

28. See also Lester to Dobie. Lester thanks Dobie for sending him some publicity information and, misspelling Mathews's last name, adds, "We would be very happy to have John Joseph Matthews of Pawhuska, Oklahoma and we will be glad to extend him an invitation to attend this meeting also."

29. See Lewandowski, *Red Bird, Red Power,* especially chapter 11, "Oklahoma." Bonnin resigned from the GFWC in 1926 after founding the National Council of American Indians (247).

30. Mathews recorded some of the evening conversations from 1959 to 1963 during their annual deer and turkey hunts at Rancho Seco, Medina County, Texas. The Western History Collection of the University of Oklahoma Libraries holds the recordings with Mathews's "Taped Diary."

31. The banter between the men includes some potentially embarrassing juvenile humor but nothing scandalous.

32. See Kalter, "Introduction," for a discussion of these various frustrations and financial difficulties.

33. The original text reads "mesqite" and "chinmey."

34. Snyder describes the "deep and heartfelt" friendship between Mathews, Dobie, and their hunting companions in his biography of Mathews, *John Joseph Mathews,* 178–79.

35. This story appears on Mathews's "Taped Diary."

36. *Querencia* is one's attachment to or longing for home. "Interfer" is the spelling in the original.

37. Dobie's correction in the first paragraph introduces some ambiguity. Johnston owned the ranch, but Dobie viewed Walker Stone, who served for years as editor in chief for Scripps-Howard newspapers, as the host during the hunting trips.

38. There are no comments by Dobie from page 120 to 446 or 463 to 718.

39. See pages 4, 19, 21, and 102 of the presentation copy of *The Osages* in Dobie's library at the Harry Ransom Center at the University of Texas at Austin.

40. See page 75 of the presentation copy of *The Osages.*

41. The Beinecke holds Riggs's teaching notes as part of the Lynn Riggs Papers. See

Baylor University Teaching Notes, Series II: Writings. In 1945, the School of Drama at the University of Oklahoma offered Riggs a visiting professorship for nine months. Rupel J. Jones, the director of the School of Drama, explained to Riggs, "Your duties would consist of one or two classes in playwriting, and the rest of your time you could devote to working on any plays you may have in mind and, of course, you would have an opportunity to present them here" (Jones to Riggs, July 16, 1945). Riggs declined the invitation.

42. The *Reviewer* was a short-lived journal founded in February 1921 in Richmond, Virginia. It moved briefly to North Carolina in 1926, where Paul Green took editorial control, but then merged the same year with *Southwest Review*. See L. Smith, "*The Reviewer.*"

43. Braunlich mentions the poetry club at Campbell's both in *Haunted by Home* (41) and her introduction to Riggs's *This Book, This Hill, These People* (7), an edited collection of Riggs's poems.

44. Riggs uses the spelling "pedlers" in the original.

45. The file, from the Western History Collections at the University of Oklahoma Libraries, also includes a one-page biography composed primarily in sentence fragments and sent to Campbell by Barrett Clark at Riggs's request.

46. The Campbell papers in the Western History Collections at the University of Oklahoma Libraries contain only two more letters from Riggs, dated in 1937 and 1948. In the first, from Hollywood, Riggs responds to a request for money from Campbell that "I am not only completely broke, but begging, myself" (Riggs to Campbell, September 8, 1937). In the latter, from New York, he again expresses regret, this time for two conflicts—a ten-day festival of three of his plays at the University of Iowa and the beginning of rehearsals in New York for *Verdigris Primitive*—that prevent him from returning to accept a citation from the University of Oklahoma and, at the same time, seeing his old friend "after how many years!" (Riggs to Campbell, April 17, 1948). For the explanation of the citation, see Braunlich, *Haunted by Home*, 173.

47. Margaret Stevenson sent the letter, which can be found in the Lynn Riggs Papers at the Beinecke, on February 18, 1935. Though she had not read *The Cherokee Night*, she concluded after reading a review of it in the *New York Times* that it was "the most significant treatment of the Indian theme in my twentieth century group." Wilson completed her thesis and earned her degree in 1957.

48. Green speculated correctly about the fate of the manuscript. After her brother died in 1954, Riggs's sister Mattie Cundiff donated his manuscripts to the Lynn Riggs Memorial in Claremore, Oklahoma. Braunlich, Riggs's biographer, found the poems for *This Book, This Hill, These People* in those papers. Riggs considered *Hamlet Not the Only* and *Of Oak and Innocence* as titles for the manuscript that he sent to Green. Poems with both titles appear in *This Book*, which suggests that Cundiff had a similar if not the same manuscript as Green and the University of North Carolina Press.

49. The less-well-known Mdewakanton Dakota writer Irene C. Beaulieu also appears with Kathleen Woodward, her Osage coeditor of *Tributes to a Vanishing Race* (1916). McNickle held an academic position near the end of his life: he taught at the University of Saskatchewan in the Department of Anthropology from 1966 to 1970.

50. See Watkins 168–170 for a comparison of Mathews's and Momaday's versions of the prayer and Chapter Four in Owens, *Other Destinies*, for an analysis of the ceremony's influence on the novel's form.

51. Momaday identifies this poem as his first publication in Schubnell, *Conversations with N. Scott Momaday*, 113. The *New Mexico Quarterly* published "The Bear and the Colt" and "The Eagles of the Valle Grande" in its Summer 1967 issue, 101–11. Silko pub-

lished "The Man to Send Rain Clouds" as Leslie Chapman. Pearce traces the origins of the *New Mexico Quarterly* to the *Southwest Review* in a letter to Dobie dated December 27, 1955. The *Southwest Review* was founded at the University of Texas at Austin as the *Texas Review* in 1915 before moving to Southern Methodist University in 1924 under the new name *Southwest Review*.

5. Crimes against Indigeneity

1. Conan Doyle read historian Francis Parkman (see the last paragraph of chapter 9 of Conan Doyle's 1907 *Through the Magic Door*, available at www.gutenberg.org/cache/epub/5317/pg5317-images.html) and novelist Thomas Mayne Reid (see the last paragraph of chapter 1 of Conan Doyle's 1924 *Memories and Adventures*, available at gutenberg.net.au/ebooks14/1400681h.html). When he recalls his 1914 travels to the United States in *Memories and Adventures*, Conan Doyle exclaims, "What deeds have I not done among Redskins and trappers and grizzlies within their wilds! And here they were at last glimmering bright in the rising morning son. At least, I have seen my dream mountains. Most boys never do" (chapter 15). See also Conan Doyle's *Our American Adventure* (1923) and *Our Second American Adventure* (1924).

2. Mourning Dove identified as Okanogan. See *Mourning Dove: A Salishan Autobiography* (1990) for her family history.

3. Downing's optimism remained evident in *The Mexican Earth*, a history of Mexico published in 1940. See chapter 3 of Cox, *The Red Land to the South*.

4. Her last name translates into English as "major mountain" or "very important mountain."

5. Rennert recalls a conversation with the doctor while on a train at an indeterminate time in the recent past. He drives himself from Texas to the hacienda in northern Mexico, and Downing does not make clear when precisely he had the opportunity to travel on a train.

6. I have been aware of laFavor's two novels since including them in the "Selected Bibliography of Novels by Indigenous Authors in the United States and Canada" in my first book, *Muting White Noise: Native American and European American Novel Traditions* (2006). However, I have not written about them until now. Since laFavor identifies as Ojibwa, I will use that spelling when referring to her and her characters.

7. Tatonetti reads laFavor's two novels "as the first of an emerging genre of texts that claim an overtly Two-Spirit erotic as well as vital precursors to the present embrace of sovereign erotics in Indigenous studies" ("Detecting Two Spirit Erotics," 375). She has also recovered laFavor's labor as an HIV/AIDS activist in the late 1980s and early 1990s. Tatonetti observes, "laFavor's cultural advocacy for Indigenous-specific HIV/AIDS education displays an embodied understanding of health sovereignty that existed long before the term was coined" ("Carole laFavor's Indigenous Feminism and Early HIV/AIDS Activism," 276–77). See also Siobhan Senier for a disability studies approach to the politics of rehabilitation, or, more specifically, the politics of the "indigenous rehabilitative contract," in laFavor's novels ("Rehabilitation Reservations").

8. LaFavor might have combined the names of the Red Lake and White Earth Reservations to form the name Red Earth. However, in the same way that Vine Deloria uses the term in *Red Earth, White Lies*, published one year after *Along the Journey River*, the name also asserts Indigenous claims to the land and to ways of knowing and living on that land.

9. For the references to LaRoche at both Alcatraz and the occupation of the Bureau

of Indian Affairs building in Washington, D.C., and the comment regarding Jenny's father's flight following a false accusation of beating an FBI agent, see *Along the Journey River*, 98. LaRoche uses the treatment of Leonard Peltier by federal law enforcement as an example of why Jenny's father remains in hiding or "underground" (98).

10. See Basil Johnston, *The Manitous*, 172, for a description of dreamers as guides and teachers in the Anishinabe world.

11. LaFavor uses both lesbian and two-spirit to identify LaRoche. The Clinton administration instituted "Don't ask, don't tell" in 1994. For the evidence that Downing was gay, see Curtis Evans, *Clues and Corpses*, and Rzepka, "Queering the Investigation" and "Red and White and Pink All Over." In the latter, Rzepka asserts that Downing was "a closeted gay man who, if the preferences of his detective heroes are any indication, was attracted exclusively to white males, especially of the Nordic type" (354). A comparison of the gender, sexual, and racial politics of Downing's and laFavor's crime novels awaits.

12. Amateur detective figures, as distinguished from professional detectives working either for the state or in private practice, appear throughout the history of crime fiction.

13. Begay appears to refer to ARPA, though the phrase she quotes does not appear in the legislation.

14. Her grandmother tells her, for example, "Everyone knows Anishanabe came from Gitchie Manitou breathing life into the *megis* shell" (laFavor, *Along the Journey River*, 31), and LaRoche remembers her grandmother's story about Nanabozho marrying one of his own daughters (89). LaFavor identifies Samantha several times as a professor and shows her at work on her writing but does not provide additional details about her work.

15. Scholars could place laFavor's novels in productive political conversation with *Last Standing Woman*, which plays a central role in Suzack's essay and includes an occupation of tribal government offices linked by LaDuke to the occupations at the Bureau of Indian Affairs in 1972, Wounded Knee in 1973, and Oka in 1990.

16. Theresa Smith defines the *windigo, windigok* (pl.) as "A Matchi-Manitou(k) who is one of the most feared, especially among northern Ojibwa and Cree. Represented as a giant ice monster and/or cannibal and said to have once been a human who died from starvation or, alternately, who ate his family in order to survive. Windigo may attack Anishnaabeg and both starvation and gluttony can cause one to suffer windigo sickness (i.e. to become windigo)" (*The Island of the Anishnaabeg*, 201).

17. We hear about Billy Walking Bear's life from LaRoche's great-aunt Lydia, her grandmother's sister. See laFavor, *Along the Journey River*, 141.

18. See, for example, Justice, *Our Fire Survives the Storm*, 28–30.

19. For a reading of the politics of King's *The Red Power Murders*, see Cox, "One Good Protest."

20. Tatonetti compares Rosa Mae Two Thunder to Freda Goodrunning, who was murdered in Edmonton, Canada, in 2014. See "Detecting Two Spirit Erotics," 382.

21. See Pettit, "A Legacy of Furious Men," in which he discusses Tomson's *Dry Lips Oughta Move to Kapuskasing* (1989), Two-Rivers's *Chili Corn* (1997; 2001), Nolan's *Annie Mae's Movement* (1998; 2006), and King's *Evening at the Warbonnet* (1994; 2006). Pettit observes, "Four Indigenous plays first staged from 1989 to 1998 evaluate the legacy of the American Indian Movement, with particular attention to AIM's history of violence against women. Using the artifice of drama to render divisive experiences coherent, the plays expose conflicts and contradictions within AIM in order to posit a top-down misogyny at odds with the organization's mission as an agent of change" (29). Following

Pettit, I have provided the date of first performance and, when applicable, the date of publication.

22. See Alexie, *Smoke Signals*, 38. Both short stories appear in *The Lone Ranger and Tonto Fistfight in Heaven* (1993).

23. Hoklotubbe mentions wild onions and grape dumplings in *Deception on All Accounts*, 33, 58–59.

24. Hoklotubbe refers to owls on page 112 and calls crawdads "traditional Cherokee food" on page 84.

25. As Beth Piatote observes, in the context of hearing the Hail Mary in Nimipuutímt, the Nez Perce language, "Liturgical texts remain one of the sites where the local indigenous languages have found a degree of refuge through many years of colonial incursion" ("Our [Someone Else's] Father," 199).

26. Bonnin's reporting on violence against Native women in *Oklahoma's Poor Rich Indians*, in which she describes meeting eighteen-year-old Millie Neharkey and hearing the story of her abduction and sexual assault (26), establishes political and literary historical links between this text and laFavor's and Erdrich's novels.

27. Holmes refers to "the scarlet thread of murder running through the colourless skein of life" in *A Study in Scarlet* (40).

Conclusion

1. See "'It Just Felt Very Wrong,'" the National Public Radio story that includes interviews with several of the women describing Alexie's abuse ("'It Just Felt Very Wrong': Sherman Alexie's Accusers Go on the Record," *All Things Considered*, March 5, 2018, https://www.npr.org/2018/03/05/589909379/it-just-felt-very-wrong-sherman-alexies-accusers-go-on-the-record), and "Falls Apart Productions LLC: For Immediate Release," Alexie's official public statement. In the statement, Alexie says, "There are women telling the truth about my behavior and I have no recollection of physically or verbally threatening anybody or their careers" (press release, February 28, 2018, https://www.indianz.com/News/2018/03/01/shermanalexie022818.pdf).

2. Bird has her own bleak view of life on the Spokane Reservation. In "Breaking the Silence," she argues that "subdued depression that manifests itself in high suicide rates, alcoholism, drug- and alcohol-related violence, and death" makes the Spokane Reservation "not the kind of place I would raise my children" (43).

3. See Green, "The Pocahontas Perplex"; Vine Deloria, "The Indians of the American Imagination"; and Vizenor, "Postindian Warriors" in *Manifest Manners*, 1–44. Deloria explains the way non-Native interest primarily in Indians of the distant past, "the ghostly figures that America loved and cherished," prevents non-Natives from understanding the cultural, social, and political issues of late-twentieth-century American Indian life (30). By focusing on the distant past, authors enable non-Native readers to assume that "real" Indigenous populations have disappeared, as promised in so many literary, historical, and scientific texts within the same colonialist storytelling traditions. Assuming the absence of any Indigenous populations that might offer resistance enables the continuance of settler–colonial policies in the present.

4. For two assessments of Alexie's subversive work, see Cox, "Muting White Noise," and Gillan, "Reservation Home Movies."

5. See Cox, *Muting White Noise*, 178–99, for an extended discussion of the politics of storytelling in *Indian Killer*.

6. See Purdy, "Crossroads," in which Alexie says, "If Indian literature can't be read

by the average 12-year-old on the reservation, what the hell good is it? You couldn't take any of his [Vizenor's] books and take them to a rez and teach them, without extreme protestation" (7).

7. These articles appear in Vizenor, *Tribal Scenes and Ceremonies.*

BIBLIOGRAPHY

Adkins, Camille. "Interview with N. Scott Momaday." In *Conversations with N. Scott Momaday,* edited by Matthias Schubnell, 216–34. Jackson: University Press of Mississippi, 1997.
Aleiss, Angela. "Who Was the Real James Young Deer?" *Bright Lights Film Journal,* April 30, 2013. https://brightlightsfilm.com/who-was-the-real-james-young -deer-the-mysterious-identity-of-the-pathe-producer-finally-comes-to-light/#. UtkhP_ucs6w.
Alexie, Sherman. *The Business of Fancydancing: The Screenplay.* Brooklyn, N.Y.: Hanging Loose Press, 2003.
———. *First Indian on the Moon.* Brooklyn, N.Y.: Hanging Loose Press, 1993.
———. *Flight.* New York: Black Cat, 2007.
———. *Indian Killer.* New York: Atlantic Monthly Press, 1996.
———. *Indian Killer.* Audiotape. Audio Literature, 1996.
———. "Introduction: Death in Hollywood." *Ploughshares* 26, no. 4 (Winter 2000–2001): 7–10.
———. Introduction to *Watershed,* by Percival Everett, vii–xii. Boston: Beacon, 2003.
———. *The Lone Ranger and Tonto Fistfight in Heaven.* New York: HarperPerennial, 1993.
———. *One Stick Song.* Brooklyn, N.Y.: Hanging Loose Press, 2000.
———. *Reservation Blues.* New York: Atlantic Monthly Press, 1995.
———. *Smoke Signals: A Screenplay.* New York: Hyperion, 1998.
———. *The Summer of Black Widows.* Brooklyn, N.Y.: Hanging Loose Press, 1996.
———. *The Toughest Indian in the World.* New York: Atlantic Monthly Press, 2000.
Allen, Paula Gunn. "Special Problems in Teaching Leslie Marmon Silko's *Ceremony.*" *American Indian Quarterly* 14, no. 4 (Autumn 1990): 379–86.
Anders, Mary Ann. "Cross of the Martyrs." *Bulletin of the Historic Santa Fe Foundation* 2, no. 1 (March 1996): 1–5.
"Annual Convention." *American Indian Magazine,* Fall 1919, 145–80.
Barnabas, Rev. Dr. Letter to the editor. *American Indian* 5, no. 3 (December 1930–January 1931): 4.
Berkhofer, Robert F., Jr. *The White Man's Indian: Images of the American Indian from Columbus to the Present.* New York: Vintage, 1979.
Bernardin, Susan. "The Lessons of a Sentimental Education: Zitkala-Ša's Autobiographical Narratives." *Western American Literature* 32, no. 3 (Fall 1997): 212–38.
Birchfield, D. L. *Black Silk Handkerchief: A Hom-Astubby Mystery.* Norman: University of Oklahoma Press, 2006.
Bird, Gloria. "Breaking the Silence: Writing as Witness." In *Speaking for the Generations: Native Writers on Writing,* edited by Simon Ortiz, 27–49. Tucson: University of Arizona Press, 1998.

———. "The Exaggeration of Despair in Sherman Alexie's *Reservation Blues*." *Wicazo Sa Review* 11, no. 2 (Fall 1995): 47–52.

Bonnin, Gertrude / Zitkala-Ša. "America, Home of the Red Man." *American Indian Magazine*, Winter 1919, 165–67.

———. *American Indian Stories*. Washington: Hayworth Publishing House, 1921.

———. "Chipeta, Widow of Chief Ouray, with a Word about a Deal in Blankets." *American Indian Magazine*, July–September 1917, 168–70.

———. "A Christmas Letter from Zit-kal-a-sa: Describes Her Community Improvement Work among the Utes." *Quarterly Journal of the Society of American Indians*, October–December 1915, 322–25.

———. "The Coronation of Chief Powhatan Retold." *American Indian Magazine*, Winter 1919, 179–80.

———. "Editorial Comment." *American Indian Magazine*, Autumn (July–September) 1918, 113–14.

———. "Editorial Comment." *American Indian Magazine*, Winter 1919, 161–62.

———. "Indian Gifts to Civilized Man." *American Indian Magazine*, Autumn (July–September) 1918, 115–16.

———. "An Indian Praying on the Hilltop." *American Indian Magazine*, Summer 1919, 92.

———. "The Indian's Awakening." *Quarterly Journal of the Society of American Indians*, January–March 1916, 57–59.

———. Letter to Carlos Montezuma, June 1, 1901. Carlos Montezuma Collection, 1877–1980. Labriola National American Indian Data Center, Arizona State University Library, Tempe, Arizona.

———. "Letter to the Chiefs and Headmen of the Tribes." *American Indian Magazine*, Winter 1919, 196–97.

———. "The Red Man's America." *American Indian Magazine*, January–March 1917, 64.

———. "A Sioux Woman's Love for Her Grandmother." *American Indian Magazine*, October–December 1917, 230–31.

———. "A Year's Experience in Community Service Work among the Ute Tribe of Indians." *American Indian Magazine*, October–December 1916, 307–10.

Bonnin, Gertrude / Zitkala-Ša, Charles H. Fabens, and Matthew K. Sniffen. *Oklahoma's Poor Rich Indians*. Philadelphia: Office of the Indian Rights Association, 1924.

Braunlich, Phyllis Cole. *Haunted by Home: The Life and Letters of Lynn Riggs*. Norman: University of Oklahoma Press, 1988.

———. "Oklahoma's Outstanding Poet-Playwright Lynn Riggs (1899–1954)." Introduction to *This Book, This Hill, These People*, by Lynn Riggs. Tulsa, Okla.: Lynn Chase, 1982. 7–8.

Brody, J. J. *Pueblo Indian Painting: Tradition and Modernism in New Mexico, 1900–1930*. Santa Fe: School of American Research, 1997.

Brooks, Joanna, ed. *The Collected Writings of Samson Occom, Mohegan: Leadership and Literature in Eighteenth-Century Native America*. New York: Oxford University Press, 2006.

Brooks, Lisa. *The Common Pot: The Recovery of Native Space in the Northeast*. Minneapolis: University of Minnesota Press, 2008.

Brown, Kirby. "Citizenship, Law, and Land: Constitutional Criticism and John Milton Oskison's *Black Jack Davy*." *Studies in American Indian Literatures* 23, no. 4 (Winter 2011): 77–115.

———. *Stoking the Fire: Nationhood in Cherokee Writing, 1907–1970*. Norman: University of Oklahoma Press, 2018.

Bruner, Joe. "A Creek's Uncles Always Selected His Companions in Life." *American Indian* 1, no. 10 (July 1927): 8.

———. "The Indian Women Served as the Official 'Scalp Takers.'" *American Indian* 1, no. 8 (May 1927): 8, 16.

———. "Interesting Legend Tells Indian Came from So. America." *American Indian* 1, no. 6 (March 1927): 10–11.

———. "Legends and Traditions of Muskogee Indians Revealed." *American Indian* 1, no. 9 (June 1927): 6, 16.

———. "Many Clans Were Formed in Ranks of Native American." *American Indian* 1, no. 11 (August 1927): 10–11.

———. "Removal of Five Tribes to Oklahoma Is Historical Event." *American Indian* 2, no. 2 (November 1927): 6.

Buford, Kate. *Native American Son: The Life and Sporting Legend of Jim Thorpe*. New York: Knopf, 2010.

Campbell, Walter S. (Stanley Vestal). *The Book Lover's Southwest: A Guide to Good Reading*. Norman: University of Oklahoma Press, 1955.

———. Letter to John Joseph Mathews, January 7, 1933. Walter S. Campbell Collection. Box 32, F-27. Western History Collections, University of Oklahoma Libraries, Norman, Oklahoma.

———. Letter to Natachee Scott Momaday, June 18, 1954. Walter S. Campbell Collection. Box 33, folder 11. Western History Collections, University of Oklahoma Libraries, Norman, Oklahoma.

———. Letter to Natachee Scott Momaday, June 22, 1954. Walter S. Campbell Collection. Box 33, folder 11. Western History Collections, University of Oklahoma Libraries, Norman, Oklahoma.

———. "Lynn Riggs: Poet and Dramatist." *Southwest Review* 15, no. 1 (Autumn 1929): 64–71.

Carroll, John M. Introduction to *The American Indian*, edited by John M. Carroll, vol. 1, unpaginated. New York: Liveright, 1970.

Carver, H. P., dir. *The Silent Enemy*. Burden-Chanler Productions, 1930. DVD, distributed by Alpha Home Entertainment.

Cohen, Matt. "The Codex and the Knife." *Textual Cultures* 6, no. 2 (2011): 109–18.

Conan Doyle, Arthur. *Memories and Adventures*. London: Hodder and Stoughton, 1924. gutenberg.net.au/ebooks14/1400681h.html.

———. *A Study in Scarlet*. Oxford: Oxford University Press, 2008.

———. *Through the Magic Door*. 1907. http://www.gutenberg.org/cache/epub/5317/pg5317-images.html.

Conley, Robert J. *The Cherokee Nation: A History*. Albuquerque: University of New Mexico Press, 2005.

Cook-Lynn, Elizabeth. "American Indian Intellectualism and the New Indian Story." *American Indian Quarterly* 20, no. 1 (Winter 1996): 57–76.

———. *Why I Can't Read Wallace Stegner, and Other Essays*. Madison: University of Wisconsin Press, 1996.

Cosandaey, Mikelle, et al. *100 Years of Filmmaking in New Mexico, 1898–1998*. Santa Fe: *New Mexico Magazine* and the New Mexico Economic Development Office, 1998.

Costo, Rupert, et al. *Indian Voices: The First Convocation of American Indian Scholars*. San Francisco: Indian Historian Press, 1970.

Coulthard, Glen. *Red Skin, White Masks: Rejecting the Colonial Politics of Recognition*. Minneapolis: University of Minnesota Press, 2014.

Coward, John M. "Promoting the Progressive Indian: Lee Harkins and *The American Indian Magazine*." *American Journalism* 14, no. 1 (Winter 1997): 3–18.

Cox, James H. *Muting White Noise: Native American and European American Novel Traditions*. Norman: University of Oklahoma Press, 2006.

———. "Muting White Noise: The Subversion of Popular Culture Narratives of Conquest in Sherman Alexie's Fiction." *Studies in American Indian Literatures* 9, no. 4 (Winter 1997): 52–70.

———. "One Good Protest: Thomas King, Indian Policy, and American Indian Activism." In *Thomas King: Works and Impact*, edited by Eva Gruber, 224–37. Rochester, N.Y.: Camden House, 2012.

———. *The Red Land to the South: American Indian Writers and Indigenous Mexico*. Minneapolis: University of Minnesota Press, 2012.

———. "Tribal Nations and Other Territories of American Indian Literary History." In *A Companion to American Literary Studies*, edited by Caroline F. Levander and Robert S. Levine, 356–72. Malden, Mass.: Wiley-Blackwell, 2011.

Cox, James H., and Daniel Heath Justice. "Introduction: Post-Renaissance Indigenous American Literary Studies." In *The Oxford Handbook of Indigenous American Literature*, edited by James H. Cox and Daniel Heath Justice, 1–11. New York: Oxford University Press, 2014.

Dahl, Robert. "The Concept of Power." *Behavioral Science* 2, no. 3 (1957): 201–15.

Davis, Steven L. *J. Frank Dobie: A Liberated Mind*. Austin: University of Texas Press, 2009.

Deloria, Ella. *Waterlily*. Lincoln: University of Nebraska Press, 1988.

Deloria, Philip J. *Indians in Unexpected Places*. Lawrence: University Press of Kansas, 2006.

———. *Playing Indian*. New Haven: Yale University Press, 1998.

Deloria, Vine, Jr. *Behind the Trail of Broken Treaties: An Indian Declaration of Independence*. Austin: University of Texas Press, 1974.

———. *Custer Died for Your Sins*. Norman: University of Oklahoma Press, 1988.

———. "The Indians of the American Imagination." In *God Is Red: A Native View of Religion*, 25–45. Golden, Colo.: Fulcrum, 1994.

———. *Red Earth, White Lies: Native Americans and the Myth of Scientific Fact*. Golden, Colo.: Fulcrum, 1997.

DeMallie, Raymond J., ed. *The Sixth Grandfather: Black Elk's Teachings Given to John G. Neihardt*. Lincoln: University of Nebraska Press, 1984.

Diamond, Neil, dir. *Reel Injun*. Rezolution Pictures, 2009.

Dobie, J. Frank. *Apache Gold and Yaqui Silver*. Boston: Little, Brown, 1939.

———. "Black Gold and Roses." Review of *Life and Death of an Oilman: The Career of E. W. Marland*, by John Joseph Mathews. *New York Times*, October 21, 1951.

———. "Can a Coyote Raise His Tail?" *Oklahoman*, March 11, 1951, 60.

———. *Coronado's Children: Tales of Lost Mines and Buried Treasures of the Southwest*. Dallas: Southwest Press, 1930.

———. *Guide to Life and Literature of the Southwest*. 1st ed. Austin: University of Texas Press, 1943.

———. *Guide to Life and Literature of the Southwest*. 2nd ed. Dallas: Southern Methodist University Press, 1952.

———. Letter to Walter Campbell, May 14, 1938. Dobie Papers, Subseries C: Recipient, 1899–1967. Vestal, Stanley. Container 182.1. Harry Ransom Center, the University of Texas at Austin, Austin, Texas.

Bibliography

———. Letter to Clarence C. Lester, December 1, 1949. Dobie Papers, Subseries C: Recipient, 1899–1967. Tub-Turnbull. Container 180.1. Harry Ransom Center, the University of Texas at Austin, Austin, Texas.
———. Letter to John Joseph Mathews, January 12, 1951. Dobie Papers, Subseries C: Recipient, 1899–1967. Mathews, John Joseph. Container 139.4. Harry Ransom Center, the University of Texas at Austin, Austin, Texas.
———. Letter to John Joseph Mathews, February 28, 1951. Dobie Papers, Subseries C: Recipient, 1899–1967. Mathews, John Joseph. Container 139.4. Harry Ransom Center, the University of Texas at Austin, Austin, Texas.
———. Letter to John Joseph Mathews, May 14, 1960. Dobie Papers, Subseries C: Recipient, 1899–1967. Mathews, John Joseph. Container 139.4. Harry Ransom Center, the University of Texas at Austin, Austin, Texas.
———. Letter to John Joseph Mathews, November 6, 1961. Dobie Papers, Subseries C: Recipient, 1899–1967. Mathews, John Joseph. Container 139.4. Harry Ransom Center, the University of Texas at Austin, Austin, Texas.
———. Letter to John Joseph Mathews, June 5, 1963. Dobie Papers, Subseries C: Recipient, 1899–1967. Mathews, John Joseph. Container 139.4. Harry Ransom Center, the University of Texas at Austin, Austin, Texas.
———. Letter to Henry Nash Smith, October 3, 1947. Dobie Papers, Subseries C: Recipient, 1899–1967. Smith, Henry Nash, 1941–1962, undated. Container 167.5. Harry Ransom Center, the University of Texas at Austin, Austin, Texas.
———. *The Voice of the Coyote*. Boston: Little, Brown, 1949.
Dormon, James H. "Shaping the Popular Image of Post-Reconstruction American Blacks: The 'Coon Song' Phenomenon of the Gilded Age." *American Quarterly* 40, no. 4 (December 1988): 450–71.
Downing, Todd. *The Case of the Unconquered Sisters*. Garden City, N.Y.: Doubleday, 1936.
———. *The Mexican Earth*. New York: Doubleday, 1940.
———. *Murder on the Tropic*. New York: Doubleday, 1935.
———. *Murder on Tour*. New York: Putnam's, 1933.
Dunbar-Ortiz, Roxanne. *Indigenous People's History of the United States*. Boston: Beacon, 2014.
Eagleton, Terry. *Literary Theory: An Introduction*. Minneapolis: University of Minnesota Press, 1996.
"'El Portal' at the Palace of the Governors." *Collector's Guide Online*, July 4, 2013. http://www.collectorsguide.com/fa/fa075.shtml.
"Emily Peake Student File." Carlisle Indian School Digital Resource Center. http://carlisleindian.dickinson.edu/student_files/emily-peake-student-file.
English, James F. *The Economy of Prestige: Prizes, Awards, and the Circulation of Cultural Value*. Cambridge, Mass.: Harvard University Press, 2005.
Erdrich, Louise. Letter to Peter Matthiessen, August 15, 1984. Peter Matthiessen Papers, Addition, Series II: Correspondence, 1975–2002. Box 24, folder 8, D–F, Erdrich, Louise, and Dorris, Michael. Harry Ransom Center, the University of Texas at Austin, Austin, Texas.
———. Letter to Peter Matthiessen, May 18, 1985. Peter Matthiessen Papers, Addition, Series II: Correspondence, 1975–2002. Box 24, folder 8, D–F, Erdrich, Louise, and Dorris, Michael. Harry Ransom Center, the University of Texas at Austin, Austin, Texas.
———. Letter to Peter Matthiessen, January 21, 1987 (postmark date). Peter Matthiessen

Papers, Addition, Series II: Correspondence, 1975–2002. Box 24, folder 8, D–F, Erdrich, Louise, and Dorris, Michael. Harry Ransom Center, the University of Texas at Austin, Austin, Texas.

———. "Rape on the Reservation." *New York Times*, February 26, 2013. http://www.nytimes.com/2013/02/27/opinion/native-americans-and-the-violence-against-women-act.html.

———. *The Round House*. New York: HarperCollins, 2012.

———. "A Time for Human Rights on Native Ground." *New York Times*, December 29, 2000. http://www.nytimes.com/2000/12/29/opinion/a-time-for-human-rights-on-native-ground.html.

Evans, Curtis. *Clues and Corpses: The Detective Fiction and Mystery Criticism of Todd Downing*. Greenville, Ohio: Coachwhip Publications, 2013.

Evans, Katherine Liesl Young. "Staged Encounters: Native American Performance between 1880–1920." PhD diss., University of Texas at Austin, 2010.

Everett, Dianna. *The Texas Cherokees: A People between Two Fires, 1819–1840*. Norman: University of Oklahoma Press, 1990.

Fallaw, Ben. *Cárdenas Compromised: The Failure of Reform in Postrevolutionary Yucatán*. Durham, N.C.: Duke University Press, 2001.

Ferguson, Mrs. Walter. "Patriots Blind to Past of United States—History Reveals Much That Is Wrong." *American Indian* 4, no. 5 (February 1930): 4.

Fisher, Dexter. Foreword to *American Indian Stories*, by Zitkala-Ša, v–xx. Lincoln: University of Nebraska Press, 1985.

Fixico, Donald L. *The Invasion of Indian Country in the Twentieth Century: American Capitalism and Tribal Natural Resources*. 2nd ed. Boulder: University Press of Colorado, 2012.

———. *Termination and Relocation: Federal Indian Policy, 1945–1960*. Albuquerque: University of New Mexico Press, 1986.

Foreman, Carolyn Thomas. "Viscount Chateaubriand's Adventures with Muscogulges." *American Indian* 4, no. 4 (January 1930): 6–7.

Foster, Tol. "Of One Blood: An Argument for Relations and Regionality in Native American Literary Studies." In *Reasoning Together: The Native Critics Collective*, edited by Craig S. Womack, Daniel Heath Justice, and Christopher B. Teuton, 265–302. Norman: University of Oklahoma Press, 2008.

Frost, Laura. "Blondes Have More Fun: Anita Loos and the Language of Silent Cinema." *Modernism/modernity* 17, no. 2 (April 2010): 291–311.

Furlan, Laura M. *Indigenous Cities: Urban Indian Fiction and the Histories of Relocation*. Lincoln: University of Nebraska Press, 2017.

Gillan, Jennifer. "Reservation Home Movies: Sherman Alexie's Poetry." *American Literature* 68, no. 1 (1996): 91–110.

González, Gilbert G. *Culture of Empire: American Writers, Mexico, and Mexican Immigrants, 1880–1930*. Austin: University of Texas Press, 2004.

González, John Morán. *Border Renaissance: The Texas Centennial and the Emergence of Mexican American Literature*. Austin: University of Texas Press, 2009.

Graham, Don. "Pen Pals: Dobie, Bedichek, and Webb." In *Giant Country: Essays on Texas*, 103–16. Fort Worth: Texas Christian University Press, 1998.

Grant, Marshall. Letter "To Whom It May Concern (for Lynn Riggs)," July 29, 1942. Lynn Riggs Papers Series 1. Correspondence. Box 6, folder 116: David O. Selznick. Beinecke Library, Yale University, New Haven, Connecticut.

Grantham, Bill. *Creation Myths and Legends of the Creek Indians*. Gainesville: University Press of Florida, 2002.

Green, Paul. Letter to Lucy Kroll, March 15, 1965. Paul Green Papers. Southern Historical Collection, Wilson Library, the University of North Carolina at Chapel Hill, Chapel Hill, North Carolina.
———. Letter to Lucy Kroll, April 21, 1965. Paul Green Papers. Southern Historical Collection, Wilson Library, the University of North Carolina at Chapel Hill, Chapel Hill, North Carolina.
———. Letter to Lynn Riggs, May 25, 1933. Paul Green Papers. Southern Historical Collection, Wilson Library, the University of North Carolina at Chapel Hill, Chapel Hill, North Carolina.
———. Letter to Lynn Riggs, September 4, 1952. Paul Green Papers. Southern Historical Collection, Wilson Library, the University of North Carolina at Chapel Hill, Chapel Hill, North Carolina.
Green, Rayna. "The Pocahontas Perplex: The Image of Indian Women in American Culture." *Massachusetts Review* 16, no. 4 (1975): 698–714.
———. "The Tribe Called Wannabee: Playing Indian in America and Europe." *Folkore* 99, no. 1 (1988): 30–55.
Guidotti-Hernández, Nicole. "National Appropriations: Yaqui Autonomy, the Centennial of the Mexican Revolution, and the Bicentennial of the Mexican Nation." *Latin Americanist*, March 2011, 69–92.
Hafen, P. Jane. *Dreams and Thunder: Stories, Poems, and "The Sun Dance Opera."* Lincoln: University of Nebraska Press, 2001.
———. "Zitkala Ša: Sentimentality and Sovereignty." *Wicazo Sa Review* 12, no. 2 (Fall 1997): 31–42.
Halpin, Joseph. Letter to James Hughes, correspondence, January 22, 1970. *A Day in Santa Fe* File. New Mexico Commission of Public Records / State Records Center and Archive.
Hamilton, Charles, ed. *Cry of the Thunderbird: The American Indian's Own Story.* New York: Macmillan, 1950.
Hammett, Dashiell. *Red Harvest.* 1929. New York: Vintage, 1992.
Harjo, Joy. *Crazy Brave: A Memoir.* New York: Norton, 2012.
Harkins, Lee F. "Culture of the Indian." *American Indian* 4, no. 4 (January 1930): 4.
———. "Dedication." *American Indian* 1, no. 1 (October 1926): 1.
———. Editorial. *American Indian* 1, no. 1 (October 1926): 4.
———. "The Indians' Vote." *American Indian* 4, no. 6 (March 1930): 4.
———. "Our Code of Ethics." *American Indian* 1, no. 1 (October 1926): 4.
———. "Sentimental Civilization." *American Indian* 4, no. 5 (February 1930): 4.
———. "Two Pulitzer Prizes." *American Indian* 4, no. 8 (May 1930): 4.
Hartshorne, Ewing. "Indian Lore Quiz." *American Indian* 1, no. 11 (August 1927): 4, 6.
Harvey, Gretchen G. "Cherokee and American: Ruth Muskrat Bronson, 1897–1982." PhD diss., Arizona State University, 1996.
Hearne, Joanna. *Native Recognition: Indigenous Cinema and the Western.* Albany: SUNY Press, 2012.
———. *Smoke Signals: Native Cinema Rising.* Lincoln: University of Nebraska Press, 2012.
———. "'This Is Our Playground': Skateboarding, DIY Aesthetics, and Apache Sovereignty in Dustinn Craig's *4wheelwarpony*." *Western American Literature* 49, no. 1 (Spring 2014): 47–69.
Hertzberg, Hazel W. *The Search for an American Indian Identity: Modern Pan-Indian Movements.* Syracuse, N.Y.: Syracuse University Press, 1971.

Hochbruck, Wolfgang. "Mystery Novels to Choctaw Pageant: Todd Downing and Native American Literature(s)." In *New Voices in Native American Literary Criticism*, edited by Arnold Krupat, 205–21. Washington, D.C.: Smithsonian Institution Press, 1993.

Hogan, Linda. *Mean Spirit*. New York: Atheneum, 1990.

Hoklotubbe, Sara Sue. *The American Café*. Tucson: University of Arizona Press, 2011.

———. *Deception on All Accounts*. Tucson: University of Arizona Press, 2003.

———. *Sinking Suspicions*. Tucson: University of Arizona Press, 2014.

Hollrah, Patrice E. M. *"The Old Lady Trill, the Victory Yell": The Power of Women in Native American Literature*. New York: Routledge, 2004.

Horak, Jan-Christopher. "The First American Film Avant-Garde, 1919–1945." In *Experimental Film: The Film Reader*, edited by Gwendolyn Audrey Foster and Wheeler Winston Dixon, 19–52. New York: Routledge, 2002.

Horsman, Reginald. *Race and Manifest Destiny: The Origins of American Racial Anglo-Saxonism*. Cambridge, Mass.: Harvard University Press, 1981.

Houghton, Louise Seymour. *Our Debt to the Red Man: The French-Indians in the Development of the United States*. Boston: Stratford, 1918.

Howe, LeAnne. *Choctalking on Other Realities*. San Francisco: Aunt Lute, 2013.

Hughes, James. Letter to Joseph Halpin, correspondence, January 26, 1970. *A Day in Santa Fe* file. New Mexico Commission of Public Records / State Records Center and Archive.

Huhndorf, Shari M. "Indigenous Feminism, Performance, and the Politics of Memory in the Plays of Monique Mojica." In *Indigenous Women and Feminism: Politics, Activism, Culture*, edited by Cheryl Suzack, Shari M. Huhndorf, Jeanne Perreault, and Jean Barman, 181–98. Vancouver: University of British Columbia Press, 2010.

Huhndorf, Shari M., and Cheryl Suzack. "Indigenous Feminism: Theorizing the Issues." *Indigenous Women and Feminism: Politics, Activism, Culture*, edited by Cheryl Suzack, Shari M. Huhndorf, Jeanne Perreault, and Jean Barman, 1–20. Vancouver: University of British Columbia Press, 2010.

Hutchinson, Elizabeth. *The Indian Craze: Primitivism, Modernism, and Transculturation in American Art, 1890–1915*. Durham, N.C.: Duke University Press, 2009.

Hutner, Gordon. *What America Read: Taste, Class, and the Novel, 1920–1960*. Chapel Hill: University of North Carolina Press, 2009.

"Introducing 'Ye Editor.'" *American Indian* 1, no. 1 (October 1926): 4.

Jameson, Fredric. *The Political Unconscious: Narrative as a Socially Symbolic Act*. Ithaca, N.Y.: Cornell University Press, 1981.

Johnson, Robinson [Whirling Thunder]. "Some 200 Signs Used Effectively in Indian Sign Language." *American Indian* 4, no. 4 (January 1930): 14.

Johnston, Basil. *The Manitous: The Supernatural World of the Ojibway*. New York: HarperCollins, 1995.

Johnston, Ralph A. Letter to John Joseph Mathews, November 17, 1960. Dobie Papers, Subseries C: Recipient, 1899–1967. Johnston, Ralph A. Container 123.5. Harry Ransom Center, the University of Texas at Austin, Austin, Texas.

Jones, Rupel J. Letter to Lynn Riggs, July 16, 1945. Lynn Riggs Papers. Series 1. Correspondence. Box 5, folder 126: University of Oklahoma. Beinecke Library, Yale University, New Haven, Connecticut.

Justice, Daniel Heath. *Our Fire Survives the Storm: A Cherokee Literary History*. Minneapolis: University of Minnesota Press, 2006.

———. *Why Indigenous Literatures Matter*. Waterloo, Ontario: Wilfrid Laurier University Press, 2017.

Bibliography

Kalter, Susan. Introduction to *Twenty Thousand Mornings: An Autobiography*, edited by Susan Kalter, xvii–lv. Norman: University of Oklahoma Press, 2012.

———. "John Joseph Mathews' Reverse Ethnography: The Literary Dimensions of *Wah'Kon-Tah*." *Studies in American Indian Literatures* 14, no. 1 (Spring 2002): 26–50.

Kaplan, Alice. *The Interpreter*. New York: Free Press, 2005.

Ke Mo Ha [Patrick Patterson]. Preface to *The American Indian*, edited by John M. Carroll, vol. 1, unpaginated. New York: Liveright, 1970.

Keys, Lucy Lowrey Hoyt. "Historical Sketches of the Cherokees, Together with Some of Their Customs, Traditions, and Superstitions (1889)." In *Native American Women's Writing, 1800–1924*, edited by Karen L. Kilcup, 71–89. Malden, Mass.: Blackwell, 2000.

King, Thomas. *DreadfulWater Shows Up*. New York: Scribner, 2003.

———. *The Red Power Murders: A DreadfulWater Mystery*. Toronto: HarperCollins, 2006.

Kirk, Betty. Unpublished and untitled article, n.d. Lynn Riggs Papers. Box 1, folder 7. Western History Collections, University of Oklahoma Libraries, Norman, Oklahoma.

Konkle, Maureen. *Writing Indian Nations: Native Intellectuals and the Politics of Historiography, 1827–1863*. Chapel Hill: University of North Carolina Press, 2004.

Kramer, Gary M. "Sherman Alexie: It's Funny That Hollywood Would Hire an Indian to Make White People More Likeable." *Salon*, October 31, 2014. http://www.salon.com/2014/10/31/sherman_alexie_it%E2%80%99s_funny_that_hollywood_would_hire_an_indian_to_make_white_people_more_likable/.

Kroll, Lucy. Letter to Paul Green, April 21, 1965. Paul Green Papers. Southern Historical Collection, Wilson Library, the University of North Carolina at Chapel Hill, Chapel Hill, North Carolina.

LaDuke, Winona. *Last Standing Woman*. Stillwater, Minn.: Voyageur Press, 1997.

laFavor, Carole. *Along the Journey River*. Ithaca, N.Y.: Firebrand, 1996.

———. *Evil Dead Center*. Ithaca, N.Y.: Firebrand, 1997.

Langdon, F. D. Letter to Lynn Riggs, November 14, 1944. Lynn Riggs Papers Series 1. Correspondence. Box 6, folder 123: Lionel Trilling, Martin Tucker, and Twentieth-Century Fox Film Corporation. Beinecke Library, Yale University, New Haven, Connecticut.

———. Letter to Lynn Riggs, December 8, 1944. Lynn Riggs Papers Series 1. Correspondence. Box 6, folder 123: Lionel Trilling, Martin Tucker, and Twentieth-Century Fox Film Corporation. Beinecke Library, Yale University, New Haven, Connecticut.

Lanier, Fanita. "A Literary Map of the Southwest." *Saturday Review of Literature*, May 16, 1942, 22–23.

Lapier, Rosalyn R., and David R. M. Beck. *City Indian: Native American Activism in Chicago, 1893–1934*. Lincoln: University of Nebraska Press, 2015.

Larré, Lionel, ed. *Tales of the Old Indian Territory and Essays on the Indian Condition*. Lincoln: University of Nebraska Press, 2012.

Layson, Geo. M. "Ancient Peruvian Civilization." *American Indian* 4, no. 4 (January 1930): 15.

Lee, Mark. "Tulsa Farm Club in Service 50 Years." *Tulsa World*, November 18, 1989. http://www.tulsaworld.com/archives/tulsa-farm-club-in-service-years/article_55eb7185-01c4-5d1d-a6b7-ffdf3acc9f7d.html.

Lesser, Wendy. "Louise Erdrich's Plains Song." *Washington Post*, August 31, 1986. https://www.washingtonpost.com/archive/entertainment/books/1986/08/31/louise-erdrichs-plains-song/97c955c2-db0b-4d36-8033-c695f0ae6625/?noredirect=on&utm_term=.7c89273c6c94.

Lester, Clarence C. (Tulsa Farm Club). Letter to J. Frank Dobie, December 5, 1949. Dobie Papers, Subseries C: Recipient, 1899–1967. Tub-Turnbull. Container 180.1. Harry Ransom Center, the University of Texas at Austin, Austin, Texas.

Lewandowski, Tadeusz. *Red Bird, Red Power: The Life and Legacy of Zitkala-Ša*. Norman: University of Oklahoma Press, 2016.

Littlefield, Daniel F., Jr. "Utopian Dreams of the Cherokee Fullbloods: 1890–1934." *Journal of the West* 10, no. 3 (July 1971): 404–27.

Littlefield, Daniel F., Jr., and James W. Parins, eds. *Native American Writing in the Southeast: An Anthology*. Jackson: University Press of Mississippi, 1995.

Lohmann, Annetta [Annette]. "Aboriginals at Dedicatory Services on Mount Thabor." *American Indian* 2, no. 5 (February 1928): 2.

———. "Christ, the World Saviour, Was Born in a Dingy Stable." *American Indian* 2, no. 1 (October 1927): 2.

———. "Holy Jerusalem Is the 'Shrine City' of the Entire World." *American Indian* 1, no. 10 (July 1927): 2.

———. "Many Denominations Vie for Supremacy in the Holy Land." *American Indian* 1, no. 12 (September 1927): 2.

———. "Many Places of Interest to Be Seen in the Holy Land." *American Indian* 2, no. 2 (November 1927): 2.

———. "Memory of Blessing Received from Eminent Pope Pius XI." *American Indian* 2, no. 6 (March 1928): 2.

———. "Mohammedans Forbid Christian Worship in Their Mosque." *American Indian* 1, no. 11 (August 1927): 2.

———. "Nazareth—Scene of Christ's Childhood—Has Cabaret." *American Indian* 2, no. 3 (December 1927): 2–3.

Lowe, Robert Liddell. "The Lyrics of Lynn Riggs." *Poetry*, March 1931, 347–49.

Lumet, Sidney. Letter to Lynn Riggs, May 14, 1951. Lynn Riggs Papers Series 1. Correspondence. Box 4, folder 79: Sidney Lumet and Alfred Lunt. Beinecke Library, Yale University, New Haven, Connecticut.

———. Letter to Lynn Riggs, June 11, 1952. Lynn Riggs Papers Series 1. Correspondence. Box 4, folder 79: Sidney Lumet and Alfred Lunt. Beinecke Library, Yale University, New Haven, Connecticut.

Lyons, Scott Richard. *X-Marks: Native Signatures of Assent*. Minneapolis: University of Minnesota Press, 2010.

Major, Mabel, and T. M. Pearce. *Signature of the Sun: Southwest Verse, 1900–1950*. Albuquerque: University of New Mexico Press, 1950.

Major, Mabel, Rebecca Smith, and T. M. Pearce. *Southwest Heritage: A Literary History with Bibliography*. Albuquerque: University of New Mexico Press, 1938.

———. *Southwest Heritage: A Literary History with Bibliography*. Rev. ed. Albuquerque: University of New Mexico Press, 1948.

Margolis, David. "An Interview with Mr. John Dorman." *A Day in Santa Fe* File, January 10, 1973, 1–6. New Mexico Commission of Public Records / State Records Center and Archive.

Mathews, John Joseph. Letter to Walter S. Campbell, December 3, 1930. Campbell, WS, Corres. Mathews. Western History Collections, University of Oklahoma Libraries, Norman, Oklahoma.

———. Letter to J. Frank Dobie, January 3, 1951. Dobie Papers, Subseries C: Recipient, 1899–1967. Mathews, John Joseph. Container 139.4. Harry Ransom Center, the University of Texas at Austin, Austin, Texas.

———. Letter to J. Frank Dobie, January 21, 1954. Dobie Papers, Subseries C: Recipient, 1899–1967. Mathews, John Joseph. Container 139.4. Harry Ransom Center, the University of Texas at Austin, Austin, Texas.

———. Letter to J. Frank Dobie, late 1959 or early 1960. Dobie Papers, Subseries C: Recipient, 1899–1967. Mathews, John Joseph. Container 139.4. Harry Ransom Center, the University of Texas at Austin, Austin, Texas.

———. Letter to J. Frank Dobie, May 9, 1960. Dobie Papers, Subseries C: Recipient, 1899–1967. Mathews, John Joseph. Container 139.4. Harry Ransom Center, the University of Texas at Austin, Austin, Texas.

———. Letter to J. Frank Dobie, January 7, 1963. Dobie Papers, Subseries C: Recipient, 1899–1967. Mathews, John Joseph. Container 139.4. Harry Ransom Center, the University of Texas at Austin, Austin, Texas.

———. Letter to J. Frank Dobie, April 18, 1963. Dobie Papers, Subseries C: Recipient, 1899–1967. Mathews, John Joseph. Container 139.4. Harry Ransom Center, the University of Texas at Austin, Austin, Texas.

———. *The Osages: Children of the Middle Waters*. Norman: University of Oklahoma Press, 1961.

———. *Sundown*. Norman: University of Oklahoma Press, 1988.

———. *Talking to the Moon*. Chicago: University of Chicago Press, 1945.

———. Taped Diary, reel 62, November 1959. Box 8: Sound Recordings. John Joseph Mathews Collection. Western History Collections, University of Oklahoma Libraries, Norman, Oklahoma.

———. Telegram to Dobie, December 15, 1949. Dobie Papers, Subseries C: Recipient, 1899–1967. Mathews, John Joseph. Container 139.4. Harry Ransom Center, the University of Texas at Austin, Austin, Texas.

———. *Twenty Thousand Mornings: An Autobiography*. Edited by Susan Kalter. Norman: University of Oklahoma Press, 2012.

———. *Wah'kon-tah: The Osage and the White Man's Road*. Norman: University of Oklahoma Press, 1932.

May, Jon D. "Bacon Rind." *Encyclopedia of Oklahoma History and Culture*. Oklahoma Historical Society. http://www.okhistory.org/publications/enc/entry.php?entry=BA003.

McAuliffe, Dennis, Jr. *Bloodland: A Family Story of Oil, Greed, and Murder on the Osage Reservation*. San Francisco: Council Oak Books, 1999.

McDonnell, Janet A. *The Dispossession of the American Indian, 1877–1934*. Bloomington: Indiana University Press, 1991.

McMurtry, Larry. "Southwestern Literature?" In *In a Narrow Grave: Essays on Texas*, 53–77. New York: Simon and Schuster, 1968.

"Memorial Erected to Brig. Gen. R. H. Pratt by Carlisle Students and Other Indians." *American Indian* 1, no. 3 (December 1926): 6.

Momaday, Natachee Scott. Letter to Walter S. Campbell, January 27, 1954. Walter S. Campbell Collection. Box 33, folder 11. Western History Collections, University of Oklahoma Libraries, Norman, Oklahoma.

Momaday, N. Scott. *House Made of Dawn*. New York: Harper and Row, 1968.

———. "Online Interview with N. Scott Momaday." *Modern American Poetry*. n.d. http://www.english.illinois.edu/maps/poets/m_r/momaday/interview.htm.

———. "Three Sketches from *House Made of Dawn*." *Southern Review*, Autumn 1966, 933–45.

Mourning Dove. *Cogewea, the Half-Blood* (1927). Lincoln: University of Nebraska Press, 1991.

———. *Mourning Dove: A Salishan Autobiography*. Lincoln: University of Nebraska Press, 1990.

Nelson, Robert M. "Rewriting Ethnography: The Embedded Texts in Leslie Silko's *Ceremony*." In *Telling the Stories: Essays on American Indian Literatures and Culture*, edited by Elizabeth Hoffman Nelson and Malcolm Nelson, 47–58. New York: Peter Lang, 2001.

Niro, Shelley, dir. *Tree*. 2005.

Okker, Patricia. "Native American Literatures and the Canon: The Case of Zitkala-Ša." In *American Realism and the Canon*, edited by Tom Quirk and Gary Scharnhorst, 87–101. Newark: University of Delaware Press, 1994.

"Open Debate on the Loyalty of Indian Employees in the Indian Service." *American Indian Magazine*, September 1916, 252–56.

Ortiz, Simon. Letter to Peter Matthiessen, August 24, 1991. Peter Matthiessen Papers, Addition, Series II: Correspondence, 1975–2002. Box 25, folder 4, M-O, Ortiz, Simon. Harry Ransom Center, the University of Texas at Austin, Austin, Texas.

———. "Towards a National Indian Literature: Cultural Authenticity in Nationalism." In *American Indian Literary Nationalism*, edited by Jace Weaver, Craig S. Womack, and Robert Warrior, 253–60. Albuquerque: University of New Mexico Press, 2006.

Ortman, Scott G. "Bowls to Gardens: A History of Tewa Community Metaphors." In *Religious Transformation in the Late Pre-Hispanic Pueblo World*, edited by Donna M. Glowacki and Scott Van Keuren, 84–108. Tucson: University of Arizona Press, 2011.

Oskison, John Milton. "The Biologist's Quest." In *Tales of the Old Indian Territory and Essays on the Indian Condition*, edited by Lionel Larré, 182–91. Lincoln: University of Nebraska Press, 2012.

———. *Black Jack Davy*. New York: D. Appleton, 1926.

———. "Cherokee Migration." In *Tales of the Old Indian Territory and Essays on the Indian Condition*, edited by Lionel Larré, 349–52. Lincoln: University of Nebraska Press, 2012.

———. "The Closing Chapter: Passing of the Old Indian." In *Tales of the Old Indian Territory and Essays on the Indian Condition*, edited by Lionel Larré, 429–36. Lincoln: University of Nebraska Press, 2012.

———. "Friends of the Indian." In *Tales of the Old Indian Territory and Essays on the Indian Condition*, edited by Lionel Larré, 362–64. Lincoln: University of Nebraska Press, 2012.

———. "In Governing the Indian, Use the Indian!" In *Tales of the Old Indian Territory and Essays on the Indian Condition*, edited by Lionel Larré, 441–47. Lincoln: University of Nebraska Press, 2012.

———. "Koenig's Discovery." In *Tales of the Old Indian Territory and Essays on the Indian Condition*, edited by Lionel Larré, 262–71. Lincoln: University of Nebraska Press, 2012.

———. "The Man Who Interfered." In *Tales of the Old Indian Territory and Essays on the Indian Condition*, edited by Lionel Larré, 305–12. Lincoln: University of Nebraska Press, 2012.

———. "The Need of Publicity in Indian Affairs." In *Tales of the Old Indian Territory and Essays on the Indian Condition,* edited by Lionel Larré, 369–71. Lincoln: University of Nebraska Press, 2012.

———. "The New Indian Leadership." In *Tales of the Old Indian Territory and Essays on the Indian Condition,* edited by Lionel Larré, 448–56. Lincoln: University of Nebraska Press, 2012.

———. "Only the Master Shall Praise." In *Tales of the Old Indian Territory and Essays on the Indian Condition,* edited by Lionel Larré, 165–76. Lincoln: University of Nebraska Press, 2012.

———. "The Outlook for the Indian." In *Tales of the Old Indian Territory and Essays on the Indian Condition,* edited by Lionel Larré, 358–61. Lincoln: University of Nebraska Press, 2012.

———. "The President and the Indian: Rich Opportunity for the Red Man." In *Tales of the Old Indian Territory and Essays on the Indian Condition,* edited by Lionel Larré, 353–57. Lincoln: University of Nebraska Press, 2012.

———. "Remaining Causes of Indian Discontent." In *Tales of the Old Indian Territory and Essays on the Indian Condition,* edited by Lionel Larré, 372–79. Lincoln: University of Nebraska Press, 2012.

———. "A Schoolmaster's Dissipation." In *Tales of the Old Indian Territory and Essays on the Indian Condition,* edited by Lionel Larré, 158–64. Lincoln: University of Nebraska Press, 2012.

———. "The Singing Bird." In *Tales of the Old Indian Territory and Essays on the Indian Condition,* edited by Lionel Larré, 331–45. Lincoln: University of Nebraska Press, 2012.

———. *The Singing Bird.* Norman: University of Oklahoma Press, 2007.

———. "A Tale of the Old I.T." In *Tales of the Old Indian Territory and Essays on the Indian Condition,* edited by Lionel Larré, 65–132. Lincoln: University of Nebraska Press, 2012.

———. "A Tale of the Old I.T." Western History Collections, University of Oklahoma Libraries, Norman, Oklahoma.

———. *Tecumseh and His Times: The Story of a Great Indian.* New York: Putnam's, 1938.

———. *A Texas Titan: The Story of Sam Houston.* New York: Doubleday, Doran, 1929.

———. "Tookh Steh's Mistake." In *Tales of the Old Indian Territory and Essays on the Indian Condition,* edited by Lionel Larré, 152–57. Lincoln: University of Nebraska Press, 2012.

———. "Walla Tenaka—Creek." In *Tales of the Old Indian Territory and Essays on the Indian Condition,* edited by Lionel Larré, 281–88. Lincoln: University of Nebraska Press, 2012.

———. "When the Grass Grew Long." In *Tales of the Old Indian Territory and Essays on the Indian Condition,* edited by Lionel Larré, 177–81. Lincoln: University of Nebraska Press, 2012.

———. *Wild Harvest: A Novel of Transition Days in Oklahoma.* New York: D. Appleton, 1925.

"Our Parish History." *The Cathedral Basilica of St. Francis of Assisi.* https://www.cbsfa.org/parish-life/about.

Owens, Louis. *Mixedblood Messages: Literature, Film, Family, Place.* Norman: University of Oklahoma Press, 1998.

———. *Other Destinies: Understanding the American Indian Novel.* Norman: University of Oklahoma Press, 1992.

Parker, Arthur C. "Indians and Freemasonry." *American Indian* 4, no. 6 (March 1930): 12.

———. Letter to the editor. *American Indian* 1, no. 2 (November 1926): 8.

———. "Editorial Comment." *Quarterly Journal of the Society of American Indians* 1, no. 1 (January–April 1913): 1–12.

———. "Editorial Comment." *Quarterly Journal of the Society of American Indians* 5, no. 1 (January–March 1917): 5–11.

———. "Editorials." *Quarterly Journal of the Society of American Indians* 6, no. 1 (January–March 1918): 5–12.

———. "The Editor's Viewpoint." *Quarterly Journal of the Society of American Indians* 1, no. 2 (April–June 1913): 103–14.

———. *The Life of General Ely S. Parker: Last Grand Sachem of the Iroquois and General Grant's Military Secretary*. Buffalo, N.Y.: Buffalo Historical Society, 1919.

Parker, Dorothy R. *Singing an Indian Song: A Biography of D'Arcy McNickle*. Lincoln: University of Nebraska Press, 1992.

Parker, Robert Dale, ed. *Changing Is Not Vanishing: A Collection of American Indian Poetry to 1930*. Philadelphia: University of Pennsylvania Press, 2011.

———. "The Garden of the Mind: An Introduction to Early American Indian Poetry." In *Changing Is Not Vanishing: A Collection of American Indian Poetry to 1930*, edited by Robert Dale Parker, 1–44. Philadelphia: University of Pennsylvania Press, 2011.

———. *The Invention of Native American Literature*. Ithaca, N.Y.: Cornell University Press, 2003.

Pearce, Roy Harvey. *The Savages of America: A Study of the Indian and the Idea of Civilization*. Baltimore: Johns Hopkins University Press, 1953.

Pearce, T. M. Letter to J. Frank Dobie, December 27, 1955. Dobie Papers, Subseries B: Letters, 1903–1964. Pearce, Thomas Matthews, 1933–1964. Container 150.10. Harry Ransom Center, the University of Texas at Austin, Austin, Texas.

———. Letter to J. Frank Dobie, March 2, 1959. Dobie Papers, Subseries B: Letters, 1903–1964. Pearce, Thomas Matthews, 1933–1964. Container 150.10. Harry Ransom Center, the University of Texas at Austin, Austin, Texas.

Perez, Domino R. "New Tribalism and Chicana/o Indigeneity in the Work of Gloria Anzaldúa." In *The Oxford Handbook of Indigenous American Literature*, edited by James H. Cox and Daniel Heath Justice, 489–502. New York: Oxford University Press, 2014.

Pérez-Torres, Rafael. *Mestizaje: Critical Uses of Race in Chicano Culture*. Minneapolis: University of Minnesota Press, 2006.

Perry, Gill. "Primitivism and the 'Modern.'" In *Primitivism, Cubism, Abstraction: The Early Twentieth Century*, by Charles Harrison, Francis Frascina, and Gill Perry, 3–85. New Haven: Yale University Press, 1993.

Pettit, Alexander. "A Legacy of Furious Men: The American Indian Movement and Anna Mae Aquash in Plays by Tomson Highway, E. Donald Two-Rivers, Yvette Nolan, and Bruce King." *Studies in American Indian Literatures* 27, no. 2 (Summer 2015): 29–61.

———. "Published Native American Drama, 1970–2011." In *The Oxford Handbook of Indigenous American Literature*, edited by James H. Cox and Daniel Heath Justice, 266–283. New York: Oxford University Press, 2014.

Pexa, Christopher J. "More Than Talking Animals: Charles Alexander Eastman's Animal Peoples and Their Kinship Critiques of United States Colonialism." *PMLA* 131, no. 3 (2016): 652–67.

Piatote, Beth H. *Domestic Subjects: Gender, Citizenship, and Law in Native American Literature*. New Haven: Yale University Press, 2013.

———. "Our (Someone Else's) Father: Articulation, Disarticulation, and Indigenous Literary Traditions." *Kenyon Review* 32, no. 1 (Winter 2010): 199–217.
Picotte, Agnes M. Foreword to *Old Indian Legends*, by Zitkala-Ša, xi–xviii. Lincoln: University of Nebraska Press, 1985.
Posey, Alexander. *The Fus Fixico Letters: A Creek Humorist in Early Oklahoma*. Edited by Daniel F. Littlefield Jr. and Carol A. Petty Hunter. Norman: University of Oklahoma Press, 2002.
Posner, Bruce. "Where the Buffalo Roamed . . . Relative Histories of an Early American Avant-Garde Film." In *Unseen Cinema: Early American Avant-Garde Film 1894–1941*, curated by Bruce Posner. New York: Anthology Film Archives, 2005.
Powell, Timothy B., and Melinda Smith Mullikin. Introduction to *The Singing Bird*, by John Milton Oskison, xix–xlvii. Norman: University of Oklahoma Press, 2007.
Prucha, Francis Paul. *Documents of United States Indian Policy*. 3rd ed. Lincoln: University of Nebraska Press, 2000.
Purdy, John. "Crossroads: A Conversation with Sherman Alexie." *Studies in American Indian Literatures* 9, no. 4 (1997): 1–18.
Rader, Dean. *Engaged Resistance: American Indian Art, Literature, and Film from Alcatraz to the NMAI*. Austin: University of Texas Press, 2011.
———. Foreword to *Choctalking on Other Realities*, by LeAnne Howe, i–vii. San Francisco: Aunt Lute, 2013.
———. "Reading the Visual, Seeing the Verbal: Text and Image in Recent American Indian Literature and Art." In *The Oxford Handbook of Indigenous American Literature*, edited by James H. Cox and Daniel Heath Justice, 299–317. New York: Oxford University Press, 2014.
Raheja, Michelle. *Reservation Reelism: Redfacing, Visual Sovereignty, and Representations of Native Americans in Film*. Lincoln: University of Nebraska Press, 2010.
Rancière, Jacques. "The Politics of Literature." *SubStance* 33, no. 1 (2004): 10–24.
Rendon, Marcie R. *Murder on the Red River*. El Paso, Tex.: Cinco Puntos Press, 2017.
Renker, Elizabeth. *The Origins of American Literary Studies: An Institutional History*. Cambridge: Cambridge University Press, 2007.
Rickard, Paul, dir. *Booming Out to NYC*. Episode 6 of the *Mohawk Ironworkers* documentary series. Montréal: Mushkeg Productions, 2016.
Ridge, John Rollin. *The Life and Adventures of Joaquín Murieta, the Celebrated California Bandit*. Norman: University of Oklahoma Press, 1955.
Riggs, Lynn. Baylor University Teaching Notes. Lynn Riggs Papers. Series II: Writings. Box 9, file 168. Beinecke Library, Yale University, New Haven, Connecticut.
———. "A Day in Santa Fe." *Cine-Kodak News*, January–February 1931, 5.
———. *The Iron Dish*. New York: Doubleday, 1930.
———. Letter to Walter S. Campbell, November 25, 1923. Campbell, WS, Corres. Riggs. Box 36, folder 8. Western History Collections, University of Oklahoma Libraries, Norman, Oklahoma.
———. Letter to Walter S. Campbell, Xmas 1923. Campbell, WS, Corres. Riggs. Box 36, folder 8. Western History Collections, University of Oklahoma Libraries, Norman, Oklahoma.
———. Letter to Walter S. Campbell, January 19, 1924. Campbell, WS, Corres. Riggs. Box 36, folder 8. Western History Collections, University of Oklahoma Libraries, Norman, Oklahoma.
———. Letter to Walter S. Campbell, June 16, 1924. Campbell, WS, Corres. Riggs. Box 36, folder 8. Western History Collections, University of Oklahoma Libraries, Norman, Oklahoma.

———. Letter to Walter S. Campbell, July 13, 1924. Campbell, WS, Corres. Riggs. Box 36, folder 8. Western History Collections, University of Oklahoma Libraries, Norman, Oklahoma.

———. Letter to Walter S. Campbell, March 13, 1929. Campbell, WS, Corres. Riggs. Box 36, folder 8. Western History Collections, University of Oklahoma Libraries, Norman, Oklahoma.

———. Letter to Walter S. Campbell, September 16, 1929. Campbell, WS, Corres. Riggs. Box 36, folder 8. Western History Collections, University of Oklahoma Libraries, Norman, Oklahoma.

———. Letter to Walter S. Campbell, September 8, 1937. Campbell, WS, Corres. Riggs. Box 36, folder 8. Western History Collections, University of Oklahoma Libraries, Norman, Oklahoma.

———. Letter to Walter S. Campbell, April 17, 1948. Campbell, WS, Corres. Riggs. Box 36, folder 8. Western History Collections, University of Oklahoma Libraries, Norman, Oklahoma.

———. Letter to Paul Green, March 5, 1939. Paul Green Papers. Southern Historical Collection, Wilson Library, the University of North Carolina at Chapel Hill, Chapel Hill, North Carolina.

———. Letter to Paul Green, September 3, 1939. Paul Green Papers. Southern Historical Collection, Wilson Library, the University of North Carolina at Chapel Hill, Chapel Hill, North Carolina.

———. Letter to Alice Corbin Henderson, March 20, 1932. Alice Corbin Henderson Papers. Box 8, folder 4. Harry Ransom Center, the University of Texas at Austin, Austin, Texas.

———. Letter to Betty Kirk, February 5, 1932. Lynn Riggs Papers. Box 1, folder 7. Western History Collections, University of Oklahoma Libraries, Norman, Oklahoma.

———. Letter to Rebecca W. Smith, September 30, 1941. Lynn Riggs Papers. Series 1. Correspondence. Box 5, folder 119: Texas Institute of Letters, Theatre Arts, and Theatre Arts Books. Beinecke Library, Yale University, New Haven, Connecticut.

———. Letter to Ann Webster, April 26, 1934. Lynn Riggs Papers Series 1. Correspondence. Box 6, folder 133: Webster, Ann. Beinecke Library, Yale University, New Haven, Connecticut.

———. Letter to Ann Webster, May 17, 1934. Lynn Riggs Papers Series 1. Correspondence. Box 6, folder 134: Webster, Ann. Beinecke Library, Yale University, New Haven, Connecticut.

———. Letter to Ann Webster, October 25, 1934. Lynn Riggs Papers Series 1. Correspondence. Box 6, folder 134: Webster, Ann. Beinecke Library, Yale University, New Haven, Connecticut.

———. "Private Showing of A DAY IN SANTA FE." Lynn Riggs Papers. Series II. Box 22, folder 364. Beinecke Library, Yale University, New Haven, Connecticut.

———. *Russet Mantle and The Cherokee Night*. New York: Samuel French, 1936.

———. "Santo Domingo Corn Dance." In *The Iron Dish*, 8–11. New York: Doubleday, 1930.

———. *This Book, This Hill, These People*. Edited by Phyllis Braunlich. Tulsa, Okla.: Lynn Chase, 1982.

———. "The Vine Theatre." *Texas Studies in Literature and Language* 59, no. 3 (Fall 2017): 274–86.

Riggs, Lynn, and James Hughes, dirs. *A Day in Santa Fe*. In *Unseen Cinema: Early*

American Avant-Garde Film 1894–1941, curated by Bruce Posner, vol. 6. New York: Anthology Film Archives, 2005.

———. "A Day in Santa Fe." Shooting script. Lynn Riggs Papers. Box 1, folder 7. Western History Collections, University of Oklahoma Libraries, Norman, Oklahoma. I-1-II-6.

Robinson, Cecil. "The Extended Presence: Mexico and Its Culture in North American Writing." *MELUS* 5, no. 3 (Autumn 1978): 3–15.

Robitaille, Emily Peake. "Carlisle Sweaters." *American Indian* 1, no. 10 (July 1927): 16.

———. "Chippewas Benefitted by the 'White Man's Education.'" *American Indian* 1, no. 2 (November 1926): 6.

———. "General Pratt Encountered Many Struggles in the Maintaining of Carlisle School." *American Indian* 1, no. 12 (September 1927): 13.

———. "General Pratt's Friendship for the Indian Led to Establishment of Carlisle College." *American Indian* 1, no. 11 (August 1927): 11.

Rodríguez, Ana Patricia. "The Fiction of Solidarity: Transfronterista Feminisms and Anti-Imperialist Struggles in Central American Transnational Narratives." *Feminist Studies* 34, nos. 1–2 (Spring–Summer 2008): 199–226.

Rogers, Will. *The Autobiography of Will Rogers.* Edited by Donald Day. Boston: Houghton Mifflin, 1949.

———. *Rogers-isms: The Cowboy Philosopher on the Peace Conference.* New York: Harper and Row, 1919.

———. *Will Rogers' Weekly Articles.* Vol. 1, *The Harding/Coolidge Years: 1922–1925.* Edited by James M. Smallwood and Steven K. Gragert. Stillwater: Oklahoma State University Press, 1980.

———. *Will Rogers' Weekly Articles.* Vol. 2, *The Coolidge Years: 1925–1927.* Edited by James M. Smallwood and Steven K. Gragert. Stillwater: Oklahoma State University Press, 1980.

———. *Will Rogers' Weekly Articles.* Vol. 3, *The Coolidge Years: 1927–1929.* Edited by James M. Smallwood and Steven K. Gragert. Stillwater: Oklahoma State University Press, 1981.

———. *Will Rogers' Weekly Articles.* Vol. 4, *The Hoover Years: 1929–1931.* Edited by James M. Smallwood and Steven K. Gragert. Stillwater: Oklahoma State University Press, 1981.

———. *Will Rogers' Weekly Articles.* Vol. 5, *The Hoover Years: 1931–1933.* Edited by James M. Smallwood and Steven K. Gragert. Stillwater: Oklahoma State University Press, 1982.

Rosenthal, Nicolas. *Reimagining Indian Country: Native American Migration and Identity in Twentieth Century Los Angeles.* Chapel Hill: University of North Carolina Press, 2012.

Round, Phillip H. *Removable Type: Histories of the Book in Indian Country, 1663–1880.* Chapel Hill: University of North Carolina Press, 2010.

Russell, Jason Almus. "Soul of the Indian Is Revealed in His Famous Orations." *American Indian* 4, no. 4 (January 1930): 10–11.

Rzepka, Charles J. *Detective Fiction.* Malden, Mass.: Polity, 2005.

———. "Queering the Investigation: Explanation and Understanding in Todd Downing's Detective Fiction." In *Murder in the Closet: Essays on Queer Clues in Crime Fiction before Stonewall,* edited by Curtis Evans, 156–72. Jefferson, N.C.: McFarland, 2017.

———. "Red and White and Pink All Over: *Vacilada,* Indian Identity, and Todd

Downing's Queer Response to Modernity." *Texas Studies in Literature and Language* 59, no. 3 (Fall 2017): 353–84.

"Santa Fe Picture at Fonda Draws Large Audience Wednesday Night." *Santa Fe New Mexican*, January 9, 1932.

Schertzinger, Victor, dir. *Redskin*. Paramount Pictures, 1929. DVD. In *Treasures III: Social Issues in American Film, 1900–1934*, collection by the National Film Preservation Foundation.

Scholtz, Christa. *Negotiating Claims: The Emergence of Indigenous Land Claim Negotiation Policies in Australia, Canada, New Zealand, and the United States*. New York: Routledge, 2006.

Schubnell, Matthias, ed. *Conversations with N. Scott Momaday*. Jackson: University Press of Mississippi, 1997.

Selznick, David O. Letter to U.S. Coast Guard Auxiliary, August 3, 1942. Lynn Riggs Papers Series 1. Correspondence. Box 6, folder 116: David O. Selznick. Beinecke Library, Yale University, New Haven, Connecticut.

Senier, Siobhan. "Rehabilitation Reservations: Native Narrations of Disability and Community." *Disability Studies Quarterly* 32, no. 4 (2012). http://dsq-sds.org/article/view/1641/ 3193.

Silko, Leslie Marmon. *Almanac of the Dead*. New York: Simon and Schuster, 1991.

———. *Ceremony*. New York: Penguin, 1977.

———. Review of *The Beet Queen*, by Louise Erdrich. *Studies in American Indian Literatures* 10, no. 4 (Fall 1986): 177–84.

———. *The Turquoise Ledge: A Memoir*. New York: Penguin, 2010.

Singer, Beverly R. *Wiping the War Paint Off the Lens: Native American Film and Video*. Minneapolis: University of Minnesota Press, 2001.

"Sioux Legend of Creation." *American Indian* 4, no. 6 (March 1930): 16.

Smith, Henry Nash. Letter to J. Frank Dobie, November 14, 1960. Dobie Papers, Subseries B: Letters, 1903–1964. Smith, Henry Nash, 1941–1962, undated. Container 167.5. Harry Ransom Center, the University of Texas at Austin, Austin, Texas.

———. *Virgin Land: The American West as Symbol and Myth* (1950). Cambridge, Mass.: Harvard University Press, 1970.

Smith, Jeanne. "'A Second Tongue': The Trickster's Voice in the Works of Zitkala-Ša." In *Tricksterism in Turn-of-the-Century American Literature: A Multicultural Perspective*, edited by Elizabeth Ammons and Annette White-Parks, 46–60. Hanover, N.H.: University Press of New England, 1994.

Smith, Leanne E. "*The Reviewer*." In *Encyclopedia Virginia*. Virginia Foundation for the Humanities, September 17, 2012. http://www.encyclopediavirginia.org/Reviewer_The#start _entry.

Smith, Paul Chaat, and Robert Warrior. *Like a Hurricane: The Indian Movement from Alcatraz to Wounded Knee*. New York: New Press, 1996.

Smith, Theresa. *The Island of the Anishnaabeg: Thunderers and Water Monsters in the Traditional Ojibwe Life-World*. Moscow: University of Idaho Press, 1995.

Smithers, Gregory D. "The Soul of Unity: The Quarterly Journal of the Society of American Indians, 1913–1915." *Studies in American Indian Literatures* 25, no. 2 (Summer 2013): 263–89.

"Snow Averts Eruption of Mt. Shasta." *American Indian* 4, no. 4 (January 1930): 11.

Snyder, Michael. *John Joseph Mathews: Life of an Osage Writer*. Norman: University of Oklahoma Press, 2017.

Spack, Ruth. "Re-visioning Women: Zitkala-Ša's Revolutionary *American Indian Stories*." *Legacy* 14, no. 1 (1997): 25–42.

Standing Bear, Luther. *Land of the Spotted Eagle.* Boston: Houghton Mifflin, 1933.
Starr, Emmet. *History of the Cherokee Indians and Their Legends and Folk Lore.* Oklahoma City, Okla.: Warden, 1921.
Stevenson, Margaret W. Letter to Lynn Riggs, February 18, 1935. Lynn Riggs Papers Series 1. Correspondence. Box 5, folder 107: S General. Beinecke Library, Yale University, New Haven, Connecticut.
Susag, Dorothea M. "Zitkala-Sa (Gertrude Simmons Bonnin): A Power(full) Literary Voice." *Studies in American Indian Literatures* 5, no. 4 (Fall 1993): 3–24.
Suzack, Cheryl. "Land Claims, Identity Claims: Mapping Indigenous Feminism in Literary Criticism and in Winona LaDuke's *Last Standing Woman.*" In *Reasoning Together: The Native Critics Collective,* edited by Craig S. Womack, Daniel Heath Justice, and Christopher B. Teuton, 169–92. Norman: University of Oklahoma Press, 2008.
Tatonetti, Lisa. "Carole laFavor's Indigenous Feminism and Early HIV/AIDS Activism: Health Sovereignty in the 1980s and 1990s." In *Global Indigenous Health: Reconciling the Past, Engaging the Present, Animating the Future,* edited by Robert Henry, Amanda LaVallee, Nancy Van Styvendale, and Robert Alexander Innes, 275–94. Tucson: University of Arizona Press, 2018.
———. "Detecting Two Spirit Erotics: The Fiction of Carole laFavor." *Journal of Lesbian Studies* 20, nos. 3–4 (July–December 2016): 372–87.
Teuton, Sean. *Red Land, Red Power: Grounding Knowledge in the American Indian Novel.* Durham, N.C.: Duke University Press, 2008.
Thrush, Coll. *Indigenous London: Native Travelers at the Heart of Empire.* New Haven: Yale University Press, 2016.
———. *Native Seattle: Histories from the Crossing-Over Place.* Seattle: University of Washington Press, 2007.
Tinkle, Lon. *An American Original: The Life of J. Frank Dobie.* Boston: Little, Brown, 1978.
Treuer, David. *Native American Fiction: A User's Manual.* St. Paul, Minn.: Graywolf, 2006.
Tucker, Mary. *Books of the Southwest: A General Bibliography.* New York: J. J. Augustin, 1937.
Updike, John. *Picked-Up Pieces* (1966). New York: Random House, 2012.
Vigil, Kiara M. *Indigenous Intellectuals: Sovereignty, Citizenship, and the American Imagination, 1880–1930.* New York: Cambridge University Press, 2015.
Vizenor, Gerald. "Aesthetics of Survivance: Literary Theory and Practice." In *Survivance: Narratives of Native Presence,* edited by Gerald Vizenor, 1–23. Lincoln: University of Nebraska Press, 2008.
———. *Fugitive Poses: Native American Indian Scenes of Absence and Presence.* Lincoln: University of Nebraska Press, 1998.
———. *Manifest Manners: Narratives on Postindian Survivance.* Lincoln: University of Nebraska Press, 1999.
———. *Thomas James White Hawk.* Mound, Minn.: Four Winds, 1968.
———. *Tribal Scenes and Ceremonies.* Minneapolis, Minn.: Nodin Press, 1976.
Vizenor, Gerald, and A. Robert Lee. *Postindian Conversations.* Lincoln: University of Nebraska Press, 1999.
Ware, Amy M. *The Cherokee Kid: Will Rogers, Tribal Identity, and the Making of an American Icon.* Lawrence: University Press of Kansas, 2015.
———. "Unexpected Cowboy, Unexpected Indian: The Case of Will Rogers." *Ethnohistory* 56, no. 1 (Winter 2009): 1–34.

———. "Will Rogers's Radio: Race and Technology in the Cherokee Nation." *American Indian Quarterly* 33, no. 1 (Winter 2009): 62–97.
Warrior, Robert Allen. *Tribal Secrets: Recovering American Indian Intellectual Traditions*. Minneapolis: University of Minnesota Press, 1995.
Watkins, Floyd C. *In Time and Place: Some Origins of American Fiction*. Athens: University of Georgia Press, 1977.
Weaver, Jace. Foreword to *The Singing Bird: A Cherokee Novel*, edited by Timothy B. Powell and Melinda Smith Mullikin, ix–xv. Norman: University of Oklahoma Press, 2007.
———. *That the People Might Live: Native American Literatures and Native American Community*. New York: Oxford University Press, 1997.
Weaver, Jace, Craig S. Womack, and Robert Warrior. *American Indian Literary Nationalism*. Albuquerque: University of New Mexico Press, 2006.
Weigle, Marta, and Kyle Fiore. *Santa Fe and Taos: The Writer's Era, 1916–1941*. Santa Fe, N.M.: Ancient City Press, 1994.
Wenger, Tisa. "Land, Culture, and Sovereignty in the Pueblo Land Dance Controversy." *Journal of the Southwest* 46, no. 2 (Summer 2004): 381–412.
Wexler, Laura. "Tender Violence: Literary Eavesdropping, Domestic Fiction, and Educational Reform." In *The Culture of Sentiment: Race, Gender, and Sentimentality in Nineteenth-Century America*, edited by Shirley Samuels, 9–38. New York: Oxford University Press, 1992.
White, Richard D., Jr. *Will Rogers: A Political Life*. Lubbock: Texas Tech University Press, 2011.
Wilkinson, Elizabeth. "Gertrude Bonnin's Rhetorical Strategies of Silence." *Studies in American Indian Literatures* 25, no. 3 (Fall 2013): 33–56.
Willard, William. "Zitkala Sa: A Woman Who Would Be Heard!" *Wicazo Sa Review* 1, no. 1 (Spring 1985): 11–16.
Wilson, Angela [Waziyatawin]. *Remember This! Dakota Decolonization and the Eli Taylor Narratives*. Lincoln: University of Nebraska Press, 2005.
Womack, Craig S. *Red on Red: Native American Literary Separatism*. Minneapolis: University of Minnesota Press, 1999.
Wright, Anne, ed. *The Delicacy and Strength of Lace: Letters, Leslie Marmon Silko, and James Wright*. St. Paul, Minn.: Graywolf, 2009.
Wright, Muriel. "Lee F. Harkins, Choctaw." *Chronicles of Oklahoma* 37, no. 3 (1959): 285–87. http://digital.library.okstate.edu/Chronicles/v037/v037p285.pdf.
Yellow Robe, Chauncey. "The Indian and the Wild West Show." *Quarterly Journal of the Society of American Indians*, January–March 1913, 39–40.
———. "My Boyhood Days." *American Indian Magazine*, January–March 1916, 50–53.
Young, Gloria A., and Erik D. Gooding. "The Haskell Celebration of 1926." In *Handbook of North American Indians*, edited by Raymond J. DeMallie, vol. 13, part 2 of 2, 1013. Washington, D.C.: Smithsonian Institution Press, 2001.

INDEX

Abeita, Louise, 175
"Aboriginals at Dedicatory Services on Mount Thabor" (Lohmann), 66
Abramoff, Jack, 193
Absolutely True Diary of a Part-Time Indian, The (Alexie), 115
Acoma Pueblo, 141, 225n31
activism, 17, 28, 49, 194; American Indian, 10, 15, 193; civil rights, 16, 196; community, 34, 40; literary, 12; militant, 211; political, 16, 26, 218n31; social, 117, 218n31
Adair, James, 88
Adams, Ansel, 118
Adams, Evan, 113, 115
Adkins, Camille, 213n9
Affair at Easter, An (Riggs), 173
African Americans: American Indians and, 36; caricature of, 98
AIM. *See* American Indian Movement
Alcatraz Island, 9, 10, 15, 72, 211; cultural segregation and, 12–13; occupation of, 11, 13, 186, 231n9
"Alcoholic Love Poems, The" (Alexie), 115
Alexie, Lillian, 141
Alexie, Sherman, 18, 19, 22, 23, 113, 114–15, 139, 140, 141, 193, 195, 201, 214n12, 223n2, 233n1; American Indian literature and, 207–8; criticism of, 208–9; literary interests / political allegiances and, 211; Native children and, 196; poems by, 223n3; Riggs and, 115, 116; sexual misconduct and, 207; skeptical liberalism and, 17; stereotypes and, 210
Allen, Paula Gunn, 7, 14, 207, 210, 213n4
Almanac of the Dead (Silko), 7, 8, 106, 108, 110
Along the Journey River (laFavor), 186, 189, 191, 193, 204
"America, Home of the Red Man" (Bonnin), 44
American Café, The (Hoklotubbe), 200, 201, 202
American Indian, 15, 18, 26, 42, 50–53, 55, 62, 71, 110; agenda of, 51; editing, 27–30; Lohmann and, 66
"American Indian Abroad Narratives" (Rader), 63
American Indian Defense Association, 49
"American Indian Intellectualism and the New Indian Story" (Cook-Lynn), 208
American Indian Movement (AIM), 5, 10, 23, 32, 186, 189, 191, 193, 194, 211, 212; FBI and, 187; rise of, 15
American Indian Stories (Zitkala-Ša), 28, 216n7
American Museum of Natural History, 48
Anders, Mary Ann, 122

Anishinabe, 188, 195, 208, 232n14
Anishinabemowin, 24, 189, 202
Annie Mae's Movement (Nolan), 232n21
Antelope Wife, The (Erdrich), 24
Apache Gold and Yaqui Silver (Dobie), 151
Apaches, 52, 138, 139, 152, 154, 197
Apela Club, 68, 70
Apess, William, 175, 227n4
Applegate, Frank C., 170
Aquash, Anna Mae, 193, 196
Aquash, Nogeeshik, 196
Archaeological Resources Protection Act (ARPA) (1979), 187, 232n13
Archambaud, Mary Alice Nelson / Molly Spotted Elk, 70
Arlington National Cemetery, 62
ARPA. *See* Archaeological Resources Protection Act
art: Indigenous, 123, 124, 125; Pueblo, 116, 117, 125
assimilation, 12, 15, 23, 25, 27, 30, 31, 34, 59–60, 68, 72, 77, 78–79, 99, 140, 144; argument for, 35; enforced, 29; process of, 82; race relations and, 36
Atlantic Monthly, 27, 31, 161, 218n36
Austin, Mary, 116, 117, 152, 154, 171, 223n6, 227n6
Austin, Stephen F., 155
avant-garde, Cherokee, 131–37
Aztecs, 54, 109

Bacon Rind, 53, 54, 55, 62, 219n45
Baker, Marie Annharte, 2
Bakos, Jozef, 119, 124, 126, 223n7
Barnabas, Reverend Dr., 71
Barrie, J. M., 153
Basilica of Mount Saint Sepulchre, 63
Battle of the Greasy Grass, 29, 39
Battle of the Little Big Horn, 196
Battle of the Washita, 196
"Battle of the Washita, The" (Ferguson), 69
Baumann, Gustave, 119
Baylor, Emmett Bledsoe, 228n16
Baylor, John R., 152, 228n16
Beach, Adam, 113
"Bear and the Colt, The" (Momaday), 230n51
Beaulieu, Irene C., 230n49
"Because My Father Always Said He Was the Only Indian Who Saw Jimi Hendrix Play 'The Star Spangled Banner' at Woodstock" (Alexie), 195
Beck, David, 53
Beet Queen, The (Erdrich), 5, 6, 7, 8; criticism of, 13–14
Bernardin, Susan, 50, 216n16
BIA. *See* Bureau of Indian Affairs
Bierce, Ambrose, 136
"Bigger Load for Educated Indians, A" (Oskison), 83
Billy the Kid, 156
"Biologist's Quest, The" (Oskison), 89, 91
Birchfield, D. L., 14, 185, 197
Bird, Gloria, 208, 209, 210, 233n2
Bird of Paradise, The (Tully), 136
Blackbird, Andrew, 175
Black Elk, Nicholas, 165, 229n25
Black Elk Speaks (Black Elk), 157, 229n25
Blackfeet, 6, 48, 177
Black Hawk, 68
Black Jack Davy (Oskison), 77, 78, 93, 94, 98, 178, 180
Black Silk Handkerchief (Birchfield), 14, 197
Bloodland (McAuliffe), 181
Blood Meridian (McCarthy), 152
Blue Duck, 8, 213n6
Boatright, Mody, 150
Boles, 92–93
Bonnin, Gertrude Simmons, 9, 18, 20, 26, 31–32, 37, 46, 61, 62, 71, 72, 161, 174, 181, 212, 213n8, 214n16, 215nn3–4, 215n16, 216nn7–8, 216n12, 217n24, 218n27, 218n31; activism of, 17, 34, 49; affiliations of, 216n10; *American Indian* and, 42; Bruner and, 59; coalitions and, 43–44; conversion of, 216n13; GFWC and, 160; Great Spirit and, 47–48; health problems for, 59; Indian cause and, 47; Indigenous beliefs and, 44; Indigenous media and, 73; investigation by, 49; Native politics and, 43; Oskison and, 73, 83; Paris Peace Conference and, 43; Pocahontas and, 218n34; SAI and, 31, 37, 41; Sioux Nation and, 45; Sioux patriotism of, 42; Utes and, 37; work of, 27–30, 31, 32, 33, 38–39
Bonnin, Raymond Telephause, 31, 48, 213n8

Index

Book Lover's Southwest (Campbell), 146, 175
Books of the Southwest (Tucker), 146, 175
borderlands, 91, 94; tribal secrets in, 151–59
Borrow, George, 162
Bowman, Arlene, 20, 116, 137, 138, 140
Braunlich, Phyllis Cole, 230n43, 230n48
Brave, Ben, 42, 218n32
"Breaking the Silence" (Bird), 208
"Broadway Pageant, A" (Whitman), 225n30
Brody, J. J., 116, 125
Broken Cord, The (Dorris), 5
Bronson, Ruth Muskrat, 19, 28, 74, 75, 110, 174, 221n8, 221n10
Brooks, Joanna, 143, 227n4
Brooks, Lisa, 16, 18, 143, 227n4
Brother's Three (Oskison), 78, 147, 175
Brown, Dee, 229n26
Brown, John, 74
Brown, Kirby, 16, 19, 28, 79, 94, 110, 221n8; Oskison and, 77
Brown, Little Sugar, 56
Browne, Sir Thomas, 153
Browns Valley Man, 188
Bruce, Louis R., 71, 72
Bruner, Joe, 18, 52, 57, 62, 220n56; assimilation and, 59–60; Creeks and, 58–59, 60, 61, 63
Buffalohead, W. Roger, 11, 12, 214n10
Bureau of Indian Affairs (BIA), 17, 71, 72, 190, 194, 232n15; Alcatraz and, 231n9. *See also* Office of Indian Affairs
Burke Act (1906), 51, 219n39
Bursum Bill, 49, 117
Bury My Heart at Wounded Knee (Brown), 229n25
Bush, George W., 203
Business of Fancydancing, The (Alexie), 115, 139, 223n3, 226n44; *Day in Santa Fe* and, 141; reading, 140
Bynner, Witter "Hal," 115, 116, 119, 147, 167, 168, 171, 223n6, 227n6

Callahan, S. Alice, 227n4
Calles, Plutarco Elías, 75
Call of the Wild, The (London), 148
Campbell, Walter S. (Stanley Vestal), 21, 144, 146, 147, 148, 166, 173, 174, 175,

176, 227n6, 229n21, 230n43, 230n45; Dobie and, 227n5; Riggs and, 167, 168, 169, 170, 171, 230n46
"Can a Coyote Raise His Tail?" (Mathews), 159
"Captain Grant" (Campbell), 169
Cárcamo-Huechante, Luis, 215n1
Cárdenas, Lázaro, 76, 183, 185, 221n14
Carewe, Edwin / Jay John Fox, 51, 116, 119, 223n4
Carlisle Indian Industrial School, 28, 29, 30, 31, 44, 52, 61, 154, 219n41
"Carlisle Sweaters" (Robitaille), 62
Carlisle University, 61, 62
Carroll, John M., 71, 219n42
Carson, Kit, 169, 170, 174
Carter, Stella LeFlore, 52, 71, 209
Carver, H. P., 225n31
Case of the Unconquered Sisters, The (Downing), 182, 187
Cathedral Basilica of St. Francis of Assisi, 122, 139
Cather, Willa, 116, 136, 167
Catholic Church, 65, 67, 102, 121
Catholicism, 28, 29, 64, 66, 122, 126, 129, 130, 134, 135
Cattaraugus Reservation, 70
Censors' Club, 168
Century of Dishonor, A (Jackson), 70, 82
ceremonies, 121–22, 140, 141; Indigenous, 126–30, 225n31
Ceremony (Silko), 7, 10, 15, 20, 106, 107, 110, 208; criticism of, 14, 210
Champan, Leslie, 231n51
Changing Is Not Vanishing (Parker), 26, 52, 168
Changing Woman, 44
"Chants Democratic" (Whitman), 225n30
Chapel of the Angels, 64
Chapel of the Ascension, 64
Chateaubriand, 209
Chaucer, 85
Cherokee Advocate, The: publication of, 84–85
Cherokee Kid, The (Ware), 228n20
"Cherokee Migration" (Oskison), 81
Cherokee Nation, 19, 73, 74, 75, 81, 85, 91–92, 94, 96, 97, 98, 99, 100, 101, 102, 105, 180, 197, 204; allotment debate

Index

and, 87–88; future of, 80, 104; sovereignty of, 77, 78
Cherokee Nation Marshal Service, 202
Cherokee Night, The (Riggs), 104, 117, 133, 135, 155, 170, 171, 173, 224n23, 230n47
Cherokee Phoenix, 26
Cherokees, 58, 60, 74, 75, 77–95, 96, 97, 110, 116, 118–19, 132, 133, 135, 198, 200, 202, 213n6; Indian Territory and, 105; Mexicans and, 104, 105; Rogers and, 99; self-exiled, 88; Texas, 92; Yaquis and, 104
Cheyennes, 29, 52
Chickasaws, 51, 56, 58, 60, 70, 72, 214n15
Chief Eagle, Dallas, 227n4
child pornography, 193, 194, 196
Chili Corn (Two-Rivers), 232n21
"Chipeta, Widow of Chief Ouray, with a Word about a Deal in Blankets" (Bonnin), 38
Chippewa County Sheriff's Department, 190, 196
Chippewas, 4, 6, 61, 208
"Chippewas Benefited by the 'White Man's Education'" (Robitaille), 61
"Choctalking" (Howe), 63
Choctalking on Other Realities (Howe), 62
Choctaws, 14, 50, 56, 58, 60, 69, 197, 213n6
Christianity, 27, 64, 65, 79
Christie, Ned, 181, 221n17
"Christmas Letter from Zit-kal-a-sa, A" (Bonnin), 37
Chrystos, poetry/politics and, 3
Church of the Pater Noster, 64
Cine-Kodak News, 123, 131
cinema, Indigenous, 113, 114, 120
citizenship, 30, 38; birthright, 33; Cherokee Nation, 78; Osages, 67; treaty rights of, 46; tribal nation, 56, 63, 96, 187
"City of Ships" (Whitman), 225n30
civilization, 31, 35, 36, 60, 87, 88, 98, 152, 217n20; Christian, 14; Indigenous, 55
civil rights, 2, 9, 17, 71, 76, 148, 166, 175, 179, 186, 193, 196, 218n29
Clark, Barrett H., 178, 230n45
Claypoole, Les, 150, 163
Clinton, Bill, 196
"Closing Chapter, The" (Oskison), 82

cloud-beings, 130
Coeur d'Alene Reservation, 113, 114
Cogewea (Mourning Dove), 178, 180
Cohen, Matt, 18, 215n1
Coler, Jack, 4
Collected Writings of Samson Occom, Mohegan (Brooks), 227n4
Collier, John, 49, 50, 69, 117, 130, 158, 185, 216n15, 223n9; OIA and, 30, 144–45; Pueblo and, 226n32
Collier's Magazine, 73, 79
colonialism, 13, 63, 126, 127, 139, 141, 143, 152, 197, 208; European, 66, 210; Spanish, 120; women and, 17
Colton, Mr.: SAI and, 37
Comanches, 52, 91, 92, 93, 152, 154
Common Pot, The (Brooks), 227n4
communities: ethnic, 85, 96; Indigenous, 2, 24, 25, 35, 76, 83, 105, 134, 144, 205, 206
Confederated Salish, 106
Congressional Record, 69
Conley, Robert, 74
Conrad, Joseph, 153
Cook-Lynn, Elizabeth, 8, 9, 32, 207, 214n10; Alexie and, 209; on Erdrich, 208
Coolidge, Dane, 222n24
Coolidge, Sherman, 217n24
Cooper, James Fenimore, 209, 210
Copway, George, 175
Corn Dances, 131, 134, 225n30
"Corn Husker, The" (Johnson), 68
Coronado's Children, 151
"Coronation of Chief Powhatan Retold" (Bonnin), 45
Cortes Rubio, Emilio, 181, 182, 183
Cortes Rubio, Salvatore, 181–82
Costo, Rupert, 11, 12
Coulthard, Glen, 179
Coward, John M., 53
Cow People (Dobie), 150, 163
coyote stories, 158, 159
Coyote Stories (Mourning Dove), 157, 159
Craig, Dustinn, 116, 138, 140
Crazy Brave (Harjo), 15
Crazy Horse, 29
Cream in the Well, The (Riggs), 133
Creeks, 57, 61, 63, 220n52; ethnographic descriptions of, 58; family formation

Index

of, 78; justice system of, 79–80; pro-Union / pro-Confederate, 60 "Creek's Uncles Always Selected His Companions in Life, A" (Bruner), 58, 59
crimes, 179, 187, 193; digital-age, 198; hate, 191; settler-colonial, 177–78, 180, 182
Cristero War, 102
Crosby, Floyd, 118, 224n14
"Crossing Brooklyn Ferry" (Whitman), 225n30
Cry of the Thunderbird (Hamilton), 175
"Cuckooland" (Rogers), 102
Culberson, James, 18, 52
culture, 13, 23, 28, 34, 44, 144, 187, 205; Anglo, 36; Anishinabe, 208; Creek, 60; Dakota, 31; ethnic, 35; Indigenous, 21, 27, 32, 68, 120, 125, 130, 155, 158, 159, 197, 219n48; majority, 32; material, 109; Osage, 147; Pueblo, 137; skateboarding, 138
Cundiff, Mattie, 230n48
"Cundiyo" (Henderson), 124, 140
Curtis, Charles D., 51, 56, 67, 219n47
Cusick, David, 175
Custer, George Armstrong, 29, 39, 69
Custer Died for Your Sins (Deloria), 14
"Custer Massacre, The" (Ferguson), 69

Dahl, Robert, 2, 213n2
Dakotas, 31, 71, 216n10
Dakota Texts (Deloria), 217n23
Darkness in Saint Louis Braveheart (Vizenor), 195
Dartmouth Alumni Magazine, 68
Daughter of Dawn, The, 226n37
David Copperfield (Dickens), 148, 149
Davis, Steven, 149
Dawes, Henry L., 83
Dawes Act (1887), 30, 83, 181, 215n6, 219n39
Dawes Commission, 72
Day in Santa Fe, A (Riggs), 19, 115, 122, 123, 131, 133, 135, 139, 141, 224n16, 226n37; avant-garde and, 132, 134; *Business of Fancydancing* and, 140; *House Made of Dawn* and, 137; Hughes and, 116–20; impact of, 119–20, 137

Death of Jim Loney, The (Welch), 204
Deception on All Accounts (Hoklotubbe), 198, 201, 202
Defense of Marriage Act (1996), 186
Delaney, James, 220n62
Delicacy and Strength of Lace, The (Wright), 20
Deloria, Ella, 174, 175, 217n23
Deloria, Philip, 51, 119, 198
Deloria, Vine, Jr., 10, 30, 210, 216n10, 216n15, 218n28, 233n3; Red Power and, 12, 14
del Río, Dolores, 51
Densmore, Frances, 145
Department of the Interior, 36
De Vargas, Don Diego, 122
development, 13; economic, 183, 192, 193; settler-colonial, 177, 179, 183, 184, 192
Diamond, Neil, 113
Diaz Bolio, José, 108, 109
Dickens, Charles, 85, 135
Dickinson, Emily, 214n9
Dietz, Angel DeCora, 45
discrimination, 21, 47
disenfranchisement, 103, 104
District of Cooweescoowee, 97, 221n8
Dix, Richard, 225n31
Dobie, J. Frank, 144, 147, 157, 173, 174, 176, 227n6, 228nn10–12, 228n21, 229nn22–23, 229nn37–38; on Aravaipa Apaches, 152; birth of, 149; Campbell and, 227n5; death of, 146; *Green Grow the Lilacs* and, 155; Indian culture and, 155; Indigenous people and, 152, 154; Lester and, 229n28; Mathews and, 145, 148–49, 150, 151, 153, 156, 158–59, 160, 161–62, 163, 164, 165, 229n34; modernization and, 163; outlook of, 156; Paredes and, 149–50; settler-colonial discourses and, 153, 155, 160; treasure hunters and, 151–52; on United States Indian Service, 229n24; work of, 21, 175
Domestics Subjects (Piatote), 227n2
Dorman, John, 118, 124, 126, 128, 129, 224n22, 224n25, 225n27
Dormon, James, 98
Dorris, Michael, 5
Douglas, Ann, 217n16

Downing, Ruth Shields, 65
Downing, Todd, 14–15, 22, 65, 75, 105–6, 110, 176, 178, 179, 181, 183–84, 185, 221n9, 227n4, 231n3, 231n5, 232n11; Indigenous transnationalism and, 17; laFavor and, 187; narrative strategies of, 188; settler-colonial crime and, 182; Smith and, 102; work of, 197
Doyle, Arthur Conan, 177, 178, 231n1
DreadfulWater, Thumps, 192
DreadfulWater Shows Up (King), 192
Dry Lips Oughta Move to Kapuskasing (Tomson), 232n21
Du Bois, W. E. B., 44
Dunbar-Ortiz, Roxanne, 177
Duncan, DeWitt Clinton, 53, 70

Eagle Dance, Pueblo Indians, 225n28
"Eagles of the Valle Grande, The" (Momaday), 230n51
Eagleton, Terry, 1, 2, 226n1
Earling, Debra Magpie, 14, 214n12
"Earth and I Gave You Turquoise" (Momaday), 176
East Lynne (Wood), 85
Eastman, Charles Alexander, 20, 28, 40, 42, 43, 44, 47, 48, 62, 78, 175, 216n8, 217n24
Eastman, Elaine Goodale, 42
Eastman, John, 217n25
Eaton, Rachel Caroline, 221n8
economic system, settler-colonial, 193
Edison Studios, 126, 225n28
"Editorial Comment" (Bonnin), 44
"Editorial Comment" (Parker), 35
education, 29, 35; knowledge-based, 70; Native, 40, 217n16
Education of Little Tree, The (Carter), 209, 210
Edwards, Jim, 71
Eliot, T. S., 228n10
Ellis, Fremont, 223n7
"E-Nah Is Said to Be the Discoverer of the Tobacco Weed" (Bruner), 58
Engaged Resistance (Rader), 9, 12
English, James F.: on economy of prestige, 21
Erdrich, Louise, 8, 23, 24, 61, 111, 178, 204, 205, 207, 208, 233n26; array generated by, 4; criticism of, 5–6, 7, 13–14; Matthiesen and, 4–5; Peltier and, 213n3
"Essay on Man, An" (Pope), 218n35
Essays (Lamb), 156
Evangeline (Carewe), 51
Evans, Florence Tsianina / Tsianina Redfeather, 51
Evans, Katherine, 32
Evening at the Warbonnet (King), 232n21
Everybody's Magazine, 27
Evil Dead Center (laFavor), 191, 193, 195, 196, 200, 204
"Exaggeration of Despair in Sherman Alexie's *Reservation Blues*, The" (Bird), 208
exceptionalism, 64, 209; Cherokee, 17; Creek, 57
Eyre, Chris, 113, 224n20

Fabens, Charles H., 49
factionalism, 11, 34, 41, 42
Fallaw, Ben, 183
Fandango (Campbell), 168–69
FBI, 186, 189, 191, 193, 194, 196, 199; AIM and, 187; Osage Indian murders and, 181
Ferguson, James E., 98
Ferguson, Mrs. Walter, 69, 70
fiction: Indigenous, 26; Native American detective, 179–80, 185–204, 205, 206
Fields, Richard, 74
First Convocation of American Indian Scholars, 10
First Nations, 2, 192
Fisher, Dexter, 216n7
Fitzgerald, F. Scott, 167
Flaherty, Robert, 118, 123, 132
Flight (Alexie), 23, 193, 196, 201, 211
Flood Control Act (1927), 95
Foreman, Carolyn Thomas, 68
Fort Belknap Reservation, 71
Foster, Tol: on Rogers, 99
Four Souls (Erdrich), 61
4wheelwarpony (Craig), 116, 138
Fox, Finis, 51
Fox, Jay John / Edwin Carewe, 51, 116, 119, 223n4
Franciscans, 120, 122
Frazier, Margaret, 42, 218n32
"Friends of the Indian" (Oskison), 82

Index

Frost, Laura, 226n45
Frost, Robert, 116, 167
Furlan, Laura M., 53
Fus Fixio Letters, The (Posey), 215n2

Galsworthy, John, 116
Gano, Richard Montgomery, 220n56
Garden of Allah, The, 137
Garland, Hamlin, 20
gender, 179, 199, 203, 204
General Allotment Act (1887), 30, 181, 215n6, 219n39
General Federation of Women's Clubs (GFWC), 49, 160, 229n29
"General Pratt's Friendship for the Indian Led to Establishment of Carlisle College" (Robitaille), 62
George Washington Gómez (Paredes), 228n11
Geronimo, 197
Ghost Dance, 29, 40
Giago, Tim, 26
"Giving Blood" (Alexie), 115
Goldwyn, Samuel, 136
Gomez, Manuel, 181, 183
González, Gilbert G., 90, 102, 221n3
Gooding, Erik D., 56, 219n47
Goodrunning, Freda, 232n20
Graham, Don, 148–49
Grandfather the Sun, 54
Grant, Marshall, 136
Grass Dancer, The (Power), 189
Gravitt, Winnie Lewis, 53
Great Depression, 51, 69, 95–96
Great Spirit, 40, 47–48
Green, Paul, 21, 104, 166, 171, 172, 173, 174, 230n42, 230n48
Green, Rayna, 210, 217n19, 219n46
Green Corn Dance, 59
Green Grass, Running Water (King), 178
Green Grow the Lilacs (Riggs), 117, 147, 169, 171, 223n12, 224n23; assessment of, 155; impact of, 114–15
Gritts, Levi, 74
Guide to Life and Literature of the Southwest (Dobie), 150, 153, 154, 155, 156, 159
Guidotti-Hernández, Nicole, 75–76
Gust-ah-yah-she, 53
Guy, James Harris, 53

Hafen, P. Jane, 31, 32, 216n10, 216n13, 216n16, 218n24
Halpin, Joseph F., 118
Hamilton, Charles, 175
Hamlet (Shakespeare), 156
"Hamlet Not the Only" (Riggs), 171, 173, 230n48
Hammerstein, Oscar, 117
Hammett, Dashiell, 205
Hanks, R. T., 52
Hanson, William F., 31–32, 216n13
Harding, Warren G.: Rogers and, 99–100
Hardy, Thomas, 170
Harjo, Joy, 15
Harkins, G. W., 56
Harkins, Lee F., 10, 26, 27, 58, 67, 69, 70, 214n15, 215n3; *American Indian* and, 18, 51; described, 50; human rights and, 71–72; Indigenous media and, 73; Indigenous modernity and, 50–53; Native voices and, 52, 53, 55–56; Tulsa and, 54
Harper's Magazine, 27
Harris, Bird, 74
Harris, James, 227n3
Hartshorne, Ewing, 15, 18, 52
Hartshorne, Mary, 53
harvest dances, 116–20, 134
Haskell Institute, 52, 56, 219n41, 219n47
Hastings, William Wirt, 56, 78
Haunted by Home (Braunlich), 230n43
Hazlitt, William, 153
Hearne, Joanna, 16, 113–14, 119, 137, 138, 223n1, 225n29
Hearst, William Randolph, 75, 221n11
Heirs of Columbus, The (Vizenor), 106, 178, 195
Henderson, Alice Corbin, 116, 119, 124, 135, 139, 140, 167, 168, 223n6
Henry, Jeannette, 26
Herrera, Velino Shije (Ma-Pe-Wi), 125, 126, 154
Hertzberg, Hazel, 33, 41, 217n24, 218n32; on Bonnin, 42
Hiawatha, 14, 68
Hiawatha, The (Treuer), 204
High Noon, 224n14
Hillerman, Tony, 212
Historical Society of New Mexico, 120
history: American Indian literary, 2,

Index

8, 15, 16, 17, 21, 24, 34, 72, 109, 145, 159, 165, 185, 186, 195, 204, 207, 209; colonial, 121–26, 151; film, 119; Indigenous, 68, 88, 133, 154, 159; political, 153; settler–colonial, 151, 185; Spanish-American, 157; tribal-nation, 172
"History of Mexico, A" (Rogers), 103
History of the Cherokee Indians and Their Legends and Folk Lore (Starr), 74
Hochbruck, Wolfgang, 14
Hogan, Linda, 178, 181, 189
Hoklotubbe, Sara Sue, 14, 22, 179, 185, 186, 199–204, 207, 233n24; novels of, 197, 198
Hollrah, Patrice, 213n3
Holmes, Sherlock, 137, 177, 178, 233n27
"Holy Jerusalem Is the 'Shrine City' of the Entire World" (Lohmann), 62
Home Mission Monthly, 44
Hoover, Herbert, 50, 68
Hopis, 157
Hopothe Yohala (Opothleyahola), 60
Horak, Jan-Christopher, 118, 123, 131–32
Horgan, Paul, 147
Hough, Walter, 48
House Made of Dawn (Momaday), 10, 14, 15, 113, 114, 137, 140–41, 145, 153, 174, 176, 208
Houston, Sam, 87, 92, 93, 94, 98
Howe, LeAnne, 62, 63, 111, 193, 214n12, 220n60
"How to Write the Great American Indian Novel" (Alexie), 115
H20, 224n16
Hughes, Christine, 117
Hughes, James, 19, 116–20, 223n11, 224n16, 224n21; Halpin and, 118; repeating/lingering by, 132–33; Riggs and, 118, 119, 121–35, 138
Hughes, Levi, 117
Hughes, Mary Christine, 117, 125
Huhndorf, Shari, 16, 17, 188
Huitzilopochtli, 109
human rights, 71–72, 219n29
Hunt, Elizabeth, 160
Hunter, Mary, 171, 172
Hurley, Patrick, 56
Hutchinson, Elizabeth, 117, 124, 224n26
Hutner, Gordon, 153, 228n18

I Am a Pueblo Indian Girl (Abieta), 175
ICWA. *See* Indian Child Welfare Act
identity, 13; Anglo, 39; gender, 188, 200; Indigenous, 14, 21; political, 19; racial, 127; sexual, 200; theft, 198
Idylls of the King (Tennyson), 149
"I Fuck Up in Japan" (Howe), 111
imperialism, 10, 63, 90, 91, 99, 133
Imprint (Linn), 120, 224n20
Improved Order of Red Men, 71
Indian Boyhood (Eastman), 20
Indian Bureau, 41
Indian Chieftain, 87
Indian Child Welfare Act (ICWA), 193, 196, 200
Indian Citizenship Act (1924), 51, 80
"Indian Code, An" (Carter), 71
"Indian Culture: Pueblos and Navajos" (Dobie), 157
"Indian Gifts to Civilized Men" (Bonnin), 44
Indian Historian / Wassaja, The (Henry), 18, 26
"Indian Hunter Prized Very Highly His Flint and Steel, The" (Bruner), 58
Indian Killer (Alexie), 23, 193, 209, 210
Indian Lore Exam for You, 52
"Indian Lore Quiz" (Hartshorne), 15
Indian New Deal, 30, 139
"Indian Praying on the Hilltop, An" (Bonnin), 47
Indian Removal Act (1830), 92
Indian Reorganization Act (1934), 30, 51, 69, 130, 139, 226n15, 229n24
Indian Rights Association, 49
Indians Are People, Too (Bronson), 174
"Indian's Awakening, The" (Bonnin), text of, 39
Indian Sentinel, 44
Indian Stories from the Pueblos (Applegate), 170
"Indians' Vote, The" (Harkins), 70
Indian Territory, 50, 72, 74–79, 81, 84, 85, 96, 97, 100–104, 110; Cherokees and, 105; representations of, 99; Rogers and, 98
Indian Trust and Treaty Funds, 83
"Indian Women Served as the Official 'Scalp Takers'" (Bruner), 58
Indigenous Americans, 69, 83, 84, 151,

Index

185; beliefs about, 27; religious beliefs/practices of, 65
"Indigenous Feminism, Performance, and the Politics of Memory in the Plays of Monique Mojica" (Huhndorf), 17
Indigenous Mexicans, 75, 76, 90–91, 102, 103, 104, 106, 110, 134, 166, 179
Indigenous peoples, 8, 30, 60, 68, 71, 79, 90–91, 92, 104, 105, 110, 120, 125, 135, 138, 143, 152, 154, 159, 166, 182, 183, 190, 192–93, 198, 199, 210; colonized, 75; crimes against, 185; dignity of, 67; dispossession of, 179; extermination of, 93; issues of, 72, 96; legal authority for, 186; mass murder of, 179; narratives of, 137; origins of, 63; politics and, 100; population of, 74, 123, 233n3; relocation of, 158; representation of, 114, 133, 211; resilience of, 139; social organization for, 160; transgressions against, 22
Indigenous Women and Feminism (Huhndorf and Suzack), 16, 188
Indigenous writers, 3, 50, 143, 150–51, 175; political contexts and, 25; rejection of, 6
"Influences" (Alexie), 115
"In Governing the Indian, Use the Indian!" (Oskison), 78, 83
integration, 29, 44, 47, 78
"Interesting Legend Tells Indian Came from So. America" (Bruner), 57
"Interesting Sioux Legend of the White Buffalo Calf Pipe" (Westbrook), 70
In the Spirit of Crazy Horse (Matthiessen), 4
Iron Dish, The (Riggs), 117, 168
IRS, 198
Irving, Washington, 52, 209, 219n40
Isleta Pueblo, 137
"It Just Felt Very Wrong" (NPR), 233n1
It Starts with a Whisper (Niro), 120, 224n20
Ivanhoe, 149
Ives, Anthony, 213n2

Jackson, Andrew, 92, 96
Jackson, Helen Hunt, 70, 82–83
James (Apostle), 64
James, King, 46

Jameson, Fredric, 1, 214n13
Jemez Pueblo, 174
Jewett, John Brown, 52
Jilinsky, Andrius, 171, 172
Johnson (Boswell), 156
Johnson, E. Pauline, 175
Johnson, James Young (James Young Deer), 119, 224n17
Johnson, Joseph, 227n4
Johnson, Pauline, 68
Johnson, Robinson (Whirling Thunder), 52, 68
Johnson, Spud, 119
Johnston, Henry Simpson, 222n28
Johnston, Ralph, 156, 161, 163
Jones, Peter, 175
Jones, Rupel J., 230n41
Julien Levy Gallery, 117
Justice, Daniel Heath, 2, 3, 88, 99, 214n12, 221n16

Kabotie, Fred, 154
Kalter, Susan, 148, 227n8, 228n13
Kanim, Swil, 140
Kaplan, Alice, 224n19
Keats, John, 153
Kellogg, Frank, 101
Ke Mo Ha (Patrick Patterson), 71
Keppel, F. P., 220n58
Kershaw, William J., 53
King, Bruce, 185, 193, 194, 197, 214n12, 214n14, 232n21
King, Thomas, 17, 22, 178, 179, 192
kinship, 143, 144, 216n8
Kiowa, 6, 52, 201, 202
Kiowa Five, 70
Kiowa Six, 154
Kipling, Rudyard, 85
Kirk, Betty, 117, 131, 226nn34–45
"Kit Carson's Last Smoke" (Campbell), 169
Knuth, Eva, 119
"Koenig's Discovery" (Oskison), 90
Konkle, Maureen, 16, 18, 227n4
Kristallnacht, 172–73
Kroll, Lucy, 173
Ku Klux Klan, 96

LaDuke, Winona, 61, 189, 207, 211, 232n15
La Farge, Oliver, 157, 170

Index

laFavor, Carole, 22, 179, 185, 186, 188, 189, 191, 194, 197, 199, 200, 202, 204, 207, 211, 215n20, 231nn6–8, 232n11, 232n15, 233n26; activism and, 193; Downing and, 187; Hoklotubbe and, 198; Native children and, 196
La Flesche, Francis, 175
Laguna Pueblo, 4, 7, 137
Lake Mohonk Conference, 83
Lakota Times / Indian Country Today (Giago), 26
Lamar, Mirabeau Buonaparte, 93
Lamb, Charles, 153
language: Cherokee, 110, 203, 222n18; Indigenous, 109, 202, 204; Nahuatl, 108, 109; Osage, 54
Lanier, Fanita, 147
Lapier, Rosalyn, 53
Larré, Lionel, 79, 215n2, 221n1; Oskison and, 73, 78, 87
Last Run of the Chili Line (Hughes), 118
Last Standing Woman (LaDuke), 61, 189, 211, 232n15
Laughing Boy (La Farge), 170
Laughing Horse, 119, 167
Lavengro (Borrow), 161–62
Lawrence, D. H., 116
Lea, Tom, 153
Leahy, T. J., 56
Leaves of Grass (Whitman), 225n30
"Legends and Traditions of Muskogee Indians Revealed" (Bruner), 59
Lesser, Wendy: *Beet Queen* and, 6
Lester, Clarence C.: Dobie and, 229n28
Letters of a Self-Made Diplomat to His President (Rogers), 63
"Letter to the Chiefs and Headmen of the Tribes" (Bonnin), 46, 59
Lewandowski, Tadeusz, 31, 32, 50, 215n4, 216n7, 218n27
Lewis, Sinclair, 116
Life and Adventures of Joaquin Murieta, the Celebrated California Bandit (Ridge), 178, 179–80
Life and Death of an Oilman (Mathews), 150, 157, 161
Life and Traditions of the Red Man, The (Nicolar), 227n4
Lincoln, Abraham, 162
Lindbergh, Charles, 75, 102, 163

Lindsay, Vachel, 116
Linn, Michael, 120
literary studies, 144, 151, 155, 174, 205, 227n3; Native American, 16, 21, 24, 148
Literary Theory (Eagleton), 1
literature: colonial, 193; Indigenous, 2, 3, 9, 16–24, 77, 109, 110, 144, 165, 170, 200, 207–8, 212; politics and, 1
Little, Brown & Company, 159, 161
"Little Chief" (Campbell), 69
Littlefield, Daniel F., Jr., 25, 87
Locke, Ben D., 53
Lohmann, Annetta, 18, 52, 57, 61, 62, 63, 64–66, 67, 72, 110, 220n62
Lomax, John, 145, 147
London, Jack, 148
Lone Bear, Samuel, 218n27
Lone Ranger and Tonto Fistfight in Heaven, The (Alexie), 113, 207, 209, 210, 233n22
Lonesome Dove (McMurtry), 8
Loney, Jim, 204
Long, Haniel, 168, 229n21
Longfellow, Henry Wadsworth, 149, 209
Long Lance, Buffalo Child (Sylvester Long Lance / Sylvester Clark Long), 62, 70–71, 154, 157–58, 220n59, 220n64, 225n31, 228n21
Lookout, Fred, 62
Loos, Anita, 226n45
Los Cincos Pintores, 116, 119
Love Medicine (Erdrich), 4, 6, 195
Lowe, Robert Liddell, 117
Luhan, Mabel Dodge Sterne, 119, 167, 223n8
Lumet, Sidney, 136
"Lynn Riggs" (Campbell), 170
Lyons, Scott, 221n16

MacLeod, Norman, 170
Major, Mabel, 146, 175
"Making an Individual of the Indian" (Oskison), 83
Manhatta (Sheeler and Strand), 123, 225n30
Manifest Destiny, 94
Manifest Manners (Vizenor), 32, 33
"Man Made of Words" (Momaday), 11

Index

"Man to Send Rain Clouds, The" (Silko), 176, 231n51
Man with a Movie Camera, 224n16, 226n34
"Man Who Interfered, The" (Oskison), 80
"Many Clans Were Formed in Ranks of Native American" (Bruner), 59
Manypenny Agreement (1877), 30
Margolis, David, 118, 129, 224n25
Marland, E. W., 100, 161
Marland Oil Company, 100
Martinez, Fred, 131, 135, 226n37
Mason, Edith Hart, 157, 158
Mathews, John Joseph, 22, 54, 55, 67, 72, 100, 106, 146, 147, 157, 169, 173, 174, 175, 176, 181, 219n45, 227–28nn6–9, 228nn12–13; on Claypoole, 163; Dobie and, 145, 148–49, 150, 151, 153, 156, 158–59, 160, 161–62, 163, 164, 165, 229n34; modernization and, 163; Native writers and, 144; Riggs and, 166; Rogers and, 163; social conservatism and, 21; Tzi-Sho chief and, 165; U.S. Army Air Service and, 148
Matthews, Washington, 175
Matthiessen, Peter, 6, 7, 20–21, 22; Erdrich, 4–5; Peltier and, 4
May, Jon, 54
Mayans, 54, 104, 135
McAuliffe, Dennis, Jr., 181, 222n31
McCarthy, Cormac, 20, 152
McCarthyism, 149
McDonnell, Janet A., 215n6, 219n39
McGee, Norman, 224n25
McGill, Mrs. W. B., 67
McGinnis, John H., 145, 146, 169, 227n6
McIntosh, James McQueen, 60
McKenzie, Fayette A., 33
McMurtry, Larry, 8, 153
McNickle, D'Arcy, 10, 20, 105–6, 175, 176, 178, 181, 230n49
Meagher, Tom, 69
Mean Spirit (Hogan), 178, 181
"Meddling in Mexico, a Summer Sport" (Rogers), 101
Medicine, Beatrice, 10, 11, 12, 216n10
"Memorial Day, 1972" (Alexie), 115
Memories and Adventures (Doyle), 231n1
"Memory of Blessing Received from Eminent Pope Pius XI" (Lohmann), 67

Menominee Reservation, 47
Meriam Report, 30, 68, 216n15
Mexican Department of Archaeology, 182
Mexican Earth, The (Downing), 14–15, 110, 227n4, 231n3
Mexicans, 1, 77–95, 96, 107, 149; Anglo Americans and, 154; Cherokees and, 104, 105
Mexico: conservative representations of, 106–7; meddling in, 95–106
"Mexico and Oklahoma in the Limelight" (Rogers), 102
MGM, 135
"Mistress White" (Campbell), 169
Mixedblood Messages (Owens), 22, 213n6
modernism, 50, 55, 125, 126, 217n16
"Mohammedans Forbid Christian Worship in Their Mosque" (Lohmann), 63–64
Mohawks, 53, 68, 71
Momaday, Natachee Scott, 174
Momaday, N. Scott, 6, 10, 11, 12, 17, 19, 21–22, 114, 115, 137, 140–41, 145, 159, 165, 167, 174, 175, 176, 205, 208, 209, 213n9
Montezuma, Carlos, 9, 26, 35, 40, 48, 214n16, 215n3, 216nn7–8, 217n24; letters to, 218n24; SAI and, 28
Mooney, James, 88
Morley, Sylvanus, 119
Morley, Virginia, 119
"Morning Walk—Santa Fe" (Riggs), 176
Morrow, Dwight, 75
Morse, Richardson, 137
Mound Builders, 58
Mourning Dove (Christine Quintasket), 157, 159, 165, 175, 178, 180, 231n2
Mruk, Walter, 223n7
Mullikin, Melinda Smith, 88
Murder on the Red River (Rendon), 212
Murder on the Tropic (Downing), 183, 192
Murder on Tour (Downing), 178, 182, 187
Murieta, Joaquín, 178, 180, 182
Murray, Laura J., 227n4
Museum of New Mexico, 123
Mussolini, Benito, Rogers and, 95
Myles, Norbert, 226n37
Mystery of Edwin Drood, The (Dickens), 135

NAGPRA. *See* Native American Graves Protection and Repatriation Act
Nanabozho, 188, 232n14
Nanook of the Desert, 118
Nanook of the North, 118
narratives, 17, 79, 137, 188; anticolonial, 9, 72, 91, 212
Nash, Willard, 223n7
Nation, 82, 115
National Association for the Advancement of Colored People (NAACP), 99
National Association of Manufacturers, 157
National Council of American Indians, 49, 229n29
National Film Preservation Foundation, 225n31
nationalism, 19, 141, 153
National Museum of the American Indian, 13
Native American Church, 29
Native American Graves Protection and Repatriation Act (U.S. Public Law 101-601) (NAGPRA) (1990), 22, 187, 188
Native American Renaissance, 9, 13, 16, 76, 88, 114, 137, 145, 150, 165, 173, 175, 204; colonial literature about, 193; function of, 210–11; Hollywood representation of, 113; legal status of, 29; Mexico and, 106–11; Native Americans, 30, 34, 37, 177, 198; Native art and, 116; sympathy for, 46
Native literary studies, 25, 205, 206; networked foundations of, 165–76
Native Recognition (Hearne), 119, 223n4, 225n29
Native voices, 52, 53, 70, 73
"Navajo" (MacLeod), 170
"Navajo Holy Song," 157
Navajo Nation, 138, 226n37
Navajo Night Chant, 175
Navajos, 100, 188
Navajo Talking Picture (Bowman), 20, 116, 137
Naya, Ramon, 171, 172, 173
"Nazareth—Scene of Christ's Childhood—Has Cabaret" (Lohmann), 65, 66

"Need of Publicity in Indian Affairs, The" (Oskison), 82
Neharkey, Millie, 233n26
Neihardt, John G., 229n25
Nelson, John Louw, 157, 158
Nelson, Joshua, 16
Nelson, Robert, 213n4
Nequatewa, Edmund, 175
New Deal, 149, 150
"New Indian Leadership, The" (Oskison), 83
"New Mexico Folk-Songs," 124
New Mexico Quarterly, 10, 176, 230n51
New Mexico State Historic Preservation Division, 122
New Mexico State Records Center and Archives (SRCA), 118
Newspaper Printing Corporation, 50
New York Evening Post, 73
New York Times, 23–24, 157, 204, 230n47
Nicolar, Joseph, 175, 227n4
Nicolar, Lucy, 51
Niro, Shelley, 116, 120, 132, 133, 137, 140
Nixon, Richard M., 72, 203
Nolan, Yvette, 194, 214n12, 232n21
"Noon Wine" (Porter), 136
No Parole Today (Tohe), 115
Nordstrom, Alanis, 212
North American Review, 83
Nutrias, José, 86

Oakes, Richard, 10
Occom, Samson, 68, 143, 175, 227n4
"Occurrence at Owl Creek Bridge, An" (Bierce), 136
O'Connell, Barry, 227n4
Office of Indian Affairs (OIA), 29, 30, 34, 38, 40, 41, 43, 45, 47, 56, 64, 144–45, 158, 185. *See also* Bureau of Indian Affairs
Of Oak and Innocence (Riggs), 230n48
"Of One Blood" (Foster), 99
oil industry, influence of, 100
Ojibwas, 14, 61, 186, 189, 196, 200, 215n20, 231n6
Okker, Patricia, 217n16
Oklahoma! (Rodgers and Hammerstein), 117, 137
Oklahoman, 159

Oklahoma's Poor Rich Indians (Bonnin), 49, 181
Old Indian Legends (Zitkala-Ša), 28, 31, 45, 217n23
"One Good Man" (Alexie), 211
One Stick Song (Alexie), 223n3
"Only the Master Shall Praise" (Oskison), 79
On Our Own Ground (O'Connell), 227n4
Ortiz, Alfonso, 10, 11
Ortiz, Simon, 7, 10, 20–21, 134, 141
Ortiz Rubio, Pascual, 182
Ortman, Scott G., 226n33
Osage Nation, 63, 100, 147, 148, 181, 228n9
Osage Reign of Terror, 30, 222n31
Osage Reservation, 54, 222n31
Osages, 54, 55, 60, 63, 66, 67, 147, 148, 156, 157, 164, 165, 181, 222n31
Osages, The (Mathews), 54, 150, 151, 161, 163, 165, 229n40
Osage Tribal Council, 148
Osage Tribal Museum, 148
Osceola, 70
Oshkosh, Alice C., 53
Oshkosh, Ernest, 219n41
Oshkosh, Reginald, 219n41
Oskison, John Milton, 14, 26, 35, 96, 147, 175, 176, 178, 180, 181, 215n2, 219n40; allotment debate and, 87–88; amalgamation and, 82; assimilation and, 79, 81–82; Bear Timson and, 222n18; Bonnin and, 73, 83; Brow and, 77–78; Cherokee exceptionalism and, 17; Cherokee Nation and, 85; Cherokees/Mexicans and, 99; Coolidge and, 222n24; education of, 76; ethnic nationalism and, 19; Indian Territory and, 105; Mexican people and, 86; Mexico and, 76, 93, 94; print media and, 73; racialism and, 78, 84; Riggs and, 94; Rogers and, 73, 74, 75, 77, 105, 221n12; settler colonialism and, 83, 90; Silko and, 110; social/political issues and, 84
Oskison, Rachel, 222n19
Ouray, Chief, 38
"Outlook for the Indian, The" (Oskison), 81
Out of Dust (Riggs), 227n4

"Over Your Shoulder" (Rogers), 103
Owen, Narcissa, 175
Owen, Robert, 96
Owens, Angie, 131
Owens, Louis, 22, 23, 145, 179, 185, 204, 208, 209, 211, 213n6
Owl in the Cedar Tree (Momaday), 174

Painter, Theophilus, 150
Paiutes, 152, 177
Palace of the Governors, 122
Palms (Riggs), 168
Pan-American Highway, 183
Paredes, Américo, 149–50, 228n11
Parins, James W., 25, 87
Paris Peace Conference, 43
Parker, Arthur C. (Gawasa Wanneh / Alnoba Waubunaki), 18, 26, 28, 33, 34, 38, 40, 42, 48, 56, 62, 70, 71, 72, 73, 175, 218n29; on Anglo culture, 36; assimilation and, 35; challenge to, 39; education and, 35; factionalism and, 41; Harkins and, 55; old ways and, 44; politics and, 37, 43; SAI and, 37
Parker, Ely S., 34
Parker, Robert Dale, 16, 18, 26, 52, 148, 168, 181, 217n17, 227n4
Parkman, Francis, 231n1
patriotism, 36, 42, 70, 156
"Patriots Blind to Past of United States—History Reveals Much That Is Wrong" (Ferguson), 69
"Paul's Case" (Cather), 136
Pawhuska, 56, 62, 147, 160
Pawnees, 177
Paytiamo, James, 175
Pearce, Roy Harvey, 152
Pearce, T. M., 146, 175, 176, 227n5
Pedley, Eric, 221n11
Peltier, Leonard, 4, 5, 23, 213n3, 232n9
Perma Red (Earling), 14
Perry, Gill, 120, 130
Pershing, John J., 100
Pettit, Alexander, 214n12, 233n21
peyote, 14, 29, 38, 40, 48, 218n27
Piatote, Beth, 16, 18, 78, 79, 80, 150, 227n2, 233n25; intimate domestic and, 144, 151, 183
Picotte, Agnes M., 216n7

Pilgrim's Progress, 149
Pine Ridge Reservation, 5, 191
Pipe, Captain (Hopocan), 68
Pipe for February, A (Red Corn), 13
Pius XI, Pope, 67
Plague of Doves, The (Erdrich), 14
Plainsman, The, 137
Plain Tales from the Hills and Soldiers Three (Kipling), 85
Plow That Broke the Plains, The, 224n14
Pocahontas, 45–46, 218n34
Poetry, 117, 124, 168
Pokagon, Simon, 175
Polatkin, Seymour, 115, 139, 140
political arrays, 1, 25; Cherokee, 19; diachronic, 3, 22; identifying/tracing, 3; profusion of, 18
political expression, 16, 17, 71
political perspectives, 25, 109, 212
politics, 9, 15, 27, 32–33, 37, 47, 71, 73, 74, 83, 97, 133, 149, 159–60, 174, 183, 191, 193, 194–95; anticolonial, 66, 81, 123; colonial, 170; conflict/power and, 2; expressive, 138; feminist, 200; gender, 109, 203, 204; Indigenous, 14, 16–24, 100, 109, 110, 200; literary, 1, 77, 114; Mohegan, 143; poetry and, 3; racial, 6, 176; Red Power, 15, 17; settler-colonial, 25, 152–53; sexual, 116, 203; spectrum model of, 23; tribal, 188
Pontiac, 10
Pope, Alexander, 218n35
Porter, Katherine Anne, 136
Portrait of a Young Man (Rodakiewicz), 118, 224n16
Posey, Alexander, 26, 175, 176, 215n2
Posner, Bruce, 118, 120, 224n15
Post, Wiley, 163
post-Renaissance, 106–11, 137
Potts, Marie Mason, 267
poverty, 6, 15, 47, 51, 66, 79, 86, 103, 228n19
Powell, Timothy B., 88
power: abuse of, 207; colonial, 120, 177; conflict and, 2; cultural, 144, 159; intellectual, 12; political, 34, 159; social, 108, 144, 159
Power (Hogan), 189
Power, Susan, 189, 207, 214n12
Powhatan, 46

Pratt, Richard Henry, 28, 40, 44, 52, 62
Preminger, Otto, 136, 226n41
"President and the Indian, The" (Oskison), 81
Pretty Weasel, 204
Price, Hiram, 56
primitivism, 20, 120, 121, 128, 129–30, 225n32
Primo de Rivera, Miguel, 95
Prince, L. Bradford, 122
"Problem of Old Harjo, The" (Oskison), 78, 79, 80
Pueblo, 117, 121, 122, 125, 129, 134, 137
Pueblo Revolt (1680), 120, 122
Pushmataha, 69, 70

Quarterly Journal of the Society of American Indians, 26, 29, 33, 37
Querry, Ron, 22, 179, 185

race, 77, 78, 84, 179; assimilation and, 36; uplift of, 35
racial awakening, 39, 40
racism, 6, 71, 74, 99, 102, 108
Rader, Dean, 9, 12, 13, 62, 115, 214nn11–12; Howe and, 63
Raheja, Michelle, 114, 119, 120, 226n38
Rainey, Homer, 150
Ramona (Carewe), 51, 116, 223n4
Ramona (Jackson), 82
Rancière, Jacques, 213n2
"Rapaho Gal" (Campbell), 169
"Rape on the Reservation" (Erdrich), 23–24
Rauh, Ida, 133, 226n39
Ray, Goldie, 202, 203
Reagan, Ronald, 6
Red Corn, Charles, 13
Red Cross, 45
Red Earth: Poems of New Mexico (Corbin), 124
Red Earth, White Lies (Deloria), 14
Red Earth Reservation, 186, 187, 189, 190, 191, 193, 194, 204; cultural/political center of, 188
Red Earth Tribal Police, 187
Red Jacket, 68
Red Lake Reservation, 231n8
Red Land, Red Power (Teuton), 9
Red Land to the South (Cox), 76

Index

"Red Man's America, The" (Parker), 38
Red Power, 1, 14, 15, 17, 50, 56, 191, 196, 211, 212; thoughts on, 10, 11, 12
Red Power Murders, The (King), 193
"Red Power: Real or Potential" (Medicine), 11
Redskin (Schertzinger), 20, 225n31, 226n37
Reel Injun (Diamond), 113, 114
Reid, Thomas Mayne, 231n1
religion, 29, 204; Indigenous, 32, 41, 127; Pueblo, 117, 129, 130
"Remaining Causes of Indian Discontent" (Oskison), 83
Removable Type (Round), 227n4
"Renaissance, The" (Wente), 113
Rendon, Marcie, 22, 185, 212
Republic of Texas, 91, 94
Reservation Blues (Alexie), 115, 207, 210; criticism of, 208–9
Reservation Reelism (Raheja), 119
resistance, 12, 32, 33, 186, 206; acts of, 9, 13; Indigenous, 15, 122
Resurrection (Carewe), 51
Revenge (Carewe), 51
Reviewer, 168, 230n42
Rhoades, Commissioner, 220n63
Rhythm for Rain (Nelson), 157
Rhythm of Rain (Riggs), 167, 168
Rickard, Clinton, 70
Rickard, Paul, 219n43
Rider, Iva Josephine (Sunshine Rider / Princess Atalie), 51, 53
Ridge, John Rollin, 175, 176, 178, 182
Riggs, Alfred, 30, 115, 140
Riggs, Lynn, 19, 20, 21, 22, 74, 90, 105, 106, 132–33, 147, 152, 155, 158, 162, 165, 166–67, 174, 175–76, 221n8, 224n13, 224n16, 224nn20–21; Alexie and, 115, 116; Campbell and, 167, 168, 169, 170, 171, 230n46; Cherokee Nation and, 104; on *Cine-Kodak News*, 123; contemporary Native film and, 137–41; death of, 136, 137, 173, 230n48; film history and, 119; film industry and, 135, 136; Green and, 171; Hughes and, 118, 119, 121–35, 138; impact of, 114–15, 137; Indigenous peoples and, 75, 76, 133, 135; Mathews and, 166; Mexico and, 99; Native literature and, 77, 144, 166; Oskison and, 94; poem by, 127, 176; politics of, 135; Rogers and, 94–95, 116; Silko and, 110; state and, 172–73; Vine Theatre and, 171, 172; work of, 116–20
Rinehart, Mary Roberts, 48
Rio Grande, 91, 93, 185
Roach, Hal, 221n11
Roadside (Borned in Texas) (Riggs), 136, 155, 171, 229n22
Robinson, Cecil, 89–90
Robinson Crusoe (Defoe), 149
Robitaille, Emily Peake, 18, 52, 57, 61, 62, 72
Rock, Howard Uyagaq, 26
Rodakiewicz, Henwar, 118, 224n16
Rodgers, Richard, 117
Rogers, Will, 17, 26, 50, 51, 63, 71, 154, 155, 162, 175, 215n2, 220n60, 221n11, 222n28; anticolonialism and, 99; Cherokees and, 99; criticism by, 101; described, 73; education of, 97; on firearms, 97–98; Great Depression and, 95–96; Harding and, 99–100; Indian Territory and, 98, 100–101; Indigenous population and, 102; Lindbergh and, 102; Mathews and, 163; Mexico and, 75, 76, 99, 103; Mussolini and, 95; NAACP and, 99; nostalgia and, 19; oil companies and, 100; Oskison and, 73, 74, 75, 77, 105, 106; politics and, 95–96; Primo de Rivera and, 95; print media and, 73; racism and, 99; Riggs and, 94–95, 116; spatial movement and, 103; vaudeville and, 98–99; Villa and, 100; Wilson and, 222n30
Rolfe, John, 45–46
Roosevelt, Franklin D., 50, 95, 150, 185, 223n9
Roosevelt, Theodore, 81, 85, 95
Rosenthal, Nicolas, 53
Ross, John, 74
Rostand, Edmond, 153
Roth, Agnes, 139, 141
Round, Phillip, 16, 18, 215n1, 227n4
Round House, The (Erdrich), 23, 178, 204, 205
Rousseau, Jean-Jacques, 130, 209
Russell, Jason Almus, 68

Russet Mantle (Riggs), 94, 133, 155, 226n39
Rzepka, Charles, 178, 179, 232n11

SAI. *See* Society of American Indians
Sandburg, Carl, 116, 162
Sand Creek Massacre, 196
Sandia Pueblo, 137
San Felipe Pueblo, 167
San Ildefonso Pueblo, 133, 134, 167
San Juan Pueblo, 10
Santa Anna, 92, 93
Santa Clara, 122, 124, 129, 130, 131, 132, 134, 135, 138, 139, 226n35; harvest dance, 120
Santa Clara Pueblo, 115, 121, 131, 132, 139
Santa Clara Tewa Language Program, 131
Santa Fe, 20, 21, 94, 109, 116, 117, 118, 120, 121, 122, 124–31
Santa Fe New Mexican, 121
"Santa Fe Picture at Fonda," 121, 224n25
Santa Fe Railway, 146
Santee Normal Training School, 29
"Santo Domingo Corn Dance" (Riggs), 115, 127, 131, 176, 225n30
Santo Domingo Pueblo, 131, 137, 167
Sarett, Lew, 48–49
Saturday Review of Literature, 146
Scalp Dance, 58
Schertzinger, Victor, 225n31
Schoolcraft, Jane Johnston, 227n4
"Schoolmaster's Dissipation, A" (Oskison), 79
Scott, Sir Walter, 85, 209
Seaton, Elise, 53
Sedillo, Juan, 119, 224n19
segregation, 22, 27; cultural, 12–13, 14
self-determination, 27, 29, 38, 56, 83, 179
Selznick, David O., 136
Seminoles, 60, 69; Black, 152, 200
Senate Indian Committee, 49
Seneca Nation, 70, 218n33
Senier, Siobhan, 231n7
"Sentimental Civilization" (Harkins), 69
Sequoyah, 71, 74, 85, 88, 89
"Sermon Preached at the Execution of Moses Paul, an Indian, A" (Occom), 68
settler-colonial contexts, 8, 59, 74, 105, 122, 143, 151, 152, 155, 165, 179, 181, 196, 197–98, 199, 205, 208, 212
settler colonialism, 77, 81, 92, 104, 120, 139, 143, 152, 158, 159, 178, 184, 185, 191, 196, 210; opposition to, 83; women and, 17
settler-colonial nation, 94, 109–10
settler-colonial states, 24, 72, 90, 177, 178, 182, 197
sexual assault, 76, 204, 205, 207
Shakespeare, William, 153
Sharpest Sight, The (Owens), 204
Shawnees, 10, 14
Sheeler, Charles, 123, 225n30
Shelley, Percy Bysshe, 153
Shell Shaker (Howe), 193
Shoshones, 177
Shuster, Will, 223n7
Signature of the Sun (Major and Pearce), 175
Silent Enemy, The (Fairchild), 20, 70, 225n31
Silko, Leslie Marmon, 4, 8, 9, 10, 15, 19, 20–21, 106, 107, 115, 141, 159, 176, 207, 208, 209; *Beet Queen* and, 5–6, 7, 13–14; Cherokee writers and, 110; criticism of, 14; Erdrich and, 7; Maya and, 109; Oskison and, 110; political concerns of, 17; Riggs and, 110
Simms, William Gilmore, 209, 210
Singer, Beverly, 119
Singing Bird, The (Oskison), 87, 88, 219n40, 227n4
"Singing Bird, The" (Oskison), 80
Sinking Suspicions (Hoklotubbe), 197–98
Sioux, identification as, 216n9
Sioux Ghost Dance, 225n28
"Sioux Legend of Creation" (Long Lance), 71
Sioux Nation, 45
"Sioux Number" (Bonnin), 38–39, 42
"Sioux Woman's Love for Her Grandmother" (Bonnin), 38–39
Sitting Bull, 29, 30, 42, 174
Six Nations, 70
Sky Woman, 226n38
Sloan, Thomas, 48, 49, 62
Smallwood, Benjamin, 56
Smart Set, 168
Smith, Al: Downing and, 102

Index

Smith, Henry Nash, 145, 147, 227n6, 228n11–12
Smith, Jeanne, 31
Smith, John, 46
Smith, Mayne, 228n11
Smith, Paul Chaat, 191
Smith, Rebecca, 146, 147, 166, 175
Smith, Redbird, 74
Smith, Theresa, 232n16
Smithers, Gregory, 33, 34
Smithsonian Institution, 89, 222n24
Smoke Signals (Hearne), 26, 113, 114, 195, 223n1
Snake Dance, 225n30
Sniffen, Matthew K., 49
Snyder, Michael, 227nn6–7
social issues, 82, 83, 160, 186, 205, 211
Society of American Indians (SAI), 18, 25, 26, 29, 31, 32, 34, 36, 37, 38, 41, 42, 43, 44, 45, 47, 49, 55, 73, 80, 83, 218n31; education and, 35; formation of, 28, 33; platform of, 40
Solar Storms (Hogan), 189
Solier, Edward, 183, 184, 185
"Song of Broad-Axe" (Whitman), 225n30
"Song of Occupations, A" (Whitman), 225n30
"Song of the Exposition" (Whitman), 225n30
Sound the Stars Make Rushing through the Sky, The (Parker), 227n4
Southern Review, 10
Southern Workman, 78, 80, 81–82
Southwest Heritage (Major, Smith, and Pearce), 146, 175
Southwest Review, 146, 169, 170, 176, 227n6, 231n51
Southworth, E. D. E. N., 85
sovereignty, 29; artistic/intellectual, 211; cultural, 186; Indigenous, 14, 114, 186; tribal-nation, 79, 223n1; visual, 114
Spack, Ruth, 217n16
"Spanish Trail, The" (Campbell), 169
"Sparkles from the Wheel" (Whitman), 225n30
Spokane Indian Reservation, 139, 233n2
Spokanes, 208
Spo-Ko-Gees, 57, 58
"Spring Morning—Santa Fe" (Riggs), 176

SRCA. *See* New Mexico State Records Center and Archives
Standard Oil Company of New Jersey v. United States (1911), 101
Standing Bear, Luther, 33, 62, 174, 175, 216n8, 218n29
Stanford University, 85, 188, 190
Starr, Emmet, 74
St. Cyr, Lillian (Princess Red Wing), 119
Steiner, Ralph, 224n16
Steiner, Stan, 12
stereotypes, 149, 167, 208, 209, 210
Stevenson, Coke, 150
Stevenson, Margaret, 230n47
Stevenson, Robert Louis, 85, 153
St. John, Michelle, 139, 141
Stoking the Fire (Brown), 110
Stone, Walker, 163, 229n37
"Story of a Misspent Boyhood" (Rogers), 97
Storyteller (Silko), 115
storytelling, 92, 210, 211
Strand, Paul, 118, 123, 225n30
Study in Scarlet, A (Holmes), 177
Summer of Black Widows, The (Alexie), 223n3
Sump'n Like Wings (Riggs), 171
Sun Dance, 29, 32, 33
Sun Dance Opera, The (Bonnin and Hanson), 31–32, 216n13
Sundown (Mathews), 150, 157, 158, 175, 181
Sunmount Sanatorium, 167
Sunset Magazine, 80
Surrounded, The (McNickle), 181
survivance, 33, 205
Susag, Dorothea, 31
Suzack, Cheryl, 16, 188, 232n15

Tabu, 224n14
Tac, Pablo, 9, 213n8
Tagaban, Gene, 140
"Tale of the Old I.T., A" (Oskison), 19, 84
Tales of the Bark Lodges (Walker), 227n4
Talking to the Moon (Mathews), 150, 151, 156, 157, 158–59, 163
Tarahumaras, 152
Tatonetti, Lisa, 186, 231n7, 232n20
Tecumseh, 10, 14, 69
Tecumseh and His Times (Oskison), 14

Teller, Henry, 56
Teuton, Chris, 215n1
Teuton, Sean, 9–10, 214n10, 221n16
Tewa, religious view of, 226n33
Texas Folklore Society, 150
Texas Institute of Letters, 166
Texas Rangers, 152
Texas Review, 146, 231n51
Texas Titan, A (Oskison), 76, 89, 91, 92, 94, 96
There's Not a Bathing Suit in Russia (Rogers), 63
This Book, This Hill, These People (Riggs), 230n43, 230n48
"This Is What It Means to Say Phoenix, Arizona" (Alexie), 113
Thorpe, Jim, 51
"Three Sketches from *House Made of Dawn*" (Momaday), 10
Through the Magic Door (Doyle), 231n1
Thrush, Coll, 53
"Time for Human Rights on Native Ground, A" (Erdrich), 23
Timson, Bear, 222n18
Tinkle, Lon, 146, 149, 150, 227n6, 228n10
To Do Good to My Indian Brethren (Murray), 227n4
Tohe, Laura, 115
Tohono O'odhams, 152
Toltecs, 68, 69
Tompkins, Jane, 217n16
Tongues of the Monte (Dobie), 162
Tonkawas, 152
"Tookh Steh's Mistake" (Oskison), 87
Toole, Lawrence, 190
Toughest Indian in the World, The (Alexie), 226n43
"Towards a National Indian Literature" (Ortiz), 8, 134, 141
Tracks (Erdrich), 61
Trail Driving Days (Brown), 229n26
Trail of Broken Treaties, 72
Treasure Island (Stevenson), 85
Treasures III (National Film Preservation Foundation), 225n31
Tree (Niro), 116, 132, 137, 226n38
Treuer, David, 24, 204, 208, 209, 210
Trial and Death of Socrates, The (Plato), 156

"Trial of Thomas Builds-the-Fire, The" (Alexie), 195
tribal-nation perspectives, 96, 105, 144, 151, 158, 159, 212
Tribal Secrets (Warrior), 21, 147
Tributes to a Vanishing Race (Beaulieu and Woodward), 230n49
Tucker, Mary, 146, 148, 175
Tully, Richard Walton, 136, 226n41
Tulsa Farm Club, 160
Tulsa Tribune, The, 50, 57
Tundra Times, The (Rock), 26
Turquoise Ledge, The (Silko), 15, 106, 108, 109
Turtle Mountain Band of Chippewa Indians, 4
Twain, Mark, 149
Twentieth Century Fox, 136, 137
Twentieth Century Pictures, 171
24 Dollar Island (Flaherty), 123, 132
Twenty Thousand Mornings (Mathews), 147, 163, 227n8
Two-Rivers, E. Donald, 194, 214n12, 232n21
Tzi-Sho lodge, 165

Uintah and Ouray Reservation, 26, 30, 33, 35, 37, 41, 51, 218n27
"Unauthorized Autobiography of Me, The" (Alexie), 115
United States Army Air Service, 148
United States Court of Indian Claims, 70
United States Indian Service, 229n24
United States–Mexican War (1846–48), 123
United States National Museum, 48
Universal Studios, 135, 136
University of Oklahoma, 26, 70, 115, 166
University of Oklahoma Magazine, 168
University of Texas, 146, 149, 150
Unseen Cinema (Posner), 118
Updike, John, 8
"Urban Scene, The" (Medicine), 12
Utes, 37, 38, 51, 83, 177

Vanity Fair (Thackeray), 148
VanNoy, Anne Turman, 52
Verdigris Primitive (Riggs), 230n46
Vertov, Dziga, 224n16, 226n34

Index

Vigil, Kiara, 16, 29, 49, 214n16, 215n3, 216n8
Villa, Pancho, 100, 222n30
Vine Theatre, 21, 104, 105, 171, 172, 173
Violence Against Women Act (VAWA), 23, 205
Virgin Land (Dobie), 145
"Viscount Chateaubriand's Adventures with Muscogulges" (Foreman), 68
Vizenor, Gerald, 18, 22, 23, 32, 106, 178, 209, 210, 211, 234n6; on Dobie, 152; Standing Bear and, 33; survivance and, 205
Voice of the Coyote, The (Dobie), 158, 160, 164
Voltaire, 209
Vultures in the Sky (Downing), 102

Wah'kon-tah (Mathews), 55, 147, 150, 151, 157, 158, 174, 175
Walcott, Derek, 20
Walker, Bertrand, 227n4
"Walla Tenaka—Creek" (Oskison), 79–80
Wand Dances, Pueblo Indians, 225n28
Ward, William T., 52, 70
War Dances (Alexie), 115
Ware, Amy, 16, 99
Warren, Robert Penn, 20
Warren, William, 176
Warrior, Clyde, 9, 56
Warrior, Ned, 77, 93, 180, 181, 221n17
Warrior, Robert, 21, 28, 147, 191, 213n4, 221n16
Washburn, Cephas, 88
Washington Post, 6
Wassaja (Montezuma), 26
Watawaso, Princess, 51
Waterlily (Deloria), 217n23
Wayne, John, 192
Way to Rainy Mountain, The (Momaday), 115
Weaver, Jace, 16, 205, 213n4, 221n16
Webb, Walter Prescott, 228n12
Webster, Ann, 135
Welch, James, 6, 10, 204
Welch, Julia Carter, 53, 70
Wente, Jesse, 113
Westbrook, Hariette Johnson (O-Jan-Jan-Win), 52, 68, 70

Wexler, Laura, 216n17
Wheeler–Howard Act (1934), 30
"When the Grass Grew Long" (Oskison), 79
White, Amelia Elizabeth, 116–17, 224n22
White, Martha, 117, 224n22
White, Richard D., 73, 95
White Earth Reservation, 61, 211–12, 231n8
White Hawk, Thomas James, 23
White's Manual Labor Institute, 30, 216n12
Whitman, Walt, 155, 209, 225n30
Why Indigenous Literatures Matter (Justice), 3
Wild Cat (Coacoochee), 60, 82, 220n55
Wild Harvest (Oskison), 77, 78
Wild West Shows, 30, 217n20
Wilkinson, Elizabeth, 218n36
Willard, William, 49
Williams, Ronald, 4
Williams, William "Old Bill" Sherley, 147
"Will Rides Back to the Good Old Times" (Rogers), 98
Will Rogers (White), 95
"Will Rogers's Radio" (Ware), 99
Wilson, Dick, 191
Wilson, Edith Bolling Galt, 45, 46, 218n34
Wilson, Eloise, 173, 230n47
Wilson, Woodrow, 45, 46, 222n30
Wind from an Enemy Sky (McNickle), 178
Winter Count (Chief Eagle), 227n4
Winter in the Blood (Welch), 10, 15
Winters, Yvor, 21, 167, 176
Wiping the War Paint Off the Lens (Singer), 119
Wirt Franklin Petroleum Corporation, 72
Wissler, Clark, 48
"With His Pistol in His Hand" (Paredes), 150
Wolfe, Patrick, 216n8
Womack, Craig, 1, 32, 213n4, 220n53, 221n16
Wood, Ellen, 85
Woodward, Kathleen, 230n49
Wordsworth, William, 153
Work, Hubert, 219n47

Works Progress Administration, 228n9
World Elsewhere, A (Riggs), 76, 94, 133
World Famous Indians basketball team, 51
Wounded Knee, 8, 23, 29, 196, 211, 216n12, 232n15
Wright, Anne, 20–21
Wright, James, 20
Wright, Muriel, 18, 50–51, 52, 175
Writing Indian Nations (Konkle), 227n4
Wynema (Callahan), 227n4

"Xmas 1923" (Riggs), 167

Yankton Reservation, 29, 31
Yankton Sioux, 49, 216n10, 216n12
Yaquis, 75–76, 89, 102, 104, 152
Year of Pilár, The (Riggs), 76, 94, 104, 133
Yellow Robe, Chauncey, 32, 70, 225n31
Yellow Robe, William S., Jr., 214n12, 217n20
Young, Gloria A., 56, 219n47
"Yours for the Indian Cause" (Bonnin), 47
Yucatán, 76, 104, 133
Yumas, 89, 152

Zanuck, Darryl, 171
Zia Pueblo, 154
Zinnemann, Fred, 137
Zitkala-Ša, 27, 31, 33, 50, 216n7, 216n16, 217n23. *See also* Bonnin, Gertrude Simmons
"Zitkala-Ša (Gertrude Simmons Bonnin)" (Susag), 31
"Zitkala-Ša: Sentimentality and Sovereignty" (Hafen), 31